Ordering Power

Like the postcolonial world more generally, Southeast Asia exhibits tremendous variation in state capacity and authoritarian durability. *Ordering Power* draws on theoretical insights dating back to Thomas Hobbes to develop a unified framework for explaining both of these political outcomes. States are especially strong and dictatorships especially durable when they have their origins in "protection pacts": broad, elite coalitions unified by shared support for heightened state power and tightened authoritarian controls as bulwarks against especially threatening and challenging types of contentious politics. These coalitions provide the elite collective action underpinning strong states, robust ruling parties, cohesive militaries, and durable authoritarian regimes – all at the same time. Comparative-historical analysis of seven Southeast Asian countries (Burma, Indonesia, Malaysia, the Philippines, Singapore, South Vietnam, and Thailand) reveals that subtly divergent patterns of contentious politics after World War II provide the best explanation for the dramatic divergence in Southeast Asia's contemporary states and regimes.

Dan Slater is Assistant Professor in the Department of Political Science at the University of Chicago. His published articles can be found in disciplinary journals such as the *American Journal of Political Science*, *American Journal of Sociology*, *Comparative Politics*, *Comparative Political Studies*, *International Organization*, and *Studies in Comparative International Development*, as well as Asia-oriented journals such as *Indonesia* and the *Taiwan Journal of Democracy*. He is also a co-editor of *Southeast Asia in Political Science: Theory, Region, and Qualitative Analysis* (2008). Professor Slater has conducted fieldwork since the late 1990s in Indonesia, Malaysia, the Philippines, Singapore, and Thailand.

Cambridge Studies in Comparative Politics

General Editor
Margaret Levi *University of Washington, Seattle*

Assistant General Editors
Kathleen Thelen *Massachusetts Institute of Technology*
Erik Wibbels *Duke University*

Associate Editors
Robert H. Bates *Harvard University*
Stephen Hanson *University of Washington, Seattle*
Torben Iversen *Harvard University*
Stathis Kalyvas *Yale University*
Peter Lange *Duke University*
Helen Milner *Princeton University*
Frances Rosenbluth *Yale University*
Susan Stokes *Yale University*

Other Books in the Series

Continued after the Index

Ordering Power

CONTENTIOUS POLITICS AND AUTHORITARIAN LEVIATHANS IN SOUTHEAST ASIA

DAN SLATER

University of Chicago

CAMBRIDGE
UNIVERSITY PRESS

CAMBRIDGE UNIVERSITY PRESS
Cambridge, New York, Melbourne, Madrid, Cape Town, Singapore,
São Paulo, Delhi, Dubai, Tokyo, Mexico City

Cambridge University Press
32 Avenue of the Americas, New York, NY 10013-2473, USA

www.cambridge.org
Information on this title: www.cambridge.org/9780521165457

First published 2010

Printed in the United States of America

A catalog record for this publication is available from the British Library.

Library of Congress Cataloging in Publication data

Slater, Dan, 1971–
Ordering power : contentious politics and authoritarian leviathans in Southeast Asia / Dan Slater.
    p.   cm. – (Cambridge studies in comparative politics)
Includes bibliographical references and index.
ISBN 978-0-521-19041-1 – ISBN 978-0-521-16545-7 (pbk.)
    1. Authoritarianism – Southeast Asia.   2. Southeast Asia – Politics and government – 21st century.
I. Title.   II. Series.
JQ750.A58S53   2010
320.530959–dc22   2010013569

ISBN 978-0-521-19041-1 Hardback
ISBN 978-0-521-16545-7 Paperback

ORDER, *v*. To arrange methodically or suitably;.... to regulate, direct, conduct, rule, govern, manage;.... To bring into order or submission to lawful authority;.... To give orders to or command; to direct authoritatively;.... to domineer over, treat as a subordinate;.... to give a.... request that (something) be made, supplied, or served.

Oxford English Dictionary

An organizer combines disparate elements into an integrated whole. He may do this *ex tempore* if his aim is simple or passing. He must make more elaborate preparations if he is confronted with a permanent and difficult task.

Karl Wittfogel, *Oriental Despotism*

The opening up of channels for the expression of manifest or latent conflicts between the established and the underprivileged classes may have brought many systems out of equilibrium in the earlier phase but tended to strengthen the body politic over time.

Seymour Martin Lipset and Stein Rokkan,
Party Systems and Voter Alignments

The cause in general which moveth a man to become subject to another, is (as I have said already) the fear of not otherwise preserving himself.... [M]en may join amongst themselves to subject themselves to such as they shall agree upon for fear of others.

Thomas Hobbes, *The Element of Laws*

[O]nce the common mind has received the impress of an acute danger, fear remains latent, as long as its ultimate cause is not removed.

Karl Polanyi, *The Great Transformation*

Contents

Map, Tables, and Figures

Map

Tables

Figures

Acknowledgments

This book examines how states and regimes in Southeast Asia have historically tried to extract and organize political and economic resources from the societies they rule. In the process of researching and writing it, I myself have accrued a rather long history of "extracting" support and encouragement from numerous sources, both personal and professional. Whether I have managed to *organize* all this generous support and encouragement into a coherent and convincing manuscript is a matter for the reader's judgment. If I have failed to bring it all together, it can only be because of my own incapacity to organize, not any lack of generosity among those from whom I have extracted so much for so long.

Although it grows out of my 2005 dissertation at Emory University, *Ordering Power* is very much a product of my five wonderful years as an assistant professor in the Department of Political Science at the University of Chicago. I simply cannot imagine a more stimulating, conducive, and egalitarian intellectual environment in which to write one's first book. It was my great good fortune to arrive in Hyde Park at the same time as an absolutely extraordinary cohort of comparativist graduate students, with whom I have shared many good times and great conversations from our days as lowly "first years" to the present. At a time when Chicago's comparativist faculty numbers have been somewhat depleted, I have gained great insights, inspiration, and sustenance from my "intra-cohort" interactions with Christopher Haid, Juan Fernando Ibarra, Diana Young-hwa Kim, Erica Simmons, and Nick Smith, as well as many other wonderful graduate students beyond this singular cohort. All of these students deserve additional thanks for leaving me to my own devices when I was finishing this book while on leave in 2008–09, despite their own ongoing advising needs. By contrast, Sofia Fenner deserves special thanks for *not* leaving me alone during this critical time, and for returning to the U of C to work closely with me as I slimmed down a rather chubby and undisciplined dissertation into the comparably svelte and sculpted tome you hold in your hands now. Throughout the rewriting process, Sofia was more like a copilot than a research assistant, often exhibiting greater command over the book's many moving parts than its own author could sustain.

There is scarcely a page of this book that did not benefit in some fashion from Sofia's considerable scholarly talents. The book has been strengthened as well thanks to research assistance from Bushra Asif, Narges Bajoghli, Adam Bilinski, Stacey Chung, John Cropper, Vikram Jambulapati, Damien Leonard, Amy Pond, Samantha Voertherms, Seth Winnie, and Allison Youatt.

My faculty colleagues at Chicago also deserve hearty thanks for pushing me to do my best work while also protecting my time to make it possible for me to do so. As the indefatigable and irrepressible chair of our department for the past three years, Lisa Wedeen has become my great personal champion and my close personal friend. Alberto Simpser's arrival as a new junior colleague during my second year served as both a jolt of new energy and a breath of fresh air. Thanks to Alberto as well as more recent faculty arrivals such as Betsy Sinclair, Jong Hee Park, and Stanislav Markus, I have been blessed with junior colleagues who are as collegial and upbeat as they are brilliant. Across the great tenure divide, my senior colleagues have always treated me in a refreshingly respectful and egalitarian spirit, free of unnecessary hierarchy or artifice of any kind. I am grateful to them all, but special thanks for extra guidance on the substance of my work go to Bob Gooding-Williams, Gary Herrigel, John Padgett, Lisa Wedeen, Steven Wilkinson, and Linda Zerilli.

My time at Chicago may have been the "critical juncture" when this book came together, but it cannot be understood without appreciating the "critical antecedents" upon which it was built. At Emory, my deepest gratitude goes to my dissertation committee – especially Rick Doner, who never failed to offer timely guidance or threatened to limit my room for intellectual maneuver. His steadfast support gave me much of the confidence I needed to embark on such a sweeping comparative-historical project. Alex Hicks served as an energetic champion as well as an expert field-guide on all matters sociological, and Carrie Rosefsky Wickham served as a consistent supporter as well as a constant reminder that in-depth fieldwork should always be a creative and transformative enterprise, not simply a "credibility check" on conclusions already drawn. Carrie also deserves thanks for introducing me to Jason Brownlee, who along with Ben Smith became my closest colleagues as we worked through graduate school at our separate institutions. For nearly a decade now, Jason and Ben have given me lesson after vivid lesson in what Gerschenkron called the advantages of backwardness. From writing our dissertations to going on the job market to completing our first books to getting tenure, I have benefited enormously from the fact that these two fine friends and brilliant colleagues have always been several steps ahead of me, showing me the way. My warmest gratitude goes as well to Tuong Vu and Erik Kuhonta, my fellow travelers in the worlds of Southeast Asian politics and comparative-historical analysis, for inspiring me to believe that this project could become part of an emerging research tradition, and not just a departure from what appeared at the time to be a shrinking "mainstream" in American political science. Digging even deeper, back into my Master's level studies at the University of Washington in the mid-1990s, I learned much of what I know about how to make rigorous causal arguments from Jim Caporaso; about how to study states and societies from Joel Migdal; and about how to blend normative concerns with analytical toughness in the study of elite politics from the late, great Dan Lev.

This book has also been shaped and improved through countless conversations with a much broader range of scholars than those mentioned above. Within the American political science community, Anna Grzymala-Busse, Steven Levitsky, James Mahoney, Hillel Soifer, Kellee Tsai, Ashutosh Varshney, David Waldner, Lucan Way, and Daniel Ziblatt have been especially helpful and influential as this project has chugged its way toward fruition. In the field of Southeast Asian studies, John Sidel and Bill Liddle have been especially keen readers and backers of this project, for which I am deeply and eternally grateful. Thanks go as well to Patricio Abinales, Jose Abueva, Benedict Anderson, Vince Boudreau, Ben Kerkvliet, Chalidaporn Songsamphan, Scott Christensen, Shawn Crispin, Jamie Davidson, Don Emmerson, Daniel Fineman, Edmund Terence Gomez, Natasha Hamilton-Hart, Paul Hutchcroft, Jomo K. S., Mike Montesano, Nipon Poapongsakorn, Patcharee Siroros, Pisit Leeahtham, Anthony Reid, Joel Rocamora, Jim Scott, and Carl Trocki for helping to guide me in various ways through the endlessly fascinating maze that is Southeast Asian political history. More impersonally but no less importantly, this project has benefited from audience feedback at more than twenty conference presentations and professional talks, including the annual meetings of the American Political Science Association (APSA), American Sociological Association (ASA), Association for Asian Studies (AAS), International Sociological Association (ISA), and Social Science History Association (SSHA); political science departments at Michigan State University, Northwestern University, the University of Florida, the University of Notre Dame, the University of Texas, the University of Vermont, the University of Wisconsin-Madison, and Yale University; sociology departments at Northwestern University and Princeton University; and Asian studies centers at the National University of Singapore, Northern Illinois University, the University of Malaya, the University of Michigan, and the University of Toronto.

Even more impersonally but also even more importantly, anonymous manuscript reviewers at Cambridge, Chicago, and Stanford provided excellent and careful feedback, which has helped improve the book greatly in its final version, if not by as much as those reviewers had every right to hope and expect. I thank Eric Crahan at Cambridge, David Pervin at Chicago, and Stacy Wagner at Stanford for soliciting such fine (and furiously fast) reviews. Eric has proven a phenomenal editor in every imaginable respect through every stage of this process at Cambridge, repeatedly re-earning the "Speedy Gonzalez" nickname with which he graciously and good-humoredly allowed me to anoint him (his regrettable lack of the "real" Speedy's "excellent accent" notwithstanding). Ken Karpinski has patiently and solicitously managed the final stages of the book's production, even when I reacted to some of his suggestions with the temperament of a neurotic bride who is informed that she needs to alter some details on her dress right before she starts walking down the aisle.

Last but not least, my many thanks to Margaret Levi for her helpful comments on the manuscript and for her flattering invitation to include my work in the Cambridge Studies in Comparative Politics series. Even though the honor was achieved through the coincidence of alphabetization more than my own efforts, seeing my name alongside Theda Skocpol's on the final pages of all forthcoming books in this series (at least until another "Sk" or "Sl" sneaks between us) will still be a genuine personal thrill.

Writing a book requires funds as well as friends, especially when extensive international fieldwork is involved. My fieldwork in Indonesia, Malaysia, the Philippines, Singapore, and Thailand has been funded by the Institute for International Education (IIE) Fulbright program, a Fulbright-Hays Doctoral Dissertation Research Abroad fellowship, the Social Science Research Council (SSRC) International Dissertation Research Fund, an Academy for Educational Development National Security Education Program (NSEP) grant, the Ford Foundation's Vernacular Modernities program, Emory University's Internationalization Fund and Department of Political Science, and the University of Chicago's Committee on Southern Asian Studies (COSAS). While living and working overseas, I have benefited from the assistance of numerous institutions. Research affiliations at the Institute for Strategic and International Studies (ISIS) in Kuala Lumpur, the Institute for Southeast Asian Studies (ISEAS) in Singapore, the Center for Strategic and International Studies (CSIS) in Jakarta, and the Institute for Popular Democracy (IPD) in Manila have proven indispensable. Above and beyond offering work space and assistance with research contacts, each of these institutions provided exceptional library resources, maintained by exceedingly helpful personnel. My research was similarly aided by outstanding collections and indulgent staffers at Chulalongkorn University's Academic Resource Center and Thammasat University's Political Science Library in Bangkok, the Freedom Institute in Jakarta, and the Lopez Memorial Museum in Metro Manila. My extended overseas stays have proven to be times of great companionship, and not just hard work, thanks to my happy extended encounters with Aries Arugay, Alice Ba, Achmad Budiman, Robin Bush, Mely Caballero-Anthony, Gladstone Cuarteros, Mohamad Hanafi, Nico Harjanto, Denis Hew, Butch and Grace Jamon, Laura Kaehler, Lee Hock Guan, Lou Joon Yee, Pornwipa Limkatanyoo, Michael and Jin Montesano, Tom Piernikowski, Patrick Pillai, Qamar Siddique, Retty Timboeleng, Christine Tjhin, C. Y. Wang, Thorsten Wohland, Zarina Zakaria, and last but not least, my unforgettable nightly dinner companions from "The Spice Guy" restaurant in Seksyen 17, Petaling Jaya.

Closer to home, my greatest personal debts of all are to my family and dearest friends. When I pause to take stock of what I have accomplished and accumulated in my life as I hurtle toward the age of 40, I count of greatest value the friendships I have built (and despite my reprehensible neglect, somehow sustained) over the years with Duffy Brook, Daryl Caid, Ben Hadary, Walter Hatch, Deirdre Karger, Mark MacDonald, Joan McCarter, Jayne Riew, Tharius Sumter, and Henry Szymonik. My late grandfather, Irwin Slater, has always served as a reminder that academic research is but one small step in the process of encouraging social and political change. My late grandmother, Elizabeth Slater, urged me since my youngest years to be her "solid citizen," and gave me much help as I tried to become one. Gene and Karen Slater have provided considerable encouragement and sound advice over the years; few uncle-aunt pairs are so engaged in a nephew's development. Lars Hanson has stubbornly insisted that everything was going to work out for me, personally as well as professionally, especially at times when it seemed obvious that it would not, and he has consistently proven correct. My beloved brothers, Matt Slater and Aaron Miller, are my constant companions in spirit – especially when I see something that I know would make them laugh, and I miss them all the more. More recently, I have been very lucky to count the wonderful, thoughtful, and generous Lockaby clan, especially (but not exclusively) Jay, Judy, and Annabelle, as my family as well.

Which brings me to my favorite Lockaby of all. Tracey was alerted to my arrival in Atlanta during my first month of PhD study by Rick Doner's charming and cunning wife, Susan Zaro. Despite the ghastly implications of my fledgling academic status for my financial solvency (I was seemingly the only Atlanta resident over the age of 16 without a car at the time), and despite Tracey's curious conclusion that I "sounded fat" on the telephone, she decided that it might not be too dangerous to invite me to go out with her and her friends for burritos. I guess maybe fat guys like burritos. In any event, she luckily found me less objectionable in person than I was on paper (and on the phone). I have now spent almost eleven years happily marveling at her lapse in good judgment. She has been my partner through every step of this process – so much so that I feel as if we both now have a Cambridge book under our belts. I only hope that this book's long-awaited completion will allow her to start focusing less on what I need, and more on what she needs. As for Ria (age 7) and Kai (age 5), they have not so much as lifted a finger to help me finish this book. All they have done is help make the years I have worked on it the most fulfilling in my entire life, by a very large margin. And I suppose they deserve some thanks for that as well.

I dedicate this book to those who have supported and suffered me the longest – my parents. If a child can receive a greater gift than to be raised by not just two, but *three* loving parents, I do not know what it is. They are collectively the reason I am who I am. (Please insert the usual disclaimer here about not blaming them for the bad parts.) My father, Paul Slater, opened my eyes to the wider world when I was still very young, and has always pushed me to think seriously about how the world works, or, more often, doesn't. My mother, Martha Hanson, instilled in me a passionate concern for political problems and, more importantly, the self-confidence to believe that I might actually succeed at helping to fix some of them. (I am far less confident about that now, but now it is too late.) My stepfather, Steve Miller, taught me by example how to approach the world with humor and humility, and how to avoid the perilous fate of taking oneself too seriously. For all their differences, they all put their children first. By dedicating this book to them, I hope in some small way to put them first as well.

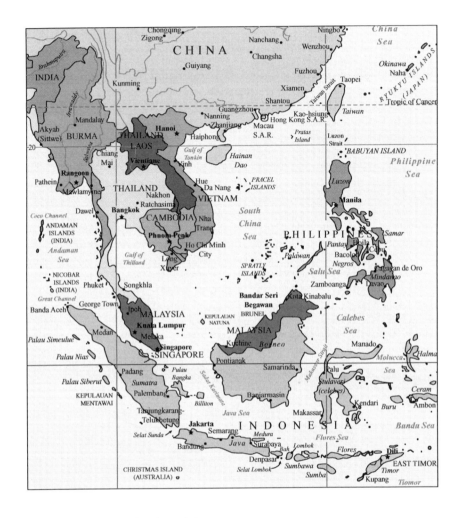

Map of Contemporary Southeast Asia

PART I

THE PUZZLES AND ARGUMENTS

I

To Extract and To Organize

The Puzzles, Arguments, and Setting

The Outcomes in Question: Ineffective States and Undemocratic Regimes

In framing a government which is to be administered by men over men, the great difficulty lies in this: you must first enable the government to control the governed; and in the next place oblige it to control itself.

James Madison

The postcolonial world is riddled with governments that must reflect Madison's worst political nightmare: They are neither enabled to control society nor obliged to control themselves. Half a century after the global struggle for decolonization reached its 1960 pinnacle, effective and democratic public authority remains a rare political commodity throughout Asia, Africa, Latin America, and the Middle East.

Yet the overarching pattern of postcolonial politics has not been one of extreme failure, but of extreme variation. The powerful "developmental states" of East Asia offer a stark contrast to the "predatory states" of sub-Saharan Africa and the numerous "intermediate states" in between.[1] Still, most postcolonial states sorely lack what Michael Mann calls "infrastructural power,"[2] or the institutional capacity to implement their political objectives. Most notably, precious few states in the developing world manage to mobilize significant revenue through income or corporate taxes on economic elites, who hold a grossly disproportionate share of wealth in developing economies.[3] Incapable of sustainably funding themselves, such states have also proven incapable of performing virtually every virtuous task that modern states ostensibly exist to fulfill. In many cases, postcolonial Leviathans have even failed to develop and coordinate the kind of coercive apparatus necessary to lay effective claim to what Max Weber considered the defining

[1] Evans (1995); Waldner (1999); Doner, Ritchie, and Slater (2005).
[2] Mann (1988): 5.
[3] Lieberman (2003).

3

trait of stateness – a *"monopoly of the legitimate use of physical force* within a given territory."[4]

Democratization has made greater headway than state-building in the post-colonial world, especially since the end of the Cold War. Yet authoritarianism remains an enduring, ubiquitous feature of global politics; the "third wave" of democratization has been far more uneven in its impact than the metaphor implies.[5] While indeed resembling that mighty metaphor in some regions (e.g., Latin America, Southern Europe, Eastern Europe), it has looked like nothing more than a faint ripple in others (e.g., Central Asia, North Africa, the Middle East. Nor have democratic transitions served as any panacea for the vast array of political and economic woes that plague most of the postcolonial world, such as crushing poverty, recurrent violence, endemic corruption, steep inequality, and shoddy public infrastructure. But by providing electoral checks on arbitrary state power, democratization has at least modestly increased some states' public accountability, pressuring them to improve their performance and curtail their most wanton, predatory abuses.

Stateness and democracy have thus proven elusive in the postcolonial world, but not entirely unattainable. Why have some states proven so much more infra-structurally powerful than others? And why have some authoritarian regimes proven so much more capable of preserving regime stability and forestalling democratization than others?[6] Since the durability of authoritarian regimes has been convincingly traced to the robustness of ruling parties and the consistent support of a loyal and unified military,[7] the regime question entails two intervening institutional questions: Why have some authoritarian regimes constructed more powerful and cohesive ruling parties than others? And why are some authoritarian regimes backed by more cohesive and compliant militaries than others?

This book commences with the assertion that these four distinct institutional puzzles – the state puzzle, the regime puzzle, the military puzzle, and the party puzzle – can be usefully portrayed as four distinct manifestations of a single coalitional puzzle: *Why are elites more prone to act collectively in some political systems than others?* States cannot successfully assert and broadcast central authority, ruling parties cannot effectively channel support to authoritarian regimes,

---

4 Cited in Gerth and Mills (1946): 78. Emphasis in original.
5 Huntington (1991). Also see Brownlee (2007).
6 Authoritarian regimes do not always become democracies when collapsing – think of the communist revolution against the Kuomintang in China, the Islamic revolution against the Shah in Iran, or coups by one set of military officers against another in Haiti. This book is solely focused on authoritarian regimes' resilience against pressures for democratization, not intra-authoritarian types of political change.
7 On parties as regime stabilizers, see Huntington (1968, 1991), Geddes (1999), Slater (2003), Brownlee (2007), and B. Smith (2007). On military splits as a prelude to authoritarian collapse, see O'Donnell and Schmitter (1986), inter alia, as well as Lee (2009), for an application to Southeast Asia. Cohesive party and military institutions thus make authoritarian regimes more durable both in the sense of temporal endurance, and of regime stability while enduring (Grzymala-Busse 2008).

and militaries cannot serve as politically reliable defenders of such regimes – leaving them highly vulnerable to collapse amid popular pressures for democratization – unless the officials commanding these institutions generate *elite collective action*.[8] When elites do not act collectively, authoritarian institutions do not function effectively. By offering an explanation for why levels of elite collective action vary so dramatically across countries, I hope to gain simultaneous analytic leverage on the political foundations of parties, militaries, states, and regimes in the postcolonial world.

My overarching argument for these multiple institutional outcomes is this: Contemporary divergence in the elite coalitions underpinning postcolonial state and regime institutions[9] has been primarily produced by historically divergent patterns of *contentious politics*. Broadly conceived as nonroutine political events involving considerable popular mobilization, contentious politics encompasses a wide range of transgressive, collective mass actions – from labor strikes to ethnic riots, from rural rebellions to student protests, from urban terrorism to street barricades, and from social revolutions to separatist insurgencies. While such plasticity in a concept can often be an analytic weakness, contentious politics proves quite useful as an umbrella term capturing the diverse types of internal conflict that have characterized and – as I shall argue and attempt to demonstrate – *shaped* the postcolonial world.

The recent profusion of research on contentious politics has almost universally treated it as an outcome to be explained – as a product instead of a producer of political institutions.[10] This book takes a different approach, inquiring into what contentious politics can explain in its own right. In contrast to most scholarship on state-building, I argue that violent internal contention can "make the state" as surely as international warfare[11] – but only when it takes especially threatening and challenging forms. Specifically, when a wide range of elites perceive the danger to their property, privileges, and persons from contentious politics to be endemic and unmanageable under relatively pluralistic political arrangements, they become prone to coalesce in *protection pacts* – broad elite coalitions unified by shared support for heightened state power and tightened authoritarian controls as institutional bulwarks against continued or renewed mass unrest.[12]

---

[8] This should in no way imply a chummy arrangement. Elites may act collectively while mistrusting, even despising each other. It also should not imply a purely consensual and noncoercive arrangement, as I discuss below.

[9] Since militaries and ruling parties are critical institutions in authoritarian regimes, I will at times refer to them under the broad rubric of "regime institutions."

[10] This is witnessed in the leading book series on the topic, *Cambridge Studies in Contentious Politics*, whose titles almost uniformly treat contentious politics as the key outcome of interest. Tilly (2004) is an important but partial exception to this rule.

[11] This language derives from Tilly's famed phrase on European state-building: "War made the state, and the state made war" (Tilly 1975: 42).

[12] Protection pacts are not simply protection rackets. My distinction echoes Tilly (1985: 170–171), who argues that the meaning of the word protection "depends mainly on our assessment of the reality and externality of the threat. Someone who produces both the danger and, at a price, the shield against it is a racketeer. Someone who provides a needed shield but has little control over the danger's appearance qualifies as a legitimate protector . . . " Tilly thus recognized the logical

My logic is perhaps most eloquently expressed by the quotations that opened this book. Challenging and threatening outbreaks of contentious politics can leave a wide range of elites, from captains of industry to captains in the military, experiencing what Polanyi called "the impress of an acute danger," which will endure "as long as its ultimate cause is not removed." Hobbes famously recognized the coalitional implications of such shared perceptions of threat – when man is stricken by "fear of not otherwise preserving himself. . . . men may join amongst themselves to subject themselves to such as they shall agree upon for fear of others." The greatest political beneficiaries of such mutual subjection would be the authoritarian commanders of Wittfogel's reorganized Leviathan – newly rebuilt not merely "*ex tempore*" for a challenge that "is simple and passing," but through "more elaborate preparations" for the "permanent and difficult task" of crafting stable institutional arrangements in what has come to be broadly perceived as an endemically unstable land.

This book dubs this political process *ordering power*. As the *Oxford English Dictionary* indicates, "to order" has multiple meanings consistent with the process of state-building under authoritarian auspices as just described. With a protection pact at their disposal, public authorities can enjoy extraordinary success in their efforts "to regulate, direct, conduct, rule, govern, manage" and "command" their vulnerable subjects. Not only do ruling political elites enjoy a rare opportunity to "combin[e] disparate elements into an integrated whole," in Wittfogel's terms. They also can leverage shared perceptions of mass threat to "request that (something) be made, supplied, or served" from society to the state. Most significantly, endemic and unmanageable contentious politics provides authoritarian regimes with extra leverage to extract tax payments from society's wealthiest figures. This comports with Lipset and Rokkan's argument that "conflicts between the established and the underprivileged classes" can ironically "strengthen the body politic over time."

In sum, protection pacts provide the strongest coalitional basis for authoritarian regimes both to *extract* resources from elites and to *organize* their most powerful allies. As an especially sturdy foundation for elite collective action, protection pacts facilitate the formation of powerful states, well-organized parties, cohesive militaries, and durable authoritarian regimes – all at the same time.

Protection pacts as I have just abstractly described them are never perfectly duplicated in real life. Yet they can be approximated, and we can learn a great deal about the divergent strength of states and durability of dictatorships by keeping this image of an ideal-typical protection pact in mind. In the pages and chapters that follow, I elaborate on and assess this conceptual and causal framework through a comparative-historical analysis of seven countries in Southeast Asia – a region exhibiting variation in state capacity, party strength, military

potential for state-building to occur through protection pacts instead of rackets; yet he treated racketeering as a defining attribute of state action. This book treats empirical variation between pacts and rackets, which Tilly acknowledged but did not explore, as causally and theoretically pivotal.

cohesion, and authoritarian durability that rivals the political variation of the postcolonial world writ large.

The Region in Question: Southeast Asia as a Zone of Anomalous Variation

The bewildering variety of language, culture, and religion in Southeast Asia.... appear[s] at first glance to defy any attempts at generalizations.

Anthony Reid[13]

The perplexing ethnic, linguistic, and religious divisions which prevail throughout [Southeast Asia] only underline the difficulties confronting us. However, diversity in and of itself need not be an insurmountable barrier to our efforts at generalization, since the diversity of Europe has not prevented more or less meaningful generalizations about the general – and the generic – course of its history.

Harry J. Benda[14]

Southeast Asia presents a perplexing political patchwork, displaying a "remarkable range of political forms."[15] This is particularly true of the political institutions under the microscope here. The Cold War era saw the region incubate extremely strong states (e.g., Singapore) and extremely weak states (e.g., the Philippines); highly robust ruling parties (e.g., Malaysia) and virtually party-less polities (e.g., South Vietnam); remarkably cohesive militaries (e.g., Burma) alongside chronically factionalized fighting forces (e.g., Thailand); as well as a seventh country (Indonesia) displaying state, party, and military institutions of intermediate capacity and cohesion. These three sources of institutional variation have shaped a fourth: the dramatically divergent durability of Southeast Asian dictatorships.[16] While selecting cases from a single region frequently entails selection bias, choosing cases in Southeast Asia helps avoid this inferential pitfall.[17] All four institutional outcomes are tabulated in rough, nominal form for these seven cases in Table 1.

---

[13] Reid (1988): 3.
[14] Benda (1962): 108.
[15] Hewison (1999): 224. Since the existence of stark variation in Southeast Asian political institutions is largely uncontroversial, the empirical chapters place somewhat greater stress on establishing the more subtle and less well-recognized variation on my independent variable – the type and timing of contentious politics. For analytic reviews of existing literatures on state, regime, and party institutions in Southeast Asia, see Kuhonta, Slater, and Vu (2008: Chs. 2–4).
[16] Following Grzymala-Busse (2008: 1), this book treats durability as "the vector of duration and stability," not as duration alone. Durability speaks not only to how *long* authoritarian regimes endure, but to how *stable* they prove to be.
[17] Geddes (1990). An additional potential regional pitfall is that Southeast Asia experienced tremendous foreign intervention during the Cold War era, raising the possibility that international factors might lie behind the region's divergent postcolonial outcomes. Yet the very ubiquity of foreign intervention throughout the region suggests that this factor is not well suited for explaining Southeast Asia's institutional diversity. While levels of foreign intervention cannot explain institutional divergence, the *type* of foreign intervention matters greatly – but since this primarily took the form of divergent state-building strategies, it is one of the outcomes this book endeavors to explain. As we will see, foreign elites were influenced as strongly as domestic elites by the types of contentious politics they confronted on the ground.

Ordering Power

TABLE I. *Institutional Outcomes in Southeast Asia*

Country Cases	State Capacity	Party Strength	Military Cohesion	Authoritarian Durability
Malaysia	High	High	High	High
Singapore	High	High	High	High
Philippines	Low	Low	Low	Low (1986)[18]
S. Vietnam	Low	Low	Low	Low (1975)
Thailand	Intermediate[19]	Low	Low	Low (1973, 1992)
Indonesia	Intermediate	Intermediate	Intermediate	Intermediate (1998)
Burma	Low	Low	High	Intermediate[20]

This sweeping political diversity within a single region should be readily famil-iar to informed laypersons with internationalist inclinations. Southeast Asia's diverse experience with democratization is especially well known, ranging from the inspirational "People Power" movement against Ferdinand Marcos in the Philippines to the notorious crackdowns by the Burmese military against protest-ing students and Buddhist monks in the late 1980s and again in late 2007. The power of the Singaporean state to regulate and control social life is as legendary as the complete collapse of the South Vietnamese state upon America's military withdrawal. Of more pressing concern to many global observers and policymak-ers, the Indonesian state has famously struggled to combat threatening infectious diseases and respond to recurrent natural disasters, while authorities in the Philip-pines have sorely lacked the capacity to manage their most serious governance challenges – from deadly floods inundating the nation's capital, to deadly militant groups infesting the archipelago nation's far southern reaches.

As an informative barometer of this regional variation, consider how much Southeast Asian states differ in their capacity to accomplish one of their

[18] Parenthesized years reflect when authoritarian regimes collapsed and transitioned to democracy – or, in the case of South Vietnam, collapsed as a state entirely. Cases with no parentheses continue as of 2010 to have authoritarian regimes in power. Regime duration is measured in this book by the year when authoritarianism collapsed, not by total years of nondemocratic rule. This is because it was much politically harder to sustain an authoritarian regime in the 1980s and 1990s than in the 1950s and 1960s. Hence the greater endurance of the Suharto regime in Indonesia than the Marcos regime in the Philippines is best indicated by the fact that Suharto outlasted Marcos by 12 years, not that he happened to seize authoritarian powers six years earlier.

[19] The Thai state proved "intermediate" because of earlier state-building legacies. Like Southeast Asia's "weak" states, the Thai state experienced no significant or sustained increase in infrastruc-tural capacity during the postwar period. See Doner (2009).

[20] Burma's military regime has exhibited similar temporal duration as Malaysia's and Singapore's party-led regimes, but it has generated far less political and regime stability during its exten-sive reign. It is precisely Burma's lack of effective civilian institutions and active civilian backing that best explains the country's recurrent lapses into massive societal unrest and violent military crackdowns – vividly illustrating Burma's relative lack of stability vis-à-vis Malaysia and Singapore. Combining high duration with relatively low stability, authoritarian durability in Burma is best conceived as intermediate. By contrast, authoritarian durability in Indonesia proved intermediate in the sense of both duration and stability.

benchmark tasks: collecting taxes. Evan Lieberman usefully locates the countries analyzed in this book (with the exception of extinct South Vietnam) alongside another hundred-plus nations in terms of their capacity to extract income and corporate taxes as a share of national income during the 1990–94 period.[21] If one were to divide this global population of cases into quadrants, this book's Southeast Asian sample would include cases from all three quadrants in which postcolonial states are predominant. Excluding the top quadrant, which is populated mostly by wealthy democracies (#1–27), the Southeast Asian cases of Indonesia,[22] Malaysia, and Singapore can be found in the strong postcolonial quadrant (#28–54); the Philippines and Thailand are positioned in the intermediate, third quadrant (#55–81); and Burma stands apart in regional terms among the world's governance basket cases (#82–107). Since theories constructed from a representative sample are more likely to prove generalizable than theories derived from a biased and truncated sample,[23] Southeast Asia provides a highly promising setting for theorizing institutional variation throughout the postcolonial world.

New theorizing is essential. While social scientists have amassed extensive knowledge on state-building and democratization, existing theories prove surprisingly unhelpful for explaining the divergent development of Southeast Asian state and regime institutions. Although I deal with alternative explanations in greater depth in the following chapter, consider for now how Southeast Asia fails to accord with some of our most familiar explanations for political development.

Table 2 (next page) obviously does not serve to falsify any of the hypotheses mentioned. Yet it suggests at a minimum that Southeast Asia's institutional variation cannot be readily explained by many of our most familiar theories. If any of these hypotheses effectively captured Southeast Asia's variation in state and regime institutions, we might not need new theorizing at all – but they do not.

The reader should also note that each of the hypotheses in Table 2 aims to explain *one* institutional outcome. Yet as we saw in Table 1, state and regime institutions in Southeast Asia have tended to be strong or weak *in tandem*. Is it merely a coincidence that states, parties, militaries, and dictatorships in the Philippines and Thailand have been fragmented and fragile across the board, while those same political institutions in Malaysia and Singapore present a consistent picture of cohesion and capacity? Might we develop a theoretical framework to explain this stark variation, while also making sense of more muddled, institutionally uneven cases such as Burma and Indonesia, and express it in general terms that can be applied and tested in other world regions?

This book attempts such an enterprise, embracing the theory-building challenge laid down by Benda to his fellow Southeast Asianists nearly half a century ago. If a region as diverse as Europe can produce general, portable theory, why not Southeast Asia? Much as Reid and Benda sought to uncover common themes and patterns in Southeast Asia's eclectic social and cultural topography, I aim to

---

[21] Lieberman (2003): 64–66.
[22] Indonesia's relatively inflated ranking is largely an artifact of its vast (and largely state-owned) mineral resources – an exceedingly easy target for corporate taxation.
[23] Slater and Ziblatt (2009).

TABLE 2. *Southeast Asia as a Challenge to Theoretical Expectations*

Theoretical Expectations	Southeast Asian "Anomalies"*
Development encourages democracy (e.g., Boix 2003)	*Malaysia, Singapore*[24] / Philippines, Indonesia
Resource rents hinder democracy (e.g., Ross 2001)	*Indonesia, Philippines* / Singapore
British colonialism fostered democracy (e.g., Weiner 1987)	*Burma, Malaysia, Singapore*
Powerful landed elites hinder democracy (e.g., Rueschemeyer et al. 1992)	*Philippines* / Singapore
Military regimes should not long endure (e.g., Geddes 1999)	*Burma, Indonesia*
Economic crises help destroy dictatorships (e.g., Gasiorowski 1999)	*Burma, Malaysia* / Thailand
External threats help build the state (e.g., Tilly 1992)	*South Vietnam* / Malaysia
Resource rents hinder state-building (e.g., Karl 1997)	*Indonesia, Malaysia*
Nation-building aids state-building (e.g., Marx 2003)	*Burma, Indonesia, Thailand* / Malaysia, Singapore
Nationalist revolutions build strong parties (e.g., Huntington 1968)	*Burma, Indonesia* / Malaysia, Singapore

* Italicized cases exhibit the hypothesized cause but not the expected outcome; nonitalicized cases exhibit the outcome without the hypothesized cause.

locate common threads capable of explaining the region's diverse political landscape. The causal framework I offer places variation in *contentious politics* and *elite collective action* at its analytic center.

From Factions to Institutions: How Contentious Politics Can Change Politics

The provision of selective incentives cannot be the general solution to the collective action problem. To assume that there is a central authority offering incentives often requires another collective action problem to have been solved already.

Jon Elster[25]

Elite collective action is as elusive as it is elemental. On the one hand, "the cohesion of the political elite is the crucial element in the search for political stability."[26] But strong elite coalitions are extremely difficult to construct and consolidate at the national level. In most places and under most circumstances, elite politics is rife with factionalism and parochialism. This book commences

---

[24] Przeworski and Limongi (1997: 161) were especially struck by this anomaly: "Singapore and Malaysia are the two countries that developed over a long period, became wealthy, and remained dictatorships until now." As Greene (2007: 22, fn. 34) notes, "Przeworski et al.'s model predicts that Singapore should have been a democracy with 98% probability," while Malaysia should have democratized "with 69% probability."

[25] Elster (1989): 40.

[26] Brown (1993): 111.

with the assumption that *factions* – not atomistic individuals, solidary organizations, ethnic groups, or economic classes – are the fundamental building blocks of
politics.[27] Whenever strong institutions arise to transcend the quotidian politics
of factions and cliques, and to organize elite collective action on a national scale,
there is a fundamental political puzzle to be explained.

How is elite factionalism tempered, and elite collective action gained? Or, to
state this question in terms of the specific institutions under consideration here
– How can state officials be induced to work collectively to extract direct taxes
from economic elites, and to channel those revenues to a central treasury, rather
than cutting self-serving side-deals with factional allies in the private sector or
pocketing most of the revenue haul for themselves? How can economic elites be
convinced that resistance to direct taxation is futile or self-defeating? Taxation
represents a monumental collective action problem – not only for individual
taxpayers with obvious incentives to free-ride, but for government officials who
must construct (or acquiesce to the construction of) effective state organizations
to make direct taxation administratively plausible in the first place.

Collective action problems plague party formation, military politics, and
authoritarian regime maintenance as seriously as they hinder state-building. How
can authoritarian rulers bring a wide range of elites into supportive relations with
their regime, and prevent them from playing oppositional roles? Building broad-
based ruling parties would appear to be the best approach. But it is inherently
risky. Such parties might ultimately be used as organized vehicles for challenging
the leadership rather than supporting it. Why not just depend on a narrow range
of personal loyalists instead, particularly in the military? Even when a regime
rests on military rather than party power, elite collective action remains essential. If military officers are not in lockstep in their willingness to use force against
democratic protestors, the regime becomes highly vulnerable to collapse in the
face of anti-regime mobilization. To pose the "regime puzzle" in the broadest
terms: Why would *any* elites provide steadfast support to a regime that does not
countenance the prospect of its own removal?

Political scientists overwhelmingly concur on a straightforward answer to this
question: People support a dictatorship when it provides them with economic
benefits.[28] Put more axiomatically, we do not expect people to bite the hands that
feed them – even if those hands also happen to be politically strangling them.
The core problem with this formulation, as Elster's previous quotation suggests,
is that the predictable provision of selective incentives or public goods requires
the prior existence of a robust political center. Elites must be effectively arranged

---

[27] Factions need not inhabit a common organizational setting, such as a political party. Following
Sandbrook, I define factions broadly as "personal alliance networks" engaged in "conflict over
access to wealth, power, and status, frequently with only minor ideological or policy implications"
(1972: 109, 115). For a similar starting assumption that politics in "natural states" exhibits a
"predominance of social relationships organized along personal lines," see North, Wallis, and
Weingast (2009: 12).

[28] "The survival of leaders and of the institutions or regimes they lead is threatened when they are
no longer able to provide sufficient resources to sustain political support" (Bueno de Mesquita
et al. 2003: 26). See also Bellin (2002) and Greene (2007), inter alia.

and capable institutions must be constructed before any predictable system of public provision can be effectively implemented.

This book seeks to uncover the origins of the institutions that channel and facilitate elite collective action under dictatorship. When trying to understand why elites have come to provide collective political support to an authoritarian regime, we are better guided by an alternative axiom to the notion that people do not bite the hands that feed them – that *the enemy of one's enemy is one's friend*. Understanding elite collective action under dictatorship requires more than "following the money." It requires recognizing how a shared "fear of enemies" can serve as "a means for the achievement of collective ends."[29]

As Hobbes argued, people are more reliably organized in collective defense against their shared *aversions* than for the collective pursuit of their shared *appetites*. In game-theoretical terms, coordinating against shared aversions tends to resemble a relatively tractable Battle of the Sexes or Assurance game, whereas cooperating for shared gains usually entails a much pricklier Prisoner's Dilemma.[30] Political theorist Ioannis Evrigenis has affirmed Hobbes' stress on shared perceptions of threat as the surest foundation for collective action, arguing that "the conditions that characterize the state of nature are such that especially initially, but also subsequently, negative association will be necessary if the barriers to group formation and collective action are to be overcome." This is why contentious politics can provide a more powerful initial spark for elite collective action and the subsequent shaping of institutional profiles than a promised abundance of shared economic benefits.[31] And the importance of shared threat perceptions for elite collective action diminishes, but does not disappear, over time. "When threats to security are distant, the pursuit of private goods rises on the list of individuals' priorities," Evrigenis notes. "This rearrangement harbors the potential for trouble."[32] Patronage can salve, but not solve, the problem of factions.

Variation in *the type and timing* of contentious politics explains national variation in elite collective action, and hence in the robustness of postcolonial state, party, military, and regime institutions.[33] To be sure, outbreaks of contentious

---

[29] Evrigenis (2008): 19.

[30] Snidal (1985). Assurance and Battle of the Sexes games are more tractable than Prisoner's Dilemmas because players face weaker incentives to cheat, shirk, or defect.

[31] In contrast to North, Wallis, and Weingast (2009), I do not see the promise of rent-sharing alone as sufficient for overcoming the fundamental Prisoner's Dilemma that stymies elite collective action in the absence of shared perceptions of threat. While "all elites have incentives to support and help maintain the coalition" (2009: 20) under such rent-filled conditions, the temptation to "cheat" and seize more resources for one's own faction against the backdrop of imperfect information remains enormous and, more important, untempered.

[32] Evrigenis (2008): 12, 19.

[33] It is not my argument that contentious politics causes democratic breakdown and authoritarian onset. It is that variation in contentious politics shapes divergence in levels of elite support for authoritarian rule and for the construction of stronger state and regime institutions to underpin it – and hence divergence in authoritarian durability. Since democracy broke down everywhere in postwar Southeast Asia, the region lacks the requisite variation to support any single systematic explanation for democratic breakdown (Slater 2008b: 59–60). For the classic argument linking class conflict to democratic breakdown and authoritarian onset, see O'Donnell (1973).

politics do not always inspire significant and sustained elite collective action – even when they take on the specific threatening and challenging attributes emphasized in this book. In a political world governed by agency as well as by structure, elites may always fail to respond to organized challenges from below. To assume that threats automatically produce effective responses would be to engage in crude and discredited modes of functionalist reasoning. Yet this does not mean that threats are causally irrelevant; it only suggests that they are not sufficient conditions for the outcomes of interest. The causal logic presented here suggests, however, that severe threats to elites' property, privileges, and persons are a *necessary* condition for the intrinsic challenge of elite collective action to be overcome.[34] One might call this "inverted" functionalism; rather than assuming "if threat, response," I assume "if *no* threat, *no* response." Given their propensity for parochialism, elites will not deemphasize their narrow factional interests on behalf of broader class interests except under extreme duress.

But how do we know extreme duress when we see it? How can we avoid the pitfalls of either (1) succumbing to post hoc reasoning and defining the severity of the threat by the seriousness of the response; or (2) naively accepting elite statements about threats from below at face value?[35] Since human perceptions are not directly observable, this book's strategy is to lay out a deductively grounded framework as to what types of contentious politics should be considered most challenging and threatening to the broadest range of elite actors. I submit that some forms of contentious politics are systematically more likely than others to inspire elite collective action toward building an increasingly powerful and unconstrained political center. The question is not simply *how much* social conflict it takes to make elites fearful, but *what type* of social conflict it takes to make elites cooperate for purposes of ordering power.

There are two key considerations. First, do state and societal elites perceive the types of contentious politics they are confronting to be *endemic* or *episodic*? Second, do they perceive these types of mass mobilization to be *manageable* under pluralistic institutional arrangements, or *unmanageable* given existing levels of state fragmentation and political openness? The source of such perceptions is difficult to formalize and doubtless depends to some degree on the historical specifics of the case in question. But in the Southeast Asian context – and, I more tentatively suggest, elsewhere – a discernible causal pattern appears to be at work.

---

[34] For other recent works portraying severe threats to elite positions and privileges as fundamental in the development of political institutions, see Collier and Collier (1991); Luebbert (1991); Downing (1992); Ertman (1997); Waldner (1999); Lopez-Alves (2000); Mahoney (2001); B. Smith (2007); and Doner (2009).

[35] Elite statements are treated as supportive evidence at times in the empirical chapters, but only when (1) there is strong intuitive reason to be confident that the statements are neither purely self-serving nor wholly disingenuous; or (2) their reception by other elites as palpably self-serving or disingenuous demonstrates the absence of a compelling sense of collective threat. In the cases of the Philippines, Thailand, and Burma, electoral victories for opposition parties during times of ostensibly unmanageable unrest are taken as evidence that urban middle classes, especially, did not accept the incumbent regime's protection logic on the eve of the origins of those countries' authoritarian Leviathans. Many thanks to Sofia Fenner for her insights on these points.

Both the type and the timing of conflict are vital. In terms of timing, the key consideration is whether contentious politics erupts *before or after* the inauguration of what I call *authoritarian Leviathans* – regimes that seek to use the full force of the state apparatus to subjugate society into a hierarchical, command-centered body politic on a presumptively permanent basis.[36] Timing is of the essence because how violent conflicts are politically perceived depends on whether they occur under a democrat's or a dictator's watch. When unmanageable contentious politics erupts under the relatively pluralistic political forms – i.e., weak states and unstable democratic regimes – that typically precede the onset of authoritarian Leviathans, emergent dictators can more credibly claim that a stronger state and a more repressive regime are necessary to preserve social peace. By contrast, when contentious politics originally erupts or significantly worsens *after* an authoritarian regime is already in power, elite opinions will vary more widely as to the helpfulness or harmfulness of authoritarianism as a tool for social order. All dictatorships may *attempt* to construct a shared sense that democracy equals chaos while authoritarianism equals stability, but only some possess the historical raw material to *succeed* at making such claims broadly credible.

Here is where the type of conflict becomes so consequential. Outbreaks of contention are especially likely to be perceived as endemic and unmanageable by an extremely wide range of elites when *class conflict* afflicts *urban areas* and exacerbates *communal tensions*. Although I elaborate on the logics underpinning this claim in the next chapter, for now it is essential to underscore the centrality of class in this argument. *Social conflict will not enhance collective action among a wide range of elites unless it emanates from a mass organization or movement making radical redistributive demands.* Clashes between vertically structured ethnic groups, or between the followers of one elite-led faction against another, are more common types of conflict in the postcolonial world than the kinds that foster elite collective action – and they are not the kinds of conflicts I have in mind.[37] Even the deadliest conflicts of such types will not elicit elite collective action, in this book's framework. Mine is not a theory of elites coalescing out of exhaustion with their incessant internecine struggles;[38] it is a theory of elites being driven by force of contentious events to perceive lower-class movements as their shared enemy, and their fellow elites as their indispensable coalitional friends.

How Power Gets Ordered: Extraction and Organization under Protection Pacts

Leading actors will have an incentive to jointly surrender their power to a strong state, only if they live in a politically divided society in which the weaker group can make a

---

[36] This concept has a slightly broader connotation than O'Donnell's (1973) notion of "bureaucratic-authoritarianism," which suggests the same sort of state-regime fusion that I wish to capture here.

[37] On elite conflict as a driver of state and regime outcomes, see Waldner (1999, 2008).

[38] For such an interpretation of elite consensus around racial exclusion in South Africa and the United States (but not Brazil), see Marx (1998). For an argument that such intra-elite armistices explain political order more universally, see North, Wallis, and Weingast (2009).

credible threat to change the rules of the game to their advantage and to the detriment of their opponents.

Michael Hechter and William Brustein[39]

To understand the influence of elite collective action on state and regime institutions, one must not only examine the tightness of a ruling coalition. One must also examine the *terms* under which it operates. Not all elite coalitions order power. Only when the terms of coalescence involve a steady flow of resources toward the political institutions of an authoritarian Leviathan, and not from the hands of public authority to actors outside the state apparatus, can ordering power be said to be occurring. When Hechter and Brustein depict elites as liable "to jointly surrender their power to a strong state" when their class enemies "can make a credible threat to change the rules of the game," they capture both the dynamics of ordering power and the causal force driving those dynamics as argued throughout this book.

This is a different reading of coalitions than the one that predominates in the comparative politics literature. In most analyses, a coalition is portrayed as the groups that benefit from government policy and support incumbent leaders in exchange.[40] Yet the defining feature of a coalition is that it provides political support – not that it receives economic benefits as an impetus to do so. When determining what kind of coalition exists in an authoritarian setting, we should not begin by asking what the government does for its coalition; we should begin by asking what the coalition does for its government.[41]

How well authoritarian leaders fare at capturing the strategic resources that elite groups possess depends on the types of contentious politics that presage the birth of the authoritarian Leviathan. Where such conflicts are widely perceived as both endemic and unmanageable, as operationalized above, authoritarian regimes enjoy an excellent opportunity to craft a *protection pact*: a pro-authoritarian coalition linking upper groups on the basis of shared perceptions of threat. At their broadest, these coalitions encompass four sets of elites: (1) *state officials*, from the top leadership to mid-level bureaucrats, including the police and armed forces and, under conditions of colonial control or foreign domination, external patrons as well; (2) *economic elites*, such as major industrialists, financiers, merchants, and landowners; (3) *middle classes*, including professionals, petty merchants, university students, and intellectuals; and (4) *communal elites*, especially leading religious and nationalist figures, as well as top figures in ethnic associations.[42] At their strongest,

[39] Hechter and Brustein (1980): 1090.
[40] As Waldner (1999: 34) puts it, coalitions "are typically constructed by means of side-payments." See also Bueno de Mesquita et al. (2003). Although this book defines coalitions differently than Waldner (2002), it still broadly fits his proposed "standard explanatory pattern" for state-building, in which conflicts shape institutions through the causal mechanism of coalitions. See Slater (2005: 11–12) for more on this point.
[41] Nor should membership in an authoritarian coalition imply policy influence (e.g., Gandhi and Przeworski 2007). Authoritarian institutions and coalitions are ultimately a regime's mechanisms to ensure societal *acquiescence* to power, not *access* to it (Slater 2003, 2010; also Kasza 1995).
[42] For more conceptual discussion of communal elites, see Slater (2009).

protection pacts institutionalize support from all four of these types of elites by organizing them into broad-based ruling parties.

Powerful postcolonial protection pacts have arisen only rarely; but when they have, as in Malaysia and Singapore, they have permitted authoritarian rulers to extract considerable compliance and resources from their fellow elites.[43] More precisely, economic elites have paid higher taxes and supplied more generous political financing to authoritarian leaders and their political vehicles. Middle classes have refrained from joining popular sectors in anti-regime mobilization, helped provide intellectual justification for nondemocratic rule, and formed the social backbone of authoritarian ruling parties. Communal elites have granted authoritarian regimes a critical imprimatur of symbolic legitimacy, mobilized followers to help suppress regime opponents, and allowed state institutions to insinuate themselves into doctrinal practices. Threatened state officials have proven loyal to ruling party or military institutions, ready to impose coercive measures on regime opponents, and willing to implement extractive tax policies in a cohesive and effective manner.

The ideal-typical protection pact is one in which all four of these upper groups reliably play these supportive roles, providing their strategic resources to incumbents and withholding them from the political opposition. Such coalitions endow states and the regimes that run them with a near monopoly on what Amitai Etzioni usefully describes as the three subtypes of power: (1) coercive, (2) remunerative, and (3) symbolic. (See Figure 1.[44]) The more of these power sources regimes lack, or lose over time, the more vulnerable they become to anti-regime mobilization and democratic transition.[45]

What Figure 1 attempts to capture is an ideal-typical protection pact working in seamless, mechanical fashion. The arrows, conveying power flows, are not meant to be exhaustive, but I have drawn them in a manner that captures the most important ways in which particular types of elites provide support to an authoritarian Leviathan (e.g., military personnel providing reliable coercion, industrialists paying taxes, religious authorities as well as secular intellectuals offering ringing public endorsements).

Of more importance is the *direction* in which power resources are flowing: from elites to Leviathan, and not the reverse. In the absence of a protection pact, authoritarian institutions are less likely to order power than to exhaust their power – especially of the remunerative sort – by buying off and otherwise

---

43 How much coercion or consent accompanies any particular process of generating compliance is an empirical question. Highly threatening and challenging forms of contentious politics can help make state officials more cohesively coercive *and* can help make economic elites more consentingly compliant with state commands.

44 Etzioni (1961). To be clear, Figure 1 is not a causal diagram, but a descriptive picture of who provides what to the authoritarian Leviathan under a protection pact.

45 See Boix (2003) and Acemoglu and Robinson (2006) for analyses similarly portraying regime outcomes as a function of the balance of power between powerholders and their opponents. This critical causal factor is exogenous in their models, whereas my framework seeks to specify it systematically, thereby proposing political foundations that I see as missing from these authors' economistic accounts.

FIGURE 1. Ordering Power (Part I): *Extracting* Power from Protection Pacts

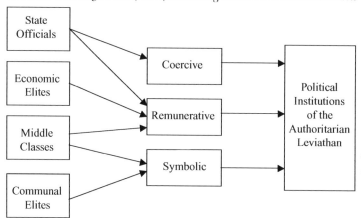

succoring potential elite opponents to stave off devastating defections. While elites are never monolithic, elites under such "provision pacts" are a much farther cry from being monolithic than elites in protection pacts. Some military officers, wealthy landowners, public intellectuals, and religious leaders will acquiesce or lend active support to the incumbent authoritarian regime, while many others will actively or clandestinely oppose it. One should thus envision the arrows in the absence of a protection pact flowing in the opposite direction as in Figure 1 or in multiple directions, with many arrows figuratively snipped by scissors, as elites deny the authoritarian Leviathan the power resources it needs to consolidate its domination.

Why are authoritarian Leviathans that order coercive, remunerative, and symbolic power more able to stabilize politics and retain power than those that do not? First, regimes with the capacity to apply coercion in an efficient and targeted manner can punish their enemies in pinpoint fashion, rather than applying repression in a haphazard way that might spark wider resistance.[46] The barebones reality of authoritarian politics is that "no transition can be forced purely by opponents against a regime which maintains the cohesion, capacity, and disposition to apply repression."[47] Stores of remunerative and symbolic power help allay the need for authoritarian Leviathans to apply repression at all, allowing political authorities to secure acquiescence and even a sense of appropriateness among their subjects.[48] For an authoritarian Leviathan to place itself in a position

[46] On how indiscriminate state violence fuels revolutionary movements, see Goodwin (2001).

[47] O'Donnell and Schmitter (1986): 21.

[48] Acquiescence to an authoritarian regime does not indicate that regime's perceived appropriateness among its subjects, however (Wedeen 1999). I consider the public actions and statements of communal elites to be a better (if still imperfect) barometer of regime appropriateness than the mere existence of public acquiescence (Slater 2009). More generally, this book focuses on the Weberian rather than the Foulcauldian face of state power because ruling elites' success at

FIGURE 2. Ordering Power (Part II): *Organizing* Power in Authoritarian Institutions

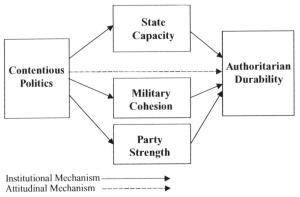

of outright and enduring political domination, it must extract as much of these three sources of power from state and societal elites as it possibly can.

Extraction is only one dimension of political domination, however – *organization* is equally vital. Having extracted coercive, remunerative, and symbolic power from the elites possessing them, how do the commanders of the authoritarian Leviathan organize them? The answer, of course, is institutions. In the absence of cohesive bureaucracies, parties, and militaries, even a purely "rightward" flow of resources toward the state will place power in the hands of a fragmented rather than a cohesive ruling apparatus. This is a recipe for endemic conflict among elites, not the ordered power that arises from sustained elite collective action.

It is primarily through the crafting of new political institutions that protection pacts gain their solidity over time. Figure 2 summarizes the role of specific state and regime institutions in my causal argument.

As Figure 2 tries to convey, contentious politics before the founding of authoritarian Leviathans exhibits path-dependent effects on authoritarian political structures through two distinct mechanisms of reproduction:[49] an *institutional* mechanism, and an *attitudinal* mechanism. The more powerful mechanism is institutional; merely by organizing actors in particular ways at the outset of a new political dispensation, leaders create structures that assume a momentum of their own. Expectations converge, relationships are forged, and interests adapt to prevailing institutional frameworks. There is a strong bias toward continuity in political institutions, which is why path-dependent causal explanations are considered so powerful in political science and historical sociology.

Authoritarian Leviathans constructed upon protection pacts do not merely maintain their original power advantages over time, however. The consistent

---

broadcasting a "state effect" (Mitchell 1991) largely depends upon their prior successes at organization and extraction. The "shabbiness" (Wedeen 1999: 3) of Hafiz al-Asad's personality cult thus exposes the deeper shabbiness of Syria's state and party institutions. For more on modern states as "repositories of symbolic power," see Loveman (2005: 1659) and Gorski (2003).

[49] On path dependence, see Mahoney (2001: 4–8); on mechanisms of reproduction, see Thelen (1999).

flow of resources from society toward the state throughout the regime's tenure provides it with "increasing returns" to power, especially on the remunerative dimension.[50] An authoritarian Leviathan that continually extracts more revenue from society than it spends to secure social support will find itself on ever-firmer fiscal footing. Dictatorships that survive strictly through patronage and spending – what I call "provision pacts" instead of "protection pacts" – will gradually squander their remunerative power and find themselves increasingly vulnerable to debilitating fiscal crises. The point is not that such regimes are incapable of enduring for long stretches of time, especially when bankrolled by oil, aid, and other nontax revenues.[51] It is that regimes founded as provision pacts suffer from the political equivalent of a "birth defect" that regimes originating as protection pacts do not.[52]

This suggests that the relative importance of shared concerns with collective protection in sustaining elite collective action should decline as an authoritarian Leviathan ages. As Evrigenis, channeling Hobbes, argued in the previous section, common threat perceptions foster collective action "especially initially, but also subsequently."[53] If a regime is founded in the absence of endemic and unmanageable conflict, it can never become a protection pact – any subsequent conflicts will as likely turn elites against the incumbent regime for its failure to provide protection as it will incite them to seek collective shelter under its continuance. But the inverse does not hold true. A regime born as a protection pact may gradually lose its protective logic as the threats of yesterday fade into the distant past.

Yet this will not automatically lead to the demise of elite collective action and consequent destabilizing of the authoritarian Leviathan. One force for continuity is habit, as collaborative elite relationships originally forged amid shared perceptions of threat might simply adapt to changing circumstances. A second is coercion, as the Leviathan's initial concentration of force might leave societal actors powerless to resist it, even as they increasingly perceive the dictatorship as an unnecessary and unwanted protection racket. A third is compensation, as the flushness of a powerfully extractive authoritarian Leviathan allows it increasingly to substitute protection with provision – a weaker and more factionalizing basis for rule, I insist, but far superior to having no basis for rule whatsoever. Much as Juan Linz and Alfred Stepan have classified contemporary regimes such as China's as "post-totalitarian"[54] – still surviving, but under a transformed logic – I refer to regimes as "post-protective" when their original protection logic fades, and gives way to rule characterized primarily by an alternative logic such as economic provision.

By now, the reader may have gotten the impression that authoritarian Leviathans born as protection pacts are utterly indestructible. Yet political coalitions

---

[50] Pierson (2004): 22–24. State infrastructural power is thus best conceived as a "stock variable" that accrues over time, not simply as a static measure. For a similar argument regarding the cumulative causal importance of democracy, see Gerring et al. (2005).

[51] Morrison (2009).

[52] To borrow Huntington's (1968: 398) evocative phrase, provision pacts are "presumptively unstable" while protection pacts are "presumptively stable."

[53] Evrigenis (2008): 12.

[54] Linz and Stepan (1996): 42–51.

and institutions *can* break down or wither over time, as the Indonesian case will most vividly testify in the chapters to come. Here is where the attitudinal mechanism of reproduction – recall the dashed line in Figure 2 – comes into play. This entails elite perceptions of earlier historical episodes of contentious politics, as well as evolving views of the probability that such mass unrest could reemerge if authoritarian controls were lifted. Such individual (but shared) perceptions are far more fluid than tangible political organizations. If state and societal elites broadly come to believe that an authoritarian leader's protestations of "après moi, le deluge" are nothing but hot air – or that a leader's perpetuation in power itself foreshadows the unleashing of such a threatening deluge – they become attitudinally available to the political opposition. It is a tortuous path from attitudinal shifts at the micro level to the coalitional and institutional shifts necessary at the macro level to physically overthrow an authoritarian regime – but it can be an important start.

Authoritarian rulers acknowledge the importance of attitudes as well as institutions in sustaining their rule when they trumpet the view, ad nauseam, that their regimes provide the only protection elites enjoy from utter chaos. Their goal is to convince social forces that *they have more to fear from each other than from the state*, nipping potential cross-class democratic coalitions in the bud. Virtually all authoritarian regimes make this pitch, but they are not all equally convincing or credible. When authoritarian rule was preceded by types of contentious politics that were widely perceived as unmanageable and endemic, anti-democratic attitudes will be easier to sustain over the long term. Without such shared historical memories, dictators confront Abraham Lincoln's famous dictum – they cannot fool all of the people all of the time. In short, some authoritarian regimes enjoy far better historical raw material with which to construct and cultivate shared threat perceptions than others.

This book's causal framework is most succinctly expressed by the template provided in Figure 2. Contentious politics is the independent variable. States, militaries, and ruling parties are dependent variables arising from contentious politics, as well as intervening variables that influence authoritarian durability in turn. The causal relationship between contentious politics and authoritarian durability is both direct (via the attitudinal mechanism) and indirect (via the institutional mechanism, or its effects on states, militaries, and parties). In sum, differing patterns of contentious politics initiate divergent pathways of party, military, state, and regime development because they produce different types of coalitions. I now aim to put empirical meat on these theoretical bones, showing how my framework makes causal sense of Southeast Asia's divergent political trajectories in the postwar era.

Southeast Asia's Counterrevolutionary Political Pathways: Domination, Fragmentation, and Militarization

A principal challenge of comparative-historical research is to push the systematic comparison of cases as far as possible without pushing it to a point where it does violence to the distinctive attributes of each case.... An important concomitant of occupying this middle ground is the recognition of a crucial point: the claim that two countries are similar or different with regard to a particular attribute does not, and is not intended to, assign to them the overall status of being similar or different cases.

Ruth Berins Collier and David Collier[55]

Southeast Asia circa 1950 appears in many ways quite strange and extraordinary from the perspective of the present. Stalinist Communists and Western colonialists – actors who have now almost completely vanished from the world-stage – were enormously important forces, sometimes engaged in life-and-death struggles, in many of the countries in the region.

Jeff Goodwin[56]

Nothing has shaped the modern world as profoundly as the emergence of mass populaces onto the political stage. In Western Europe, World War I signaled the bellwether moment beyond which elite politicians could no longer ignore the mounting clamor from ordinary citizens for political inclusion. Wartime mobilization to salvage national sovereignty gave way to peacetime mobilization to secure popular sovereignty. To say that Western European elites did not accept this development passively would of course be a colossal understatement. As Carl Schmitt put it, "the approach of democracy appeared a chaotic storm against which a dam had to be built."[57] Yet the region-wide challenge of mass politics wrought a wide variety of elite responses at the national level – there was more than one way to build Schmitt's dam against what continental elites feared would culminate in unbridled mob rule. As Gregory Luebbert so masterfully detailed, liberal democracy, social democracy, and fascism would be the three institutional pathways through which interwar European elites would save themselves from full-blown democratic or – far worse – socialist revolution.[58]

This book ventures the argument that World War II unleashed broadly analogous and similarly defining political dynamics in Southeast Asia as World War I spawned in Europe. "The second wave of world social revolution emerged out of the Second World War, as the first had emerged out of the First – though in an utterly different way," Eric Hobsbawm has written. "This time it was the waging of war and not the revulsion against it which brought revolution to power."[59] Yet in Southeast Asia, the most common outcome of postwar contentious politics was not the triumph of revolution, but *counterrevolution*. We can profitably conceive of the diverse counterrevolutionary reactions to the explosion of mass unrest that rocked most of Southeast Asia in the postwar years in terms of three primary pathways, much as Luebbert so fruitfully attempted in the European context.

What this book thereby offers is a stab at staking a Collier and Collier–style "middle ground" between implausibly stylized cross-case patterns and inscrutably

---

[55] Collier and Collier (1991): 13, 14.
[56] Goodwin (2001): 75.
[57] Schmitt (1985) [1923]: 51.
[58] Luebbert (1991).
[59] Hobsbawm (1994): 80. The parallel between communist revolutions emerging in Russia out of World War I and in China out of World War II – vividly haunting conservative elites in Western Europe and Southeast Asia, respectively – is especially important here.

ideographic case specifics. As the Goodwin quote above attests, the countries and colonies of Southeast Asia suffered a simultaneous region-wide exogenous shock with Japan's wartime occupation and its unstable aftermath. Yet as in Europe, these postwar tremors of mass politics were experienced in subtly different ways in different parts of Southeast Asia – and the consequences remain visible today. Again to invoke Hobsbawm: "Even where the experience of communism has been reversed, the present of the ex-communist countries, and presumably their future, bear, and will continue to bear, *the specific marks of the counter-revolution which replaced the revolution.*"[60] In Southeast Asia, the lasting footprints of counterrevolution can even be seen in countries where leftist forces fiercely fought, but finally failed, to reshape politics in the mold of Marxist-Leninism.[61] To understand the sharp divergence between two of Southeast Asia's three counter-revolutionary pathways of political development, one must pay careful attention to the subtle differences in the intentions, impacts, and implications of leftist mass mobilization in the region's broad popular upsurge in the wake of World War II.

Pathway #1: Domination

The first counterrevolutionary political pathway, which I will call *domination* for shorthand, is most clearly witnessed in Malaysia and Singapore. There, the Japanese occupation did not pit occupier against occupied so much as it pitted the largely collaborationist indigenous Malay population against armed anti-Japanese communist insurgents, who were mostly ethnic Chinese. When Japan suddenly surrendered after the atomic annihilation of Hiroshima and Nagasaki in August 1945, both British Malaya[62] and Singapore experienced a chaotic, stateless, and bloody interregnum in which ethnic Chinese– and communist-led insurgents briefly stood as the only organized political force on the Malayan Peninsula, before European rule could be restored on the ground. Radical leftist mobilization continued in both cases throughout the 1950s, and urban race riots emanating from economic underclasses augured the collapse of pluralist politics and the birth of authoritarian Leviathans in the 1960s.

Postwar contentious politics in Malaysia and Singapore thus broadly fits the stylized description of endemic and unmanageable social conflict offered earlier in this chapter. As ever, it was the type rather than the raw intensity of conflict that

---

[60] Ibid. 83. Emphasis added.

[61] As a work of comparative *counter*revolution, this book does not examine the left-revolutionary Southeast Asian cases of Cambodia, Laos, and post-unification Vietnam. (I do consider the relative durability of revolutionary and counterrevolutionary regimes in the following and concluding chapters, however.) Since South Vietnam was the most likely among these three cases to have developed a taxation-funded protection pact, given its relative national wealth, I consider its failed counterrevolution in depth. In other words, the inability of state elites in Cambodia and Laos to collect direct taxes might well be overdetermined, given the tiny size of those countries' private sectors. Southeast Asia's other two countries, Brunei and East Timor, did not commence their decolonization processes until long after the postwar upsurge in contentious leftist politics had ceased, greatly complicating their comparability as well.

[62] Malaya was renamed Malaysia in 1963.

mattered most. Mass movements *preceded* the rise of authoritarian Leviathans, *presented* radical demands, *penetrated* the polities' urban core, and *provoked* ethnic and religious tensions. New elite coalitions arose in active support of both increased state centralization and open-ended authoritarianism, as the imperative of restabilizing what appeared to be an endemically destabilized social and political order outweighed the perceived risks of giving free rein to a potentially predatory authoritarian Leviathan.

These are the types of coalitions I call protection pacts. In Malaysia and Singapore, such high levels of elite collective action have served as the social foundation for highly cohesive ruling parties, states with considerable fiscal power, and militaries of solidaristic and subservient stock. With preponderant advantages over any and all potential opponents on every dimension of political power, successive leaders of the Malaysian and Singaporean Leviathans have commanded authoritarian regimes of remarkable durability – even as threat perceptions gradually fade and authoritarian politics takes on an increasingly "post-protective," provision-driven dynamic in both cases.

Pathway #2: Fragmentation

In a second set of Southeast Asian cases, the types of contentious class politics following World War II exhibited much less of a centripetal impact on national elites, and factions rather than institutions remained the bedrock of politics. Mass leftist mobilization preceding the rise of authoritarian Leviathans in these cases was either virtually nonexistent (as in Thailand from 1945–57); driven mostly by reformist, lower-class demands for democratic rights and inclusion (as in the Philippines from 1945–53); or characterized by cross-class appeals for national independence (as in South Vietnam from 1945–55), rather than by purely redistributionist programs and demands.[63] In all three cases, furthermore, leftist rebellions in these periods lacked both urban impact and communal implications, given their purely rural character and the backdrop of weakly politicized ethnoreligious divisions against which rebellion occurred.

Intensely violent such episodes of contentious politics often were. Yet the types of conflict they entailed generally led elite groups to perceive the danger to their property, privileges, and persons to be relatively episodic and manageable under somewhat pluralistic political conditions. Comparatively confident in their capacity to deploy their own social power to defeat the leftist threat – without needing to "join amongst themselves to subject themselves" to a more centralized political authority in the Hobbesian sense – they provided nothing more than tepid and temporary support for authoritarian rulers' projects of state-building, party formation, military subjugation, and regime maintenance.

Flimsy coalitions produced flimsy institutions. Authoritarian leaders enjoyed precious little success at building robust ruling parties, taxing upper groups' incomes, enlisting military support in cohesive crackdowns, and ultimately

[63] Leftists' willingness to subsume themselves into cross-class *nationalist* movements in the immediate aftermath of World War II – as seen in Vietnam, Indonesia, and Burma – will be treated as empirical evidence of a reformist approach.

TABLE 3. *Classifying Contentious Class Politics in Southeast Asia*

	Urban Impact?	
	Yes	**No**
Yes **Communal** **Implications?**	Singapore 1945–48, 1955–65 Malaysia 1945–57[#], 1969 Indonesia 1964–66[#]	Empty Set[+]
No	Burma 1946–48 Philippines 1970–86[*] S. Vietnam 1968–75[*] Thailand 1973, 1976[*]	Burma 1946–85 Philippines 1945–53 S. Vietnam 1960–68[*] Thailand 1968–73, 1976–77[*]

[*] Peaked *after* the onset of authoritarian Leviathans (Burma 1962, Indonesia 1966, Malaysia 1969, Philippines 1972, Singapore 1965, South Vietnam 1955, Thailand 1958).
[#] Even when class conflict was *predominantly* rural, its urban impact was significant.
[+] "Immigrant" minorities mostly settled in urban areas during Southeast Asia's colonial era.

securing their regimes' survival in the face of cross-class anti-regime mobilization. In all three cases, contentious class politics looked far more threatening *after* the birth of authoritarian Leviathans than beforehand. Such worsening mass unrest splintered ruling coalitions rather than cementing them, as authoritarianism could be readily perceived by many elites as a *source* of violence instead of its essential *solution*. As seen in Table 3, contentious class politics in the Philippines, South Vietnam, and Thailand differed markedly from the postwar leftist upsurge in Malaysia and Singapore in terms of its political timing, urban impact, and communal implications. Bound by nothing besides elites' shared but zero-sum appetites for economic largesse, the provision pacts of the Philippines, South Vietnam, and Thailand proved a far weaker social foundation for authoritarian durability than the protection pacts of Malaysia and Singapore. Instead of ordering power *from* elites, highly personalized regimes in these cases mostly squandered power *to* elites in their desperate attempts to salvage their own incumbency through their control of an inexorably shriveling public purse. Given the shared feature of institutional incoherence that links these three otherwise radically different cases, I refer to their overarching postwar political trajectory as one of *fragmentation* rather than domination.

In short, authoritarian regimes built upon protection pacts enjoyed more success at ordering power than their provision-driven counterparts. Power was ordered both in the sense of being *extracted* from society, especially through tax revenue; and in the sense of being *organized* into political institutions, such as centralized states, cohesive and subservient militaries, and powerful and hierarchical ruling parties. Elite collective action produced stronger party, military, state, and regime institutions in the first set of cases, while elite factionalism persistently debilitated these same institutions in the second set.

This contrast between domination and fragmentation captures the sweeping institutional divergence between five of the seven cases in this book. Malaysia, the Philippines, Singapore, South Vietnam, and Thailand all developed state, party, military, and regime institutions that were either weak or strong *in tandem*. However, my causal framework aims not just to capture the stark contrast in political processes and outcomes between these two sets of cases. It also endeavors to explain why patterns of contentious politics and elite collective action in Burma and Indonesia produced more uneven institutional profiles. As summarized in Table 1, Burma's authoritarian regime has experienced extraordinary endurance, despite the lack of political stability resulting from the absence of either a strongly extractive central state or a robustly organized ruling party. And authoritarian institutions in Indonesia proved to be neither as powerful as those of the domination cases, nor as divisive and debilitated as parties, militaries, states, and dictatorships in the fragmentation examples. The next section tackles the analytic challenge of tracing what I argue to be a third counterrevolutionary political trajectory, without abandoning the analytic focus on contentious politics and elite collective action characterizing the domination and fragmentation pathways.

Pathway #3: Militarization

A causal framework centering on class conflict alone cannot apprehend the full range of ways in which contentious politics shapes the coalitions and institutions underpinning authoritarian Leviathans. To understand coalitional contours and institutional outcomes in Burma and Indonesia, one must consider the causal implications of another type of contentious politics that has ravaged so much of the postcolonial world: *regional rebellions*, or violent "struggles over the establishment of central authority" marked by "provinces rebelling against control by the capital."[64]

Armed movements aiming to *escape* the state should tend to build different elite coalitions than mass mobilization seeking to *seize* the state. Whereas "bottom-up" conflicts can spur a wide range of upper groups to perceive a shared interest in organizing for common class protection, regional rebellions generally present less of a direct physical threat to economic elites, middle classes, and communal elites, who in postcolonial settings largely huddle in major cities. If such peripheral violence sparks increased collective action among any elite group, it is most likely to be military leaders, who typically shoulder the actual responsibility of quelling regional unrest.

Regional rebellions should thus tend to exhibit a unifying effect on the national military, but not upon the other elite groups who can potentially constitute a protection pact. The most likely institutional result is a highly unified but militarized state with weak links to societal elites and – given military officers' disinclination either to prioritize the bureaucratic minutiae of civil governance themselves, or to

---

[64] Centeno (2002): 62. This encompasses armed struggles for regional autonomy as well as outright separatism.

defer to civil servants on matters of internal governance[65] – weak administrative capacity to boot. Yet the relative cohesion of military elites will still contribute to regime durability, so long as the state's coercive apparatus remains willing to use violence to compensate for the regime's lack of social support. The upshot is neither Malaysia-style domination nor Thailand-style fragmentation, but a third trajectory: what I will call *militarization*.

Burma provides the consummate example of such causal dynamics. Regionalist insurgencies raged between independence in 1948 and the establishment of open-ended military rule in 1962, and civilian authorities' chronic incapacity to deal with such armed movements provided a primary rationale for the military's political intervention. As in Malaysia and Singapore, unmanageable contentious politics in Burma on the eve of the definitive authoritarian takeover helped produce a tight, cohesive elite coalition. The boundaries of this coalition have been no broader than those of the military apparatus itself, however, as upper groups in urban areas have never had reason to perceive the military as a necessary protector from any organized mass rivals. Absent shared enemies, Burmese urbanites and soldiers have never been friends.[66]

With no social foundation for either a strong central state or a broad-based ruling party, Burma's military leaders have bunkered themselves in, sustaining their illegitimate regime with the main weapon at their disposal – organized violence. Having consistently ordered coercive power from their military personnel, Burma's leaders have survived without ordering remunerative and symbolic power from societal elites. The elite collective action necessary for authoritarian durability in Burma is not channeled through the sort of state and party institutions that order power in Malaysia and Singapore; but what sustains Burmese military rule is elite collective action – originally forged in response to specific types of contentious politics – nonetheless.

The distinction between class and regional conflict is equally critical in comprehending intermediate patterns of political development in Indonesia, which confronted a *combination* of class and regional conflicts after World War II that knows no parallel in Southeast Asia. One cannot understand the militarization of state power that commenced in the late 1950s without recognizing the unifying effect that regional rebellions had on the Indonesian army, or ABRI. As in Burma, territorial conflict in Indonesia made the army a more unified political actor. Yet these rebellions never packed the separatist punch of Burma's border wars, and had been effectively curbed before Sukarno's semipluralistic "Guided Democracy" was violently overthrown by Suharto's "New Order" authoritarian Leviathan in the mid-1960s. It was the dramatic rise of contentious *class* politics

---

[65] As Silberman (1993: 423) argues, it does not "seem possible for military leadership to set about constructing a civil bureaucracy as a mirror image of itself. To do so would be to create another relatively autonomous institution with great powers." When soldiers do take up administrative positions, as we will see in Indonesia, they tend to prioritize coercive tasks such as surveillance over more administrative tasks.

[66] For the definitive argument along these lines in the Burmese context, see Callahan (2004).

in the mid-1960s, via the mobilization of a powerful, grassroots communist party with a massive rural *and* urban membership, that spurred a remarkable increase in elite collective action upon the birth of the Suharto regime.

This sequential layering of regional and class conflict explains, first, why the military played so much more of a leading role in Indonesia than in the party-dominant protection pacts of Malaysia and Singapore; and additionally, why military rule in Indonesia was inaugurated with much broader elite backing than military rule in Burma. Wide-ranging elite support provided the Suharto regime with the social foundations necessary for building a relatively robust ruling party and improving the performance of the central state. Indeed, few authoritarian regimes have ever ordered power more impressively than Indonesia's New Order during the late 1960s and early 1970s, as the country's "urban/communal" positioning in Table 3 should lead us to expect.

Yet the fact that the Indonesian military came to power by completely annihilating its communist rivals had a critical unintended consequence. While the leftist threat was widely perceived as *unmanageable* upon the establishment of the new authoritarian Leviathan, it was not widely perceived as *endemic* once the organized Left had been wiped out in a pogrom claiming upwards of half a million souls.[67] The three-plus decades of New Order rule involved countless political twists and turns; but it also displayed a consistent long-term decline in the tightness and breadth of the ruling coalition. As his coalition eroded, Suharto became less inclined to *strengthen* regime institutions than to *balance* increasingly rivalrous party and military institutions against each other.[68] From a base of elite support initially approximating the Malaysian and Singaporean protection pacts, Indonesia's authoritarian coalition slowly withered to more closely resemble the personalized provision pact of Ferdinand Marcos' Philippines by the mid-1990s.

In sum, the core empirical task for this book is to explain variation in political order and democratization throughout Southeast Asia's noncommunist polities, as seen in these three broad political pathways: (1) *domination* in Malaysia and Singapore; (2) *fragmentation* in the Philippines, South Vietnam, and Thailand; and (3) *militarization* in Burma and Indonesia. To have any hope of being broadly applicable, however, any such explanation should be expressible in terms of deductive, theoretical reasoning that transcends regional specificities. This chapter's final section details how I aim to strike this delicate balance between the particular and the general in my research design and methodological approach.

Research Design and Methodological Approach: The Chapters to Come

Any attempt at comparative analysis across so many divergent national histories is fraught with grave risks. It is easy to get lost in the wealth of fascinating detail, and it is equally easy to succumb to facile generalities and irresponsible abstractions. Scholarly prudence prompts us to proceed case by case, but intellectual impatience urges us to go beyond the

---

[67] I am grateful to Anna Grzymala-Busse for helping me fine-tune this basic point.
[68] Slater (2010).

analysis of concrete contrasts and try out alternative schemes of systematization across the
known cases.

Seymour Martin Lipset and Stein Rokkan[69]

The following chapters seek to establish the internal validity of my arguments
in seven Southeast Asian cases, while pursuing a research design geared toward
maximizing the potential for generating external validity. Readers familiar with
qualitative and comparative-historical methodology in political science and sociology will have already recognized that this is a consummate example of both
a "controlled comparison" research design and a "critical juncture" argument.[70]
Yet my research design aims to build upon these classic explanatory frameworks
in several ways, as my discussion of the chapters to come will hopefully make
clear.

Before switching gears to the empirical chapters in Part II, Chapter 2 concludes Part I by situating my arguments in relevant theoretical literatures on state
and regime institutions. This theoretical discussion has an explicit and essential
methodological purpose. When conducting a controlled comparison of a limited
number of cases, one cannot know if one has achieved theoretical control without
meticulously considering all of the most important rival explanations.[71] Table 2
earlier in this chapter took a first cut at this, but it was far from sufficient. Hence
Chapter 2 engages directly and more deeply with leading theoretical works in
the state-building and democratization canons, specifying why our best existing explanations are not the best explanations for these institutional outcomes
in Southeast Asia.[72] In contrast to most existing works, this book does not treat
state, party, military, and regime institutions as wholly separate phenomena, but
attempts to apprehend them as multiple reflections of a single coalitional phenomenon – elite collective action.

The primary analytic purpose of Chapter 2, however, is to sharpen the five
main theoretical "hooks" of this volume. First, I show how my argument on
contentious politics might shift existing scholarly consensus on internal conflict
being the "wrong kind of war" for building states. Second, I present the case that
nation-building may not facilitate state-building as is often presumed – to the
contrary, it may forestall state-building by reducing elites' interest in a stronger
Leviathan to bridle communal conflict. Third, I argue that the structuralist literature on democratic transitions has problematically conflated social forces with
social classes and overstated the importance of economic factors in driving democratic protest. We might better understand recent "democratic revolutions" by
paying closer attention to communal elites, and the emotive appeals to shared
nationalist and religious identifications they use to mobilize cross-class coalitions

---

[69] Lipset and Rokkan (1990) [1967]: 123.

[70] The best interdisciplinary reader on comparative-historical analysis is Mahoney and Rueschemeyer (2003); on controlled comparisons, see Lijphart (1975); on critical junctures, see Collier
and Collier (1991).

[71] Slater and Ziblatt (2009).

[72] For a more extensive treatment of a wider array of alternative explanations, see Slater (2005:
27–55).

against authoritarian incumbents.[73] Fourth, I argue that shared fears and felt needs for state protection better explain elite support for dictatorship than the most common explanation: economic benefits. Finally, I present the case that authoritarian ruling parties might not grow their strongest roots through leftist and nationalist revolutions, but through conservative counterrevolutions, and by fusing themselves with a highly extractive state instead of a highly mobilized society.[74]

It is in Part II, "Contentious Politics and the Institutions of Order," that my empirical analysis of Southeast Asia begins. Yet it does not commence with the "critical juncture" immediately following the Japanese occupation, when subtly divergent types of contentious politics sent Southeast Asian countries on such widely divergent institutional trajectories. Causal processes often begin *before* critical junctures, with "critical antecedents" predisposing different cases to follow different trajectories in later years.[75] Conceptually distinct from other types of antecedent conditions, these critical antecedents *combine* with causal factors during the critical juncture – in this book, contentious politics – to produce the ultimate outcomes of interest.

Chapter 3 is devoted to tracing these critical antecedents in the Southeast Asian context. In brief, I argue that *prewar* social and territorial cleavages predisposed Southeast Asian colonies toward the types of conflict they would endure in the *postwar* period. The seeds of ethnicized class struggle were sown by the colonial construction of "plural societies" in urban British Malaya and Singapore, while the prewar muting of communal tensions in Thailand and the Philippines meant that postwar class conflict would be class conflict alone. Finally, deeply politicized territorial cleavages were carved into Burmese and Indonesian soil by particularly invidious prewar colonial practices of regional divide and conquer. In sum, variation in *prewar nation-building* proves essential for explaining divergent patterns of *postwar state-building* in Southeast Asia. After examining the causal importance of prewar *cleavages* as critical antecedents, I explain why variation in prewar colonial *institutions* cannot outperform my own explanation for postwar institutional divergence. This addresses a vital alternative explanation that I am unable to address adequately in Part I.

Once these critical antecedents are established, I conduct a chronological, multichapter "structured, focused comparison" of postwar contentious politics and elite collective action *across* cases, as well as a "process-tracing" exercise to apprehend the causal mechanisms linking conflicts with subsequent institutions *within* cases.[76] To make the narrative details of process-tracing more digestible, I split my seven cases into two categories. Throughout the remaining chapters in Parts II and III, my empirical attention will rest squarely on three cases: Malaysia,

[73] Slater (2009).
[74] Slater and N. Smith (2009).
[75] First developed in Slater (2005), this concept receives a more thorough elaboration in Slater and Simmons (2010).
[76] See McKeown and George (1985) on how these methods work together in qualitative causal inference. Also see Mahoney (2003b).

the Philippines, and Indonesia. This allows me to convey the dynamics of one *domination* case, one *fragmentation* case, and one intermediate case best depicted as an example of *militarization*. My other four cases will be set aside until Part IV as "congruent" cases, largely mimicking the causal trajectories – if by no means the political particulars – of my three primary cases: Singapore as a case of domination; South Vietnam and Thailand as instances of fragmentation; and Burma as an additional (indeed, the paradigmatic) militarization case.[77]

Chapter 4 commences this comparative-historical analysis by comparing processes of contentious mobilization and elite countermobilization in the decade and a half following World War II in British Malaya, the Philippines, and Indonesia. Leftist unrest penetrated urban areas, exacerbated ethnic tensions, and incited major new efforts at state-building and party formation in late-colonial Malaya, while a more distant and less threatening rural insurgency in the Philippines exhibited much less of a centripetal political effect on national elites. Meanwhile, Indonesia went from violent nationalist mobilization against the Dutch in the late 1940s to violent regionalist mobilization in the late 1950s. This instigated a process of political militarization that had no parallel in Malaya or the Philippines, even though those cases had been as profoundly shaped in their own ways by their own distinct patterns of counterinsurgency.

Chapter 5 concludes Part II by comparing and tracing the subtle differences in contentious politics during the years immediately leading up to the emergence of authoritarian Leviathans in all three countries: Indonesia in 1966, Malaysia in 1969, and the Philippines in 1972. Pluralist politics was extinguished in all three cases against the backdrop of worsening unrest and rising political violence, but the differences were more important than the similarities. Malaysia witnessed urban electoral race riots, borne in part from frustrations among the relatively impoverished majority Malay population with Malaysian democracy's lack of redistributive content, and in part from Chinese working-class parties' aggravation with their ethnic community's second-class political status. The upsurge in political violence in the Philippines ushering in Marcos' declaration of martial law was based far more on faction than class, with much of it perceived to have been committed by the aspiring autocrat himself. Finally, Indonesia experienced a leftist upsurge surpassing anything witnessed in Malaysia or the Philippines, and Sukarno's populist "Guided Democracy" was destroyed amid an orgy of

---

[77] The generating and testing of hypotheses are not sharply demarcated in most comparative-historical research, since a major analytic goal is to *refine* initial hypotheses through the "interactive processing" of theory and evidence (McKeown 1999: 188). Nevertheless, the congruent cases of Singapore, South Vietnam, and Thailand were only analyzed in depth after my hypotheses on domination and fragmentation had been generated and refined through a combination of deductive theorizing and detailed inductive analysis of Malaysia and the Philippines. Hence these three congruent cases can fairly be considered theory-testing cases. By contrast, Burmese empirics helped generate and refine my arguments on militarization in Indonesia, so neither of these cases can be considered theory-testing cases by usual standards. It is also worth noting that most of this book's detailed within-case evidence on Malaysia and the Philippines was collected *after* my hypotheses had been generated and refined. Thus not even my original cases were purely "theory-generating" cases.

counterrevolutionary violence claiming the lives of hundreds of thousands of suspected communists and communist sympathizers in late 1965 and 1966.

The political consequences of these divergent types of contentious politics *before* dictatorship for coalitional politics *under* dictatorship are the subject of Part III, "The Foundations and Fates of Authoritarian Leviathans." Chapter 6 considers the question of foundations, showing how coalitional differences were visible across the three regimes *from their inception*. Malaysia's dominant-party regime built upon the extractive successes of previous years, ordering power from all types of elite groups to consolidate its political hegemony. Marcos could only dream of ordering such power flows from society to state in the Philippines. Saddled with a weak postcolonial Leviathan to begin with, Marcos initially abolished all political parties in recognition of his relative lack of elite support. Protection would never serve as a credible defining logic of Marcos' unstable dominion. Suharto's New Order in Indonesia was an intermediate case. Although it was born with very broad coalitional backing, many of its elite supporters hoped for a restoration of the competitive electoral politics that had preceded the communists' rise, and the coalitional cement of anti-communism quickly weakened in the aftermath of the anti-communist genocide. As his protection pact faded, Suharto increasingly worked to secure his position by personalizing power and pitting military and civilian elites against each other, with corrosive coalitional and institutional consequences.

Chapter 7 considers the fates of these divergently empowered authoritarian Leviathans during their times of greatest political crisis. The critical question to be addressed is how much elite support oppositionists were able to generate for anti-regime mobilization. The critical actors in these dramas, I argue, were communal elites. Where these actors remained tightly wedded to the authoritarian regime through a protection pact, as in Malaysia in 1998, democratic protest never reached critical mass and was easily crushed. Where protection pacts either were absent (as in the Philippines in 1986) or had expired (as in Indonesia in 1998), popular and middle classes rallied behind communal elites in cross-class democratic revolutions. In contrast to works portraying such "end-game" dynamics in highly contingent terms, I show that patterns of elite opposition and support during moments of crisis were quite consistent with coalitional behavior over the course of these authoritarian Leviathans' decades-long tenures.

Part IV concludes the book with some broader applications of my core arguments. Chapter 8 provides an overview of the political pathways traveled by this volume's four "congruent cases." In brief, Singapore roughly approximates Malaysia's pattern of intense class conflict with urban impact and communal reverberations before the onset of an authoritarian Leviathan. As in Malaysia, robust state and regime institutions and durable authoritarian rule – in a word, *domination* – have been the result. Thailand's political institutions broadly resemble the Philippine pattern of *fragmentation*, which is attributable to the muted nature of class and communal conflict in Thailand throughout the 1940s and 1950s. While South Vietnam experienced immeasurably more *intense* contentious politics than Thailand during the postwar period, the *type and timing* of conflict left it as a second congruent case of fragmentation. Specifically, the cross-class

character and lack of urban and communal impact of the anti–French Resistance in the 1945–54 period, plus the worsening of the leftist threat *after* South
Vietnam's post-1955 era of authoritarian Leviathans began, combined to pre-
clude the emergence of a protection pact and robust political institutions. Finally,
evidence from Burma echoes the lesson from South Vietnam that nationalist revolutions tend to splinter rather than unify elites, and suggests additionally that
regional rebellions tend to build narrow elite coalitions and militarized authoritarian Leviathans. Subsequent military cohesion has sustained authoritarian rule
in Burma, despite the absence of the sort of robust state and party institutions
that have stabilized nondemocratic politics in Malaysia and Singapore – but
only through levels of murderous military violence against fellow elites (e.g.,
Buddhist monks, university students) not witnessed in authoritarian Leviathans
able to order power in multiple ways.

   Chapter 9 concludes the book with some initial thoughts on the applicability of
its arguments beyond Southeast Asia. Broadly analogous examples can be located
from all three political trajectories, seemingly supporting the deductive intuitions
upon which my causal framework was built. It also appears that fragmentation
rather than domination or militarization has been the predominant postcolonial
trajectory, affirming this book's stress on factionalism as the defining feature of
politics. Elite collective action has been the exception rather than the rule, while
the never-ending factionalism of unstable dictatorships and fragile democracies
continues to characterize most of the postcolonial world. This does not mean
that Madison's dream of democratic Leviathans is unattainable – it simply means
that in most postcolonial settings, effective and democratic government were not
secured simultaneously, and will have to be secured sequentially. The ultimate
lesson of Southeast Asian political development is that state strength has been
a product of robust mass politics, not authoritarian politics.[78] State-building in
other postcolonial regions will seemingly require the revitalization of mass political engagement, not the reentrenchment of authoritarian regimes.

[78] Slater (2008a).

2

States and the Regimes That Run Them

Introduction

We are driven by a common desire to understand what makes for good governments and how to build them. Good governments are those that are (1) representative and accountable to the population they are meant to serve, and (2) effective – that is, capable of protecting the population from violence, ensuring security of property rights, and supplying other public goods that the populace needs and desires.

Margaret Levi[1]

The state.... is the vexed institution that is the ground of both our freedoms and our unfreedoms.

James Scott[2]

Few if any political challenges are as persistently portentous as those of democratization and state-building. Wherever citizens are denied the opportunity to remove government officials through competitive elections, they lack an important (if imperfect) institutional means for pressuring public authority to govern in ways commensurate with popular interests. Wherever the state is hamstrung by particularistic demands, or lacks infrastructural power, citizens chronically lack access to even the most basic public goods. It should thus come as no surprise that state-building and democratization have long represented core theoretical concerns in comparative politics.

This is a book about Southeast Asia – but not Southeast Asia alone. As an examination of states and regimes, it speaks to issues that engage the interest of scholars and practitioners working on every region of the postcolonial world. Given the importance of democratization and state-building in the shaping of "the West," these topics continue to attract the attention of students of European and American political development as well. Before turning our focus to the specifics of Southeast Asia, therefore, it is important to ask what we know about

[1] Levi (2006): 5.
[2] Scott (1998): 7.

33

states and regimes in general. Only then can this book's arguments be properly situated and its theoretical contributions appropriately assessed.

We have learned a great deal about why authoritarian regimes do or do not democratize, and why states do or do not effectively assert authority. Yet the three most compelling theoretical literatures on the core themes of this book – those on (1) war and state-building, (2) democratic coalitions and transitions, and (3) authoritarian institutions – cannot better explain variation in state and regime institutions than my own framework centered on contentious politics and elite collective action. In arguing that states arise from war, democracy emerges from elite splits and cross-class coalitions, and dictatorships endure through powerful ruling parties, comparative scholars have placed elite collective action at the heart of their arguments – yet without recognizing the overlap. Our rightful concern with theorizing *different types of institutions* has blinded us to the fact that their strength can be predicated upon *similar types of coalitions*. One broad analytic purpose of this chapter is to show how elite collective action runs like a common thread through these distinct literatures in comparative politics.

In so doing, I highlight five surprising causal patterns that might prompt political scientists and sociologists to reconsider how state-building and democratization have occurred in other world regions. First, I show that *internal conflicts can make states* to a degree rarely recognized in the state-building literature – but only when they assume the threatening and challenging forms most likely to spur elite collective action in response. Second and relatedly, although successful nation-building is generally presumed to be useful if not essential for successful state-building – indeed, external war is often thought to make strong states by unifying the nation – Southeast Asia shows that *weak nations can produce surprisingly strong states*, and vice versa. Third, I question the focus of the democratization literature on class actors and economic factors in driving mass democratic mobilization, highlighting the central role of *emotive appeals to nationalist and religious sentiments and solidarities* in Southeast Asia's democratization struggles. Fourth, I argue that recent scholarship has overemphasized the importance of economic benefits and has underappreciated the significance of *shared perceptions of endemic threat* in holding authoritarian coalitions together. And fifth, I dispute the notions that strong ruling parties are necessarily the best backstops for authoritarian regimes, and that such institutions typically arise from revolutionary struggles. Instead, I see *counterrevolutionary party, military, and state institutions* as similarly conducive to authoritarian durability because of their shared capacity to order power and sustain elite collective action.

War and the State   .

Taxation and State Infrastructural Power

He who knows how to listen to [fiscal history's] message here discerns the thunder of world history more clearly than anywhere else.

                                                                                    Joseph Schumpeter[3]

---

[3] Schumpeter (1954) [1918]: 7.

Taxation has generally been perceived as a sine qua non of statehood. Yet most states in the developing world exhibit tremendous difficulty at mobilizing domestic revenue, and some barely manage to collect taxes at all. The consequences of this widespread fiscal powerlessness have been enormous. Throughout much of the postcolonial world, states cannot extract enough revenue from their own populations to escape punishing cycles of unserviceable national debt. Lacking sufficient revenue as well as the knowledge of social conditions that often develops through the revenue collection process, these states often fail to provide even the most rudimentary social services, including basic physical protection from violence, hunger, and disease.

In short, revenue collection may not be a perfect barometer of state power; but it is the next best thing. As Margaret Levi puts it in political science's locus classicus on the subject: "The greater the revenue of the state, the more possible it is to extend rule. Revenue enhances the ability of rulers to elaborate the institutions of the state, to bring more people within the domain of those institutions, and to increase the number and variety of the collective goods provided through the state."[4] Revenue is thus fundamental to the extension of what Michael Mann calls the state's "infrastructural power," or "the capacity of the state to actually penetrate civil society, and to implement logistically political decisions throughout the realm."[5] Since taxation lies at the heart of state infrastructural power, this book will largely rely on revenue data to assess divergence in the capacity of Southeast Asian states.

We must remain as attentive to *how* states generate revenue as to *how much* revenue they generate, however. Different types of taxes entail different political implications and impacts. Assessing a state's *fiscal power* thus requires both quantitative and qualitative measurement. In quantitative terms, I measure fiscal power by the total tax revenue as a share of gross domestic product. More qualitatively, I consider a state's fiscal power to be a function of its shift from indirect means of extraction (i.e., trade and consumption taxes) toward direct forms of taxation (i.e., income and corporate taxes).[6]

The type of taxation is important, first, because direct taxes proved to be the biggest revenue earner of the twentieth century.[7] Postcolonial states that impose them with some degree of effectiveness have an enormous fiscal advantage over those that cannot. Direct taxes also provide the best measure of a state's power to extract from economic elites. Income tax especially exhibits "the desirable property of being 'equitable,' as it could be collected with progressive rate structures."[8] Given the highly skewed distribution of incomes that exists in the vast majority

[4] Levi (1988): 2.
[5] Mann (1988): 5.
[6] This four-part typology of taxes – trade, consumption, income, and corporate – derives from Zee (1996).
[7] Lieberman (2001): 515.
[8] Ibid. Like many others, Hobson (1997) treats direct taxes as more progressive than indirect taxes by definition.

of developing countries,[9] postcolonial states must ultimately impose significant taxes on upper groups if they hope to escape the vicious cycle between chronic dependence on externally derived revenues, and the fiscal crises that recur when such outside funds periodically dry up.

This book therefore paints the core challenge of postcolonial state-building as one of *asserting* the state's authority over societal elites, rather than *broadcasting* the state's authority across the broad expanses of national territory. Ever since state-led industrialization fostered the rapid growth of enormous "primate cities" throughout the developing world, societal elites have increasingly made their residence in national capitals, not in hard-to-reach hinterlands. Furthermore, the advent of the United Nations system in 1945 has given existing national borders "juridical" standing, relieving postcolonial states of much of their concern with actively administering their territorial periphery.[10] Extending the state's writ beyond the capital city clearly remains problematic; but postcolonial states are more deeply incapacitated by their general inability to avoid "capture" by those closest to them than by their inability to impose control over those furthest away. *What matters most is not the length of the state's infrastructural reach, but the strength of its infrastructural grip.*

My analysis of state power also departs from existing literature in proposing new causal mechanisms linking taxation and regime type. Many political scientists and economic historians have argued that negotiations between rulers and wealth holders over taxation give rise to "fiscal contracts," in what has been described as "the interlocking iron triangle of revenue extraction, institutional development, and representative politics."[11] In Southeast Asia, however, this triangle has proven to be anything but iron. The two states with the most fiscal power in the region – Malaysia and Singapore – are the region's two most durable authoritarian regimes. Yet we lack theoretical guidance on how authoritarian regimes might manage to impose taxation without offering democratic political representation.

Fiscal power and authoritarian durability can prove highly compatible for two reasons. First, when states extract large amounts of revenue from the domestic economy, ruling regimes are the greatest beneficiaries. *It is regimes, after all, that run the state.* With more revenue at their disposal, authoritarian regimes enjoy greater capacity to co-opt potential dissent and to develop and bankroll organizations for social control. A state's infrastructural power provides the very institutional tools that authoritarian regimes need to suppress potential challenges. Strong states facilitate authoritarian consolidation as surely as they facilitate democratic consolidation.[12]

---

9 This ubiquity of inequality leaves me doubtful that variation in this factor might shed much explanatory light on variation in postcolonial political outcomes (e.g., Acemoglu and Robinson 2006, Boix 2003).

10 R. Jackson (1992).

11 Vandewalle (1998): 20. North and Weingast (1989), Levi (1988), and Bates and Lien (1985) provide the classic arguments on fiscal contracts.

12 Linz and Stepan (1996) rightly argue that stateness is a necessary condition for workable democracy. Levitsky and Way (forthcoming) provide one of the most explicit theoretical statements that strong states help sustain dictatorship. See also Slater (2008b).

This explains why authoritarian regimes might prove especially durable if they can impose direct taxes on societal elites. But why would upper economic groups be willing to pay taxes to a regime that accepts no democratic electoral controls on its behavior?[13] The answer, I argue, is that economic elites will do so *if and only if they perceive unbridled mass mobilization as a more imminent threat to their persons, property, and privileges than a strong, centralized state*. And if these elites might support state centralization as a bulwark against political instability, might they not also support open-ended authoritarian rule for the same reason? Under conditions of endemic and unmanageable threat, upper groups become especially liable to provide authoritarian leaders with the resources they need, not only to assert state power, but to stabilize and sustain their regime.

Yet it is state officials, not economic elites, who drive the state-building process. *The bourgeoisie can beckon Leviathan, but not build it.* Hence the most important mechanism through which contentious politics facilitates state-building is by inciting elite collective action within the state apparatus itself. This typically begins with improved coordination and invigorated deployment of the state's coercive apparatus. Only when this proves insufficient for bridling contentious politics should we expect to see the political leadership undertaking the complex and controversial effort to reshape and retool the state's administrative institutions, including its tax-gathering apparatus. In the chapters to follow, we will repeatedly see outbreaks of contentious politics sparking new state efforts to build more cohesive and capable coercive institutions. It will only be where contentious politics assumes endemic and unmanageable forms that we will witness the rise of a highly extractive tax state, grounded in the construction of a newly empowered administrative Leviathan.

Can Internal Conflicts Make States?

For were the impulses of conscience clear, uniform, and irresistibly obeyed, man would need no other lawgiver; but that not being the case, he finds it necessary to surrender up a part of his property to furnish means for the protection of the rest.

Thomas Paine

But in order that these antagonisms, these classes with conflicting economic interests, might not consume themselves and society in fruitless struggle, it became necessary to have a power, seemingly standing above society, that would alleviate the conflict and keep it within the bounds of "order."

Frederick Engels

A benchmark assumption of the literature on state formation is that fiscal power tends to increase amid the presence or imminent threat of political violence. However, the consensus is that extractive capacity grows in response to international rather than domestic conflict. As Charles Tilly famously put it in his mammoth edited volume on state formation in Western Europe: "War made the

---

[13] Barzel (2002) suggests that economic elites will only accept the rise of a strong state after devising a vehicle for their own collective action (i.e., a parliament), to prevent predation. I argue that in times of unmanageable mass threat, economic elites might provide resources to public authorities out of desperation, and be forced to hope for the best where state predation is concerned.

state, and the state made war."[14] This view that international warfare stimulated state-building by forcing monarchs to step up revenue collection to meet the rising costs of modern military conflict stands as conventional wisdom in most prominent studies of European fiscal history.[15]

If Europe's powerful states arose in response to geopolitical threats, it stands to reason that the postcolonial world is littered with weak states because of the relative rarity of cross-border military conflict since 1945. This reasoning dominates current thinking on state weakness in sub-Saharan Africa.[16] Scholars specializing in Latin America and the Middle East have challenged this consensus; yet their analytic focus either remains exclusively on cross-border war,[17] or provides no systematic answers for how different types of conflicts might have divergent political effects.[18] We are thus left pondering the question Miguel Angel Centeno pointedly raises, but ultimately cannot answer: Has the postcolonial world mostly had "the 'wrong' kinds of wars?"[19]

Given the greater prevalence of internal than external conflict in the post-1945 era, it behooves scholars to consider whether civil wars can make states in the same way foreign wars evidently did in Europe. Such inquiry seems especially overdue when one considers the recognition by seminal political theorists that the state serves not only to combat foreign enemies, but to contain social conflict – a point around which thinkers as disparate as Paine and Engels could agree. Even a scholar as associated with an "externalist" understanding of state formation as Tilly defines "statemaking" as the process of "attacking and checking competitors and challengers *within* the territory claimed by the state."[20] As an empirical matter, Tilly did not portray variation in these internal practices as vital to divergence in European state forms. In defining these early states as protection rackets, Tilly treated such processes as universal, not uneven.[21] Yet as a theoretical matter, Tilly offers reason to suspect that variation in states' struggles to extend internal protection might help explain divergence in postcolonial state power.

Scattered bits of theoretical argumentation and empirical research suggest that internal conflicts can have an impact on state-building, but these are yet to be woven into any coherent theoretical statement. This book aims to advance this literature by suggesting that *only some types of internal conflicts build states because only some types of internal conflict inspire elite collective action in response.*

---

[14] Tilly (1975): 42.

[15] See Ertman (1997), Tilly (1992), Downing (1992), and Mann (1988).

[16] For instance, see Herbst (2000).

[17] Barnett (1992) and Gongora (1997).

[18] Centeno (2002, 1997) and Lopez-Alves (2000).

[19] Centeno (1997): 1591–92.

[20] Tilly (1992): 96. Emphasis added. Thanks to Jason Brownlee for his suggestions on this front.

[21] Tilly (1985). The same can be said of North, Wallis, and Weingast's (2009) argument that political order arises from elite efforts to curb social violence – an insight with which this author is in complete agreement. Yet much as Tilly treats all states as similarly racket-based by nature, North, Wallis, and Weingast treat all "natural states" as similarly violent by nature. In contrast, I argue that variation in the causal factor that North et al. treat as universal (types of violence) explains variation in an outcome that Tilly treats as universal (states as protection rackets). Thanks to Sofia Fenner for her helpful thoughts on North et al.'s arguments and their points of overlap and tension with my own.

The most sophisticated theoretical statement in support of the notion that internal conflict can build strong states was written three decades ago by Michael Hechter and William Brustein. As noted in Chapter 1, these authors suggest that elites are unlikely to "jointly surrender their power to a strong state" unless "they live in a politically divided society in which the weaker group can make a credible threat to change the rules of the game."[22] Absent credible internal threats, economic elites will vigorously resist paying direct taxes to state authorities, and will attempt to handle any challenges to their status primarily through their own sources of social control, with only minimal assistance from a barebones state apparatus.[23] Low-conflict polities tend to be marked by "elite rigidity" and "unrestricted self-dealing" between state officials and economic elites, with each side making only minimally challenging demands of the other.[24]

Although Hechter and Brustein targeted their argument at scholars placing an "unwarranted emphasis on the exogenous determinants of initial state formation in western European history,"[25] they did not suggest that geopolitical conflicts had been unimportant in the European context. Rather, they offered the corrective that internal conflict could serve as a *functional equivalent* for international warfare. This is the perspective adopted here. By arguing that internal conflicts can make states, this book does not reject the finding that external wars can do the same. In the postcolonial world as in Europe, different types of conflicts can strengthen the state – but this causal effect depends on whether conflicts spark increased elite collective action in self-defense.

Unfortunately, Hechter and Brustein's analysis has been largely overlooked by contemporary scholars of the postcolonial world. An exception is Carmenza Gallo, who employs the Hechter-Brustein model to explain why the Bolivian state intermittently succeeded in imposing taxes on the country's tin-mining elite. "The need a privileged class has for an organization to help it pursue its interests and preserve its privileged position is directly dependent on the opposition that these objectives encounter among the other classes," Gallo argues. "Or, to put it differently, class conflicts. . . . induce an upper class to organize itself in the defense of its interests."[26] This usefully points our attention toward contentious politics as a causal influence on fiscal power. Yet Gallo's analysis raises as many questions as it answers. Is class conflict the only type of contentious politics that can lead to expansion in the state's fiscal power? If so, why did most Latin American states remain captured by upper groups, even after the emergence of powerful leftist movements during the Cold War? Do economic elites always organize to defend their interests by calling forth a more powerful Leviathan, or might they find other, lower-cost means of preserving their positions? Does ethnic conflict have different effects than class conflict on relations between states and societal elites?

Given the lack of empirical variation that Gallo captures in her one-country study, her analysis provides little guidance in addressing these puzzles. Even

---

[22] Hechter and Brustein (1980): 1090.
[23] On resistance to state-building by societal "strongmen," see Migdal (1988).
[24] Lachmann (2000): 164–65.
[25] Hechter and Brustein (1980): 1063.
[26] Gallo (1991): 12.

when specialists on Latin America *do* make a determined effort to trace state capacity to different types of social conflict, they are hamstrung by the region's lack of variation in fiscal power. Miguel Angel Centeno and Fernando Lopez-Alves' recent studies of war and state-building in Latin America search hard for systematic causal patterns linking types of wars to types of states. Yet they ultimately find no evidence that war's effect on the state might fundamentally depend on what type of war it is (e.g., external, internal, class, communal, regional, factional).[27]

To date, several scholars of Southeast Asian politics have produced empirical studies of internal conflict and state-building, and have made initial efforts to inform broader theoretical frameworks. In a volume edited with Paul Rich, Richard Stubbs suggests that postcolonial states have sometimes grown stronger through the process of quelling domestic insurgencies.[28] Yet Rich and Stubbs' explanation for why some counterinsurgent states become stronger than others – those adopting a "political" approach strengthen, while those taking a "military" approach weaken – is unsatisfying on several counts. First, scholars should "at the very least abandon false dichotomies such as 'the economic' vs. 'the military' approach to counter-insurgency,"[29] as Karl Jackson has argued, because state responses invariably combine elements of both.

More fundamentally, this emphasis on political-economic as opposed to military responses does not answer the big question so much as it rephrases it: Why do some states manage to devise effective political strategies for containing mass insurgency, while others flounder politically and lash out militarily? This theoretical puzzle takes empirical form within the Rich and Stubbs volume itself, as one chapter lauds Malaysia's effective state response to domestic insurgency, while an adjacent chapter remarks on the Philippine state's continued ineffectiveness in the face of growing insurgent violence.[30] I address this empirical divergence directly and in depth in the chapters to come.

The most ambitious efforts to trace variation in Southeast Asian states' power vis-à-vis societal elites to the intensity of contentious politics come from David Brown and Donald Crone. Brown's analysis is especially valuable for present purposes, as he directly connects state-building to elite collective action. "Within a dominant class," Brown argues, "elite cohesion arises firstly from the concern of class members to preserve their common economic interests against *threats from below*." Although elite collective action can take various forms, "*the state* provides the organizational basis whereby the whole system is stabilized, and the

---

[27] Centeno (2002, 1997); Lopez-Alves (2000). Centeno seems convinced that such variation should exist, but he does not find it. When contrasting internal and external conflict, Centeno first insists, "The distinction between these two types of conflict is critical," insofar as their "consequences may be radically different." Yet he concludes soon thereafter: "the type of war appears to make an insignificant difference on its effects" (Centeno 2002: 34).

[28] Rich and Stubbs (1997).

[29] K. Jackson (1985): 4. His definition of "economic" responses to insurgency mirrors what Rich and Stubbs call "political" responses.

[30] Stubbs (1997) and Abinales (1997).

fractional tensions within the dominant class are resolved or contained."[31] Crone
recognizes that threats from below cannot be assumed, and vary across cases. He
echoes Brown – and foreshadows the analysis here – in suggesting that elite factionalism will prevail in nonthreatening times, and that broader elite collective
action is nearly impossible absent shared perceptions of threat:

> Political leaders require motivation to oppose the interests of important actors among the
> elite.... A threat to the stability of the system, and especially to the ability of the current
> regime to maintain itself in power, is an extreme motivation for state elites to take some
> action. Mere political opposition (where that is tolerated) is unlikely to provoke a crisis
> mentality, but severe rioting or insurgency movements, for example, put the regime in a
> crisis that may threaten its continued existence.[32]

As with the other studies mentioned here, however, Crone's framework does
not systematically consider how different types of conflict might have different
effects on the state. This is why Crone's argument fails to apprehend much of the
variation *within Southeast Asia itself*. For instance, states in the Philippines, South
Vietnam, and Burma have all clearly faced severe episodes of domestic insurgency.
Yet none of these states responded with sustained efforts to develop institutional
capacity, as Malaysia and Singapore did. South Vietnam even collapsed entirely
as a sovereign entity.

   The key to unraveling the puzzle of divergence in state power in Southeast Asia
is the same key that helps solve the puzzle of regional divergence in authoritarian
durability: the different *types* of contentious politics that rocked the region after
1945. If any type of internal conflict is "the wrong kind" for state-building, it is
regional rebellions, because they are especially likely to drive a political wedge
between civilian and military elites rather than bringing them together, and to
elicit a purely military as opposed to an administrative response. And neither
class nor communal conflict alone appears sufficient to galvanize state officials
and upper economic groups into deemphasizing their factional interests for the
sake of broader elite interests. What Roger Gould calls "the intertwining of class
and community"[33] in severe episodes of urban unrest seems to be what triggers
the causal chain from contentious politics to growth in the state's infrastructural
power.

Different Conflicts, Different Coalitions
Crises.... fostered an atmosphere of desperate experimentation that helped leaders to
discover policies that joined former antagonists in a partnership. They also created an
atmosphere in which it was easier for leaders to sell a realignment to their followers.

                                                                  Gregory Luebbert[34]

A common spiritual enemy can also produce the most remarkable agreements.

                                                                      Carl Schmitt[35]

[31] Brown (1993): 123, 124. Emphasis added.
[32] Crone (1993): 58.
[33] Gould (1995): 10.
[34] Luebbert (1991): 312.
[35] Schmitt (1985) [1923]: 75.

State infrastructural power and authoritarian durability both ultimately rest on elite coalitions supporting the increased concentration of public authority. Why do some authoritarian regimes have more success at assembling such coalitions than others? Specifically, why are some regimes more successful than others at extracting tax payments and political financing from economic elites? Why do middle classes display greater unwillingness to join popular sectors in mobilizing against some authoritarian regimes than others? Why do religious authorities and nationalist icons actively legitimize some authoritarian regimes, but not all? And why do state officials in only some authoritarian settings set aside factional agendas and reliably play their formally defined roles, providing political leaders with the infrastructural power necessary to sustain stable domination?

These elite groups only surrender these strategic resources to an authoritarian Leviathan – granting it with a preponderance of coercive, remunerative, and symbolic power that makes its position hegemonic – when they perceive contentious politics as a more endemic threat to their core interests than state predation. The trick is to specify the type of conflict that is likely to have such a political effect without succumbing to post hoc reasoning: viz., measuring the seriousness of conflict by the seriousness of the response. One must go beyond Luebbert's invocation of crises as transformative moments, and specify *what kind* of crisis is most likely to induce elite collective action among "former antagonists." It is more important *how* conflict takes place than *how much* conflict takes place. Specifically, protection pacts only arise when a mass movement with revolutionary aims penetrates the urban sphere, threatening to explode a communal powder keg in the process.

What drives these theoretical expectations? First, I expect urban conflict to be perceived as more *physically threatening* than rural conflict. This is because even the most rusticated postcolonial landowners tend to own urban property as well, where they can safely reside during outbreaks of purely rural unrest.[36] Second, urban conflict should be perceived as more *administratively challenging* than rural conflict. To understand why, it is useful to consider James Scott's explication of "patron-client relations," or the vertical exchanges of loyalty and dependency that define most pre-industrial polities.[37] These ties should be more difficult to elaborate on an all-encompassing basis in cities than in the countryside. The logic, to invoke Scott's more recent work, is one of "legibility."[38] Postcolonial societal strongmen can construct local near-monopolies of force and political knowledge in the gemeinschaft of the village or hinterlands town; but the chaotic gesellschaft of the postcolonial city, choked with unregistered migrants from multiple rural provinces, will tend to be far more "illegible" to the most powerful elites residing there. The implication is that rural elites enjoy a greater arsenal of weapons for social control than urban elites, and will be less willing to cede control and

---

[36] In the prewar era, rural elites were almost certainly more deeply rooted to the land, and might have been more directly threatened by rural than urban violence (as Luebbert [1991] implies).

[37] Scott (1972).

[38] Scott (1998).

surrender resources to central state authorities in the face of contentious mass mobilization.

This is especially true if class conflict remains class conflict alone, and does not spill over into communal violence. Societal elites have less difficulty managing threats from below when those threats derive from the same ethnic or religious community, because shared language and belief systems improve legibility. Only when mass mobilization arises from groups over which societal elites have weak or nonexistent social control will it tend to strengthen the central state at the expense of splintered, self-serving societal elites.

Whereas class cleavages can often be salved with clever elite combinations of repression and accommodation, furthermore, communal cleavages tend to be perceived as comparatively immutable. Since deep communal divisions represent a seemingly permanent political challenge, fears of communal strife should make societal elites especially willing to provide resources to a permanent protector. It was not by accident that Schmitt saw "the most remarkable agreements" emerging historically as a collective response to a perceived "spiritual enemy."

The particular historical circumstances of the postcolonial world compound this general causal logic. The worldwide wave of democratic breakdowns between the 1950s and the early 1970s occurred against the backdrop of the global Cold War at its hottest. Communism was a widely feared ideology for a broad cross-section of postcolonial elites. But the decline of communism as a revolutionary ideology by the 1980s left the Left in a far less threatening pose, from Latin America to Africa to Asia. In cases where authoritarian Leviathans emerged to combat *communism* but not *communalism* – Chile and South Korea leap to mind – dictatorship lost whatever credible protective logic it once had with the Cold War's end. By contrast, authoritarian Leviathans forged to snuff out not just class but communal strife experienced the 1990s' global upsurge in ethnic conflict as a new lease on life, rather than a death knell.

My argument that ethnic divisions can prove surprisingly conducive for political order resonates with leading works on identity politics and taxation. As Evan Lieberman has argued in the South African case, shared perceptions of an impoverished and threatening racial other can foster increased elite willingness to bankroll the state in collective self-defense. Where such endemic racial discord was absent, as in Brazil, elites remained regionally fragmented, and Leviathan failed to draw provincial wealth toward the political center.[39] Kiren Aziz Chaudhry has contrarily emphasized the importance for direct taxation of ascriptive distance between state officials and economic elites, which allowed the state in Yemen but not Saudi Arabia to avoid capture by the local bourgeoisie.[40] In both instances, wide-ranging and active elite support for state-building projects has been predicated on elite perceptions of the state as a necessary bulwark against perceived communal foes.

---

[39] Lieberman (2003) stresses the causal significance of constitution-making processes rather than social conflicts in shaping these divergent taxation outcomes in Brazil and South Africa, however. See Slater and Simmons (2010) for a fuller discussion.

[40] Chaudhry (1997).

This contradicts the conventional and seemingly commonsensical notion that strong states are predicated upon strong nations.[41] Even more than the absence of warfare, the absence of nationalism has been presumed to be a hindrance to post-colonial state-building. Indeed, it is largely through the strengthening of national consciousness that cross-border wars are expected to strengthen the power of centralized states. Yet Southeast Asian countries marked by stronger ethnic than nationalist identifications (Malaysia and Singapore) have produced especially strong states, while those countries where nation-building before World War II was most effective at muting identity cleavages (Thailand and the Philippines) have ironically seen much weaker postwar state-building efforts. This is not to say that communal heterogeneity presents no real barrier to state consolidation – it is to say that such diversity can serve as a structural opportunity, and not simply as an insuperable obstacle, to the emergence of capable central authority.[42]

In sum, endemic and unmanageable contentious class politics can strengthen Leviathans by pressuring economic elites to pay more taxes in exchange for invigorated state protection, and by providing state officials with leverage to impose formal institutional hierarchies over factions within the state apparatus itself.[43] When such conflicts occur under conditions of relative political pluralism, they discredit democracy among middle classes and communal elites as well, with powerful repercussions for authoritarian durability – the question to which I now turn.

Democratization and Authoritarianism

Coalitional Foundations of Political Regimes
The fate of classes is more frequently determined by the needs of society than the fate of society is determined by the needs of classes. . . . [T]he chances of classes in a struggle will depend on their ability to win support from outside their own membership, which again will depend upon their fulfillment of tasks set by interests wider than their own.

Karl Polanyi[44]

Ever since Barrington Moore unveiled his sweeping historical argument regarding "the social origins of dictatorship and democracy," political scientists and sociologists have tried to determine which classes and what coalitions are responsible for originating and sustaining political regimes.[45] A "voluntarist" literature emerged in response to this "structuralist" canon, arguing that contingent splits within a regime rather than structural shifts in society offered the best explanation

---

[41] See, especially, Herbst (2000) and Centeno (2002).
[42] Inverting Wedeen's (2008) argument that nationalism can emerge in the absence of a strong state, I argue that strong states do not require the existence of a strong nation.
[43] Darden (2008) has intriguingly argued that informal practices such as blackmail can preserve institutional hierarchies as well. Yet if blackmail were sufficient to craft lasting political order, the postcolonial world would look far more orderly than it does.
[44] Polanyi (1944): 159.
[45] B. Moore (1966). See Mahoney (2003a) for the best review of this research tradition.

for democratic transitions.[46] For all their differences, these two bodies of thought share a fundamentally coalitional approach to politics, portraying elite collective action as highly conducive for authoritarian durability. If protection pacts solidify elite collective action, they should impede both the *internal regime splits* emphasized by voluntarists and the *cross-class coalitions* stressed by many structuralists. The framework here thus aims to reconcile structuralist and voluntarist perspectives in a novel way.

In terms of the structuralist literature, this book picks up on two lines of critique leveled against "the Moore hypothesis": namely, that a powerful bourgeoisie was a necessary condition for democracy because of its role in breaking the social hegemony of reactionary landed elites. This thesis has come under fire from within the structuralist camp for understating the importance of working-class mobilization for the instauration of democracy.[47] New research in the political economy tradition similarly portrays democratic transitions as the triumph of redistribution-seeking masses over anti-redistributive elites.[48]

This book concurs that mass mobilization is a major, often essential, stimulant to authoritarian collapse. Yet a shared weakness of these works is their tendency to portray democratic mobilization as the product of one class attacking another, rather than the fluorescence of a *cross-class coalition*. As Polanyi argued above, single classes rarely shape history on their own, but require the assistance of other classes to force political change – especially when change involves the kind of collective action witnessed in democratic revolutions, when hundreds of thousands of citizens come together to bring an authoritarian regime to its knees.

A few authors have transcended the "carrying class" model of democratization and highlighted the role of cross-class coalitions in shaping regimes. An early example was Gregory Luebbert, who explained Europe's interwar regime divergence as an outcome of varying cross-class responses to the eruption of mass politics.[49] In the very different context of postwar Central America, Deborah Yashar similarly argues that cross-class coalitions emerged during "democratizing moments" when mass mobilization and elite divisions arose simultaneously.[50] What thus appears necessary as a complement to mass mobilization is either the sort of elite divisions that Yashar emphasizes, or the sort of active middle-class support for democracy that Luebbert highlights. Where pro-authoritarian collective action can be sustained among such upper groups, democratic transition becomes practically unthinkable. Although structuralist, my coalitional argument is consistent with the core insight of the voluntarist literature: "there is no transition whose beginning is not the consequence – direct or indirect – of important divisions within the authoritarian regime itself."[51]

---

[46] Rustow (1970) gave birth to this "transitology" literature, and O'Donnell and Schmitter (1986) gave it new life.

[47] See Rueschemeyer, Stephens, and Stephens (1992), R. Collier (1999), Bermeo (1997), and Wood (2000).

[48] Boix (2003), Acemoglu and Robinson (2006).

[49] Luebbert (1991).

[50] Yashar (1997): 15–17.

[51] O'Donnell and Schmitter (1986): 19.

My stress on cross-class coalitions should help explain why I discount the role of popular sectors in bolstering authoritarian Leviathans, even as I depict their role as fundamental in inspiring their creation and as vital in ushering in their destruction. It is ultimately the collective action of elites that makes authoritarianism durable, and the defection of elites that makes democratization possible.[52] A democratic uprising from below makes authoritarian collapse far more likely, but only when it enjoys or can secure sanction and support from some segment of a fragmented elite stratum.

Communal Elites and Democratic Mobilization

[A] real threat from the citizens requires the juxtaposition of many unlikely factors: the masses need to solve the collective-action problem necessary to organize themselves, they need to find the momentum to turn their organization into an effective force against the regime, and the elites – who are controlling the state apparatus – should be unable to use the military to effectively suppress the uprising.

Daron Acemoglu and James Robinson[53]

[Democracy and liberty] are only possible where they are backed up by the determined *will* of a nation not to be ruled like a flock of sheep.

Max Weber[54]

It is on the sources and not the significance of democratic mobilization that the regimes literature proves deficient. Most scholarly attention focuses on the role of *social classes* and their purportedly objective *economic interests* in driving mass protest. This book counters that a class-rationalist perspective exhibits major analytic problems as a lens for understanding democratic mobilization, both logically and empirically. First, class itself cannot logically explain the kind of *cross*-class coalition that seems so important in securing democratic change. Again, Polanyi gets it right: "There is no magic in class interest which would secure to members of one class the support of members of other classes. Yet such support is an everyday occurrence."[55]

Democratic revolutions are far from "an everyday occurrence." But they occur more frequently than a purely rational-choice account of democratic mobilization seems capable of allowing.[56] The trouble is immediately visible in Acemoglu and Robinson's depiction of democratic mobilization above as requiring "the juxtaposition of many unlikely factors." To be more precise, democratic mobilization requires a combination of causal factors that their redistributive model ignores. Democratic revolutions rarely look like class warfare, but like a sudden flowering of cross-class cooperation. Given the personal risks and interpersonal

---

52 Since I consider "middle classes" to qualify as elites in postcolonial settings, this formulation is less elite centered than it might initially sound.
53 Acemoglu and Robinson (2006): 25.
54 Cited in Kurzman (2006: 127). Emphasis in original.
55 Polanyi (1944): 160.
56 Rationalist accounts of mass protest often stress "focal points" or "tipping mechanisms" as solutions to collective action problems (e.g., Tucker 2007). Yet such arguments still do not satisfactorily solve the intrinsic free-rider problem introduced by Olson (1965).

dynamics intrinsic to anti-authoritarian protest, one might more broadly critique individualistic rational-actor models as ill suited for the explanatory task. As Mara Loveman argues, "rational choice models are particularly *un*helpful for explaining participation in collective action in situations involving high levels of risk or contexts of extreme instability and unpredictability."[57]

The culturalist literature on social movements proves a far more fruitful starting point. Unlike most rational-actor models, arguments in this vein begin with the notion that "individuals share prior bonds with others that make solidaristic behavior a reasonable expectation."[58] Yet the puzzle of collective action pertains to broad coalitions *against* dictatorship as much as to broad coalitions *supporting* dictatorship; the shift from narrowly factional to broadly organized politics remains anything but automatic. Much as protection pacts provide the best explanation for *pro*-regime collective action, the ability of communal elites to mobilize religious and nationalist communities through emotive appeals to shared identities helps unravel the puzzle of *anti*-regime collective action.[59]

Chapter 7's empirical discussion of democratic revolutions and authoritarian crackdowns in Southeast Asia will lend credence to Weber's culturalist insight above. *Much as it can take a state to preserve authoritarianism, it can take a nation to tear it down.* This depends upon the support of communal elites, who possess especially strong credentials to mobilize cross-class democratic protest through nationalist and religious appeals. Like other types of elites, however, they do not become structurally available to democratizing coalitions unless a protection pact is absent or has withered away.

Provision vs. Protection in Authoritarian Coalitions

The notion that authoritarianism (in some form) is aggravated (somehow) by conditions of (some kind of) threat actually has a long and venerable history.... authoritarians prove to be relentlessly sociotropic boundary maintainers, norm enforcers, and cheerleaders for authority whose classic defensive stances are activated by the experience or perception of threat to those boundaries, norms, and authorities.

Karen Stenner[60]

[P]olitical and military leaders judge the risks of democracy by looking at how ordinary people use the freedoms that democracy affords.

Nancy Bermeo[61]

The question then becomes: Why do cross-class alliances turn against authoritarian regimes in some settings, but not others? I see the macrostructural stability

---

[57] Loveman (1998): 480. Emphasis in original. The reader should of course not infer authorial hostility to rationalist arguments entirely. My argument on the political origins and attitudinal microfoundations of authoritarian Leviathans fundamentally depends on a rationalist logic.

[58] Polletta and Jasper (2001): 289.

[59] For more on this theoretical argument, including a historical framework for how communal elites gain or lose political autonomy from authoritarian regimes in the first place, see Slater (2009).

[60] Stenner (2005): 26, 32.

[61] Bermeo (2003): 4.

of authoritarian regimes resting on the same microfoundations that political psychologists such as Stenner have pinpointed as the source of individuals' authoritarian predispositions: "the experience or perception of threat." This insight has occasionally informed comparativists' understanding of non-democracies, as when Robert Kaufman notes the role of shared threat perceptions in dampening elite opposition to authoritarian rule in Latin America:

> The "threat from below" – activated during periods of political-economic crisis – is the lowest common denominator and the most important bond of cohesion within bureaucratic-authoritarian coalitions. In the context of antipopulist or counterrevolutionary fear, broad exclusionary policies have been accepted at least initially not only by the armed forces and "big business," but also by many white-collar, professional, and local entrepreneurial groups that otherwise suffer considerably from most aspects of bureaucratic-authoritarian rule.[62]

If shared elite foreboding of renewed mass mobilization is "the most important bond of cohesion" for authoritarian Leviathans, regime durability should vary with the perceived severity of such threats. Eva Bellin goes furthest in incorporating this notion into her theory of authoritarian durability.[63] Her primary argument is that industrialization has generally failed to generate elite support for democratization in the postcolonial world because the state tends to play such a large role in guiding late development. State sponsorship makes elites highly dependent on authoritarian rulers for the contracts and licenses that make their enterprises viable. Meanwhile, mass politics threatens to introduce newly organized threats to property rights and the overall investment climate. Bellin thus attributes democratic diffidence among postcolonial capitalists not only to their dependence on the state, but also to their fear of chaos amid any political transition. Authoritarian durability arises from elite perceptions that the regime is both a good *provider* and a good *protector*.

Capitalists' perceived need for protection is more pronounced under conditions of late development, Bellin argues, because democratization can no longer be tempered by restrictions on universal suffrage. Yet this gives us little guidance in explaining variation in levels of elite trepidation toward democratization *within the postcolonial world itself.* All postcolonial elites know that democratization entails granting immediate universal suffrage to a society marked by generalized poverty. Their willingness to open these political floodgates, I submit, cannot be explained by their level of dependence on state patronage. Rather, as Bermeo's formulation above implies, upper groups' perceptions of *prospective* threat under a future democratic regime are shaped by *retrospective* consideration of how mass politics looked before an authoritarian Leviathan was established. Where patterns of contentious politics fostered the creation of protection pacts, authoritarian regimes enjoy the coalitional foundations to withstand even severe economic crises, which sharply curtail the state's capacity to meet the material interests of economic elites. This book thus sees the capacity of authoritarian regimes to

---

[62] Kaufman (1986): 86–87.
[63] Bellin (2002): 1999.

protect upper groups from any shared fears of mass unrest as the best predictor of authoritarian durability. *A protection pact is sturdier than a provision pact.*

Why does protection serve as a stronger basis for authoritarian coalitions than provision? First, no regime has ever been a perfect purveyor of patronage. Resources are always limited – unlike elites' material wants – so ruling groups distribute selective benefits that bring some groups in and leave others out. State sponsorship might enhance the political loyalty of the regime's biggest beneficiaries; but what about those fractions of the upper class that remain outside the regime's charmed inner circle? Nor does it logically follow that *state* sponsorship always fosters *regime* loyalty among its recipients, who might expect to receive even more patronage under a new political leadership it helps to install. In sum, state sponsorship can cultivate loyal class *fractions*, but fear of renewed unrest and instability can cultivate loyal upper *classes*, writ large.

Another reason to suspect that protection trumps provision is that economic elites are by no means the only type of elites whose support underpins authoritarian durability. Military officers have the greatest capacity of all to bring a regime down by refusing to use force against a democratic opposition. But if regime loyalty derives from state sponsorship, how can we explain defection by these *state personnel*, whose very livelihood depends on the continuation of that sponsorship? Once again, the key points are that threats can unify elites in a way that patronage cannot, and that elites' need for state largesse will not necessarily cement their attachment to a particular regime.

Nor is the uniting effect of a credible threat of renewed mass unrest limited to economic elites and state officials. Middle classes and communal elites should find unbridled contentious class politics to be similarly threatening to their basic interests. As a coalitional currency in the hands of an authoritarian Leviathan, therefore, fear has two main advantages over patronage: (1) fear is indivisible, whereas state sponsorship of one elite faction leaves fewer resources for others; and (2) fear can generate broad support for authoritarian rule among groups whose interests transcend the material (i.e., religious elites), and who are hard to reach with targeted state patronage (i.e., urban middle classes).

A focus on the role of patronage alone in sustaining authoritarian rule suffers from another shortcoming as well. Such a perspective assumes that authoritarian durability can be sustained with particular *policies*, regardless of the capacity of underlying *institutions* to implement policies efficiently.[64] Yet a regime that enjoys access to a state with significant fiscal power has more capacity to keep patronage flowing than a regime that does not.[65] Similarly, a regime organized into a

---

[64] On the institutional requirements of difficult economic policies, see Doner, Ritchie, and Slater (2005) and Hamilton-Hart (2002). See Pepinsky (2008) for an argument that variation in economic policies rather than institutional capacity best explains divergence in authoritarian durability, with an emphasis on Indonesia and Malaysia.

[65] As Thachil and Herring (2008: 451) adroitly argue: "The problem with patronage-based systems is one of aggregation: there is never enough to go around, or there is serious fiscal crisis if attempts are made to ensure patronage trickles down." While agreeing with this point in general, this book also stresses how variation in state fiscal power produces variation in regimes' ability to deliver patronage widely without rendering themselves vulnerable to fiscal crisis.

cohesive ruling party will be better able to manage the "insatiable wants" of leading figures and their personal networks, dampening the factional disputes that
inevitably arise over the distribution of patronage. Regimes that appear to rest on
"remunerative power" alone thus often rely on effective state and party institutions to keep resources flowing in a targeted way to those figures whose support
is vital to regime survival. Variation in the strength of these regime institutions,
as with state institutions, is best explained by variation in counterrevolutionary
elite responses to the divergent threats posed by contentious politics.

Political Institutions and Authoritarian Durability

One of the reasons regime transitions have proved so theoretically intractable is that
different kinds of authoritarianism differ from each other as much as they differ from
democracy.

Barbara Geddes[66]

[T]he nightmare of all founders is that their organizational creation will walk away from
them.

John Padgett and Christopher Ansell[67]

It has long been recognized that stable and effective democracy rests upon workable states and parties. Only recently have scholars evinced a similar recognition
of the role of party and – to a far lesser extent – state institutions in shaping the
stability and duration of authoritarian regimes. This book is squarely situated
within this emerging institutionalist consensus. Yet it aims to build upon it with
new perspectives on the relatively neglected importance of state institutions for
authoritarian durability; the counterrevolutionary origins of robust ruling parties;
and the importance of elite collective action in sustaining not only single-party
regimes, but military regimes as well.

The fortifying effect of robust ruling parties on authoritarian regimes is well
established.[68] There are two main reasons why parties count. First, they are ideal
mechanisms for organizing mass participation.[69] Second – and of more consequence here – ruling parties can help order elite politics as well. By channeling
elite support to the ruling regime and channeling benefits of state power to elite
backers, ruling parties serve as ideal mechanisms for preventing elite defection.[70]
In other words, parties fortify authoritarian regimes in large measure because
they serve as institutional vehicles for elite collective action. The finding that
single-party regimes systematically outlast military regimes has been attributed
to ruling parties' presumptive superiority to ruling armies as facilitators of elite
collective action in defense of dictatorship.[71]

---

[66] Geddes (1999): 121.
[67] Padgett and Ansell (1993): 1260.
[68] Recent works include Geddes (1999), Slater (2003), B. Smith (2005), Brownlee (2007), Gandhi
and Przeworski (2007), and Levitsky and Way (forthcoming).
[69] Huntington (1968) is of course the classic argument to this effect.
[70] Brownlee (2007).
[71] Geddes (1999).

This consensus on the importance of ruling parties is not wrong, but it is incomplete. Its first shortcoming is that it understates the role of *the state* in shaping authoritarian durability.[72] Where states are well organized and effectively extractive, ruling parties gain more political mileage by colonizing the state apparatus with party appointees. Where states are disorganized and weak, party membership confers fewer tangible privileges. This suggests that strong *party-state complexes* rather than parties alone serve as the sturdiest institutional foundation for durable authoritarianism.[73] When dissident politicians get expelled from the ruling party in such systems, they are relegated to "the political wilderness." One often hears this phrase in discussions of elite politics in Malaysia and Singapore. When leading politicians have gotten sacked in more disordered political systems such as Thailand and the Philippines, they have typically enjoyed alternative routes to the political summit. *Where power is not ordered, there is no political wilderness.*

A second shortcoming of most current institutionalist research is that it cannot tell us why party and military regimes exhibit so much *intra-type* variation in durability.[74] It is a valuable insight to recognize that party regimes systematically outlast military regimes; but it is no stopping point. Ruling parties are generally, but by no means universally, more cohesive than ruling militaries. If we adjust our target of inquiry to the elite collective action that authoritarian institutions facilitate, rather than the institutional types themselves, we might discover common sources of durability in military-led and party-led authoritarian regimes alike.

In sum, authoritarian regimes vary dramatically in their institutional foundations, as Geddes argues above – but those institutions have coalitional foundations that exhibit independent causal significance. Indeed, where an authoritarian leadership lacks broad elite support at the onset of its rule, it is unlikely to take the political risks inherent in building stronger states and parties in the first place. When broad elite support is lacking, the founders' nightmare invoked by Padgett and Ansell becomes especially vivid – a newly formed institution will tend to organize a leadership's rivals as well as its allies, and potentially take on a regime-subverting life of its own. And it is only when unmanageable and endemic forms of contentious politics loom on the political landscape that elites are likely to eschew factional interests and forge broader patterns of elite collective action to begin with.

[72] Whereas Greene (2007) stresses the importance of state *size* in sustaining authoritarianism, my argument stresses state *strength*. As Owen (2004: 36, 37) notes: "the huge size of the bureaucracy in most Middle East and Third World countries has been taken as a sign of a very strong state"; but in most cases, "the state's apparent coherence was more a matter of presentation than reality."

[73] Also see Levitsky and Way (forthcoming) and Slater (2008b). On the role of powerful party and state institutions in driving more equitable development outcomes in Malaysia than Thailand, see Kuhonta (2003).

[74] B. Smith (2005) provides the best argument for intra-*party* variation. My framework aims to build upon his by offering an explanation that is at once more parsimonious (setting aside Smith's stress on resource endowments) and more precise (sharply distinguishing the effects of elite vs. mass opposition, which Smith at times comes close to conflating).

This provides a novel explanation for *the origins* of strong ruling parties. Contrary to Samuel Huntington's classic and subsequently unchallenged argument that intense revolutionary struggles yield especially durable parties,[75] this book suggests that *counter*revolutionary parties should prove particularly robust as sources of enduring elite collective action.[76] Revolutionary parties tend to fragment once their shared enemy is vanquished – especially when that enemy is a departed colonial power, as in Burma and Indonesia.[77] Counterrevolutionary parties retain their deepest source of institutional cohesion so long as the authoritarian Leviathan continues to be perceived as a powerful protector against the endemic enemy of radical mass mobilization. Elites' historical memories and evolving perceptions of the threat of contentious politics best explain the strength not only of ruling parties, but of authoritarian institutions more generally.

Conclusion

By situating this book's arguments in major literatures on war and state-building, democratic coalitions and transitions, and authoritarian institutions, this chapter has aimed both to assess the most important rival explanations and to clarify its most novel theoretical claims. The chapters to follow present empirical evidence from seven Southeast Asian cases that (1) internal conflict can make the state; (2) weak nations can facilitate and not just stymie state-building; (3) communal elites and identity politics are key drivers of democratic mobilization; (4) protection sustains dictatorships more reliably than provision; and (5) the strongest authoritarian institutions are born in counterrevolution rather than revolution. These arguments all derive from a causal framework centering on contentious politics as the strongest shaper of elite collective action, which in turn shapes the institutional strength and durability of authoritarian Leviathans. How well these theoretical claims stand up beyond the Southeast Asian context will be the primary concern of this book's concluding chapter. Until then, I focus my attentions on the region where my causal arguments were born and first developed: Southeast Asia.

---

[75] Huntington (1968, 1970).

[76] Brownlee (2007) provides a compelling argument that ruling parties can also be strengthened by decisive factional victories at their origin point. For a similar logic on state-building, see Vu (2004). Yet I submit that the *transcendence* of factions trumps the *triumph* of any single faction as an enduring source of party cohesion.

[77] To the extent that regimes resting on revolutionary parties exhibit impressive duration, I hypothesize that this occurs either because nationalist revolutions wedded communal elites to the regime and made them unavailable to lead any democratic opposition, as in post-1975 Vietnam (Slater 2009); or because subsequent outbreaks of anti-regime contention led these historically revolutionary regimes to undergo a counterrevolutionary "turn," as in post-1958 Mexico and post-1989 China (Slater and N. Smith 2009).

PART II

CONTENTIOUS POLITICS AND THE INSTITUTIONS OF ORDER

3

Colonialism, Cleavages, and the Contours of Contention

From Why to When: Critical Antecedents in Historical Causation

As detailed in Part I, this book's core proposition can be summarized as follows: *Authoritarian Leviathans will only be able to generate the kind of elite collective action that underpins strong state and regime institutions when contentious class politics preceding their onset is perceived by a wide range of upper groups as an endemic and unmanageable threat.* How threatening and unmanageable such mass mobilization is perceived to be depends less on its raw intensity than on the specific forms it takes. Contentious class politics will most likely be perceived by multiple types of elites as an endemic threat requiring root-and-branch institutional transformation when it: (1) destabilizes major urban centers; (2) mobilizes radical redistributive demands; and (3) exacerbates communal tensions in the process. When contentious politics takes the form of regional rather than leftist rebellions, elite collective action is more likely to be enhanced within the military alone, permitting the rise of a long-lasting military regime despite a weak supporting coalition.

This may explain *why* postcolonial Southeast Asia diverged onto separate domination, fragmentation, and militarization pathways; but the question of *when* this divergence took place requires more explicit analytic attention. At one level, my answer is simple. The period of relatively pluralistic politics between the end of World War II and the inauguration of authoritarian Leviathans serves as the "critical juncture" in my argument.[1] In a cross-case study such as this, critical junctures can fairly be defined as periods in history when variation in a specified causal force pushes multiple cases onto divergent long-term pathways.[2] The

[1] See Lipset and Rokkan (1990 [1967]) and Collier and Collier (1991) for classic treatments, and Capoccia and Kelemen (2007) for a valuable overview of the critical juncture concept.
[2] The methodological literature is divided over whether contingency and choice are defining attributes of critical junctures. This book treats divergence across cases as the defining trait, and the importance of choice and contingency as an empirical question.

causal force at issue in this book is contentious politics, which varied during the postwar critical juncture across Southeast Asia in subtle ways, but with powerful and path-dependent political consequences.

It is common practice in comparative-historical analysis to commence one's causal analysis during a critical juncture. After all, this is when one's primary causal factor was operative. While intuitive, such an approach is problematic. Is it really plausible that everything preceding a critical juncture can be considered causally irrelevant? Can "background conditions" always be "held constant" across different countries? Such lab-like control is virtually impossible to attain in comparative politics – especially when studying a region as diverse as Southeast Asia. Clearer thinking is needed as to how conditions preceding a critical juncture might combine with factors operating during that critical juncture to produce divergent long-term outcomes.

I call such preexisting conditions *critical antecedents*.[3] When examining the "antecedent conditions" preceding a critical juncture, one should clearly distinguish critical antecedents from (1) *background similarities*, which cannot logically explain cross-case divergence; and (2) *rival explanations*, which provide a longer-term argument – and typically an earlier critical juncture – for the divergent outcomes of interest. This chapter wrestles with the inferential difficulty that Southeast Asia exhibits precious few background similarities upon which to construct a quasi-experimental "controlled comparison." The concept of critical antecedents allows one to embrace rather than elide antecedent cross-case variation, bringing conditions before a critical juncture into one's causal analysis in a systematic and transparent way.

The seven Southeast Asian countries analyzed in this book clearly *varied* in multiple ways before they *diverged* in their institutional trajectories. This chapter assesses which kinds of antecedent variation were causally relevant and which were not. It shows that variation in prewar practices of nation-building shaped variation in postwar social and territorial cleavages throughout Southeast Asia. One cannot understand cross-case variation in postwar patterns of contentious politics – i.e., my key causal variable – without understanding cross-case variation in prewar cleavage formation. Since this factor *combined* with postwar eruptions of contentious politics to produce long-term political divergence, it is a critical antecedent.[4] By contrast, any argument that variation in prewar practices of state-building directly carried over into postwar variation in state power – i.e., one of my key outcome variables – would be a rival explanation. The remainder of this chapter argues that prewar *nation-building* must be understood as a causally relevant critical antecedent, while prewar *state-building* is a rival explanation that cannot outperform my own causal framework centering on divergent types of contentious politics after World War II.

---

3 Slater and Simmons (2010).
4 Readers concerned with infinite regress should note that prewar cleavages did not *cause* postwar conflicts, but helped determine what shape those later conflicts – themselves more a product of Japanese invasion than preexisting conditions – would take.

How Cleavages Shaped Contention: Prewar Nation-Building as a Critical Antecedent[5]

The Japanese military's conquest and occupation of Southeast Asia during World War II was nothing short of a shared regional cataclysm. In a manner that was shockingly sudden and practically simultaneous, Western-run colonial states were demolished, and Japanese occupying forces would build precious little infrastructure for systematic rule in their place. Unlike Korea and Taiwan, where the Japanese constructed powerful state apparatuses over decades of imperial control, Southeast Asia would experience Japanese overlordship primarily as a time of brutal ransacking, not bureaucratic routine. Unlike colonial zones spared the Japanese onslaught, Southeast Asia would find the infrastructural lid of European colonial power blown to bits, granting extraordinary if temporary space for new forms of mass politics – especially when ousted colonial powers provided arms and equipment to Southeast Asian mass organizations for combating their shared enemy: Japanese occupying forces.

Yet for all its sweeping and simultaneous quality, Japan's violent arrival on Southeast Asian shores took place against sharply distinctive social and political backdrops. Mass politics would become far more contentious virtually everywhere – but *what form* such contentious politics took depended upon social cleavages predating the Japanese invasion. Where prewar colonial rule had neglected nation-building efforts and fostered the emergence of sizable urban immigrant minorities and deeply divided "plural societies,"[6] as was most clearly the case in British Malaya and Singapore, the postwar explosion of mass politics would have both urban impact and communal reverberations. Where prewar rulers had pursued and achieved greater ethnic, religious, and linguistic integration at the national level – as in the American Philippines, precolonial Vietnam, and noncolonized Thailand – postwar class conflict would primarily take place within rather than across identity groups. And where colonialists had practiced especially invidious forms of territorial divide-and-conquer, as in British Burma and the Netherlands East Indies, postwar conflicts would not only take on an ethnic coloration characteristic of the "plural society" model, but a regionalist dimension as well.

Plural Societies as a Harbinger of Urban Communal Conflict
If the national museum is the paradigmatic showcase for modern states to parade their triumphant narratives of national spirit and solidarity, Malaysia and

---

[5] It is not my claim that nation-building is necessarily the *only* critical antecedent for postwar institutions. Any other prewar factor predisposing these cases to experience the forms of contentious politics that they did – e.g., well-established electoral politics as an incorporative check against radical redistributive demands in the Philippines (e.g., Sidel [1995]: 142; Kerkvliet [1998]: 171; Slater [2005]: 107–108), or the relative prewar strength of nationalist vis-à-vis leftist movements in Burma and Indonesia – serves to complement rather than contradict my causal framework. Lest one think this makes my argument unfalsifiable, I hasten to add that any scholar proposing a *direct* causal connection between some prewar factor besides state-building and the postwar institutions I examine would indeed be threatening to disconfirm my central argument.

[6] The term was coined by Furnivall (1944: 304), and entails a society in which diverse social groups "mix but do not combine.... living side by side, but separately, within the same political unit."

Singapore have built rather curious variants of the political form. Visitors to the Malaysian National History Museum in downtown Kuala Lumpur barely set foot inside before confronting a display of the legendary fifteenth-century Malay warrior Hang Tuah, his hand poised on a ceremonial keris dagger, crowned with his famous if perhaps apocryphal slogan: "the Malays shall not vanish from the earth." One of the postcolonial world's most ethnically diverse polities thus features not a call for national fellow-feeling, but the rallying cry of a single ethnic group. This incantation has been repeatedly mobilized as a collective rhetorical defense against Malaysia's sizable ethnic Chinese minority – the only community recently accused of threatening the political supremacy of the ethnic Malay majority.

Singapore's national museum makes no such brash symbolic appeal to any single ethnic identity group. Yet its national spirit is rather wanting. Look no further than the hall dedicated to formal, reverent portraits of Singapore's stuffy succession of British colonial governors. One might think that an independent nation-state would be a bit more sheepish about openly celebrating its former imperial overlords. One imagines that a museum curator proposing a similar exhibit in any other Southeast Asian capital would be roundly ridiculed and summarily sacked.

Such curatorial displays attest to the relative weakness of nationalist identifications superseding ethnic loyalties and emotively unifying the body politic in both Malaysia and Singapore. This shared condition is deeply rooted in these neighboring countries' shared colonial experience. Prewar British colonial authorities fostered the rise of ethnically plural societies without undertaking the hard political work of bridging "indigenous" Malays with "immigrant" Chinese and Indians. The colonial state's political and economic practices not only yielded steep class stratification, which broadly characterized societies throughout Southeast Asia[7] – they also created veritable communal tinderboxes. The exceptional sharpness of communal cleavages would make postwar contentious politics much more threatening and difficult to manage than outbreaks of conflict in neighboring countries, notably the Philippines.

Far more than their colonial counterparts elsewhere in Southeast Asia, British authorities in Malaya[8] and Singapore relied on imported manpower – primarily Chinese, and secondarily Indian – for cheap labor in the colonies' lucrative tin mines, rubber estates, and urban ports and enterprises. Colonialism thereby spawned an enormous alien underclass. The British also encouraged the in-migration of Chinese capitalists to manage tax farms and export ventures, as well as Indian professionals and civil servants to staff the colonial state. Malaya's indigenous majority group, ethnic Malay Muslims, remained somewhat of a collective bystander to these demographic and economic shifts. In short, "urbanization in

---

7 Prewar class cleavages are thus considered a background similarity rather than a critical antecedent in this study.

8 The federated states on the Malayan Peninsula were known as "Malaya" until 1963, when their merger with Singapore and the territories of Sabah and Sarawak ushered in their renaming as "Malaysia." Singapore exited Malaysia amid rising Malay-Chinese tensions in August 1965.

Malaya was unusually extensive and essentially Chinese."[9] With the Malay masses concentrated in peasant production, and Malay elites predominantly employed in aristocratic service, relatively little social interchange took place among the colony's sizable Malay, Chinese, and Indian communities before World War II. Since the British did nothing whatsoever to foster new political associations transcending communal lines, colonial Malaya rapidly became a paradigmatic plural society utterly lacking institutions to manage inter-ethnic relations.

In institutional terms, communal fragmentation was most importantly expressed in the field of education. Whereas prewar national language policies fostered the integration of Chinese minorities in Thailand and the Philippines, British authorities made little effort to use English as an integrator of Malaya's diverse communities. "The Chinese community continued to enjoy considerable autonomy in educational affairs despite attempts by the government to regulate the proliferation of Sino-centric activities in Chinese schools by requiring them to register with the Education Department after 1920," Heng Pek Koon has written. "However, the government was unsuccessful in this effort," because "the colonial government did not have the necessary Chinese-speaking administrators to effectively supervise the activities of the Chinese schools."[10] This captures both the severe ethnic fragmentation of prewar Malayan society, as well as the relative standoffishness of the prewar Malayan state – a theme I revisit later in this chapter. Each ethnic community was essentially self-governed, when governed at all.

The price of this expedient approach became apparent as war with Japan loomed. Having failed to facilitate the emergence of any sort of cross-communal organizations or identities in Malaya and Singapore, the British had no local allies with nationalist credentials to enlist for support in their war effort. After years of cracking down on the Chinese-dominated Malayan Communist Party (MCP), the British were forced into a reluctant shift in strategy; they "turned to the illegal and detested MCP for assistance in providing labor for essential services and volunteers for guerrilla squads and local defense corps."[11] That the MCP could generate ample anti-Japanese fervor was beyond question, given Chinese Malayans' outrage at Japanese aggression and atrocities in mainland China. But by aiding and abetting the mobilization of the MCP, the British fostered the rise of a radical group with no more affinity for the colony's Malay sultans – Malaya's ostensible rulers – than for the hated Japanese.

Japan's invasion and occupation transformed Malay-Chinese relations from a pattern of relative indifference into one of violent hostility. "The occupation's main political legacy to Malaya was its worsened inter-communal relations."[12] This was due to Japan's differential treatment of its Malay and Chinese subjects. Malay aristocrats were succored in exchange for active collaboration. By contrast,

---

[9] Stenson (1974): 129.

[10] Heng (1988): 22. As of 1947, five times as many young Chinese studied in Chinese-language schools as in English-language schools (Ibid. 23).

[11] Stenson (1974): 132.

[12] Tarling (2001): 204.

the Chinese population in both Malaya and Singapore was the target of three-and-a-half years of horrific violence. After the rapid and unceremonious expulsion of the British in early 1942, moreover, Allied forces provided material support to the Malayan People's Anti-Japanese Army (MPAJA), a resistance force led by communist Chinese. Collaborationist Malays – far softer military targets than the Japanese – bore the brunt of this resistance movement, which was nearly as anti-Malay as anti-Japanese. Wartime communal violence set the stage for dramatically worsened communal relations in the postwar period.

As it happened, the British had no opportunity to prevent wartime bloodshed from spilling over into postwar violence. Japan surrendered suddenly in August 1945, in the wake of the atomic attacks on Hiroshima and Nagasaki, at a time when no Allied personnel were in a position to reassume control over Malayan territory. The Japanese were ostensibly entrusted with maintaining law and order until Allied personnel could physically reclaim their colonial possessions. In practice, Japanese soldiers mostly withdrew from their policing responsibilities and allowed the existing balance of local political forces to play out.

This resulted in the granting of virtually unchallenged authority to heavily armed communist resistance movements in two areas of Southeast Asia. The first and most famous site of such clear leftist advantage was northern Vietnam, where relative ethnoreligious homogeneity meant that communist mobilization had no significant communal repercussions and was perceived by many elites to be nationalist, and not merely communist, in its intent. But the second such site was the Malayan Peninsula, including Singapore at its southern tip, where communist mobilization equaled ethnic Chinese mobilization, thus combining class and communal unrest in explosive ways.

In sum, prewar British policies helped produce deeply divided polities in Malaya and Singapore. The Japanese occupation badly exacerbated these cleavages, violently pitting lower-class Chinese against Malays as well as Chinese elites. By actively supporting the MPAJA, the British spawned a well-armed, radical leftist organization that they were in no position to control. These critical antecedents provide the essential backdrop for the outbreaks of contentious politics that followed the Japanese occupation, which posed threats and challenges to British and Malayan elites that far surpassed those confronting elites in countries such as Thailand and the Philippines.

Prewar Nation-Building and the Taming of Identity Politics

No society in Southeast Asia could reasonably be described as anything approximating homogenous – even in the constructed fiction and fantasy world of the national museum. Yet national identifications have made more headway at superseding narrower ethnic attachments in some countries than others. In the Philippines, Thailand, and Vietnam, prewar nation-building practices yielded polities that were less linguistically fragmented and more religiously unified than neighboring Malaya and Singapore. This would ultimately make the region-wide postwar upsurge of mass politics less threatening to elites' "way of life," leaving them less desperate for immediate or ongoing protection from a powerful and centralized authoritarian Leviathan.

Linguistic and religious unification commenced in all three cases long before the British began "pluralizing" their possessions in Malaya and Singapore in the late nineteenth century. In the Philippines, Spanish rule (1565–1898) was largely conducted through religious authorities, under whose watch "a vast proselytization was launched which has resulted in the contemporary Philippines being 90 per cent Christian."[13] Furthermore, many unconverted Chinese immigrants were expelled in the mid-eighteenth century, and Spanish authorities subsequently kept a much tighter lid on new Chinese arrivals. Chinese-indigenous mestizos converted to Christianity en masse, and became the backbone of the Philippines' new landed elite.

Long before the American takeover at the turn of the twentieth century, therefore, the Philippines' geographic center had largely rid itself of the deep ethnic and religious cleavages just beginning to emerge at the very heart of the Malayan and Singaporean colonial polities.[14] The American imperium did nothing to reverse these Spanish legacies, while doing much to overcome the archipelago's linguistic fragmentation: first by introducing widespread primary education in English in the 1900s, and later by permitting Philippine elites to propagate Tagalog as a lingua franca in the 1930s. To be sure, American officials deserve considerable opprobrium for stifling the development of a meaningfully independent postcolonial state in the Philippines. Yet prewar colonial practice helped in some ways to consolidate the very Philippine nation that would later chafe under America's postcolonial domination.

Nation-building projects began much earlier and achieved even greater success in Thailand and Vietnam. The rise to power of Thailand's Chakkri dynasty[15] in 1782 and Vietnam's Nguyen dynasty in 1802 marked the emergence of what would quickly become the two most administratively centralized and territorially consolidated kingdoms in mainland Southeast Asia. Their relative success at prewar state-building will be addressed shortly. For now, the key point is that Thailand and Vietnam both underwent significant prewar nation-building processes that had no equivalent in Malaya and Singapore.

In terms of ethnic diversity, Thailand rivals the Philippines for its effective assimilation of ethnic Chinese. This was hardly a frictionless process. Chinese business enterprises suffered harsh discrimination throughout the early decades of the twentieth century, and Chinese-language schools were severely restricted in the wake of the 1932 overthrow of Thailand's absolute monarchy. Yet as discrimination worsened, historian K.P. Landon argued, "the natural tendency among the Chinese was to seek Thai citizenship in larger numbers than previously."[16] As a foremost scholar on the politics of Chinese minorities throughout Southeast Asia once (over)stated, Thailand is "[s]ingularly fortunate as the result of its

[13] B. Anderson (1998) [1988]: 194–195.
[14] The marginalization of the Philippines' sizable Muslim minority in the far-southern islands of Mindanao and Sulu would not give rise to separatist violence until after Ferdinand Marcos was in power, as I discuss in Chapter 5.
[15] Thailand was known as Siam until 1939; for the sake of non-Southeast Asianists, I tend to use anachronistic rather than additional country names.
[16] Cited in Purcell (1965: 136).

ethnic homogeneity."[17] Having dodged formal colonialism altogether, Thailand avoided the pluralizing effects of unrestrained immigration under conditions of imperial political aloofness.

Also like the Philippines, Thailand has long possessed a hegemonic national religion.[18] More than 90% of Thais are practicing Buddhists, and throughout the Chakkri era, the Thai state has consistently insisted that nation, religion, and monarchy "form a threefold moral bond" and that "the stability of the nation and religion cannot be separated."[19] Such nationalist socialization has been facilitated by both linguistic unification and educational centralization. "The centralized educational system provided the vehicle," argues Prudhisan Jumbala. "The Thai language, in the form of the Bangkok dialect, became the only medium of instruction," as textbooks "introduced the modern idea of a territorial nation but based on traditional cultures and structures."[20]

As relatively integrated polities, Thailand and the Philippines are but infants alongside the oldest surviving state in Southeast Asia: Vietnam. Separated from China in the tenth century A.D., the Vietnamese state has anchored the southeastern corner of mainland Southeast Asia for over a millennium. In comparative terms, Vietnam has been noteworthy for the historical rootedness of nationalism and the relative insignificance of ethnic, linguistic, and religious divisions. Even the endemic geographic division between northern and southern Vietnam has been more political and economic than cultural in character: northerners and southerners overwhelmingly speak the same language and identify with similar religious beliefs and practices. French colonial efforts to construct a Catholic cultural and political counterweight to Vietnam's syncretistic Buddhist and Confucian supermajority gained only limited traction in the southern reaches of its "Indochinese" possessions. Confucianism has long served as a revolutionary ideology that "consolidated Vietnam's national spirit and facilitated resistance to foreign invaders."[21] The contrast with Malaysia – where Hang Tuah's spirited battle cry is ethnically exclusive and inwardly targeted – is stark.

Hence when class conflict struck the Philippines, Thailand, and Vietnam in the post–World War II era, it did not take place against a backdrop of endemic ethnic divisions, as happened in Malaysia and Singapore. Substantial *prewar nation-building* ironically undermined *postwar state-building*. Relatively unified ethnic and religious structures left postwar leaders in Manila, Bangkok, and Saigon with little leverage for extracting resources from relatively assimilated economic elites, and left the dictators who eventually emerged in those countries without the necessary historical raw material to divide and conquer their opponents along communal lines.

[17] Osborne (1970): 192.
[18] On the concept of a hegemonic national religion, see Friedland (2001) and Slater (2009).
[19] Somboon (1981): 1.
[20] Prudhisan (1992): 13.
[21] Woodside (1999): 26–27. On the importance of Confucianism in Vietnam's nationalist movement, see McHale (2004).

Territorial Cleavages as a Centrifugal Omen

The gravest challenges to national integration do not always strike at a polity's heart – they can also threaten to tear a polity apart from its extremities. As argued in Part I, Burma and Indonesia were the only Southeast Asian countries to face major regional rebellions during the pluralist interlude between World War II and the emergence of authoritarian Leviathans, setting them on a pathway toward militarization rather than domination or fragmentation. We must again look to variation in prewar colonial policies and practices to understand divergence in the types of contentious politics that roiled Southeast Asia in this critical postwar period.

To be sure, Burma and Indonesia were not the only Southeast Asian polities to develop sharp territorial cleavages before Western powers began their collective retreat. The French artificially divided the ancient Vietnamese state into three provinces; the British governed their Malayan possessions as a quasi-federation through three distinct formal logics of rule; and the southernmost provinces of the Philippines and Thailand were similarly characterized by local Muslim majorities lacking significant demographic presence in their national heartlands. Yet it was only in Burma and Indonesia where colonialists constructed state institutions that successfully drove a political wedge between territorially divided identity groups through a purposeful policy of divide-and-rule – cleavages that the Japanese interregnum would seriously exacerbate, especially in Burma. Although virtually any Southeast Asian polity could have conceivably suffered regionalist violence in the wake of gaining independence – and the Philippines and Thailand would indeed suffer such conflicts decades down the road – Burma and Indonesia were more primed and predisposed for near-term territorial disintegration than any of their Southeast Asian neighbors.

Burma is the extreme case. As in Malaya and Singapore, British colonialism spawned a hyperpluralized society in prewar Burma. The critical difference would be the British colonial state's differential treatment of the "indigenous" populations it confronted. While Singapore lacked either a sizable native population or entrenched local authority structures, and Malaya was ruled by sultans who proved relatively amenable to British overlordship, Burma's monarchy and majority ethnic Burman population would resist British imperial encroachments tooth and nail. It would take three Anglo-Burmese Wars in the nineteenth century to overthrow Burma's Konbaung dynasty and impose an extraordinarily coercive form of direct rule in its stead. Without a reliable political toehold in the majority Burman community, the British looked to collaborationist ethnic minorities and armed Indian sepoys to secure their colonial grip.

Divide and rule found expression, first of all, in the formal administrative separation of Burma into highly segregated geographic zones. While the predominantly Burman population of "Lower" Burma was governed directly and repressively by foreign forces, the ethnic minorities of "Upper" Burma were placed in the hands of non-Burman local elites who were protected and bolstered by the British as recompense for their collaboration. Unlike in Malaya and Singapore, where Britain's communal complacency left Malays and Chinese standing cheek to jowl throughout much of the geographic landscape, colonial favoritism toward non-Burman and non-Buddhist groups such as the Christian Karens produced deepset political and cultural divisions that were not just ethnic, but territorial.[22] "Administrative simplifications along territorial and racial lines resulted in political, economic, and social boundaries that continue to divide the country today," Mary Callahan has written. "The residents of central Burma.... had no contact with the juridically distinct 'frontier' or 'excluded' areas, where other ethnic groups resided and remained largely forgotten by the colonial state."[23]

The spirit of divide et impera was most blatantly and fatefully witnessed in colonial practices of military recruitment. As of 1931, ethnic Burmans made up over 75% of the total population but barely 12% of army recruits.[24] The Burma Army enlisted more than three times as many Karens and nearly twice as many Kachins and Chins as Burmans, even though none of those three ethnic groups represented even ten percent of Burma's population. By 1941, as Japanese invasion loomed, Burmans surpassed the enlistment rates of Kachins and Chins, but still lagged badly behind the Karens, even though Burmans outnumbered Karens in the general population by a factor of eight.

Japan's occupation exacerbated the regional dispersion of political identities and power that had characterized Burma under British rule, much as it exacerbated preexisting communal divisions in Malaya. Thanks to "Allied dumps" of heavy weaponry to "a dizzying array"[25] of anti-Japanese insurgent movements during the occupation from 1942–45, British authorities discovered upon their return to Burma that "arms were scattered across the country from a wide variety of sources and were thus available to virtually anyone who wanted them."[26] Of greatest consequence for the conflicts to follow, British operatives rather impetuously provided both heavy weaponry and empty promises of future self-rule to Karen militias, who "simply never returned the great quantity of arms"[27] they had received from Allied forces once Japan's occupation came to a close.

While the British armed Burma's ethnic minorities, the Japanese armed the majority Burmans, mobilizing the Burma Independence Army (BIA) in Thailand in 1941 to assist in their invasion of British-ruled Burma. "As BIA troops marched northward and westward from the Thai border, they swept into their ranks mainly Burmans of Lower Burma," writes Callahan. "Karens of the delta did not enlist nor did the BIA recruit them, probably because of Burman resentments about the overrepresentation of that ethnic group in the prewar colonial army and bureaucracy."[28] Even worse, ethnically Burman BIA forces unleashed horrific violence against Karen civilians during their march on Rangoon. "BIA troops may have killed as many as eighteen hundred when they destroyed four hundred Karen

---

[22] As discussed in Chapter 8, significant pockets of Karens in and around Rangoon would briefly give the Burman-Karen conflict more of a "centripetal" dynamic in the late 1940s.
[23] Callahan (2004): 16.
[24] All figures in this paragraph are from Callahan (2004: 36, 42).
[25] Ibid. 3.
[26] Maung Maung (1990): 195.
[27] Ibid. 186.
[28] Callahan (2004): 53.

villages in early 1942," Callahan notes. As Karen leader Saw Tha Din described relations between his minority community and the Burman majority on the eve of independence: "How could anyone expect the Karen people to trust the Burmese after what happened during the war – the murder and slaughter of so many Karen people and the robbing of so many Karen villages? After all this, how could anyone seriously expect us to trust any Burman government in Rangoon?"[29] Since the Burman-dominated BIA would ultimately become the core of the postcolonial Burmese army, it is hardly surprising that Karen organizations took the separatist path – with other ethnic groups from the prewar "Excluded Areas" not far behind.

Postcolonial Indonesia's inherited territorial tensions were far less severe. But Dutch colonial practice in its "East Indies" exhibited similarities in kind if not degree. As in Burma, imperialism in Indonesia produced not just communal pluralization but territorial fragmentation. To some degree this was inevitable – Indonesia is the world's most sprawling and diverse archipelago, and what is most noteworthy is not how the Dutch politically splintered it, but how much their dominion politically unified it. Nevertheless, the Dutch saw political opportunities, not just obstacles, in Indonesia's spectacular diversity.

Dutch distrust of Indonesia's Muslim, Javanese majority broadly mirrored British distrust of Burma's Buddhist, Burman majority. "The Dutch, recognizing that Islamic leaders and institutions posed the greatest potential for resistance to colonial domination, waged a 350-year campaign to confine Islam to the realm of domestic relations and private conscience."[30] Collaborationist non-Muslim minorities were succored. As in Burma, this divide-and-conquer approach was expressed through formal territorial divisions; the political preservation and protection of ethnic minority elites; and a military apparatus dominated by ethnic and religious minorities hailing from the colony's far geographic reaches.

Indonesia's political parallelism with Burma would continue under the Japanese flag. Long a unitary state in de jure if not de facto terms, Indonesia underwent formal territorial division for the first time during World War II. The Japanese interlude in Indonesia was a world turned upside down – ethnic and religious majorities long "balanced" by collaborationist minorities finally received what they saw as their political due. While much of the Dutch-built and non-Javanese–dominated colonial army went into anti-Japanese resistance, predominantly Javanese nationalists broadly collaborated with the Japanese occupiers in expectation of an eventual granting of independence. The Japanese drew heavily on the Javanese as they mobilized Indonesia's first indigenous army. As we will see in the following chapter, tensions between armed units mobilized by the Dutch before the war and those mobilized by the Japanese during the war would quickly prove explosive after Indonesian nationalists declared independence upon Japan's surrender in August 1945.

In sum, Burma and Indonesia both experienced territorially ominous divide-and-conquer machinations under long-term European and short-term Japanese

---

[29] Ibid. 75.
[30] Madrid (1999): 19. One could get the mistaken impression when visiting Amsterdam's colonial Tropenmuseum that Indonesia was more than 90% *non*-Muslim rather than Muslim.

rule – with minority/peripheral and majority/central populations taking turns as the preferred tool of occupation. This primed both countries for territorial conflicts with the retreat of colonialism. By contrast, the other five Southeast Asian cases in question here would need to wrestle more immediately with the sharp class and (in Malaya and Singapore) communal cleavages bequeathed by empire. The seeds of postwar conflicts had thus been unevenly laid across Southeast Asia before the end of World War II.

The next section argues that the same cannot be said for Southeast Asia's colonial state apparatuses. While prewar *nation*-building was a critical antecedent, indirectly shaping postwar state power through its causal influence on postwar conflict, variation in prewar *state*-building does not offer a compelling comparative explanation for postwar divergence in state strength. It is an important rival explanation, but not the right explanation. What would eventually become Southeast Asia's strongest postwar Leviathans showed surprisingly little relative potency vis-à-vis their regional neighbors in the prewar era.[31]

The Lateness of Southeast Asian States: Prewar State-Building as a Rival Explanation

This book's causal framework encompasses multiple types of political institutions. Yet one is especially pivotal: the state. Variation in postwar contentious politics produced divergence, first and foremost, in the character and capacities of state apparatuses throughout Southeast Asia. With a stronger and more effectively extractive Leviathan in place, it would prove easier to construct and consolidate a robust and cohesive ruling party, to bring and keep the military under civilian wraps, and to sustain authoritarian rule over many decades.

It would thus be inferentially perilous for my entire causal framework if Southeast Asia's variation in postcolonial state capacity had its origins in the prewar era. While prewar social cleavages are a critical antecedent and thus a *complementary* explanation, prewar state institutions are a *rival* explanation to my own. Yet any such "continuity hypothesis" cannot in fact outperform my own framework centering on postwar contentious politics and resultant elite collective action – not only because it offers no direct or determinative predictions on the other institutional outcomes this book endeavors to explain, but because it cannot explain postwar variation in state strength itself. *British Malaya and Singapore were no more destined to have infrastructurally strong postcolonial states by the time of Japan's occupation than Burma, Indonesia, the Philippines, South Vietnam, and Thailand were doomed to have relatively weak ones.*

The first reason is the Japanese occupation itself. Anyone positing that postwar Malaysia and Singapore simply inherited powerful Leviathans from the prewar period must reckon with the reality that Japan's occupation annihilated the Leviathans that the British had constructed. Whatever state cohesiveness that

---

[31] I focus on state-building rather than on party or regime institutions because Southeast Asia exhibited virtually no variation in either party or regime institutions before World War II. State institutions varied more and were more clearly inherited by postwar, postcolonial leaderships.

existed before the war was undermined, among other ways, by the occupation's fostering of postwar conflict between "those 'in the bag' (i.e., Japanese POWs) and those 'not in the bag' (i.e., those who escaped from Malaya)."[32] Even the most optimistic chronicler of prewar Malayan state strength calls the process of postwar state-building one of "starting again."[33] As will become evident in Chapter 4 and Chapter 8, British colonialists needed to retool the Malayan and Singaporean Leviathans in dramatic ways after World War II to cope with the novel challenges of mass urban mobilization and communal conflict.

Of primary interest for this volume, this would include a significant revamping of the Malayan and Singaporean taxation systems. Tax data for Southeast Asia during the pre-1945 period are spotty and inconsistent, but it does not appear that British Malaya or Singapore enjoyed any appreciable edge on their neighbors before the Japanese occupation in terms of overall tax collection. More important evidence of Malaya's and Singapore's lack of antecedent institutional advantage derives from the *mix* of taxes before the Japanese occupation. Recall that this book defines state fiscal power not simply in terms of tax/GDP ratios, but by the share of direct taxes in the total revenue haul. It is thus of exceeding importance that prewar British rulers depended almost entirely on indirect trade and consumption taxes for their tax revenues, rather than direct income or corporate taxes.

Most telling of all, Malaya and Singapore were the only cases studied in this book that did *not* put in place a significant and sustained system of direct income and corporate taxation before World War II. According to United Nations data of the time, direct tax collections amounted to only 1–2% of total tax revenue in British Malaya and less than 5% of total taxes in Singapore as of 1947, before skyrocketing with the imposition of income and corporate taxes in December of that year (see Figure 3, next page).[34]

How contentious politics shaped this major fiscal shift after 1945 is a topic for later chapters. For now, the key point is that the powerful and comparatively progressive tax systems witnessed in postwar Malaya and Singapore simply did not exist during the prewar era. Even Singapore was more of a tax haven than a tax state before World War II, as suggested by the *Straits Times'* invocation of prewar Indonesia as a model for postwar Singapore and Malaya on the eve of progressive tax reform in 1947:

In the Netherlands East Indies before the war, income tax had been in force for many years. The Dutch are hardheaded people and their administration in the N.E.I. before the war was second to none.... In point of fact, they enforced income tax so effectively that one of the richest multi-millionaires of the N.E.I., the late Oei Tiong Ham, came to Singapore to escape it. What the Dutch could do in the N.E.I., the British can do in Malaya.[35]

---

[32] Zakaria (1977): 66.
[33] Heussler (1983).
[34] United Nations (1953): As Martin Rudner (1994 [1975]: 22) has written: "Prior to World War II Malaya had acquired a highly fragmented and socially regressive tax system."
[35] "An Expert on Income Tax," *Straits Times*, 21 August 1947.

FIGURE 3. The Postwar Origins of Fiscal Power in Southeast Asia

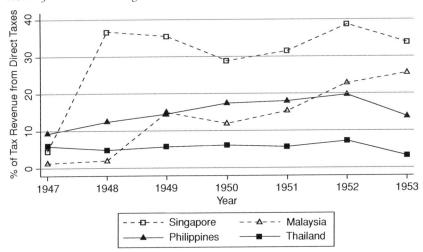

Sources: U.N. Statistical Yearbook and U.N. Economic Survey of Asia and the Far East (multiple years)

British officials made only halfhearted attempts to build a centralized and bureaucratic Leviathan before World War II, as Malaya retained "a bewildering array of different administrative authorities" on the eve of war – what one historian has described as "an administrative morass."[36] In prewar Malaya's relatively placid political climate, the indigenous sultans of individual Malay states had no incentive to surrender greater powers or resources to the British-ruled center. "Despite British frustration with the constitutional heterogeneity of Malaya, it proved difficult to subsume state identity, as represented by the Rulers, within a more unified state structure."[37] The upshot was a congeries of "Malay states dominated by regional elites, *comparable in some respects to the caciques of the Philippines*"[38] – a supposedly paradigmatic case of prewar state fragmentation and capture. Nor did the Malayan state comprise an especially impressive Weberian bureaucracy before the Japanese occupation, given the importance of royal descent in shaping administrative recruitment. "The main characteristic of the system was that it was dependent upon nomination and not upon competition," as "it was considered that competitive examinations would not ensure the selection of suitable candidates" for the subservient, indigenous arms of Malaya's civil service.[39]

To be sure, Singapore's prewar state was considerably more centralized and bureaucratized than that of its Malayan neighbor. Yet there are two important reasons why a powerful postwar Singaporean Leviathan was not a foregone conclusion either. First, effective state centralization and bureaucratization are

36 S. Smith (1995): 21.
37 Ibid. 201.
38 Rich and Stubbs (1997): 14. Emphasis added.
39 Khasnor (1984): 49.

conceptually distinct from – if also, in my view, nearly necessary conditions for – the extension of state infrastructural power.[40] Prewar British authorities patently lacked the political incentive, will, and personnel to elaborate the kind of intrusive and extractive tax bureaucracy that would become a key sinew of the postwar Singaporean state – as the earlier vignette from Singapore's *Straits Times* indicated. Nor did prewar Singapore boast either the highly extractive provident funds or the sweepingly effective public housing provision that would emerge as signs of the state's infrastructural reach and grip in the postwar era. As Virginia Thompson wrote in 1945, "up to the time when Malaya was invaded provident funds for Asiatic employees were still the exception, not the rule," while "[t]he housing situation in the Straits ports resembled that of Rangoon."[41]

A second reason for skepticism is that Singapore was not unique in the Southeast Asian context for being a relatively centralized and bureaucratic prewar polity. Vietnam was provincially fragmented in name only, with all decisions emanating from the French governor-general in Hanoi. "In terms of administrative structure," Truong Hoang Lem has argued when examining Vietnam, "the French colonial administration is the most centralized compared to that of other colonial powers, for instance, the Dutch and the British."[42] The French also long preserved centuries-old Confucian practices of meritocratic recruitment to the Vietnamese bureaucracy, and constructed a powerful prewar police force, the Sûreté, which was notorious for its frequent and fearsome interventions in Vietnamese civil society. The dramatic splintering of the Vietnamese state along both territorial and factional lines would primarily be a product of political dynamics following rather than preceding World War II.

Unlike Malaya, furthermore, Thailand and the Philippines were unitary rather than federal systems in the prewar era. Prewar administrative centralization was no harbinger of postwar infrastructural power. Of Southeast Asia's future fragmentation cases, Thailand enjoyed especially fortuitous antecedent state capacity, thanks to the Siamese monarchy's avoidance of colonization through concerted responses to British and French geopolitical pressures in the second half of the nineteenth century. In short, "the Thai political system was transformed from a basically feudal state to a centralized bureaucratic polity" after 1873.[43] Bureaucratic principles and practices were almost certainly more deeply ingrained in Siamese than Malayan statecraft before World War II. Yet this head start at state-building did not yield the powerful postwar Leviathan in Thailand that a continuity hypothesis from prewar to postwar institutions would posit.

The Philippines is a trickier case and warrants closer attention. Most contemporary experts argue that the Philippine state apparatus was irretrievably weakened during the first decades of the twentieth century, in the early years of American rule. By introducing representative political structures such as elections

---

[40] See Soifer (2008), Slater (2008a), and the other articles in the special issue of *Studies in Comparative International Development* on state infrastructural power for more discussion of these distinctions.
[41] Thompson (1945): 21, 36.
[42] Lem (1971): 86.
[43] Chai-Anan (1971): 18–35.

and legislative bodies before building a strong administrative apparatus – argue Benedict Anderson, Paul Hutchcroft, and John Sidel[44] – the American colonists ensured that civil servants would be captured by, and beholden to, the provincial politicos who appointed them. According to this view, the initial era of municipal and national elections represents the true "critical juncture" when the Philippine state's weakness was produced. The challenge of this argument to the present study is clear. It suggests that, since American colonialism produced a bureaucracy with no effective autonomy from provincial politicos, the postcolonial state could not reasonably have been expected to impose significant direct taxes on this wealthy political class, regardless of postwar patterns of contentious politics.

The causal linkage from prewar elections to postwar fiscal powerlessness does not stand up very well to broader comparative analysis, however. Sidel seems to acknowledge its limitations when he suggests that the Philippines' "putatively 'weak' postcolonial state curiously resembles that of contemporary Thailand, which in the nineteenth century had a monarchical state 'strong' enough to avoid direct colonial subjugation."[45] Variation in prewar state-building cannot explain this "curious" postwar convergence, but postwar patterns of contentious politics can.

To be sure, the Philippines' unusual prewar legacy of "precocious electoralism" helped shape the *contours* of the postcolonial Philippine state by molding it into a "politicos' polity,"[46] in stark contrast to Thailand's famed "bureaucratic polity."[47] But it did not predetermine the Philippine state's postcolonial *capacities*. Even if post-independence politics "essentially reconstructed the institutional legacies of American colonial rule,"[48] one must still endeavor to explain why postwar events failed to overturn these prewar legacies. The Philippines' first postwar secretary of the interior, Tomas Confesor, "was stridently opposed to rehabilitating elite collaborators and wanted to rebuild the Philippine polity on the basis of a strong chief executive."[49] The next chapter aims to explain why any such centralizing impulse in the postcolonial Philippines would face implacable and effective elite resistance. For now, the key point from the comparison of future domination and fragmentation cases is that state-building legacies are not always forever – especially when an occupying wartime army fractures the arc of history by shattering every institution in its path and neglecting to construct new institutions capable of taking their place.

---

44 See B. Anderson (1998 [1988]: 201–203); Hutchcroft (2000); and Sidel (1999: 12, 16–18). These authors' intellectual debt to Shefter (1994) is evident and explicit.

45 Sidel (1999): 11.

46 The absence of repeated elections in prewar Malaya surely meant that the postwar Malayan state was not as inclined as the postwar Philippine state to become the plaything of *elected politicos*; but keeping in mind the sultans' strong influence over prewar civil service recruitment, the Malayan state could well have become a plaything of *provincial royalty* after the British withdrawal if postwar contentious class politics had not taken the form that it did.

47 Riggs (1966) coined the term in reference to postwar Thailand. Again, the distinction between bureaucratization and infrastructural power as types of state strength is critical to keep in mind.

48 Sidel (1999): 18.

49 Franco (2000): 113.

Does this hold true for Burma and Indonesia as well? Did either prewar or Japanese state-building predispose these cases toward militarization? As noted above, the topsy-turvy quality of military mobilization under imperial auspices – first European favoritism toward peripheral minorities, then Japanese favoritism toward central majorities – paved the way for territorial warfare after World War II's end. Yet it was by no means self-evident that the Burman- and Javanese-dominated armies organized by the Japanese would come to dominate their respective political systems. First of all, both Burma and (especially) Indonesia had relatively well-developed prewar administrative apparatuses, which could have been resurrected and revitalized for postwar governance. As Benedict Anderson has argued, the prewar Dutch *beamtenstaat* served as a historical model for Suharto's New Order Leviathan, even after "Japanese military rule (March 1942 to August 1945) came close to destroying this iron cage" and "the state almost disappeared in the face of popular insurgence."[50] Meanwhile, in Burma after the war, "the government's activities – tax collection, criminal investigation, disease inoculation, customs inspection, and census taking – were all undertaken by bureaucrats who had worked for the British colonial regime and who relied on the same methods they had used prior to independence."[51]

Failure of the administrative state and a full-blown political takeover by the military were by no means a foregone conclusion in either Burma or Indonesia – not only because both countries had reasonable stocks of preexisting state capacity, but also because as of the end of World War II, vanguard nationalist parties looked like the prime contenders to capture political power after independence. Indonesia's Nationalist Party (PNI) and Burma's Anti-Fascist People's Freedom League (AFPFL) were fronted by charismatic national heroes and backed by massive, mobilized memberships. They were far better organized than their military brethren, who had been institutionally and ideologically fractured more than unified by their involvement in occupation and decolonization politics. It would only be with the outbreak of regionalist rebellions *after* World War II that civilian-military tensions would reach a boiling point, and military officers in both Burma and Indonesia would overcome factional schisms to combat rebellious regional commanders and supersede the political power of those countries' civilian leaders.

Conclusion

This chapter has set the stage for the arguments and evidence to follow by showing what prewar factors in Southeast Asia can and – equally important – cannot explain. Stark variation in prewar social and territorial cleavages was critically important in shaping the contours of conflict that erupted throughout Southeast Asia after World War II. By contrast, the British did not engage in any exceptional prewar practices of state-building in Malaya and Singapore before World War II that might have presaged the comparatively powerful Leviathans

---

[50] B. Anderson (1983): 480.
[51] Callahan (2004): 7.

that ultimately emerged. Like the variation in regime institutions that emerged in their wake, the divergent capacity of Southeast Asia's postcolonial state institutions is fundamentally a postwar, not a prewar phenomenon. Hence we now turn to postwar factors – specifically, variation in contentious politics, as influenced by the social and territorial cleavages just discussed – to explain how Southeast Asia's divergent institutions of political order came about.

4

Mobilization and Countermobilization amid Colonial Retreat

Introduction

[A]fter Japan's capitulation in August 1945, the Europeans could not make an effective comeback. Nothing like this happened anywhere else in the colonized zones of Asia and Africa. It also meant that Southeast Asia was the one colonized region – after Spanish America 140 or so years earlier – where armed struggle for independence – and more – was commonplace.... No other region of the world – not Latin America, not the Near East, not Africa, and not South Asia – had this kind of alarming profile.

Benedict Anderson[1]

"Small" events early on may have a big impact, while "large" events at later stages may be less consequential.

Paul Pierson[2]

Between the end of World War II and the birth of the authoritarian Leviathans that are the core concern of this book, Southeast Asia traversed an extraordinary era of mass political contention. What often appeared to outsiders as a singular, region-wide explosion of armed communism involved subtly distinctive types of contentious politics both across and within Southeast Asia's emerging polities. Anderson's invocation of a uniform "alarming profile" for the region accurately captures a widely held gestalt as World War gave way to Cold War – but it obscures the significant variation in how alarmed different types of Southeast Asian elites in fact were by the different types of conflict reverberating across the region's inchoate political landscapes.

This chapter traces variation in the first postwar wave of contentious politics, from 1945 until roughly the mid-1950s, in Malaya, the Philippines, and Indonesia. As subtle as this variation was, the patterns of elite collective action that arose in response would be strikingly divergent, with profound and lasting consequences

---

[1] B. Anderson (1998): 6, 7.
[2] Pierson (2004): 45.

for the institutions of political order. In line with Pierson's insight above, minor early differences would mean major differences down the road. Well before a second wave of contentious politics commenced in the mid-1960s, ushering in the demise of pluralist politics and the emergence of new authoritarian Leviathans, these three countries began traveling divergent political pathways: domination in Malaya, fragmentation in the Philippines, and militarization in Indonesia. Stark variation in elite collective action had yielded state, party, and military institutions of widely varying cohesion and capacity by the late 1950s. These institutions would later become the political bedrock of authoritarian Leviathans: regimes bearing the birthmarks of contention, deeply determining their durability during the worldwide wave of democratization to come.

Social Conflict and Elite Organization: Communism and Communalism in Malaya, 1945–1957

> If the Japanese are famous for their latent fear of earthquake, we call it the earthquake syndrome; in Malaysia, one could say that we have an ethnic-quake syndrome.
>   Chandra Muzaffar[3]

Of the seven countries in this book, Malaysia is perhaps the most compelling. This is because it defies conventional theoretical wisdom in virtually every respect. The country has long enjoyed abundant natural resources and has faced a complete absence of external threat; yet it has developed one of the strongest and most extractive state apparatuses in the developing world. It has experienced substantial capitalist development, lacks a labor-repressive landlord class, and suffered a severe buffeting during the Asian financial crisis of 1997–98; yet authoritarianism has endured amid only modest pressures for democratization. Malaysia also has electoral rules that typically privilege dispersed individual candidates over centralized parties, and lacks a legacy of revolutionary anti-colonial struggle for party elites to draw upon for legitimacy. Yet the country's ruling parties have stood as rock-solid pillars of institutionalization throughout more than five decades of independence. Such extraordinary political and institutional stability has been the product of consistent patterns and practices of collective action among Malaysia's political and economic elites.

These surprising outcomes have a surprising source. Put simply, *stability at the elite level* originated in reaction to particular patterns of *instability at the mass level*. Mass unrest has consistently entailed the intertwining of class and communal grievances. Such episodes of social conflict have consistently been countered by new forms of elite organization and collective action. Malaysia's strong central state, robust ruling party coalition, cohesive and subservient military apparatus, and durable authoritarian regime have their shared historical roots in elite responses to especially challenging pressures from below.

The discussion of Malaya in this chapter surveys elite responses to four distinct episodes of contentious politics during the 1945–57 period: (1) the anarchic interregnum that followed Japan's surrender; (2) mass mobilization to influence

---

[3] Chandra (1998): 47.

debates over the terms of Chinese citizenship in the mid- to late 1940s; (3) the urban strike wave that shook the foundations of the colonial economy during the same period; and (4) the period of Emergency from 1948–57, when the British and their local allies struggled to quell a Chinese-led leftist rebellion from the "illegible" confines of squatter settlements along the jungle fringes. Although scholars commonly trace the strength of Malaysian political institutions to the Emergency period, I argue that the outbreaks of urban conflict between 1945 and 1948 had an equal if not greater political impact.

Communist Power and Communal Chaos: The Postwar Interregnum, 1945–1946

For most residents of Southeast Asia, Japan's surrender in August 1945 marked a welcome end to a period of tyranny and state terror. But for most residents of Malaya, the sudden Japanese withdrawal meant being cast from the frying pan of brutal wartime occupation into the hellish fires of political anarchy and communal chaos. For nineteen frightful days (August 15th–September 3rd), British authorities remained absent from the scene, and the heavily armed Malayan Communist Party (MCP) – having enjoyed direct wartime British support in its guise as the Malayan People's Anti-Japanese Army (MPAJA) – essentially had the field to itself. As one British officer described the scene upon his return to Malaya: "the Chinese communists were roaming the countryside and taking up positions in towns. Well armed and unopposed by the Japanese for over a month they had things pretty much their own way."[4]

Armed and ascendant Chinese communists exacted revenge upon the majority Malay population throughout late 1945 and early 1946, repaying their rivals for their general attitude of accommodation toward Japan's occupying forces. Instead of using its momentary control to prove its capacity to govern, the MCP turned its attentions to "settling old scores against Japanese informers and collaborators, brandishing weapons, threatening people, and generally creating a mood of fear, even a reign of terror."[5] This was consistent with the communists' punitive treatment of the Malay population during the Japanese period. As Cheah Boon Kheng describes one set of Malay villagers' recollections of the MPAJA's wartime conduct:

Some of the Chinese men would abduct Malay women, molest them, or keep them as mistresses.... Chinese are also said to have slaughtered pigs in the mosques, and forced Malays to eat pork. Without a trial Chinese guerrillas would kill Malays on the slightest suspicion of being collaborators. Many Malay policemen, *penghulu* (district headmen), *ketua kampung* (village headmen), and government officials were said to have been tortured and executed in a cruel and inhuman manner. Wives and children would also be shot along with the suspected collaborators. Bodies of victims were said to have been mutilated beyond recognition, an act which offended the Islamic religion.... The Chinese would also prevent the Malays from congregating and attending Friday prayers, for fear that the Malays were gathering to attack the Chinese.[6]

---

[4] Quoted in Heussler (1983: 83).
[5] Cheah (1983): 295.
[6] Ibid. 197.

It was against this immediate backdrop that ethnic Chinese communists came not merely to challenge the colonial state, but to replace it. As one leading official in the returning British Military Administration (BMA) declared in his summary report in September 1945: "There is no doubt that in all the villages throughout the Malay States the Chinese Resistance Forces are in command."[7] Even after British rule was ostensibly restored, "the MCP operated alongside the BMA as an alternative government," and "the BMA was overstretched even in its limited objective of restoring stability."[8] Although this period of MCP ascendancy and quasi-statelessness was brief, its effects were anything but. "Their short administration left an indelible impression on the minds of most people of how frightening communist rule might be," writes Cheah. "For Malays especially, *distrust of Chinese and distrust of communism intertwined.*"[9]

While the Malay majority was on the defensive, it was by no means defenseless. Violent Chinese actions invited violent Malay reactions, in what quickly deteriorated into "a vicious cycle of reprisals and counter-reprisals."[10] Malay reactions against Chinese communists were especially fearsome in areas where MPAJA guerrillas had gained a foothold during the Japanese occupation, and where fears of an imminent Chinese communist takeover were greatest. The populous southern state of Johor witnessed the emergence of a violent invulnerability cult under the leadership of Kiyai Salleh, who gained the active support of no less a figure than the Sultan of Johor "to destroy the enemy of religion once [and] for all"[11]:

The intensity of the Malay resistance was now partly due to Malay fears that the Chinese would seize political power in Johor and throughout the country. Rumors had spread among the Malays, and were generally believed, that the British government had promised the Chinese and the MPAJA that Malaya would be handed over to them after the Japanese surrender.... At this critical moment the Sultan of Johor is believed to have turned to Kiyai Salleh as the Malays' savior.... He asked Kiyai Salleh to "menjaga negeri kita" (guard our country).[12]

Communism and communalism thus combined to make an extraordinarily lethal cocktail of contentious politics. And if the short-lived experience of communist ascendancy had left an "indelible imprint" on many Malays, Malay religious violence had no less of a lasting effect upon many Chinese. "The Malay-Chinese clashes also meant that Malays would resort to widespread extremist violence if pushed," Cheah argues. "The long-term implications of this extremism were very great: the overall Malayan polity might always be held subject to ultimate Malay recourse to mass bloodshed."[13]

---

[7] Quoted in Heng (1988: 39).
[8] White (1996): 80.
[9] Cheah (1983): 295. Emphasis added.
[10] Heng (1988): 42.
[11] Ibid. 215.
[12] Ibid.
[13] Ibid. 298.

The Citizenship Controversies: Mobilizing for Communal Advantage, 1945–1948

This chaotic interregnum colored every outbreak of mass contention – and hence every organized elite response – that was to follow. In an effort to weaken popular Chinese resistance and replace "the ramshackle administrative structures of prewar days"[14] with "a new single, unified, centralized structure,"[15] British authorities pressured the colony's Malay sultans to accept a new constitution in late 1945. The Malayan Union plan had two key elements: "The Malay rulers were to be stripped of even the symbolic and ceremonial political powers they had hitherto enjoyed and reduced to the status of priest-kings with some control over religious affairs," writes Chandra Muzaffar. "The recently-domiciled non-Malay communities were to be granted citizenship on very liberal terms."[16]

Against the backdrop of mass mobilization among the armed forces of Chinese communism, these proposals hit the Malay population like political dynamite. Only a vigorous, concerted Malay response could possibly force the British to rescind their plan once it had received official local consent. Yet the Malay population lacked mass organizations of any kind, and the Malay aristocratic and administrative elite remained splintered along provincial lines. The felt need for a broader organization to defend Malay interests was compounded by the fact that no political organization in Malaya could begin to rival either the grassroots presence or the national scope of the MCP. What emerged in response to this threat from below was the organization that would become Malaysia's ruling party:

> The Malays, already deeply insecure because of their economic position and the communist challenge, felt betrayed by the British, who were seen as the vital protectors of Malay society.... *Numerous Malay associations rapidly transcended their particularistic local village and state identities and coalesced against the Malayan Union scheme.* The oppositionist movement, which culminated in the United Malays National Organization (or UMNO), was led by the elite stratum of Malay administrators. Using their links with district level Malay authorities right down to the Malay headman, the elites succeeded in mobilizing most of the Malay population and, in doing so, laid the basis for UMNO as a mass political party.[17]

Although UMNO is often portrayed as having been a vehicle for anti-British sentiment at its inception, it is more accurate to see it as an instrument for anti-*Chinese* ends.[18] The irony is that "a strong, pro-British party sprang on to the political scene to oppose a British proposal."[19] Quite unlike nationalist parties that emerged to front anti-colonial struggles in Indonesia, Burma, or Vietnam, Malaya's UMNO did not even press a claim for *eventual* national independence at

[14] Heussler (1983): 92.
[15] Chandra (1979): 53.
[16] Ibid. 53–54.
[17] Jesudason (1996): 42–43. Emphasis added.
[18] For similar interpretations, see Stenson (1974: 138); Chandra (1979: 61); and Heng (1988: 42).
[19] Jesudason (1996): 43.

its birth in early 1946. To the contrary, the mobilization of UMNO represented a clarion call for reinforced British protection from a dreaded Chinese bid for power.

Further evidence that Malay anxiety centered on the liberalization of Chinese citizenship, far more than the diminution of the sultans vis-à-vis British officialdom, derives from the eventual outcome of the Malayan Union controversy. When British and Malay leaders hammered out the compromise Federation Agreement in 1947, it continued to contain the Malayan Union's provisions regarding the centralization of state power; but the proposed liberalization of prewar restrictions on Chinese citizenship had been thrown by the wayside. So long as the British did not use their powers to favor the Chinese, the Malay leadership was willing to see the British accrue the added political powers they desired. Indeed, the 1945–57 period consistently shows Malay leaders welcoming, even inviting the expansion of the colonial state's powers in response to the challenge of Chinese mass mobilization.

Closer attention to the micro-dynamics of UMNO's rise similarly supports the perspective that the party emerged for anti-Chinese purposes. Given the geographical fragmentation of Malay politics, the movement needed to flower at the local level before it could conceivably blossom into a national party. The first days of 1946 saw the sprouting of a new Peninsular Malay Movement of Johor, under the leadership of Onn bin Jaafar, the Malay District Officer in the district of Batu Pahat: *the district where racial violence during the postwar interregnum had been the most severe.* The purpose of the new association was to "facilitate the organization of the Malays in order that their security could be assured, for by that time serious Sino-Malay clashes had broken out in Batu Pahat." In sum, "these racial clashes between the Malays and Chinese gave a greater sense of urgency to the Malays to organize themselves. The clashes also emphasized the fear of the Malays that one day they would be overwhelmed and ruled by the Chinese."[20]

This palpable sense of ethnic anxiety explains the fervor with which mobilization occurred – not only in Johor, but across the Malay population. Just two days after Onn bin Jaafar convened the new Malay association in Johor, the Malay-language daily *Majlis* cried out for similar communal rallying nationwide:

Join and take part in associations as soon as possible if you love your grandchildren. Look at your people – what will befall them – they will be left far behind. *There is no other remedy than to organize ourselves into associations through which we unite to face the danger.*[21]

By mobilizing literally hundreds of thousands of Malays in opposition to the Malayan Union plan, however, Malay elites produced parallel trepidation and dread among the Chinese.[22] Just as Malays mobilized across class lines to limit Chinese citizenship, Chinese initially did likewise to expand it. This took the form of a nationwide work stoppage (hartal) in October 1947 to oppose the

---

[20] Ishak (1960): 59.
[21] Quoted in Ibid.
[22] As of September 1947, UMNO's total membership was estimated at over 115,000 (Ibid. 90).

constitutional proposals. "The whole of the Chinese community stayed indoors," Charles Gamba writes. Communal threat thus served to unify Chinese Malayans across class and geographic boundaries. "The groups taking part in the Malaya-wide hartal formed a colorful mixture where the MCP found common fellowship with Chinese millionaires."[23]

Labor Unrest and the Reordering of Coercive and Administrative Institutions, 1945–1948

For a brief moment in late 1947, therefore, it appeared that Malayan politics might be defined by collective action *within* communal groups, while failing to generate elite collective action *across* communal boundaries. This is a recipe for strife, not stability. But Malay and Chinese elites alike were pressed to find common cause by the persistence of class-based mobilization throughout the mid- to late 1940s. In a direct spillover from the chaotic postwar interregnum, a powerful, urban-based, communist-led labor movement mushroomed throughout Malaya (and Singapore) between late 1945 and 1948: the Pan-Malayan General Labor Unions (PMGLU) federation.

This movement was noteworthy for its cohesion, scope of membership, and radicalism. As early as September 1945, a British planter remarked upon "the existence of 'a very strong Trade Union structure' which 'originally purported to be Anti-Japanese but it now appears to have switched over, and is anti everything purporting to progress and rehabilitation.'"[24] By 1946, "the labor movement appeared to be in a position of dominance,"[25] prompting a BMA police adviser to warn the Colonial Office that Malaya was "heading for disaster"[26]; and "by March 1947, the Pan-Malayan GLU constituted a powerful movement combining a major section of the industrial workforce under a single leadership. Had its progress continued in the inexorable fashion of the previous year it would perhaps, as the MCP hoped, have forced a revolutionary change in the forms of economic organization and probably also of government."[27] The Singapore-based *Straits Times* nervously agreed, editorializing in April 1947 that the MCP was "not content merely to be the spearhead of the trade union movement but is deliberately aiming at causing such economic and political disintegration, by strikes and other means, as will bring down our social order in ruins, and the Malayan Government with it."[28]

This continuation of class conflict did not so much overshadow the communal frictions of 1945–48 as it exacerbated them: "labor unrest had also a peculiar communal flavor."[29] The PMGLU was dominated by non-Malays, especially Chinese. In the wake of the bloody communalism of the postwar interregnum, any Chinese-led labor movement was bound to be perceived as a renewed threat

---

[23] Gamba (1962): 242.
[24] Quoted in White (1996: 86).
[25] Stenson (1970): 132.
[26] Quoted in Heussler (1983: 159).
[27] Stenson (1970): 126.
[28] Quoted in Stenson (1969: 23, fn. 45).
[29] Gamba (1962): 225.

to the Malay community. Most Malays were unconvinced that "socialist equality provided an adequate safeguard against racial extinction."[30]

The ethnic composition of the labor movement not only made it especially threatening to the Malay population; it also made it exceptionally difficult for British authorities and their Malay collaborators to manage. Whereas the citizenship controversies had sparked party organization among the Malays, labor militancy sparked new state-building efforts by the British. This initially took the form of reorganizing the state's coercive apparatus. However, we also see state authorities pushing through major reforms in the civilian administration and new forms of direct taxation on economic elites, putting the state on firmer fiscal footing for the foreseeable future.

British authorities patently lacked the capacity to police the labor movement as it emerged, emboldened, from the ashes of Japanese occupation. "Many police records had been lost because of the War and consequently, in the area of security and criminal intelligence especially, the organization was in a state of debility."[31] British officials reorganized Malaya's seven prewar police forces into a single national force, but the PMGLU was too strong of an organization to be coerced into submission: "even if Government had wished to prevent the formation of a central trade union organization, it would not have been in a position to do so."[32]

Hopes for bridling the PMGLU rested upon a vigorous effort to register its member unions, as a prelude to tighter state supervision and control. With widespread labor mobilization a fait accompli, the best that state authorities could hope for was to wean individual unions from the PMGLU's radicalizing influence. This was a job for administrative institutions; yet such bodies simply did not exist. The British were thus "obliged to create a new and more elaborate administrative structure,"[33] commencing with the appointment of an adviser and registrar of trade unions, as well as the creation of a centralized Department of Labor in early 1946. The registration effort initially foundered, as these new institutions suffered mightily from their lack of personnel equipped to navigate the complexities of governance across communal divides. As of November 1946:

The registration campaign had become by this time a virtual comedy of errors. It was, perhaps inevitably, begun in great haste and with little knowledge of the problems involved. For the first time Malayan officials were faced with the problem of conveying complicated instructions to the vernacular-educated or illiterate leaders of the Chinese and Indian workers.... [R]egistration was, at that stage, largely a matter of form because the registrar's and adviser's departments had not the staff to explain and to supervise the operations of the law.[34]

Effective labor registration and control required heightened efforts to recruit and train non-Malay (particularly Chinese) locals to serve on the front lines of the

---

[30] Funston (1980): 36.
[31] Zakaria (1977): 68.
[32] Gamba (1962): 120.
[33] Stenson (1970): 134.
[34] Ibid. 137, 164.

state apparatus. The Trade Union Adviser took the lead, as he "built up a staff of local officials to tour the country persuading managers of the advantages of non-militant unions." Such meetings provided a venue in which "the laborers discussed their own grievances with sympathetic officials who were of their own community and could speak their own language."[35] By early 1948, state efforts to register and de-radicalize the labor force had proven a considerable success; of 289 registered unions, 117 remained under the umbrella of the successor to the PMGLU, the Pan-Malayan Federation of Trade Unions (PMFTU). The remaining 172 were evenly split between unions of "independent" and "doubtful" standing. The non-radical unions possessed a larger total membership than the PMFTU and "doubtful" unions combined, by a margin of 82,000 to 67,000.[36]

This administrative success would have been unthinkable were it not for growing perceptions of the need for elite collective action both within the colonial state itself, and between the state and economic elites. This resolve to cooperate grew in direct response to the worsening of Malaya's strike wave:

The concerted unionization and the many successful but disruptive strikes of 1946 finally provoked from early 1947 a strong and equally concerted reaction. Employers, who had been divided and disorganized as never before in the generally anarchical struggle for profits, were *driven together by what had come to constitute a full-scale attack on their traditionally dominant and privileged position.* . . . Whereas the strikes of 1946, irritating though they were, merely necessitated an element of profit sharing, those of 1947 were seen as posing a threat to the traditional structure of Malayan industry and employment.[37]

Economic elites urged state officials to restore labor control with an iron fist rather than a velvet glove. In a meeting with Malaya's British governor in October 1947, a delegation from the Integrated Society of Planters insisted that union rabble-rousers face a more "ruthless application of the sentences of death, banishment, and particularly of flogging."[38] Yet the business community's growing pleas for protection provided the state with growing leverage to deal with labor as it saw fit. State officials doggedly resisted pressures to deny official recognition to radical unions, recognizing that registration would give the state more capacity to monitor labor over time.

State elites were thus acting collectively with economic elites to manage labor unrest – but essentially on the state's terms. The vulnerability of the business community to state demands became starkly evident during the colonial government's push to impose direct, progressive income and corporate taxes in late 1947. Although such fiscal reform had long been on the drawing board, the impetus to push it through at this historical juncture came from the worsening of labor unrest. As an official fact-finding commission studied the proposed levy of direct peacetime taxes for the first time in Malayan history, even the conservative *Straits Times* editorialized that Malaya could no longer remain "the only country in the

[35] Gamba (1962): 191.
[36] The raw totals come from Gamba (1962): 155.
[37] Stenson (1970): 153. Emphasis added.
[38] Ibid. 162.

world which does not impose direct taxation on individual incomes and company profits for the benefit of the community as a whole."[39]

Pressures from below weighed heavily on the minds of tax reform's backers. "It is not difficult to imagine the propaganda which the Malayan Communist Party, and also the Left-wing parties of AMCJA and PUTERA,[40] are already cooking up for the consumption by the working classes, in the event of heavy retrenchment and a standstill of social services in the Union," the *Straits Times* argued, after detailing the fiscal impossibility of stepping up public services without an influx of new revenue. As its parting shot to the fact-finding commission on direct taxation, the *ST* concluded: "Let us hope that its members are *sufficiently sensitive to the ominous groundswell of Malayan politics* to take into account the social facts as well as the financial ones."[41]

The most ominous element in this groundswell was chronic strike activity throughout 1947 in the public sector – a realm that had been relatively sealed off from communist influence. If demands from such reformist quarters could not be met, and government workers carried through on their threat to hold a general strike throughout Malaya and Singapore, the entire British strategy of tempering labor radicalism by fostering labor reformism would have been called into question.

While business representatives bewailed the prospect of direct taxes, labor organizations announced their support for fiscal reform, directly linking such progressive taxes to civil servants' demands for a pay increase. "Support for the income tax came from labor representatives in the Advisory Council as well as from various quarters outside," writes Martin Rudner. "Organized labor, including the Pan-Malayan Council of Government Workers, the Malayan Teachers Union and large Communist-led Pan-Malayan Federation of Trade Unions declared strongly for the introduction of income taxation as the 'most equitable' source of public finance."[42]

Direct taxation represented a win-win proposition for colonial officials. Revenues would grow, and the air would be taken out of a controversy that threatened to radicalize the labor movement even further. When business representatives on the Advisory Council outvoted labor representatives 13–2 in rejecting the tax proposals, British officials vetoed the decision, imposing direct taxation by fiat in December 1947. The shift would prove to be among the most significant in Malaya's economic history, as "the introduction of income taxation underlined a fundamental change in colonial Malayan fiscal objectives," notes Rudner. "Henceforth the government would pursue increased progressivity in revenue collection," by "placing the burden squarely on the broadest shoulders."[43]

By early 1948, then, the colonial government had responded to the postwar outbreak in worker militancy with considerable state-building efforts. By

39 "An Expert on Income Tax," *Straits Times*, 21 August 1947.
40 These were Chinese- and Malay-dominated movements, respectively, that emerged to protest the aforementioned Federation proposals.
41 "The Unofficial Audit," *Straits Times*, 2 October 1947. Emphasis added.
42 Rudner (1994) [1975]: 29.
43 Ibid. 26.

reorganizing its coercive institutions, co-opting the labor movement's more reformist elements, and securing precious new sources of revenue from the ample pockets of Malaya's "well-fed, racehorse-owning, cinema-building"[44] economic elites, the state placed itself in a much stronger position to confront PMFTU radicalism. Confrontation intensified in the wake of the PMFTU's annual conference in April 1948, which "left no room for doubt that the PMFTU intended to turn to a far more militant policy." After the conference opened "with the singing of the internationale in a hall decorated with the hammer, sickle, axe and star symbol," labor leader Lam Swee pronounced that "workers now know that they cannot get anything by relying on trade union specialist advisers and Commissioner for Labor: our only salvation lies in our own unity to fight." Concluding that "as long as capitalism remains there is the cause for war," Lam dramatically proclaimed: "The conference has become a war conference."[45]

Less than a month later, British authorities outlawed the PMFTU's planned May Day protests, prompting the MCP to declare in its broadsheet: "No more open and lawful means; there is only one way to pursue – the secret and unlawful one."[46] Radical rhetoric rapidly became reality, as an upsurge in strike activity "resulted in more lost working days during the months of May and June than ever before."[47] This labor militancy was associated with increased violence, and produced ever louder cries from economic elites for a concerted government response:

As May wore on, the violence was stepped up, strike breakers being murdered in a few instances, managers threatened with death if they did not grant concessions, and recalcitrant laborers being beaten.... The government was *patently unable to provide protection* for workers wishing to return and was equally unable to prevent attacks upon supervisors or managers who defied the MCP or PMFTU. Employers therefore demanded, by means of representations to the High Commissioner and petitions to the Secretary of State, far more effective control of trade union activities.[48]

Colonial authorities responded forcefully, introducing a highly restrictive Trade Union Ordinance in late May. After the assassination of three British planters in the state of Perak in mid-June, the British declared a colony-wide state of Emergency and banned the MCP and PMFTU outright. With its coercive power firmly reestablished in all of Malaya's major towns, the state quickly succeeded in uprooting communist elements from their familiar urban nests. "The whole of the trade union structure had now collapsed and the Party, being isolated in the jungle, had lost touch with the majority of the working class."[49] This would present British and Malayan elites with a whole new set of challenges in the years to come. For now, the critical point is that the crushing defeat of Malaya's once-mighty urban labor movement had not come easily, as state officials and

---

[44] This colorful description was offered by one of the two labor representatives on the Advisory Council, M.P. Rajagopal, in July 1947. Quoted in ibid. 30.

[45] All cites in this paragraph are from Stenson (1970: 214–215).

[46] Ibid. 219.

[47] Ibid. 220.

[48] Ibid. 221, 224. Emphasis added.

[49] Gamba (1962): 373.

economic elites had stepped up collective action and fundamentally reordered
their relationships to cope with the threat from below.

An "Illegible" Rebellion between City and Countryside: The Emergency, 1948–1957

When the British declared a state of emergency in June 1948, "Malaya did not
move from peace to war. Malaya had in fact not been at peace."[50] The importance
of violence between 1945 and 1948 is commonly overlooked, however, in analyses that portray social conflict as commencing with the onset of the "Malayan
Emergency." Another common misconception is that the Emergency was a rural
rebellion, fitting within the same category of contentious politics as the countless
peasant and sharecropper revolts that have shaken Europe, Latin America, and
Asia throughout modern history.

Yet this particular communist rebellion was not a revolt of the peasantry, or
sharecroppers, or agricultural producers of any kind. To the contrary, the MCP
was generally considered a mortal enemy by the Malay peasantry, even as it
confronted an equally hostile British state apparatus in Malaya's cities. Malaya's
communists thus lacked both an urban *and* a rural base. Then how could it be, as
Nicholas White claims with only mild hyperbole, that in Malaya: "The level of
violence was more intensive and protracted than in any other colonial territory
in the decolonization era"?[51]

Denied a mass base in both the peasantry and the urban workforce, the MCP
mobilized most of its support among Malaya's enormous population of ethnic Chinese squatters. This population reached an estimated 150,000 by 1940,
and ballooned to 500,000 by 1945, as urban Chinese fled Japanese massacres.
Although many squatters returned to urban settings after Japan's defeat, most
did not. At the time Emergency was declared in June 1948, the squatter population was still estimated at over 300,000.[52]

That these demographic statistics are only rough estimates helps explain why
the squatter problem was so difficult for the British and their local allies to manage. Unlike workers on estates or plantations, squatters in Malaya were almost
completely ungoverned, and highly "illegible" to state authorities. "During the
immediate post-war years, squatters had opened up huge tracts of land miles away
from government administrative centers, and the Malayan Union Government
found it lacked manpower in the District Offices and Agricultural Department
to control and administer them."[53] Thus the Deputy Chief Secretary lamented,
even before the MCP began reasserting its violent grip over squatter settlements
after June 1948, that the squatter problem was a "vast and complicated" one.[54]

---

50 Tregonning (1979): 56.
51 White (1996): 97. This assessment seems fair for the British empire, but not the postcolonial
    world as a whole (e.g., Vietnam). Malaya indeed confronted Britain with "the longest and fiercest
    resistance it ever faced in the history of its modern empire" (B. Anderson [1998]: 7).
52 Sandhu (1973): xxxii.
53 Heng (1988): 102.
54 Ibid.

The squatter population served as an opaque swamp in which communist guerrillas could swim. Located along Malaya's jungle fringes, squatter settlements provided an ideal staging ground for attacks on tin mines and rubber estates, the twin pillars of Malaya's export economy. Since expatriate planters often maintained residences on their estates as well as in the cities, "British managers were in the front line of insurgency."[55] An estimated 10% of the British planter population would be assassinated by communist guerrillas during the decade-long Emergency.[56] So although the insurgency was not primarily based in urban areas, it combined the administrative illegibility and direct elite impact that tend to make urban forms of contentious politics more challenging and threatening than rural conflict.

And Malaya's cities were hardly untouched. "Assassination was not confined merely to the rubber estate foreman or tin dredge operator," as the Emergency saw "many anti-Communist Chinese killed in the towns of Malaya."[57] The most prominent Chinese political and business leader in the land, Tan Cheng Lock, suffered serious wounds in a bomb attack at a rally in the city of Ipoh in April 1949. Tan later became besieged in his home city, writing in October 1951 that "there is no rail, sea or air transport out of Malacca, and car travel is fraught with difficulties."[58] Considering that the insurgency exacerbated communal tensions and mobilized revolutionary demands, it accords rather closely with this book's conceptualization of unmanageable class contention.

The MCP could not be wiped out until the British and their neocolonial allies mustered the elite collective action necessary to counter the communists' edge in Malaya's squatter settlements. This was expressed through the continued strengthening of the colonial state, the birth of a robust Chinese political party, and the construction of a broad party coalition linking elite figures across Malaya's communal chasms. Yet these new political institutions emerged only gradually – even grudgingly – as lower-cost means of fighting the Emergency repeatedly proved inadequate to the challenge.

The Emergency Leviathan: State-Building under Duress, and in Fits and Starts

The so-called squatter problem was allowed to grow, mainly as the result of administrative "tidakapathy" (from the Malay tidak apa, meaning "never mind"). The Government saw no urgency in the need to deal with the squatters, who were virtually out of sight.

Kernial Singh Sandhu[59]

State-building in response to mass mobilization again involved the retooling of both coercive and administrative institutions. Extending even basic police and intelligence capacity into Chinese squatter settlements presented an enormous task. Intelligence-gathering authority was entrusted to the police's Special

---

55 White (1996): 97.
56 Ibid. 125, fn. 3.
57 Tregonning (1979): 63.
58 Ibid. 67.
59 Sandhu (1973): xxx.

Branch, but the unit got off to a "meager 1948 start," as it still only employed a paltry staff of "12 officers and 44 inspectors (few of them speaking Chinese)."[60] The Special Branch was thus described as "chronically understaffed," and "failed to generate enough intelligence – in some areas virtually any intelligence – to make army action effective."[61] Nor did British authorities initially make headway in coordinating the colony's multiple coercive agencies. When the police rather than the military were granted authority to lead all Emergency operations in October 1948, Malaya's top military official huffed that "it was completely unacceptable for a general to accept orders from a policeman."[62]

Little effective reorganization took place during the opening years of the Emergency because elite opinions differed widely on the rebellion's manageability. "Tidakapathy" remained rampant. Most British elites belittled the insurgency as "the work of a few agitators and extremists, probably directed from outside the country."[63] On the other hand, an official report released in January 1949 by a special committee on the squatter problem helped to lay the groundwork for the state-building effort to follow. It concluded that "one of the most striking features of the squatter communities was the fact that they were outside the normal processes of administration."[64] Whenever squatters were confronted by pressures to comply with both insurgent and British commands, they "necessarily succumb to the more immediate and threatening influence – the terrorist on their doorstep against the vague and distant authority of the Government." The report insisted that, for counterinsurgency to be effective, "the provision of effective administration is a *sine qua non*." This would "entail the provision of adequate communications, police stations, schools and health facilities and the like."

The committee endorsed the wholesale resettlement of Malaya's squatters into "New Villages," secured from communist raids and provided with improved public services. Yet such a comprehensive initiative was still neither administratively nor politically feasible. A major political obstacle was presented by Malay-run state governments, which urged mass deportation and imprisonment to combat the insurgency. Resettlement would entail new federal incursions into issues of land management (historically a state-level concern), as well as the provision of public goods to ordinary Chinese that ordinary Malays were still denied. Administratively speaking, the British lacked the capacity to *explain* resettlement, let alone to *enact* such an ambitious plan. "The Public Relations Department did little more than drop leaflets along the jungle fringes," reports Richard Stubbs, "many of which lodged in the tree canopy or quickly rotted once they reached the ground – and sent out loud-speaker vans which were described by the Chinese as 'loud but empty voices.'"[65]

---

[60] Hack (1999): 7.
[61] Ibid. 5.
[62] Stubbs (1989): 71.
[63] Ibid. 69.
[64] All cites in this paragraph are from Osborne (1965: 12).
[65] Stubbs (1989): 85.

From 1948 until early 1950, the British approach to insurgency was one of "coercion and enforcement." But by February 1950, "it was becoming evident that the Government was losing ground to the MCP," prompting British High Commissioner Henry Gurney to recommend the creation of a new post of Director of Operations. Upon his arrival in Malaya the following month, Lieutenant General Harold Briggs' first task was "to co-ordinate the activities of the police and the military" for the first time.[66] Given the failure of coercive tactics at reducing the insurgent threat, such concentration of authority was insufficient (if clearly necessary) for the tide to be turned.

Briggs was convinced that victory over Malayan communism required stronger institutions as much as strong-armed repression. More important, he found considerable elite support both locally and among his Western backers for his efforts to elaborate a more administrative approach to counterinsurgency. The core of the new approach was squatter resettlement. In 1948 such a "perceived intrusion into what was considered to be state jurisdiction was hotly contested as a matter of principle,"[67] but by 1950, the deteriorating security situation had broken Malay resistance. Briggs "encountered little of the initial recalcitrance shown by the state governments on the subject of resettlement. He was therefore able to concentrate the resources of both federal and state governments on the comprehensive New Village resettlement scheme known as the Briggs Plan. Two years after Briggs' arrival in Malaya, the plan had largely been implemented: 470,509 squatters were now resettled in 440 New Villages."[68]

Even this did not suffice to take the wind out of the insurgency. Most "New Villages" did not receive their promised public services between 1950 and 1952, as colonial officials hesitated to post civil servants to rural bailiwicks that Malay officials still considered their own. Forced resettlement thus worsened rather than alleviated squatters' antagonism toward the state. "Rather than enjoying the blessings of a sound administration and a wide variety of social services, it seemed to most of them that they were being placed behind the barbed-wire fences to make it easier for the police to screen, detain, and deport suspected communist sympathizers, and for the security forces to intimidate them."[69]

Such population control measures probably helped the British win the war in the long term.[70] But in the short term, the MCP responded to the disruption of its supply networks by undertaking more desperate and dramatic acts of violence. This increasingly convinced British and Malayan elites alike that the war was in danger of being lost altogether. The long stretch from June 1950 to December 1951 marked the darkest and deadliest phase in the war. "There seemed to be no end in sight to the tensions and stresses created by *the constant threat which lurked in the jungle only yards away*." After his visit to Malaya in July 1951, travel writer Graham Greene concluded that "there was defeat in the mind," and that

---

[66] Ibid. 98.
[67] Ibid. 79.
[68] Ibid. 104.
[69] Ibid. 106–107.
[70] Hack (1999).

"Malayans appeared to be condemned to *a chronic state of fairly intense guerrilla warfare for years to come.*"[71]

The nadir was reached in October 1951, when High Commissioner Gurney was assassinated in an ambush on his motorcade by MCP guerrillas. Further attacks made the subsequent six weeks the bloodiest since the beginning of the Emergency. Britain's Secretary of State for the Colonies, Oliver Lyttleton, toured Malaya immediately after Gurney's assassination and was informed by a business delegation in Kuala Lumpur that "they had completely lost confidence in the police."[72] Lyttleton grimly concluded that the government was "on the way to losing control of the country and soon."[73] The *Far Eastern Economic Review* concurred:

The war in Malaya continues relentlessly. Ambushes and scores of fatalities week after week have become routine developments. The British have failed to suppress the insurrection and they now have to admit that it cannot be suppressed. . . . The commercial community, irrespective of race, is taking a growingly somber view of developments but they now understand that accusing the authorities of inefficiency and what not [sic] will not bring peace one step nearer.[74]

Worsening conditions inspired the appointment in February 1952 of Gerald Templer to serve simultaneously as Director of Operations for the Emergency (a la Briggs) and as High Commissioner of Malaya (a la Gurney). Hence, "from the beginning, Templer was armed with some of the most comprehensive powers ever given a British colonial official."[75] Given the growing unmanageability of the MCP rebellion, elites from all groups welcomed the concentration of power in the hands of this new "civil-military supremo."[76] After Templer's first address to Malaya's Legislative Council, UMNO leader Onn bin Jaafar reported that "what he was really saying was: 'If anyone gets in my way he'll be trod on.' Onn noted that this approach is 'exactly what we need.'"[77]

This broad elite support helped Templer erase the manifold institutional divisions between military and civilian policing and intelligence functions. Meanwhile, aggressive recruitment – notably of Chinese to serve in the Special Branch – made the Malayan police grow "from around 11,000 (1948) to over 73,000 (1952 peak),"[78] or "easily larger than the rest of the British colonial police force combined."[79] Such growth was not permitted to compromise either capacity or coordination: "At the same time that there was expansion, training was not curtailed."[80] It was the persistence of a highly threatening and challenging threat

---

[71] Stubbs (1989): 126–127. Emphases added.
[72] White (1996): 109.
[73] Quoted in Stubbs (1989: 136).
[74] *Far Eastern Economic Review*, 6 March 1952.
[75] Stubbs (1989): 140.
[76] White (1996): 123.
[77] Quoted in Stubbs (1989: 144).
[78] Hack (1999): 8.
[79] Zakaria (1977): 79.
[80] Ibid. 73.

from below that helped the Malayan police overcome the factional tensions that had divided the forces since World War II. As Zakaria Haji Ahmad states the counterfactual: "for all the bitterness and schisms that existed, the exigencies of the Emergency situation evaporated those conflicts that *otherwise would have led to an enduring lack of cohesion* in the officer corps as a whole."[81]

While important, this retooling of coercive institutions could not allay the administrative challenges that lay at the root of the insurgency. The British commission on Chinese squatter communities had recognized this back in early 1949; but it was only after the chronic failure of the original "coercion and enforcement" approach that political elites came to the broadly shared "realization that the MCP guerillas could not be beaten by force alone."[82] Templer received widespread elite support for his call to build new civilian institutions capable of winning the "hearts and minds" of potential recruits to the communist cause.

The administrative complexity of delivering new public services to more than 600 New Villages entailed not just the promulgation of new policies, but the construction of new institutions. The Emergency witnessed a "forced growth in administrative capacity," because "the greater emphasis to be placed on delivering services, especially to the rural population, required an administrative capability that was obviously not yet in place." Initially little more than prison camps, New Villages were to be refurbished with public goods such as "a modicum of agricultural land and the granting of long-term land titles, an adequate water supply.... a school which could accommodate at least a majority of the children.... roads of passable standards and with side drains," and "reasonable conditions of sanitation and public health."[83]

Implementing these programs from scratch was complex and costly. Thanks in large measure to the "freakishly high commodity prices"[84] that attended the Korean War from 1950–52, British authorities enjoyed ample funds to finance their new programs. This influx of revenue represented not merely a windfall, but a handsome return on earlier efforts to impose direct income and corporate taxes on economic elites:

British business was a major contributor to the Federal revenues used for counter-insurgency operations. It is impossible to quantify the exact burden of taxation which fell on British business during the Emergency, but what is clear is that the demands were ever increasing. Corporation tax was first instituted in Malaya at the end of 1947 before the Emergency was declared. The original rate of 20 per cent of gross profits was increased to 30 per cent in 1951. Meanwhile, revisions to export duty schedules were introduced just in time to capture the massive surpluses generated by the Korean boom.... [T]he improved fortunes of rubber and tin during the Korean war, *combined with fiscal reforms*, provided the funding needed for the Federation's resettlement policy, the seven-fold increase in police numbers, the raising of 240,000 Home Guards and an extra four battalions of the Malay

[81] Ibid. 71. Emphasis added.
[82] Stenson (1970): 237.
[83] Stubbs (1989): 169.
[84] White (1996): 112.

Regiment, and additional funds for social and economic development. In other words, British business financed Templer's "hearts and minds" campaign.[85]

With economic elites largely prostrate to state demands, colonial officials seized the opportunity in 1951 to introduce Malaya's Employees' Provident Fund (EPF) – the first such fund in the developing world. The compulsory contribution scheme registered 500,000 employees and 12,000 employers in its first year alone.[86] Given the long time-lag between collections and payouts, the EPF has consistently padded the country's public savings, providing considerable economic benefits to the state apparatus and concomitant political benefits to the party leaders who command it, as we will see in the chapters to come.

The Emergency Coalition: Building Parties from Above to Bridle Threats from Below

The building of state and party institutions can exhibit a strikingly parallel logic. In Malaysia, as elsewhere, parties have been strong for the same basic reason that the state has been strong: both types of institutions have consistently managed to organize and channel elite collective action. It was unmanageable pressures from below that galvanized the creation of strong parties in Malaysia, just as they served as the original stimulant for strengthening the central state.

We have seen that the birth of UMNO as a mass Malay party in 1946 was an elite-led assertion of ethnic claims in the face of mass Chinese mobilization. The emergence of the Malayan Chinese Association (MCA) three years later was similarly inspired by a worsening of contentious politics. "The immediate impetus for the formation of the MCA was the outbreak of the Emergency," argues Heng Pek Koon. "Faced with a militant Communist challenge, Chinese conservative leaders sought to consolidate their position within the community. Meanwhile, the colonial government actively encouraged them to centralize their resources through the formation of a political party in order to garner Chinese support behind its anti-insurgency campaign."[87]

Even leading Malays urged Chinese elites to create a new political party – a move that only makes sense in light of the shared perception of threat among Chinese and Malay elites qua elites. In July 1948, UMNO leader Onn bin Jaafar proclaimed that "law-abiding Chinese should band together in a political party to help the government in the fight against Communism.... I would appeal to the leaders of the Chinese community to organize themselves and to come in together with us, and we can stamp this danger out."[88] One of the MCA's cofounders, Tan Cheng Lock, expressed the party's raison d'être in similar terms: "I am perfectly positive that without some such Chinese organization as the MCA

[85] Ibid. 120. Emphasis added. Elite taxpayers were largely compliant with these burgeoning exactions, protests notwithstanding. "There were, of course, rumblings of opposition to such moves, but the actions of the European planters and miners in particular seemed to belie their protestations" (Stubbs 1989: 83).
[86] Salehuddin (1994): 258.
[87] Heng (1988): 54. "The MCA was encouraged to form branches in all squatter areas where Communist activities were discernible" (Ibid. 105).
[88] Ibid. 59.

as a counter to the MCP, the danger of communism establishing its rule over Malaya will be increased ten-fold."[89]

The Emergency thus presented the kind of palpable pressure for collective action among Chinese elites – along with a clear rationale for Malay and British elites to support such collective action – that was sorely lacking before the eruption of mass mobilization. It is difficult to overstate the political fragmentation and factionalism that characterized Malaya's Chinese population before the postwar eruption of mass politics. "The most salient fact about the Chinese in Malaya before the war was their dividedness."[90] Yet the Emergency placed Chinese elites squarely – and collectively – on the defensive. Not only were elite Chinese collaborators the primary victims of MCP violence; the predominantly Chinese nature of the insurgents kept the entire community under chronic suspicion. The MCP was widely perceived by Malays as "a Chinese attempt to capture Malaya. Race relations plunged to a new low. Everywhere, the Chinese were isolated, hated, suspected, and feared."[91] No wonder, then, that Tan Cheng Lock described the success of the MCA in private correspondence as a "matter of self-preservation,"[92] and publicly called upon his fellow Chinese in a December 1948 address to unite behind the MCA, "to save themselves from disaster."[93]

Such calls did not go unheeded. At the elite level, the diversity of the party's 32 founding members bore witness to the MCA's support across dialect divides: "12 were Hokkiens, 11 Cantonese, 6 Hakkas, 2 Hainanese, and 1 Teochew."[94] Equally impressive was the MCA's success at mobilizing a cross-class membership, allowing it to rival the grassroots power of UMNO:

> In November 1949, a mere eight months after the Association's inauguration, the party boasted an impressive membership of 103,000. The support given to the new party by Chinese association and business leaders, who became office-holders in the party, immediately drew a large proportion of the membership of Chinese associations to the MCA. When the party embarked on its Emergency welfare work, its membership increased dramatically. In May 1950, there were 145,000 members. ... In February 1953, the party membership reached the quarter million mark. By 1957, on the eve of Malaya's independence, the MCA claimed well over 300,000 members, making it by far the most widely based party in the country.[95]

If Chinese elites had limited their collective action to their own ethnic community, the MCA's explosive growth would have destabilized Malayan politics along communal lines. But the MCA enjoyed strong support from British and Malay elites, stabilizing Malayan politics along *class* lines. Elite collective action across the Malay-Chinese divide was facilitated by British authorities beginning in early 1949, when Malcolm MacDonald, the Commissioner-General for Southeast Asia, convened a meeting of leaders from all three major ethnic communities.

[89] Ibid. 130.
[90] Soh (1960): 29.
[91] Tregonning (1979): 57.
[92] Heng (1988): 57.
[93] Soh (1960): 43.
[94] Heng (1988): 67.
[95] Ibid. 78.

The rationale, yet again, was that with radical mass mobilization exacerbating communal tensions, MacDonald and his fellow colonial officials perceived an urgent "need to bring the conservative Malay, Chinese and Indian leadership together *to confront the MCP insurrection.*"[96]

This could not have succeeded unless Malay and Chinese elites found such collective action to be in their own interests. Shared perceptions of endemic threats from below provide the most compelling explanation both for the internal strength of Malaysia's ruling parties, and for the robustness of the coalition adjoining them. Certainly the two leading figures, UMNO's Onn bin Jaafar and the MCA's Tan Cheng Lock, were not brought into partnership by any sense of natural affinity. "They had come to realize that there was an urgent need for co-operation between the Malays and non-Malays in order to ward off racial conflicts in Malaya," argues Ishak bin Tadin. "It was also imperative that racial harmony should exist in Malaya so that the various races could form a united front against the Communist insurrection."[97] No communist insurrection with explosive communal implications, no urgent need for such a united elite front.

Electoral successes then compounded the incentives for UMNO and MCA leaders to sustain their coalition. Having teamed up to sweep a series of municipal elections in 1952, the two parties joined hands with the Malayan Indian Congress (MIC) in creating "The Alliance" in August 1953. This party coalition would win 51 of 52 seats on the Legislative Council in the national elections of July 1955, paving the way for Britain's handover of power in August 1957. The Alliance's smashing electoral victory was a testament to its constituent parties' success in recruiting the elite figures who could deliver large banks of votes, not only across Malaya's major ethnic groups, but throughout the colony's eleven states.

Electoral pressures pressed UMNO and the MCA to build stronger organizations at the grassroots level.[98] Yet electoral pressures cannot explain the origins of the parties themselves. Considering the geographic fragmentation of Malayan politics and the absence of a party-list voting system, one should have expected to see the same sort of weak parties and localized electoral fiefdoms that emerged in the postwar Philippines. What was missing in the Philippines, but present in Malaya, was an insurgency that proved unmanageable under existing political arrangements, pressing elites to create institutions facilitating elite collective action at the national level.

Conclusion: Malaya's Proto-Protection Pact

The preceding analysis has traced the political origins of Malaya's strong state and robust party coalition to the social conflicts of the 1940s and 1950s. It has thereby helped set the stage for an examination of the "protection pact" that has stabilized authoritarian politics in Malaysia since the birth of its authoritarian Leviathan in 1969. The elite coalition of the 1950s was not a protection pact by this book's definition, since it did not organize elite support for authoritarianism per se. From 1957–69, Malaysia combined the free and fair elections and

---

[96] Ibid. 147–148. Emphasis added.
[97] Ishak (1960): 72.
[98] Slater (2008a).

basic civil liberties that mark the minimum procedural definition of an electoral democracy. Yet the Alliance's primary political purpose was to keep mass politics from spinning out of control. This would make it relatively easy for elite collective action to persist under more authoritarian forms of politics after racial riots struck Kuala Lumpur in May 1969. Malaysia's regime type would change, but the logic of elite collective action would remain much the same.

An Orderly Handover and a Manageable Rebellion: Elite Fragmentation and State Weakness in the Philippines, 1944–1954

The danger to the stability of the Philippines.... has been exaggerated, showing the high degree of nervousness prevailing in foreign circles friendly to the Manila govt. In certain parts of Luzon there is considerable insecurity and the Huks are in a position to control or otherwise to terrorize the countryside.... [Yet] there is no doubt that the govt. is in no danger whatsoever.... [The communists] are not really as disruptive as has been often depicted.

Far Eastern Economic Review, 6 March 1952[99]

If the foremost scholars of Philippine political history are unanimous on anything, it is their shared portrayal of the Philippine "state" as barely worthy of the name. Bureaucratic officials in Manila have exhibited a perpetual incapacity to fend off the predatory intrusions of provincial elites – commonly called "caciques" – who use personal fortunes to win elective office, and use elective office to pad their personal fortunes. The Philippine state has been "choked continually by an anarchy of particularistic demands from, and particularistic actions on behalf of, those oligarchs and cronies who are currently most favored by its top officials."[100] It has been "captured by its supporters, with little room for state action independent of their interests,"[101] and chronically "unable to assert its own autonomy, much less implement its own agenda."[102] These patterns of authority have perpetuated themselves because "caciques prospered well under weak state structures."[103]

Provincial elites' capture of the Philippine state is most importantly expressed, for our purposes here, by the state's chronic incapacity to impose significant direct taxes – or even more mildly extractive policies, such as land reform – on the country's richest citizens. Arrangements linking state and societal elites have remained highly factionalized and relatively devoid of power flows from society toward the state. Philippine political parties failed to cement elite collective action as in Malaya, while the Philippine military developed none of the collective will to rule that emerged in Indonesia during the same period.

This trajectory of political fragmentation has its roots in the character of contentious politics in the immediate postwar era. Regional rebellions were yet to erupt, and leftist mobilization was broadly perceived as episodic and manageable. The contrast between such perceptions and contemporaneous elite perceptions

---

[99] Untitled editorial, pp. 301–302.
[100] Hutchcroft (1994): 217.
[101] Crone (1993): 60.
[102] Abinales (1997): 29.
[103] Ibid. 44.

of leftist insurgency in Malaya is nicely captured by the March 1952 report of the fiercely anti-communist *Far Eastern Economic Review* quoted above. In the same article depicting how the Malayan Emergency "continues relentlessly" and "cannot be suppressed," the editors argue that the rural rebellion in the Philippines by the leftist Huk movement could not credibly threaten to overturn the sociopolitical order, even at its peak. Provincial economic elites proved capable of handling this unrest through local mechanisms of social control, some limited and temporary revamping of the coercive apparatus of the state, and the implementation of freer and fairer elections. The Huk Rebellion thus induced only a minor increase in elite collective action and temporary improvements in public authorities' capacity to order power from societal elites.

Manageable Transitions: America Regains and Rescinds Sovereignty, 1944–1946

Like Malaya, the Philippines was militarily occupied by Japanese forces during World War II, sparking the emergence of a powerful, armed, leftist anti-Japanese guerrilla resistance force. Upon Japan's surrender, the challenge for American and Philippine elites – as for colonial and neocolonial elites in Malaya – was to demobilize these leftist insurgents and to reassert their political authority. The puzzle is how they were able to do so without being pressed, as their counterparts in Malaya would be, to place more effective social power in the hands of a more centralized Leviathan.

To understand how the "caciques" and their American champions pulled this off, one must first understand the relative continuity of colonial infrastructure throughout the Japanese interregnum. For starters, the People's Anti-Japanese Army (Hukbalahap) in the Philippines never had the field to itself as the Malayan Peoples' Anti-Japanese Army (MPAJA) did. The United States managed to mobilize approximately 100,000 Filipino troops into the MacArthur-led United States Armed Forces in the Far East (USAFFE) shortly before Japan conquered the Philippines in early 1942. Although the USAFFE played a lower-profile role during the occupation than the Hukbalahap, it provided a basic infrastructure of coercive power upon which returning American officials and their local allies could build. Since the USAFFE had been "led by American officers who were unable or unwilling to be evacuated in the wake of the Japanese invasion,"[104] American authorities never lacked a presence on the ground throughout the war. MacArthur made his mythic return in October 1944, nearly half a year before Japan's surrender of the Philippines in February 1945. The contrast with Malaya, where British forces could not return to restore order for weeks after Japan's defeat – and struggled to do so even then – is stark indeed.

The non-revolutionary character of mass politics as American rule was restored is also underscored by the divisions within the Philippine Left. These schisms were both tactical and social. First, there was a clear cleavage between reformist and revolutionary segments of the leftist anti-Japanese resistance. Hukbalahap responses to the reassertion of American control over their local wartime

---

[104] Goodwin (2001): 44.

bailiwicks suggest that the group could scarcely be characterized as radical nationalists, let alone radical leftists:

> Because Hukbalahap leaders had never planned to hang on indefinitely to these towns and because they regarded the Americans as allies, the Hukbalahap welcomed the American troops when they arrived in these towns and, as two United States military sources reported, cooperated with those American officers responsible for providing a transitional government until the Philippine government in Manila was secure again. "Once liberation was underway.... *the Hukbalahap planned to disband because there was no longer any reason to fight.*" Symbolic of the Hukbalahap's intentions were the American and Filipino flags that fluttered over the municipal buildings as American soldiers walked into the towns which Hukbalahap guerrillas had liberated.[105]

Any revolutionary tendencies within the Hukbalahap were tempered by its alliance with the Philippine Communist Party (PKP), which had ostensibly founded the Hukbalahap resistance in March 1942. Based primarily in Manila's educated (ilustrado) class, the PKP took a very different approach to the Japanese occupation than its rural Hukbalahap allies. While the Hukbalahap eschewed any alliance with landholders, the PKP sought to forge a "United Front" encompassing any and all anti-Japanese elites. This precluded any possibility for an urban-rural revolutionary alliance to emerge during the occupation and to confront Philippine and American officials upon Japan's withdrawal.

Beyond such tactical schisms, the Left exhibited weak social foundations, particularly in its urban wing. Urban and rural leftists had no significant history of cooperation before the war, and Japan's coercive blanketing of Manila prevented the urban PKP from expanding beyond its ilustrado base and playing an active role in the resistance. Particularly noteworthy was the PKP's failure to mobilize urban labor, with PKP leader Jesus Lava admitting that his party "had only a limited number of cadres among the labor movement even before the war, and, because of the Japanese, it was too difficult and dangerous for any kind of labor movement or communist education."[106] This relegated the Hukbalahap to a wartime strategy of hit-and-run strikes on landed elites "in the remoter rural areas," from which most managed to run before they could be hit. In short, "peasants joined hands with the guerrillas in forming the Hukbalahap armies which harassed the Japanese and assassinated such collaborators as they could reach," notes Benedict Anderson. "Unsurprisingly, *many of the oligarchs abandoned their haciendas to their unlucky bailiffs and retreated to Manila.*"[107]

Even if the Hukbalahap and the PKP had united behind a strategy of armed struggle in response to the Americans' return, they lacked the urban penetration necessary to put Philippine elites into an immediate state of highest alert. Rather than facing the threat head-on, parochial elites could simply "abandon their estates for the safer confines of the cities."[108] Furthermore, the fact that rural elites shared the same language and religion as rural leftists meant that they

---

[105] Kerkvliet (1977): 108. Emphasis added.
[106] Quoted in Kerkvliet (1977: 101).
[107] B. Anderson (1998) [1988]: 204–205. Emphasis added.
[108] Abinales (2000): 115.

enjoyed a wider array of mechanisms for social control than Malayan elites, who faced the specter of bottom-up challenges *across* communal divides. Caciques' confidence was exemplified by rampant landlord non-compliance with a crop-sharing arrangement brokered by President Sergio Osmeña to restore rural peace in late 1945.[109] This confidence only grew as American forces demobilized the Hukbalahap forces in ample time to hand over power to their Philippine allies in July 1946.

Leftist Remobilization, Elite Response: State-Building and Repression, 1946–1954

Although largely compliant with orders to lay down their arms, Hukbalahap forces did not intend to retire quietly into the good night of post-independence politics. With the elimination of colonial restrictions on suffrage, the Left hoped it could influence democratic policymaking through its mass organizations, or even win power outright through the ballot box.

The Left took two main institutional forms: the National Peasants' Union (PKM), and the Democratic Alliance (DA). As a direct descendant of the Hukbalahap army, the PKM enjoyed immediate organizational strength, mobilizing an estimated 500,000 members shortly after its formation in May 1945. As a successor to the Communist Party's (PKP's) urban-rural anti-Japanese front, the DA was a much weaker creature as it mobilized voters for national elections in April 1946. Urban leftists continued to flounder in their efforts to transcend their ilustrado roots and bring labor into the DA fold. A new federation called the Congress of Labor Organizations (CLO) emerged, but its "role apparently remained minor."[110] The urban Left "never established itself as an important central political force in the postcolonial arrangement."[111]

Yet the rural PKM appeared to be a powerful enough workhorse to pull the DA to a strong showing in the April 1946 vote. Even though the Left was eschewing violent means in the run-up to the election, provincial and national elites perceived the DA's potential voter power as a considerable threat:

Given the peasant unity and organization that the PKM represented, the landed elites of Central Luzon did, indeed, have cause to be worried – even afraid – of what might happen to their society. They had never had to cope with such a peasant movement before. . . . To make matters even worse for the elites, the PKM became strong enough to threaten elite political power.[112]

Before detailing the response of Philippine and American elites to this perceived leftist threat, it is worth briefly recalling how Malayan and British elites responded to mass mobilization at a similar historical juncture. British officials granted official recognition to urban labor unions, imposed direct taxation on economic

---

[109] Kerkvliet (1977): 146.
[110] Ibid. 138.
[111] Boudreau (2002): 548.
[112] Kerkvliet (1977): 132–133.

elites, midwifed the creation of new broad-based political parties and coalitions to facilitate elite collective action both within and across communal groups, and began building the administrative infrastructure for a much stronger and more centralized state.

By contrast, American and Philippine elites responded to mass mobilization, first, by allowing USAFFE troops to melt into provincial elites' "civilian guards,"[113] and by channeling firearms to the municipal police forces that these local bosses controlled. In January 1946, in response to instances of refusal by Hukbalahap remnants to surrender their firearms – as landlords returned to their fiefdoms and demanded back rent – the secretary of the interior "had five thousand machine guns distributed to municipal and provincial police forces in Central Luzon."[114] The Philippine Constabulary – the most basic coercive arm of the central state – became increasingly irrelevant. As "Manila's control over the countryside weakened, provincial politicians demanded neutralization of the Constabulary as a condition for the delivery of their vote banks to presidential candidates, thereby fostering a de facto local autonomy and endemic political violence."[115]

In short, leftist mobilization did not press the caciques to "crawl together under the apron of the military,"[116] or to support the building of stronger national-level institutions more generally. This was not because Americans and Philippine elites failed to take the Left seriously; rather, the point is that the nature of the threat was such that the caciques perceived they could manage it with existing, decentralized institutions. Unrest in the 1945–46 period was entirely rural and lacked central coordination. Provincial elites could combine their control over local clients' manpower with an infusion of American and USAFFE firepower, and smother rural unrest with force. Far better to cultivate a local coercive clientele (which would prove useful at election time as well) than to surrender higher taxes to central administrators who might use such resources in unwelcome ways. Nor did mass mobilization inspire any Malaya-style strengthening of Philippine political parties, as the prewar "rivalrous political class housed in the prevailing Nacionalista Party"[117] splintered into a fluid and purely patronage-based two-party system of factionalized notables.

So long as the Left had no powerful, revolutionary urban presence, the caciques felt little pressure to overcome their factional rivalries or build new institutions. Their calculation that coercion alone could carry the day led to a fateful decision to deny elected office to six victorious DA candidates in the April 1946 vote. When confronted by a combination of electoral exclusion and growing violence by "civilian guards" and municipal police, former Hukbalahap forces were left,

---

[113] Kerkvliet describes "civilian guards" as "armed groups that landlords used and that the local government and Military Police sanctioned. Illustrative of this arrangement was that landlords and the Military Police paid the civilian guards' wages" (Ibid. 125).
[114] Goodwin (2001): 148.
[115] McCoy (1993): 14.
[116] B. Anderson (1998) [1988]: 225.
[117] Brownlee (2007): 74.

as Jeff Goodwin would say, with "no other way out." Starting in late 1946, the
anti-Japanese army began gradually remobilizing into the People's Liberation
Army (HMB), or "Huks."

Whereas the PKM and DA had presented a credible threat to win power
through constitutional means, the Huks seemed by 1950 to pose an increasingly
credible threat to seize the state through armed rebellion. "In March and August
of 1950, the Huks – who had as many as fifteen thousand armed guerrillas and
one hundred thousand active supporters – launched coordinated and generally
successful raids on fifteen and eleven towns, respectively. Huk leaders were confident that a relatively quick seizure of power was possible, perhaps within as little
as two years."[118] Such confidence was overblown, given the rock-solid American
commitment to keeping the Philippines (with its strategic military facilities) in
non-communist hands. But in the immediate aftermath of the Chinese Communist Party's vanquishing of the Kuomintang – and with the benefit of post-
Vietnam hindsight – it was not utterly absurd. As the Huks gathered strength,
it began to appear for the first time that the Philippines' weak and decentralized
state might not be up to the task of protecting the caciques' (or the Americans')
basic interests.

This burgeoning rural rebellion indeed pressured the central state to expand
its capacities. Some American advisers showed signs of panic, as exemplified by
the conclusion of two U.S. reports – the Treasury Department's Bell Mission in
1950, and the Mutual Security Agency's Hardie Report of 1952 – that military
force alone would not quell the Huk threat. But whereas British efforts to centralize state authority in Malaya were pursued with relative vigor and received with
relative acquiescence and even acclaim among provincial elites, American proposals to curb cacique power met significant elite defiance. The recommendation
of the Bell and Hardie reports that "land redistribution was necessary to address
the problem effectively, mark[ed] a significant departure from the elite political mainstream and galvaniz[ed] landlord opposition politically."[119] Provincial
politicos remained unconvinced that breaking the Huk resistance could require
better governance, and not just a harsher crackdown.

The caciques might have had little choice but to submit to the redistributive
recommendations of the Bell and Hardie reports if American pressure to do so
had been consistent and forceful:

But the arrival in the country in 1950 of the Central Intelligence Agency's Edward
Lansdale to direct counterinsurgency operations introduced an alternative approach to
the Philippines' agrarian problem that integrated military action with populist promises
of political and socioeconomic reform. The country's *hacendero* elite, who were adamantly
opposed to any change in the agrarian structure, as well as many U.S. policymakers who
regarded the Bell Mission as "soft" on Communism, seized upon Lansdale's counterinsurgency program as a way to eliminate the problem without having to resort to actual
land redistribution.[120]

---

[118] Goodwin (2001): 77.
[119] Franco (2000): 120.
[120] Ibid.

Lansdale's strategy was implemented by his Filipino right-hand man, Ramon Magsaysay, upon his appointment as defense minister in September 1950. Up to that point, the government's approach to the Huk insurgency had been purely coercive. Military methods had been deployed to meet military objectives. By contrast, the new strategy complemented coercion with rejuvenated efforts at rural co-optation. It is critical to note, however, that *the military, rather than any civilian agency, was the sole institutional basis for this strategy*. Military methods would now serve political objectives, as opposed to purely military goals. But in institutional terms, the military was the only institution whose performance would need to be improved to implement Lansdale's new approach.

In an interview with *The Manila Times* on the night of his appointment, Magsaysay seemed to suggest that times were ripe for the state to make new demands on a population rendered vulnerable by a worsening rural insurgency. And yet, as defense minister, Magsaysay only controlled the military, and could use only that institution to implement his counterinsurgency strategy. "Today our people are crying out to have their lives, their property, protected," he declared. "This is a big job, and will be my first concern. It is so big that it demands the joint effort of *everyone in the armed services*, from the youngest private to the commanding general."[121]

Magsaysay appeared convinced that defeating the Huks depended not merely on military strengthening, but on socioeconomic and political reform. His strategy was to pursue the former as a means to the latter. As rural rebellion neared its apex, Magsaysay imposed hierarchical order on the Philippine military. Given the extreme fragmentation of coercive institutions, this was no small feat. As Defense Minister, "Magsaysay merged the twenty-two-thousand-man Philippine Constabulary with the army, which included another thirty-three thousand troops, thereby creating a single chain of command."[122] This housecleaning and reorganization provided Magsaysay with more military muscle to implement Manila's directives in the provinces.

The Defense Minister's growing clout was manifested in several ways. Most significantly, "the 'civilian guards' – essentially the private armies of large landowners who were notorious for their mistreatment of villagers – were disbanded."[123] This represented a stark about-face in government policy, as President Elpidio Quirino had been encouraging the formation of "citizen armies" before Magsaysay's appointment.[124] During Magsaysay's first tour of rural Luzon, he found that "the villagers are armed with a substantial number of licensed firearms which even the gawky teen-ager of the barrio could fire with a certain degree of skill."[125] Disarming such groups proved to be an arduous and expensive process. Military officers typically had to buy "loose weapons" rather than confiscating

---

[121] "Humble and Proud, Says Magsaysay, on Appointment," *The Manila Times*, 1 September 1950. Emphasis added.

[122] Goodwin (2001): 118.

[123] Ibid. 119.

[124] See "Guerrillas Set To Oppose Huks," *The Manila Times*, 11 April 1950.

[125] "Defense Chief Starts Tours," *The Manila Times*, 4 September 1950.

them; in Cavite province, the governor retained armed "special agents" until at least mid-1952, much to Magsaysay's consternation.[126]

Nevertheless, Magsaysay's success in demobilizing such private armies represented a temporary bite out of provincial politicos' power. Not only did this limit caciques' capacity to control their own workforce; it weakened their stranglehold on local voters. While Lansdale was lukewarm toward the Bell Report's endorsement of land redistribution, he shared Magsaysay's view that the Huks had gained considerable mileage from the fraudulent and violent national elections of 1949. Making the midterm elections of November 1951 a cleaner affair thus became a top priority. In the confrontation that followed, Magsaysay's interest in a clean vote won the day over provincial politicos' interest in winning re-election through any means necessary. Magsaysay retained his post and eventually won the presidency in 1953. Yet his disbanding of provincial civilian guards and reorganization of the Philippine military proved to be his only accomplishments as a state-builder.[127]

Marshaling a country's capacity for large-scale violence into a state monopoly is merely the beginning of state-building, not its culmination. "Because governments faced with insurgencies also tend to be burdened with corrupt, inefficient, or abusive armies, the first reform must be in training the untrained and disciplining unruly troops and local police."[128] Magsaysay accomplished this, but little more, when taking on entrenched interests. Even his own staff remained in the grip of parliamentary patronage prerogatives, as "Magsaysay was rebuffed by Congress when he asked for powers to reorganize the executive department."[129] Nor did his housecleaning of the military survive his untimely death in a plane crash in 1957. With the Huk rebellion under control, Magsaysay's successor, Carlos Garcia, "replaced the 'Magsaysay boys' with his own partisans, often favoring fellow Boholanos or other Cebuano speakers from his native Visayas," and installed his wife's classmate as chief of the national police.[130]

Magsaysay's failure to assert state authority becomes even more glaring when we turn our attention to the issue of taxation. To sense both the extent and the limitations of the state's growing extractive demands upon upper groups during the Huk rebellion, consider the parlous postwar state of the Philippines' Bureau of Internal Revenue (BIR):

The number of people with incomes sufficient to require filing of reports increased greatly after the war, and yet the government had neither space nor equipment adequate to take care of the needs. The filing system was so inadequate that taxpayers' records could not be found, and many of the assessments and payments remained unposted for years. Provincial treasurers often failed to send in reports, and the Bureau was in no position to press for effective compliance. Assessment notices, unposted receipts, and other papers were literally

---

[126] "AFP Units Hit by Magsaysay," *The Manila Times*, 13 July 1952.
[127] For more discussion of this Magsaysay-led exercise in state-building for purposes of implementing freer and fairer national elections, see Slater (2008a).
[128] K. Jackson (1985): 26.
[129] Doronila (1992): 124.
[130] McCoy (1999): 137.

piled up in filing cabinets, desk drawers and boxes, and on shelves, cabinets and on the floor. In brief, no one knew to what extent the tax liabilities of the postwar period had been paid.[131]

To be more precise, no one in the tax bureaucracy had any idea what proportion of owed income taxes had actually been paid. The Central Bank produced an educated guess regarding the scale of tax evasion among the estimated 88,000 Philippine citizens with sufficient incomes to owe income tax. Of that narrow upper income group, just over 9,000 had filed taxable returns at all – barely 10% of the total – and their declared combined income amounted to only 13% of their estimated gross income. Astonishingly, the Central Bank collected nearly five times more revenue from its surcharge on foreign-exchange transactions in 1952 than the BIR accumulated through income taxes. More anecdotally, *The Philippines Herald* reported in the same year that even "a cursory study of the professionals who pay taxes... reveals a more or less rampant tax evasion." For instance: "Two-thirds of the representatives of Congress were not assessed; and of the 24 senators and 10 Cabinet members, only eleven were assessed income taxes."[132] Given the correlation between wealth and officeholding in Philippine society, this provides a vivid picture of the BIR's incapacity to collect income taxes from economic elites.

Even as the Huk rebellion approached its zenith, the Philippine state failed to impose new fiscal demands on the very economic elites it was helping to protect from rural unrest. In 1949, while the Malayan fisc was being rebuilt, "the Philippine state nearly collapsed. Rehabilitation assistance was plundered by the oligarchs to pay for duty-free imports of consumer durables, and the government lacked the means to stem the haemorrhage of foreign exchange."[133] In short, the state continued to exhibit a woeful "inability to extract revenue from the oligarchy."[134]

As in Malaya during this period, external assistance to the Philippines served as a stimulant rather than a suppressor of tax effort. This slight spike in state resolve to collect income taxes was facilitated by the Mutual Security Agency – *the same American agency* that produced the aforementioned Hardie Report in 1952, warning that administrative reform was essential to avoid a looming Huk takeover. Underlining the causal connection between contentious politics and this burst in state centralization, this agency led this new state-building effort during *the same year* when it issued the Hardie Report:

In 1952, with the assistance of tax advisors provided by the Mutual Security Agency of the United States, the Bureau began a program of clearing income tax delinquencies and of putting its tax administration machinery in operating condition. By the end of that year the tax accounts for post-war years were listed and a program of follow-up on delinquencies was undertaken.[135]

[131] Stene and Waldby (1955): 199.
[132] Ibid. 200–201.
[133] Hutchcroft (1994): 226.
[134] Ibid. 238, fn. 20.
[135] Stene and Waldby (1955): 199.

This enforcement effort intensified with the transfer of presidential power in 1953. "Shortly after his inauguration, President Magsaysay directed that [sic] National Bureau of Investigation to examine into the many charges of corruption in the Bureau of Internal Revenue. After its initial investigation the NBI decided to maintain a permanent staff of agents in the Finance building."[136] Yet as with Magsaysay's efforts to clean up the military, his bid to clean up the tax bureaucracy was limited in both scope and duration. State resolve faded as the Huk threat fizzled. "With the collapse of the Huk rebellion by 1954, the only incentive for central authorities to mobilize state resources against regional authoritarian elites was removed."[137] Taxes stayed mired below 10% of gross domestic product throughout the 1950s, with direct taxes generally accounting for less than 20% of that paltry total.[138]

Patterns of land reform during the Huk rebellion appear broadly similar to patterns of military reorganization and taxation. Rural insurgency inspired spikes in the central state's capacity in all these realms, but not to any great extent, and not for very long. Although he "projected a concern for the common man, and even lent enthusiasm to the agrarian reform program, up to a point,"[139] Magsaysay could not dent deep-set elite resistance to any significant redistribution of land. Rather than confronting caciques in this period with demands for land redistribution, the government avoided confrontation by emphasizing land *resettlement*, co-opting former Huks by providing them with virgin public lands in Mindanao and other peripheral regions. Since this program was implemented by the military, it involved no capacity-building among the state's administrative institutions.

As with his reorganization of the military and his attempted revamping of the tax bureaucracy, Magsaysay's push for land reform is inexplicable except as a consequence of worsening contentious politics. The only reason Magsaysay and his American backers evinced any enthusiasm for land reform at all was because they "were desperately trying to halt the Huk rebellion."[140] As mass political unrest waned, so did elite political will: "most Filipino politicians and U.S. State Department advisors intended to concede only enough legislation and funding for agrarian projects *to keep rural discontent to a manageable level.*"[141] The timing of both the burst in land reform and the bursting of the reform bubble supports the argument that contentious class politics can have a significant impact on the shape of the state and the extent of its extractive powers.

Conclusion: Rural, Reformist Rebellion and the Limited Growth in State Power

Why did the Huk rebellion, for all its intensity, fail to leave a bigger imprint on the Philippine state? Once again, I locate the answer to this puzzle in the *character*

---

[136] Ibid. 202.
[137] Franco (2000): 123.
[138] See Asher and Kinantar (1989: 129, fn. 5) and Thompson (1995: 23).
[139] Wurfel (1985): 233.
[140] Kerkvliet (1979): 117–118.
[141] Ibid. Emphasis added.

of contentious politics that the rebellion represented. Although the resistance became far more intense in the 1949–53 period than it had been in the 1944–46 period, it remained plagued by an inability to make its presence felt in the major urban centers that upper groups called home. Even at its peak, "the major Huk concentration" came no closer than eighty-five miles from "the seat of national power, Manila."[142] This constituted a source of serious concern, but not imminent personal threat, to most caciques, who had been "leaving their haciendas in the hands of sons-in-law and bailiffs and moving into palatial new residential complexes on the outskirts of the old capital."[143]

Critically, the capital remained calm. Urban labor showed no signs of mimicking the militancy of the rural Left, as exemplified, at the height of Huk strength in 1950, by the "CLO request for a permit to run two jeeps with loudspeakers in Manila.... during the Labor Day celebrations."[144] Even as Huk forces crept closer to Manila in April 1950, Manila's mayor warned the city's residents not to engage in "Huk-hysterics."[145] Nor did rumors of Huk attacks on the upland resort city of Baguio crimp elite lifestyles. "Undaunted by rumors of an impending Huk attack, summer vacationists continued to flock in the Pines City, overcrowding its hotels, apartments and private residences."[146]

Elite self-confidence reflected not only the parochial character of the rebellion and the Huks' persistent internal tensions, but the media's consistent portrayal of the situation as utterly manageable. "To those of us in Manila," journalist and scholar Amando Doronilla recalls, "the rebellion seemed very far away."[147] The media's lionization of Magsaysay as a one-man wrecking crew undermined any sense among elites that defeating the Huks required shared sacrifice. "We were under the impression," scholar Jose Abueva recollects, "that Magsaysay was taking care of it."[148] In a meeting with President Truman in Washington, the Philippine ambassador to the United States gushed that "Without Magsaysay.... the Huks would have attacked Malacañan" – the presidential residence in downtown Manila – "at the height of their ferocity two years ago."[149] With the newfound potency of the Philippine military perceived in such personal rather than institutional terms, it is little wonder that Magsaysay was relegated to pleading with Congress merely to *maintain* total force levels, even as the Huk rebellion continued to rage in rural areas.[150]

This book's argument that rural rebellion tends to be perceived by state and societal elites as more manageable than urban unrest thus appears to hold up for the Huk rebellion. One might also find empirical ballast for my arguments in the absence of any *communal* implications arising from this intense rebellious

[142] K. Jackson (1985): 22.
[143] B. Anderson (1998) [1988]: 209.
[144] "City Alerted," *The Manila Times*, 31 March 1950.
[145] "Manila Security Assured, Says Mayor," *The Manila Times*, 8 April 1950.
[146] "New Strategy in Field Effective, Says Brass; Amnesty Plan Wins Okay," *The Manila Times*, 6 April 1950.
[147] Interview with the Author, Quezon City, Metro Manila, 1 November 2003.
[148] Interview with the Author, Marikina, Metro Manila, 29 October 2003.
[149] "Sec. Mag'say Bares Methods," *The Manila Times*, 14 June 1952.
[150] "Magsaysay Would Keep AFP As Is," *The Manila Times*, 31 July 1951.

episode. Contentious class politics is more likely to spur state-building when it exacerbates ethnoreligious divisions because elites tend to perceive such conflicts as more *endemic* than episodic. The emergence of politicized, mobilized communal cleavages thus gives economic elites a particularly acute need for long-term state protection.

From this perspective, it is telling that Magsaysay's success at demobilizing private armies was merely *temporary*. Provincial elites had no lasting reason to seek protection through the national police – or any national institutions – rather than their own local "muchachos."[151] Class conflict had become so severe that patron-client relations and local coercive institutions lacked the capacity to manage it, at least in certain locations. Yet even those caciques who perceived a need to relinquish their sources of coercive power only saw the need to make a tactical retreat, not a strategic withdrawal. The discourse of the period suggested the impermanence of the disarming of such units, as in the mayor of Lipa City's revealing request for the surrender of all local firearms to military personnel for "safe-keeping."[152] Caciques would only "crawl together under the apron of the military" for as little time as absolutely necessary.

One may also question whether the Huks had the revolutionary credentials to inspire counterrevolutionary state-building. When reflecting on their participation in the rebellion, former Huks justified their actions as a means to "'stop the civilian guards and PC from beating up my family' and 'let the DA congressmen hold office'"[153] – not to seize the means of production. As one villager put it:

I went underground in 1946. The next year I was in the guerrillas again. But it wasn't like during the Japanese occupation. *We weren't against the government.* We wanted reforms, true. But so did the PKM. *We were fighting to save our lives.*[154]

One need not take these peasant pronouncements at face value to perceive the Huks' reformist character. More convincing evidence comes from the readiness of elite factions to ally with the Huks to enhance their position in factional disputes. After Quirino's blatant use of fraud and intimidation to secure the presidency in the 1949 election, there emerged "an uprising by followers of cheated challenger Jose P. Laurel, Sr.," which "may have begun to explore a link with the Huk revolutionary movement." Laurel did not intend to seize power through violent means, but "the continued threat of violence gave him leverage over the administration."[155] As we will see in the next chapter, this pattern of oddball alliances between cacique politicians and ostensibly communist rebels became much more common in the late 1960s, as President Marcos began using violent means to win elections. The fact that provincial elites have been recurrently willing to join forces with armed leftists, and that armed leftists have been recurrently amenable to such alliances, suggests either the questionable revolutionary

---

[151] Hutchcroft (2000): 293.
[152] "PC Successes Slow Up Huk Activities," *The Manila Times*, 23 April 1950.
[153] Kerkvliet (1977): 164.
[154] Ibid. 165. Emphasis added.
[155] Thompson (1995): 16, 25.

credentials or the nonthreatening character and positioning of the Philippine Left.

Finally, one finds evidence of striving for political rights, rather than efforts to overthrow capitalism, in the timing of the Huks' rise and decline. The rebellion first gathered force in the wake of the "fraud and terrorism of the 1949 polls," which "made the Huk guerrillas' cry of 'bullets, not ballots' more compelling." It was immediately after the 1949 vote that "their membership expanded rapidly, reaching a peak of 12,000 to 15,000 soldiers and a peasant support base of 1.5 million to 2 million shortly after the election."[156] Much as the betrayal of democratic principles made the rebellion swell, the apparent restoration of democratic practices had a deflating effect. As David Wurfel argues, "electoral processes from 1951 on became more honest and open, thus making government both more legitimate and more responsive."[157] "After subsequent elections proved to be more democratic," Kerkvliet concludes, "a new government (Ramon Magsaysay's) that permitted dissent and public debate on agrarian issues had been elected and seemed likely to push for additional tenancy reforms, and the rapacious behavior of the military had abated, the rebellion subsided as well."[158] In sum, peasant rebellion ultimately triggered little state-building in the Philippines because it was the Huks whose backs were against the wall, not the caciques.

Not only was the Huk rebellion the wrong kind of leftist insurgency to give rise to a trajectory of political domination as witnessed in Malaya. It was also not the kind of rebellion likely to induce the sort of political militarization we are about to see in Indonesia. Rather than driving civilian and military elites apart, the Huk threat brought them together – if only weakly. By privileging military institutions in the counterinsurgency process, Magsaysay helped guarantee that military officers would not broadly perceive a collective need to overthrow civilian power to protect their operational interests. Military elites remained as prone to factionalism and backroom intrigue as their civilian counterparts, while lacking the kind of institutional cohesion that would have been necessary to pursue a thoroughgoing militarization of the Philippine polity.

Regionalist Violence before Communist Uprising: Political Militarization in Indonesia, 1945–1959

Thus far this chapter has considered cases exhibiting one overarching type of contentious politics – contentious *class* politics. Indonesia complicates our causal narrative by forcing us to consider the consequences of two very different types of violent conflict occurring in the same case. The radical Left would pose a much more credible threat to seize national power in Indonesia than in Malaysia or the Philippines, spawning an elite protection pact in many ways comparable to the Malaysian case. Yet it would not do so in the time-period under analysis in this chapter. During the first postwar wave of contentious politics, regionally based

---

[156] Ibid. 25.
[157] Wurfel (1985): 232–233.
[158] Kerkvliet (1998): 172.

rebellions were a more pressing problem than the gathering national strength of the Indonesian Communist Party (Partai Komunis Indonesia, or PKI). These centrifugal conflicts posed an especially imminent concern and a particularly potent incitement for heightened collective action among *military* elites.

The upshot by the late 1950s was a military apparatus of increased operational cohesion and political centrality. Ensconced at the heart of national power by President Sukarno's declaration of martial law in 1957, the Indonesian military would seize power in its own right in the mid-1960s in response to the gathering strength of the PKI – quite unlike the *civilian*-commanded counterrevolutions against leftist insurgents in Malaya and the Philippines. How the exigencies of contentious politics originally helped elevate the military into this leading political role in Indonesia – a position of predominance it would maintain even as it joined forces with civilian allies under Suharto's New Order in the late 1960s – is the subject for the remainder of this chapter.

Perjuangan and Provincialism: National Revolution as Unifier and Divider, 1945–1949

While the end of Japanese occupation in Malaya and the Philippines brought communists into violent conflict with anti-communists, the principal struggle in Indonesia pitted colonialists against anti-colonialists. As in Burma and Vietnam, nationalist forces in Indonesia quickly declared independence upon Japan's surrender in August 1945. Like the British and the French, the Dutch vigorously resisted, sparking one of the world's bloodiest wars of decolonization. This violent anti-colonial struggle witnessed the same sort of cross-class nationalist mobilization in Indonesia that we will see later in Burma and Vietnam, culminating in Indonesian nationalist forces' securing of sovereignty over their war-shattered land in December 1949.

The anti-Dutch revolution has attained mythic status in Indonesian historiography. Since most political groups stake their historical legitimacy at least in part on their purported role in the great nationalist struggle (or perjuangan), it is easy to overemphasize the subsequent effects of the four-year war on postcolonial politics. In reality, violent revolution wrought in Indonesia what it does in most places – a wrecked polity and intense internal conflicts, as disparate elite actors vie for supremacy in the unsettled atmosphere of a brand-new political entity. Perjuangan helped give most Indonesians a sense of shared nationhood, but it did nothing to resolve the core political questions of how state and society should be ordered.

As elsewhere, postcolonial order in Indonesia would be determined by patterns of elite collective action, which would be shaped primarily by the character of contentious politics. For our purposes here, therefore, the most important causal impact of the revolution was its greater tempering of class cleavages than territorial tensions. The PKI generally assumed a low profile, as leftist elements in the anti-Dutch resistance tended to adhere to the consensus that "[t]he needs of the national revolution must take precedence over those of the social revolution."[159]

159 Quoted in Goodwin (2001): 87.

The common enemy of the Dutch gave communists and noncommunists grounds for cooperation, unlike in postwar Malaya. "Leftists did play a role in many of the local 'social revolutions' that broke out across the archipelago following the surrender of Japan," notes Jeff Goodwin; but "although they involved popular mobilizations, they did not attempt to seize land, factories, or other property."[160] To the extent that the PKI was subsumed within a cross-class nationalist struggle, there was no prospect of a Malaya-style protection pact coalescing a broad cross-section of counterrevolutionary elites against revolutionary leftist masses.

This subsumption of communist forces within a nationalist movement would prove less complete in Indonesia than in Vietnam, however. In contrast to the Vietnamese revolution, which was consistently led by a single vanguard party, the Indonesian revolution was a splintered struggle. Revolutionary forces were often inspired but rarely mobilized by the charismatic personage of Sukarno, whose Indonesian National Party (Partai Nasional Indonesia, or PNI) represented but one mass organization among a panoply of groups combating Dutch forces, and whose putative Republic exerted little control over fragmented revolutionary forces. Instead of a centralized insurgent organization, it was "a highly localized popular resistance.... expressed through a myriad of extrastate politico-military organizations"[161] that eventually prevailed – thanks in part to American diplomatic pressure – in Indonesia's national perjuangan.

The revolution was thus a time of division as much as unity. The schism between communist and anti-communist streams of the struggle reared its head in the East Javanese city of Madiun in 1948, when a putsch by pro-PKI officers erupted against the Sukarno-led revolutionary government, and was quickly crushed by nationalist troops (hence helping to assure the aforementioned American support for Indonesian independence). An important long-term effect was to make Madiun a codeword for communist treachery, and a memory to be mobilized for propaganda purposes by anti-communist forces. But in the shorter term, the failed revolt at Madiun meant the political decimation of the PKI and the party's irrelevance to political developments until Indonesia's parliamentary election in 1955.

Revolution would in some ways exacerbate regional tensions, even as it mitigated class conflict. As discussed in Chapter 3, the Dutch had long favored non-Javanese minority groups such as the predominantly Christian Ambonese and Minahasa in their military recruitment. The outbreak of revolution on Java convinced Dutch officials that their best hope for victory rested on bolstering the non-Javanese counterweight they had tried to nurture. As Dutch military actions gained momentum, colonial policy came to rest upon "a three-fold strategy":

First, it called for the application of sufficient military force to destroy the Republic and administer a decisive defeat to its armed forces. Second, it called for an over-all program of divide-and-rule, maintained through a skillfully operated form of indirect rule of the fifteen to twenty states into which Indonesia was to be divided and which together were

[160] Ibid. 86.
[161] B. Anderson (1983): 481.

to be known as the United States of Indonesia. Third, it called for obtaining international sanction of this program through the granting of sovereignty to this indirectly Dutch-controlled federal Indonesia.[162]

Like the British in Burma, the Dutch calculated that one of the best ways to throw sand in the gears of decolonization in Indonesia was by privileging the political periphery. Provincialism would be pitted against perjuangan. This eleventh-hour favoritism for the provinces left many regionally based actors with a taste for regional autonomy – and distaste for the more Java-centric politics that independence was to bring. "The Javanese elite saw in independence an opportunity, as it were, to fulfill the ambitions and promises of Javanese civilization in the new national state," Daniel Lev has written, "while the smaller and more particularistic societies of the rest of Indonesia recoiled before the vision of their eventual subordination or assimilation in a Javanese-dominated nation."[163]

Fragmentation and Creeping Militarization: The Parliamentary Era, 1950–1957

Unlike Malaya and the Philippines, Indonesia gained independence with a ruling coalition that could as well be described as revolutionary as counterrevolutionary. Still shaken by its disaster at Madiun, the PKI was not a powerful force outside of government but a secondary partner within it. There was not yet a looming social revolution for elites to come together to counter. To the extent that any common enemy existed to unify Indonesian elites during the 1950s, it was not the communists but the Dutch, who retained control of most revenue-earning export enterprises as well as the hotly contested western half of New Guinea. As spiritual leader of Indonesia's new parliamentary republic, the nationalist revolutionary Sukarno sought to unify the body politic through ongoing appeals to anti-colonialism, rather than trying to solidify a broad elite coalition through appeals to anti-communism.

Having failed to cement wide-ranging elite collective action during the heady days of the revolution, anti-colonialism could hardly serve such a unifying role after independence was secured. A politically fragmented revolution carried over into a politically fragmented postcolony. Unlike Burmese and Vietnamese nationalist parties that had built up massive popular support through anti-Japanese resistance, Sukarno's PNI had collaborated with the Japanese and made only limited headway at recruiting a mass base transcending Indonesia's formidable religious, regional, and ideological divides. The PNI competed for support with the PKI as well as two Islamic mass parties – the Japanese-created Masyumi (which mostly appealed to Indonesia's urban, "modernist," and non-Javanese Muslims) and the Nahdlatul Ulama (based in the rural, "traditionalist" heartland of Central and East Java). With a powerful and revolutionary Left still yet to emerge as a common enemy, Indonesian elites were unfettered in pursuing their factional interests during the period of parliamentary democracy. The major political syndrome in

[162] Kahin (1952): 349.
[163] Lev (1966): 3.

Indonesia in the 1950s was fragmentation, as parliamentary politics spawned factional strife and struggle rather than a Malaya-style collective elite project in search of political order.

Elite fragmentation helps to explain why the Indonesian state, widely considered a model of centralized fiscal power during colonial times, failed to assert its authority during the parliamentary period. "About one-third of all tax revenues accrued from personal and corporate income taxes" under the "diversified revenue system"[164] that characterized the waning days of Dutch rule. Yet Sukarno-era governments chronically suffered from "an inability either to reimpose the colonial fiscal system or to evolve a new regime capable of funding public expenditure growth in a non-inflationary way."[165]

Parliamentary politicking entailed pressure to build new political clienteles and hold together unwieldy governing coalitions. This counseled massive spending on patronage and public works – not increased extractive demands from economic elites who could support whichever party or party faction offered them the best deal. Fiscal extraction would be debilitated by state-business relations that were overwhelmingly dyadic, clientilistic, and disorganized. "State organizations at this time lent themselves to the development of collaborative, informal relationships between largely ethnic Chinese entrepreneurs and government powerholders."[166] In light of the causal framework proposed in this book, such patterns of elite interaction were as predictable as they were dysfunctional. Absent any powerful common enemy to facilitate elite collective action, state-business relations can typically be expected to be highly factionalized and devoid of common purpose or shared sacrifice.

The coercive institutions of the Indonesian state were nearly as splintered and factionalized as its administrative and representative institutions. Although military leaders typically locate the historical source of their relative cohesion in the war against the Dutch, neither ideological nor institutional cohesion was much in evidence within ABRI before the outbreak of regional rebellions in the late 1950s. Aside from chronic "competition between the three services, the army, navy and air force,"[167] the army itself was plagued by deep factional, ideological, and territorial divisions. Efforts by ABRI leaders to reorganize the guerrilla units of the national revolution into a more centralized fighting force were consistently thwarted. The main barrier was civilian elites who feared the concentration of military power, wished to retain the authority to make military appointments for patronage purposes, and even sought – in Philippine style – to cultivate local ABRI commanders for muscle in their own election campaigns.[168]

Early signs of military esprit de corps and political ambition were evident amid the disarray, however. "During the early years of independence, the army was poorly organized, poorly disciplined, and poorly equipped," Lev notes. Yet the

---

[164] Booth (1997): 296.
[165] Ibid. 286–287.
[166] Hamilton-Hart (2002): 40.
[167] Kingsbury (2003): 141.
[168] Utrecht (1972): 58.

immediate flareup of low-level territorial conflicts after independence meant that ABRI officers could not readily retreat from their role as anti-colonial revolutionaries into the postcolonial barracks:

The revolution was too fresh in the minds of most officers; they saw themselves as having played too crucial a role in it to retire into the background immediately. Moreover, units of the army were constantly deployed after 1950 against various groups involved in violent internal disturbances: the fanatic Darul Islam in West and Central Java, Atjeh, and South Sulawesi; the Republic of the South Moluccas; the supposedly Communist-inspired rebels in the north-central hill areas of Central Java.... and other groups creating disorders and minor rebellions. As a result, army officers remained impressed with their responsibility for saving the state, whose creation, some believed, was mainly the army's doing.[169]

Both the extent and limits of military camaraderie and cohesion were displayed in a major demonstration by ABRI forces in Jakarta in October 1952. Sparked by frustration with parliamentary interference in military affairs, the protestors demanded that Sukarno dissolve parliament and give full support to their campaign for *"re-dan-ra"* (reorganization and rationalization). Sukarno stood firm and purged the officers responsible for the protests. "The consequences of the 17 October 1952 Affair were severe," writes Ernst Utrecht. *"Re-dan-ra*, which had progressed only half-way, could not be resumed until 1958.... But the most serious fact was that the Army was split up into two groups, the 'pro-17 October 1952 military' and the 'anti-17 October 1952 military.'"[170] When military leaders renewed their call for operational autonomy in the Jogja Charter in February 1955, "the Government did not take the Jogja Charter seriously. The stubborn Minister of Defense, Iwa Kusumasumantri, who planned to purge the Army of 'pro-17 October 1952 elements,' continued his policy of appointing military functionaries on mere political considerations."[171]

The gathering strength of both leftist and regionalist challengers would enhance military cohesion and alter the balance of military-civilian power in ABRI's favor. It would be of enormous consequence for long-term patterns of political development, however, that *the regionalist challenge became threatening first.* The PKI came in fourth place in the national elections of 1955, and was "domesticated"[172] by the exigencies of electoral politics throughout the parliamentary period. Even when Sukarno invited the PKI into the cabinet in 1957, the party remained "prepared to play a subordinate role in any parliamentary coalition and to defer to their major alliance partner, the PNI."[173] For all their anti-communist fervor, most military elites remained somewhat sanguine so long as elections and parliamentary coalitions diluted PKI power among Indonesia's other popular, noncommunist parties:

A part of the military elite feared the influence of the communists not only on the affairs of the Government in general, but also specifically on the cleavages inside the Army.

[169] Lev (1966): 5.
[170] Ibid. 59.
[171] Ibid.
[172] The phrase is Donald Hindley's, as quoted in B. Anderson (1996: 29).
[173] Mortimer (1974): 59.

However, the numerous rifts among the politicians themselves in the period which immediately followed the elections and Sukarno's growing dislike for the unstable party system
diminished the "threat" expected from the PKI and its associated mass organizations.[174]

As in the Philippines, democratic procedures in Indonesia contained the powers of the radical Left more than they unleashed them. Conversely, Indonesia's
period of postwar parliamentarism saw regionalist tensions inflamed. Pressures
for territorial integration arose after the Dutch retreat in the form of a "unitarian
movement," involving "popular demands for a scrapping of what was conceived
to be an alien-imposed federalism and for the liquidation of these states and
their merger with the old Republic."[175] While widely popular among the general public, Indonesia's quick moves toward unitary government threatened old
provincial elites and – more ominously – non-Javanese officers of the old colonial
army (the KNIL). Armed revolts led by ex-KNIL forces broke out in West Java
and the South Moluccas within months of formal independence. Although easily
repressed by ABRI loyalists, these revolts only strengthened the conviction of the
"unitarians" that Indonesia suffered from deep territorial cleavages and required
a strong political center to hold the fledgling Republic together.

Neither effectively centralized nor decentralized, Indonesia's inchoate territorial structure incubated suspicions on all sides. For many politicians and military
officers in the "Outer Islands," parliamentary democracy meant taking orders
from Jakarta, and suffering the effects of economic policies perceived as benefiting Javanese importers at the expense of non-Javanese commodity exporters. The
view from the center was predictably inverted. Parliamentary democracy seemed
to give non-Javanese party politicians undue influence over national affairs, stifling the Sukarno-led pursuit of economic policies that were too nationalist and
redistributionist for non-Javanese tastes. This poisoned the democratic atmosphere and left Indonesia vulnerable to eruptions of territorial conflict. It would
be regional rather than leftist insurgency that would usher in the collapse of parliamentary democracy in the late 1950s – with the military as the prime political
beneficiary.

Regional Rebellions and the Origins of Military Ascendancy, 1957–1959
Rather like a volcanic eruption, the eruption of regional rebellions in Indonesia in 1957 marked the culmination of long-simmering pressures more than an
instantaneous reaction to sudden events. The underlying conflicts involved military as well as civilian actors. On the civilian side, "Outer Island" politicians from
the Masyumi party in particular had grown accustomed to de facto regional self-
rule as a result of Jakarta's internal tensions and attenuated territorial control.
They tended to forge alliances with regional military commanders (panglima),
who shared provincial politicos' interest in raising as much revenue as possible
from local commodity sources and sharing as little of it as possible with central authorities. As Sukarno veered increasingly to the Left – in large measure
out of frustration with the Netherlands' continued intransigence over western

---

[174] Utrecht (1972): 59–60.
[175] Kahin (1952): 450–451.

New Guinea and domination over the commanding heights of the Indonesian economy – these regional Masyumi-military alliances found increasing external support from the United States, who feared that Indonesia was going the way of communist China.

Two regional rebellions – initially separate, but later conjoined – would shatter the fragile interregional peace. The first would commence with the formal demand for greater regional autonomy by the Permesta movement, centered in South Sulawesi, in February 1957. The second would be sparked by the declaration of a new and alternative national government, or PRRI, in West Sumatra in February 1958. Neither would be particularly bloody, especially in comparison to Indonesia's revolution of the late 1940s and anti-communist pogrom of the mid-1960s. Quite unlike the regionalist insurgencies in Burma, to be discussed in Chapter 8, the PRRI-Permesta rebellions mobilized demands for territorial autonomy rather than outright separation, and did so without significant recourse to violence. Herbert Feith and Daniel Lev described the PRRI wing of the rebellion in West Sumatra as "something of a phoney war," exhibiting a "remarkable absence of ruthlessness" in what almost appeared at times to be "a war between friends." They conclude that "the quip that this was history's most civil civil war has a large grain of truth."[176] Karl Jackson concurs that the PRRI "spawned a fairly anaemic mass following in a rebellion that never really took hold in its three-year long existence."[177] Barbara Harvey refers to the Permesta portion of the regional uprising in Sulawesi, a bit dismissively, as "half a rebellion." The manageability of regional rebellion in the late 1950s helps explain why Indonesia underwent a less thorough process of political militarization than Burma, which was confronted with far more unmanageable separatist pressures.

Nevertheless, it is the *type* more than the *intensity* of contentious politics that determines the contours of elite collective action most likely to emerge in response. Mild as they were, Indonesia's regional rebellions of the late 1950s induced significant political militarization for three main reasons. First, the rebellions enhanced the operational and ideological foundations for solidarity within ABRI itself. They incited ABRI leader A.H. Nasution to elaborate the concept of *dwifungsi*, or dual function, which would later be used to justify the military's active and leading political role throughout the New Order. Second, regional uprisings provided an opportunity for Javanese ABRI units to purge non-Javanese rivals, further improving military cohesion. As in Burma in the late 1940s, the regionalist mutinies in Indonesia in the late 1950s gave rise to a more sociologically cohesive set of top generals. "After the 1958 rebellion, the Javanese element in the army leadership became absolutely dominant."[178] Combating regional *contention* meant eliminating regional *factions*. "Each military success meant the elimination of competitors for intramilitary ascendancy," writes Benedict Anderson. "The grip of Java-based officers on the high command increased, while Javanese troops became de facto occupiers of much of the Outer Islands."[179]

---

[176] Feith and Lev (1963): 42, 43.
[177] K. Jackson (1985): 8.
[178] Utrecht (1972): 60.
[179] B. Anderson (1983): 483.

A third reason why regional rebellions sparked political militarization was that they discredited a major party, Masyumi, as complicit in the rebellions, as well as the parliamentary system more generally as a source of political divisiveness rather than decisiveness. They thus strengthened the power position of Indonesian generals vis-à-vis civilian politicians, producing quick institutional repercussions. "In 1958 professionalization of the Army resumed. The rebellion in the Outer Islands offered the long-awaited opportunity to commence a new 'reorganization and rationalization' plan."[180] Whereas Sukarno had nixed such efforts in 1952 and 1955, the regional rebellions had definitively shifted the political landscape. Since ABRI had quashed the unrest, and non-Javanese parliamentarians had been blamed in part for instigating it, Sukarno became much more beholden to a military that was "far stronger and more united"[181] than it had been before the PRRI-Permesta mutinies erupted.

This shift toward political militarization accelerated with Sukarno's declaration of Guided Democracy in 1959, terminating Indonesia's experiment with parliamentary rule. The military consolidated its control over many of the country's assets in the plantation, mining, and petroleum sectors, which Sukarno had begun nationalizing in late 1957. Meanwhile, "military occupation of the bureaucracy also increased."[182] In short, the transition to Guided Democracy marked a "partial military take-over."[183]

Conclusion: Militarization and the Pathway to Semi-Ordered Power

To apprehend the causal effects of contentious politics on the institutions of political order in Indonesia, one must be attentive to more types of conflict and more types of institutions than in other Southeast Asian cases. A focus on contentious class politics alone would fail to explain why the military seized a political leadership role in Indonesia during the 1950s – quite unlike in Malaya and the Philippines, where it remained a background player. ABRI's leading role in the nationalist revolution against the Dutch provided an important basis for *ideological* cohesion, but it would take a decade of struggles with armed regional rivals before ABRI would begin to exhibit the *institutional* cohesion necessary to militarize politics in any significant way. Regional rebellions would also shatter Sukarno's limited tolerance for parliamentary democracy and lead him to perceive the military as a more reliable partner in his never-ending nationalist revolution than the civilian sources of division in Indonesia's parliament.

Once ABRI gained this central position in Indonesian politics, it would not loosen its grip. As we will see in subsequent chapters, the explosive growth of the PKI under Sukarno's Guided Democracy gave rise to a broad elite coalition in support of state-building under more deeply authoritarian auspices – in other words, a protection pact. Yet this pact would manifest itself in a distinctive institutional manner, with military institutions remaining pivotal and providing a check against the building of a strong new civilian ruling party and administrative

---

[180] Utrecht (1972): 60.
[181] Feith and Lev (1963): 46.
[182] Emmerson (1978): 88.
[183] Utrecht (1972): 61.

state apparatus. Indonesia's New Order would order power more impressively than Marcos' Philippines, but not as extensively as Malaysia under UMNO and its partners.

Conclusion

Southeast Asia's postwar upsurge in contentious politics took subtly different forms in different countries. Malaya suffered a succession of contentious and violent events in which revolutionary lower-class mobilization penetrated urban areas and exacerbated ethnic tensions. A new state and new parties were gradually (and grudgingly) crafted in response, providing the institutional foundations for the authoritarian Leviathan to come. Leftist unrest in the Philippines was perceived as more reformist, episodic, and manageable, exhibiting a much milder centripetal effect on elites and leaving state and party institutions far weaker than their Malaysian counterparts. Finally, Indonesia suffered more significant outbreaks of regional than class contention in the decade-plus following World War II, elevating the military to a position of power and influence that had no parallel in Malaya or the Philippines.

The next chapter discusses how a second wave of contentious politics, commencing in the mid-1960s, pushed Malaysia and the Philippines ever further along the domination and fragmentation pathways, while pushing Indonesian politics in a dramatically – but not entirely – new direction.

5

Varieties of Violence in Authoritarian Onset

Introduction

Pluralist politics and mass mobilization did not end in Malaysia, the Philippines, and Indonesia with the conflicts discussed in the previous chapter. A second wave of contentious politics would crash over all three countries beginning in the mid-1960s, helping to justify elite projects to construct new authoritarian Leviathans. These new regimes would not simply fail to meet minimal requirements of procedural democracy; they would actively endeavor to demobilize popular sectors through a significant increase in repression and a revamping of centralized state power, with no promise that a return to democracy was forthcoming in the foreseeable future.

These regimes would vary widely in their durability. Ferdinand Marcos would fail to construct a viable authoritarian Leviathan and be overthrown in 1986; Suharto would undertake much more extensive institution-building and survive politically until 1998; and the UMNO-led regime in Malaysia would leverage its command over Southeast Asia's strongest authoritarian Leviathan (save Singapore's) to endure in power until today. Chapter 7 will explore these regimes' divergent fates during times of political crisis; Chapter 6 will examine the strength of elite coalitions before those crises struck.

This chapter aims to explain the origins of those authoritarian coalitions themselves. It does so by comparing the types of contentious politics that struck Malaysia, the Philippines, and Indonesia – and the divergent elite perceptions of those contentious outbreaks – as pluralist politics was brought to a violent end. Even more than in the previous chapter, the focus here will be on leftist rather than regional unrest. As before, the varying coalitional effects of contentious class politics preceding the attempted construction of an authoritarian Leviathan depend upon whether it *presents* revolutionary demands, *penetrates* urban areas, and *provokes* communal tensions.

From Social Conflict to Electoral Conflict: Malaysia, 1957–1969

It is a truism in the study of Malaysian politics that the country gained its independence through a peaceful, negotiated transfer of sovereignty. Unlike their counterparts in Indonesia, political elites in Malaya did not need to raise arms to win self-rule. As Syed Farid Alatas captures this comparative consensus: "the Indonesian state was created by a revolution while the Malaysian state emerged peacefully."[1]

This truism obscures more than it reveals. While the handover of power in August 1957 was indeed a cordial affair, it was a moment of calm – like the eye of a temporal hurricane – between gales of communal conflict. The twelve years preceding independence had seen British and Malayan elites struggling to manage an urban labor movement and communist insurgency that had triggered powerful communal reverberations. The twelve years following independence witnessed Malay and Chinese elites struggling to hold their coalition together amid pressures from hardliners in both camps. UMNO and MCA leaders had been successful at muzzling extreme communalist voices so long as the communist insurgency presented both Malays and Chinese with a tangible threat from below. With the defeat of the MCP and the advent of competitive electoral politics, the voices of communal assertion became harder to keep in check.

From a comparative perspective, it is useful to recall the relationship between competitive elections and leftist extremism analyzed in the Philippines in Chapter 4. The Huk rebellion intensified in direct response to the government's flouting of democratic principles during the elections of 1949, then weakened in the wake of freer and fairer elections in 1951. Mass unrest in the Philippines was strongly and directly associated with *declining* electoral competition. As we will see later in this chapter, the same would hold true for the Philippines in the late 1960s and early 1970s, as Ferdinand Marcos sparked worsening urban unrest with his increasingly undemocratic behavior.

By contrast, the worsening of communal tensions in Malaysia throughout the 1960s was directly related to *increasing* electoral competition. Most significantly, it was the communal reverberations of an unexpectedly close national election in May 1969 that sparked deadly Malay-Chinese riots in Kuala Lumpur, ushering in the birth of Malaysia's authoritarian Leviathan. Malaysian elites have therefore generally lacked the confidence of their Philippine counterparts that democracy and stability can go together – making them more suitable fodder for incorporation into the protection pact that has sustained Malaysian authoritarianism for four decades and running.

Tremors before the Quake: Communalism Strains the Alliance, 1959–1967

By the time the British relinquished sovereignty over Malaya in August 1957, Malaya's postwar "ethnic-quake" had come to a halt. This returned the Malay and Chinese communities from their state of active friction to one of passive tension. By permitting the continued concentration of political power in the hands of

[1] Alatas (1997): 38.

Malay elites and economic power in the hands of Chinese elites, the Alliance bargain produced considerable irritation among Malay and Chinese communalists alike.

The first major sign of communal strain came before the national elections of 1959, when MCA leader Lim Chong Eu demanded that his party be allowed to compete in 40 of the 104 races that the Alliance would be contesting. UMNO leaders held firm in allowing the MCA to compete for only 31 seats. They "were convinced that it posed a threat to the political position of the Malay community itself," Chandra Muzaffar argues. "In fact, this was how the issue was presented to the Malay community at large. And to a great extent, the community stood solidly behind the UMNO leadership."[2] Lim bolted the MCA in protest, but few defectors followed suit, in a sign of how institutionalized party politics had already become. "For these businessmen-cum-political leaders, continued membership in an MCA which belonged to the ruling coalition was a much better proposition than being cast out into the political wilderness."[3]

Neither UMNO nor the MCA fared as well in the 1959 vote as in pre-independence elections. The MCA won only 19 of the 31 races it contested, while UMNO suffered an even greater shock, losing outright in the Malay heartland states of Kelantan and Terengganu. UMNO's struggles in those states where the Chinese population was the smallest in the country testified to the party's dependence on an anti-Chinese, protection logic for its support. With no major Chinese presence to threaten Malay interests, Malay voters in Kelantan and Terengganu flocked to the Pan-Malayan Islamic Party (PAS), which condemned UMNO for its cozy relationship with its non-Islamic Alliance partners.

The MCA found itself losing even more ground to parties expounding a harder communalist line, with many Chinese voters feeling inspired by Lim Chong Eu's example to demand more out of the Alliance bargain. These electoral results spelled trouble for elite collective action across communal divides. The underlying premise of the Alliance bargain, after all, was that each member party would secure the electoral support of its own ethnic community.

The peaceful resolution of the 1959 UMNO-MCA dispute would ease communal tensions only momentarily. In Alatas' apt phrase, "the dust did not settle."[4] Communal anxieties were reignited in 1961 when Malaya's first prime minister, Tunku Abdul Rahman, proposed the integration of Singapore into a new Federation of Malaysia. Incorporating Singapore entailed absorbing a predominantly Chinese city where leftist ideology remained extremely strong (as we will see in Chapter 8). The Tunku's move was "a response to the growing communist threat in Singapore posed by the *Barisan Socialis* (Socialist Front); alarmed that he might be faced with a 'Cuba' at his doorstep, Tunku acceded to requests by the ruling PAP [People's Action Party] of Singapore to merge the two countries."[5] The Malaysian merger was consummated in September 1963,

---

[2] Chandra (1979): 79.
[3] Heng (1988): 257.
[4] Alatas (1997): 135.
[5] Funston (1980): 53.

diluting the strength of the Singaporean Left in a wider, more conservative peninsular polity.

While the Malayan and Singaporean leaderships shared a strong distaste for
communism, they held radically different visions as to how communal peace
should be preserved. As the representative of Malaysia's most heavily Chinese
major city, PAP leader Lee Kuan Yew rejected the notion that ethnic harmony
necessarily rested on Chinese acquiescence to Malay political hegemony. Rather
than a "Malay Malaysia," he proposed the evolution of a "Malaysian Malaysia,"
in which all groups would enjoy unfettered access to state power and resources.
As unobjectionable as such non-communal rhetoric might seem, to Malay ears
it expressed a cloaked form of communalism, since the Chinese would be the
prime beneficiaries of any withdrawal of pro-Malay preferences. Lee's talk of
"non-communalism" and "meritocracy" implied that ethnic Chinese should be
permitted to occupy the political pinnacle in Malaysia, and not just dominate its
economic commanding heights.

This was anathema not only to Malaysia's ethnic Malay leaders, but to their
Chinese partners in the ruling Alliance. The son of MCA founder Tan Cheng
Lock, Finance Minister Tan Siew Sin, struck a dramatic chord in his public
warning to the PAP in April 1964 not to endanger the existing elite consensus
on the inviolability of Malay political hegemony:

The Malays, from the Tengku [Tunku Abdul Rahman] downwards, feel strongly that the
retention of this special position is their only hope of survival. The Tengku himself has
stated repeatedly that he and his people regard agreement on this question as the acid test
of our sincerity towards the Malays. Any erosion of this principle could make the Malays
desperate and you know, as well as I do, what desperate people can resort to.[6]

Given Malaysia's recent history of communal violence, Tan knew that anyone
reading his comments in the *Straits Times* would understand his meaning. It
would not be long before his prophecy (or threat) was realized. In July 1964, a
procession in Singapore celebrating the prophet Muhammad's birthday turned
violent, triggering three days of communal rioting. The riots came on the heels
of a fiery war of words pitting the Malay-dominated Alliance against the Chinese-
dominated PAP. Leaflets distributed at the procession provide a good sense of
the apocalyptic tone in which some Malays were portraying the PAP's bid to
compete for national power:

These called on Malays to "destroy" the "Chinese" PAP government. "If we Malays do
not oppose the PAP Government from now, within 20 years there will be no more Malays
in Malaysia and there will be no more Sultans because the PAP Government does not
want Malay Sultans," one charged. Another warned of Chinese "planning to kill Malays"
and urged Malays to unite and "wipe out the Chinese from Singapore soil because if we
leave them alone they will make fools of the Malays. . . . Before the blood of Malays flows
on Singapore soil it would be better to see the blood of Chinese flooding the country. Let
us fight to the last drop of blood!"[7]

---

[6] Quoted in Lau (2003): 114.
[7] Ibid. 162.

Erupting just under a year after Singapore's incorporation into Malaysia in September 1963, and just over a year before the city's expulsion from Malaysia in August 1965, the July 1964 riots were only the bloodiest expression of the exacerbated communal tensions that characterized the two-year merger period. Riots again rocked Singapore in September 1964, bringing the total number of people killed in the two eruptions to 36, the number injured to 560, and the number detained to 5,962.[8]

The political effect of these riots was magnified by the fact that the PAP's interest in challenging the Alliance for national power was galvanized rather than tempered by the violent experience. When Lee Kuan Yew tried in 1965 to mobilize a grand coalition of opposition parties called the Malaysian Solidarity Convention in support of his "Malaysian Malaysia" concept, the Alliance's tolerance was pushed to its limits, and Singapore's expulsion became virtually inevitable. But not before the two-year challenge by the Chinese-dominated PAP to the Malay-dominated Alliance had reactivated the specter of Chinese political domination throughout the Malayan peninsula. "Political competition between Chinese and Malays in a union of Malaya and Singapore had brought the racial situation to an intolerable tension," Alvin Rabushka summarizes. Expulsion resulted from "a growing Malay fear that Singapore's ambitious Prime Minister Lee Kuan-yew sought to increase Chinese control over the public sector."[9] This sense of communal threat was not purely a partisan concoction of UMNO leaders to justify their control – even the opposition Islamist party, PAS, "saw the entry of the PAP as 'aimed towards the elimination of Malay power.'"[10]

If the PAP rise had mainly spooked the Malays, the Singapore riots had primarily spooked the Chinese. It was the *type* of violence that was most politically significant. The urban upheaval showed in dramatic fashion that nowhere in Malaysia – and by logical extension, no *one* in Malaysia – was immune from communal bloodletting if elite consensus were to crumble. Underscoring the point, severe riots shook the city of Penang in late 1967, sparking a month of violence that saw 29 people killed, more than 200 injured, more than 1,000 arrested, and the imposition of a month-long 24-hour curfew by federal troops.

Even more than the Singapore riots, the violence in Penang witnessed a tight coupling of class and communal elements. A general strike declared by the left-wing, Chinese-dominated Labor Party had turned bloody, and "it soon became evident that continuing outbreaks of violence had rapidly assumed communal overtones. This was not too surprising given the highly urbanized and racially tense atmosphere of Penang."[11] Considering that Penang was far from the only "highly urbanized and racially tense" city in Malaysia, this local outbreak had national implications. The Dean of the University of Malaya's economics department, Ungku Abdul Aziz, warned that the country was facing the specter of a "spiral of violence" on a national scale.[12] Indeed, Penang was not alone in

[8] Numbers calculated from Ibid. (175, 197).
[9] Rabushka (1973): 103.
[10] Chandra (1979): 81.
[11] Snider (1968): 965.
[12] Ibid. 969.

confronting leftist agitation that threatened to spill over into renewed communal bloodshed in late 1967:

Kuala Lumpur itself was being swept by persistent rumors and threats of a general strike – again organized and generated by left-wing elements of the Labor Party. . . . Police and military units, including light armored vehicles, spread throughout the capital city from a staging area at the Stadium Negara. Soldiers with rifles at ready were stationed at ten-foot intervals along many of Kuala Lumpur's busy shopping streets. There is little doubt that it was these strict preventive measures which made intimidation ineffective. The city was very tense, but the shops stayed open.[13]

Malaysian authorities thus proved capable of forestalling unrest in Kuala Lumpur when a Chinese-dominated leftist party attempted to trigger a general strike. Less than two years later, they would fail to prevent urban communal violence when Chinese-dominated opposition parties made surprising gains in national elections. Even more than the PAP's electoral challenge to the Alliance from 1963–65, the success of anti-Alliance Chinese parties in 1969 raised fears that competitive democratic elections were an avenue to instability rather than political order.

Unmanageable Contention at the Polity's Heart: Elections and Riots, May 1969

Communal politics remained on a knife's edge throughout the 1960s because parties continued to use communal appeals to vie for power. The ruling Alliance had constructed a loose internal consensus on the proper boundaries for communal politicking. This consensus frayed, but did not unravel, in the UMNO-MCA crisis of 1959. But opposition parties were neither invested in this bargain nor beholden to its constraints. Competitive national elections in 1959, 1964, and 1969 served less to reconcile ethnic cleavages than to pour salt into perceived communal wounds.

The PAP's bid for power in 1964–65 had already served as a dramatic example. While the PAP leadership had been expelled from Malaysia along with its home base of Singapore (indeed, the Malaysian government expelled Singapore mostly *to* expel the PAP leadership), the party's Malaysian arm lived on in the form of the Democratic Action Party (DAP). Another Chinese-dominated party called Gerakan emerged after the Penang riots in 1967, pushing for non-Malays to be better represented in Malaysia's plural society. Both the DAP and Gerakan presented frontal challenges to the elitist MCA. While these parties tapped into non-Malay discontent with Malay political domination, PAS continued to tap into Malay discontent with Chinese economic domination. So long as most Chinese felt sealed off from political power and most Malays felt sealed off from economic opportunities, communal grievances – emanating primarily from the lower classes – remained sharp.

National elections in May 1969 revealed the acuteness of these grievances. PAS captured an unprecedented share of Malay voters in urban and suburban constituencies, while Gerakan and the DAP made even bigger inroads among

---

[13] Ibid. 966.

the Chinese. At the national level, the Alliance's majority shrunk from 89 to 66 out of 104 total seats, endangering its two-thirds majority for the first time. This electoral turnabout "called into question the hitherto widely held assumption that the UMNO was and would always remain the neutral party of government, *the assured center of an otherwise unstable political system.*"[14]

It was in Malaysia's capital city where the elections had their most explosive implications. To be sure, the Chinese opposition parties' gains were less dramatic in the state of Selangor, where Kuala Lumpur was located, than in Penang, where an 18–6 Alliance advantage in state seats was suddenly converted into an opposition advantage of 20–4. Selangor produced a deadlock instead of an opposition landslide, with Alliance forces and opposition forces securing 14 seats apiece.

The key difference was not in the raw numbers, but in their political meaning. Since Penang had been ruled directly by the British, the state had no Malay sultan. Selangor had been ruled indirectly, retaining a Malay sultan. It was one thing for Malays to countenance a Chinese takeover of Penang, where Malay sovereignty had been snatched away nearly two centuries before. It was quite another to ponder the symbolic and substantive significance of a Chinese oppositionist becoming Chief Minister of Selangor, seizing the top executive position in the nation's capital, and gaining greater de facto power than the Sultan himself. "This is a bad omen to the future of the Malay race," the Malay-language daily *Utusan Melayu* opined gravely.[15]

Widespread Malay anger at the voting results was directed not only at top Chinese oppositionists, but at the broader Chinese population who had supported them. It was of enormous significance that Chinese voters had abandoned the Alliance in greater numbers than the Malays. According to the estimates of K.J. Ratnam and R.S. Milne, 54.2% of Malays voted for Alliance parties, compared to only 40.4% of non-Malays.[16] In Selangor, UMNO won 12 out of 13 Malay-majority districts; but the collapse in Chinese support for the MCA turned a 24–4 Alliance edge into a 14–14 tie. These voting patterns led many Malays to conclude that the Chinese had abandoned the constraints of the Alliance bargain and renewed their bid for full political equality, or even supremacy. The results "gave rise to anxiety and even alarm among UMNO activists and sympathizers that political power was 'slipping out' of 'indigenous' into 'immigrant' hands."[17]

As in the postwar interregnum of 1945–46, the Emergency of 1948–57, and the PAP confrontation of 1963–65, communal bloodshed was unleashed in May 1969 amid what many Malays perceived to be a Chinese bid for political power. This time, Kuala Lumpur itself was the epicenter. As Goh Cheng Teik describes the linkage from elections on May 10th to the riots on May 13th:

The Selangor results had evoked feelings of anger, frustration and anxiety with the local UMNO branches. Anger was stirred up by the perceived pattern of voting in the state. While the Malays rejected the "extremist" PAS and solidly supported UMNO as evidenced

---

[14] Kessler (1980): 7. Emphasis added.
[15] Goh (1971): 16.
[16] Calculated from figures in Von Vorys (1975: 305).
[17] Goh (1971): 19.

by UMNO's loss of only 1 out of 13 seats, the Chinese and Indian voters rejected MCA and MIC and flocked to the "extremist" Opposition parties.... The UMNO anger was, therefore, vented on the Chinese and the Indians in the state for "deserting" the Alliance Party – the vehicle of "multi-racialism" – *en masse*.[18]

Violence was triggered not just by how Chinese voted, but by how they gloated. Crowds of Chinese reportedly marched to the home of Selangor Chief Minister Harun Idris on May 11th–12th and demanded that he vacate the residence. "They are reported to have shouted slogans like 'the Malays have fallen,' 'Malays do not have power anymore,' 'we are now in control,' 'Kuala Lumpur now belongs to the Chinese,' 'Malays can return to their villages,' 'this country does not belong to the Malays,' 'we want to chase out all the Malays' and so on."[19] As Goh describes the local Malay reaction to these celebrations:

These visits to Dato Harun's house and the slogans shouted at the processions registered vigorous reactions among Dato Harun's supporters in particular and Malay inhabitants in the Greater Kuala Lumpur district in general. They felt outraged that they, the natives of the soil, should have been asked to withdraw from Kuala Lumpur, the capital of *Tanah Melayu*, into Red-Indian-style reservations so that the immigrant communities could gain dominance over it.[20]

It was during the pro-UMNO counterdemonstration on the night of May 13th, attended by an estimated 5,000 protestors, that violence first erupted:

Some of the intending participants brought with them makeshift weaponry (sticks, rocks, knives and a few parang and kris) in case of trouble. Before the demonstration had started rumors reached the assembled crowd that Malays had already been attacked in another part of town, causing hundreds to run off on indiscriminate punitive raids. It was beyond the powers of the police to quickly control the ensuing violence since they had not prepared for attacks on the UMNO procession and were not in the immediate vicinity.[21]

The political impact of the May 13th riots cannot be measured in lives lost alone, but in the political implications of ethnic violence in the Malaysian context. John Funston draws on Anthony Reid in portraying May 1969 as a time when the whiff of genocide was in the air and was sincerely feared by many Chinese and Malays alike. In his ethnography of the riots, Reid details "the prominence of Malay magico-religious leaders, stories of invulnerability, and the enormous demands for talismans" in Kuala Lumpur. Reid observes that

May 13 fits the traditional pattern of violence within the Malaysian-Indonesian region. Characteristically, such outbursts occur when *the very identity if not existence of the community is felt to be threatened*. It is not mere coincidence that prior to May 13 the last occasion on which magico-religious leaders gained widespread prominence was immediately after the Second World War when large numbers of Malays were killed and humiliated by the communist, predominantly Chinese, Malayan People's Anti-Japanese Army: in both

[18] Ibid. 18.
[19] Chandra (1979): 83.
[20] Goh (1971): 21.
[21] Funston (1980): 209.

instances Malays perceived a direct threat to their identity and retaliated with the fanaticism of the religiously possessed in a holy war.[22]

Conclusion: Sacrificing Democracy on the Altar of Communal Stability

Throughout the 1960s, competitive elections allowed Chinese communalists (and, to a lesser extent, Malay communalists) to gain political ground at the expense of the multicommunal Alliance. Elites from across Malaysia's ethnic spectrum thereby perceived electoral democracy to be an igniter rather than a dampener of communal mass mobilization. Whereas competitive democratic elections were widely seen as part of the solution for social instability in the Philippines, in Malaysia they came to be perceived as part of the problem. "In short, the terrifying experience of open racial strife provided the UMNO-led government with *a legitimate reason for the adoption of authoritarian government control*."[23]

The government enjoyed wide-ranging elite support when it disbanded parliament, declared martial law, and ruled through an UMNO-dominated National Operations Council (NOC) from May 1969 until February 1971. When parliamentary rule was ostensibly restored at the end of the NOC's 21-month rule, it was a desiccated version of the electoral democracy that existed in Malaysia from 1957–69.[24] In its first act upon reconvening, parliament passed a bevy of new constitutional restrictions on speech and assembly. UMNO pressed parliament to amend Malaysia's security laws, broadly expanding the coercive content of draconian regulations such as the Internal Security Act (ISA), Official Secrets Act, Sedition Act, Printing Presses Act, and University Act. These laws provide the UMNO leadership with the wherewithal to silence and imprison anyone it deems a threat. Most importantly, "the selective use of the ISA against political leaders, academics, trade unions, NGO activists, and any critical individuals has effectively muted immediate and/or potential political dissent."[25]

By making politics more illiberal, the Malaysian government made politics more undemocratic. Parliamentary elections were reintroduced in 1974, in a move described in some circles as a bona fide return to democracy.[26] In reality, UMNO leaders only permitted the reintroduction of electoral politics because they felt supremely confident – given their broadened coalition and strengthened authoritarian powers – that elections could not possibly unseat the party as "the assured center of an otherwise unstable political system." This confidence proved to be entirely warranted, as we will see in the next two chapters. For now, the key point is that elite perceptions of endemic and unmanageable conflict *preceding* authoritarianism dampened elite resistance *to* authoritarianism.

---

[22] Cited in ibid. 210–211. Emphasis added.
[23] Hwang (2003): 100. Emphasis added.
[24] The reconvening of parliament was entirely due to elite calculations, not public pressure to do so. "The NOC could probably have extended its tenure, there being no apparent or serious challenge to its rule" (Khoo [1997]: 54).
[25] Hwang (2003): 107.
[26] See, for instance, Alatas (1997).

This would provide Malaysia's leaders with leverage to order power through the new authoritarian Leviathan's key institutions.

Marcos as Firefighter, or Arsonist? Contentious Urban Politics in the Philippines, 1968–1972

As in Malaysia and Indonesia, the project to construct a new authoritarian Leviathan in the Philippines would immediately follow a considerable upsurge in urban unrest. Yet unlike his regional counterparts, "Marcos clearly failed to build a class coalition" in support of open-ended authoritarian rule.[27] To understand why, one must take a closer look at the character of contentious politics that preceded Marcos' declaration of martial law in September 1972. Patterns of conflict not only gave elites little reason to perceive any need for a permanent protector; they also undermined Marcos' claims to be the protector the Philippine elite needed.

For heuristic purposes, this discussion is usefully framed by a simple metaphor: Was Marcos properly seen as a *firefighter*, deploying martial law to douse the flames of leftist and regional rebellion? Or was he more justifiably perceived as an *arsonist*, igniting social conflict and fanning the flames of violence with his anti-democratic practices? The purpose of this discussion is not to resolve this historical debate, but to establish that Marcos' role in these conflicts was highly debatable. By tracing patterns of contentious politics when President Marcos still ruled through electoral legitimation rather than dictatorial decree, we can better understand the limited and qualified nature of elite support for authoritarian rule from its very inception.

Twilight of an Oligarchic "Heyday": Stirrings of Conflict in the Late 1960s

When Marcos won presidential power through the ballot box in late 1965, the Philippines had just enjoyed more than a decade of social stability. The 1954–65 period was the apex of what Benedict Anderson calls "the full heyday of cacique democracy in the Philippines. The oligarchy faced no serious domestic challenges,"[28] as the Huk rebellion had been laid to rest, and urban labor remained as weak as ever.

By the time Marcos ran for re-election in 1969, warning signs of renewed instability had begun to appear. The foundation of the Movement for the Advancement of Nationalism (MAN) in 1967 "broadened the issue base of the nationalist movement to include redistributive themes,"[29] and the launching of a new Communist Party of the Philippines (CPP) in 1968 raised the specter of a revitalized radical Left. The CPP established a peasant-based New People's Army (NPA) in 1969, threatening to renew Huk-like rural rebellion against oligarchic interests.

[27] Interview with Joel Rocamora, Quezon City," Metro Manila, 27 October 2003.
[28] B. Anderson (1998) [1988]: 207–208. For evidence of the Philippine state's failure to impose taxes on elites during this "heyday" period, see Slater (2005: 166–167).
[29] Doronilla (1992): 162.

Yet these stirrings of discontent hardly amounted to a populist upsurge. For instance, the passage of the "Magna Carta of Social Justice and Economic Freedom" by nationalist forces in Congress in 1969 might have been "full of redistributive, nationalist, and statist rhetoric"; yet it also endorsed the importance of "State responsibility to maintain a favorable investment climate," and contained no concrete proposals to redistribute income.[30] As for the NPA, it boasted "fewer than 50 armed men" upon its founding in 1969.[31] Nor was the CPP an impressive vehicle for bottom-up politics:

> Of the 13 founding members of the new communist party, 10 came from middle class families and the founding chairman, Jose Ma. Sison, while born into a landed clan, worked as a university professor. Moreover, during the formative years of the new party, the overwhelming majority of the party's initial core of cadres were university students and intellectuals from middle class families.[32]

From the beginning, the CPP and NPA exhibited the same uncertain revolutionary intentions as their Huk forebears. They "forged an alliance with bourgeois nationalists,"[33] specifically elite oppositionists such as Benigno (Ninoy) Aquino, who sought mass allies for their fight to deny President Marcos a second term. Aquino went so far as to introduce peasant rebel "Commander Dante" to CPP founder Sison, midwifing the birth of the CPP/NPA alliance. "Aquino reportedly let Dante and his armed band use Hacienda Luisita (his wife's family plantation) as a training ground, provided the rebels with food and medicine, and printed Dante's book on good guerrilla behavior."[34] This courtship of avowed communists might seem quixotic, given Aquino's status as the scion of one of the Philippines' wealthiest landowning families. But his ambitions were factional, not revolutionary: "Aquino was hoping that out of this seemingly paradoxical alliance a strong guerrilla army would emerge to help him fight the dangerously powerful Philippine president."[35]

Growing societal perceptions of Marcos as "dangerously powerful" help explain rising levels of societal dissent in the late 1960s. This was witnessed not only in the resurgence of leftist conflict, but in regional unrest. Muslim-Christian violence erupted in 1968 in the Muslim-majority island of Mindanao, well before Marcos declared martial law. Yet the conflict was smeared with Marcos' fingerprints from the outset. The formation of the Mindanao Independence Movement (MIM) in May 1968 represented a response to a scandal pertaining directly to Marcos just two months before. As Patricio Abinales describes it, "deteriorating Muslim-Christian relations took a critical turn when the media exposed a massacre of Muslim military trainees in a secret training camp outside Manila."[36] Media reports and congressional investigations revealed "evidence of a covert

---

[30] Ibid. 129.
[31] Ibid. 161.
[32] Rivera (2001): 234.
[33] Doronilla (1992): 161.
[34] The argument is Gregg Jones', but it is paraphrased here by Thompson (1995: 40).
[35] Ibid.
[36] Abinales (2000): 166.

apparatus operating under executive control," which opposition leader Aquino denounced as a "secret strike force under the president's personal command, to form the shock troops of his cherished garrison state."[37] This raised public consciousness of Marcos' capacity to manipulate military force for personal purposes, and influenced public perceptions of the urban violence that arose in the early 1970s.

Our analytic attentions thus turn to the social conflicts that rocked Manila, before martial law, during the "parliament of the streets" period from January 1970 until September 1972. Quite unlike the Huk rebellion, this was a decidedly urban uprising. Vincent Boudreau rightly calls this "the Philippines' first *urban* movement to make national and integrated demands" for sweeping political change.[38] With its leftist tone and urban impact, this period of strife more closely resembled this book's profile of unmanageable contentious class politics than any previous episode in Philippine history.

Yet Marcos would enjoy far less success at ordering power from upper groups than his authoritarian contemporaries in Malaysia and Indonesia. In the next two chapters, I detail this failure and trace its effect on authoritarian durability. But first, I trace the origins of Marcos' weak authoritarian coalition to the character of social conflict that presaged his declaration of martial law. More factional than ideological and more top-down than bottom-up in nature, and devoid of any communal implications whatsoever, violence in Manila in the early 1970s was not of a type liable to inspire the development of a broad elite protection pact. This was true of all three predominant types of urban unrest that occurred: (1) student protests and riots, (2) labor strikes and activism, and (3) terrorist bombings.

Urban Unrest (Part I): Student Protests and Riots

During the first three months of 1970, student activism surged beyond the leafy confines of Manila's universities and exploded violently throughout the capital. This "First Quarter Storm" was largely inspired by popular anger over Marcos' inauguration to a second term in late 1969. The first Philippine president to win re-election, Marcos was widely perceived as having secured his incumbency with levels of fraud and intimidation not seen in decades, if ever.

Student protests during Marcos' first term were mostly minor and disjointed affairs, as "their number was small as their grievances were many."[39] The arrival of US Vice-President Spiro Agnew for Marcos' second inauguration in December 1969 inspired a major student rally at the American embassy. After it was forcefully dispersed, student anger over police brutality sparked a series of marches to the presidential palace, Malacañang. Besides Marcos' marred re-election campaign, students were galvanized by the President's retraction of his campaign pledge not to send troops to aid the American war effort in Vietnam, and by fears

---

that Marcos would rig the upcoming Constitutional Convention to his personal advantage.

Anger turned to bloodshed on January 26th, following Marcos' State of the Nation address. Student militants confronted Marcos as he exited Congress, thrusting two cardboard likenesses – one of a crocodile, symbolizing corruption, and another of a coffin, symbolizing the death of democracy – toward the President and First Lady. In the imbroglio that followed, riot police chased the protestors through the streets of Manila. Attacks and counterattacks throughout the night, described as a "club-swinging, placard-throwing melee," left an estimated 72 officers and 300 students injured.[40]

This merely marked the beginning of the "Storm." On January 30th, a student-led rally at Malacañang turned even more violent, as militants commandeered a fire truck that had been sent to disperse them, and crashed it through one of the palace's main gates. While some protestors lobbed Molotov cocktails onto the Malacañang grounds, others fled and were pursued into the Manila night by riot police. In the ensuing street battle, which pitted stones and bottles against tear gas and live ammunition, four students were killed and 162 were injured. Looting and vandalism struck downtown businesses, as "hoodlums and professional thieves" evidently "took advantage of the disorder."[41] "This is no longer a riot," one police officer declared. "This is an insurrection."[42] Marcos predictably agreed. The violence, he proclaimed, represented "a revolt by local Maoist Communists," hell-bent on burning down Malacañang and toppling his democratic government.[43]

But perceptions differed – dramatically. Even as the student protests maintained their momentum through February and March – sometimes ending peacefully, sometimes culminating in renewed violence and vandalism – upper groups were far from unanimous in adopting Marcos' panicked tones.

To be sure, class defensiveness was palpable. The upscale downtown shopping and commercial districts of Ermita and Malate were "transformed into a plywood jungle."[44] The national police chief ordered the redeployment of constabulary forces, including two rifle companies, to the "millionaire's row" of high-priced residential areas in the financial center of Makati, such as Bel-Air and Forbes Park. Such governmental precautions failed to mollify members of the Forbes Park Association, who held an emergency meeting to consider a plan "to organize and arm themselves."[45] Rather than trusting their fate to a militia of their prosperous peers, "Refugees from Forbes Park nervously paced the carpeted floors of the Hotel Inter-Continental."[46]

Yet student protesters successfully dissociated themselves from the worst instances of violence. For all his bluster, even Marcos felt forced to differentiate

---

[40] "MPD Tags Red Agents, Studes Cry Brutality," *The Manila Times*, 27 January 1970.
[41] "Property Damage Estimated at P1M," *The Manila Times*, 3 Feburary 1970.
[42] Lacaba (2003) [1982]: 62.
[43] "FM Blames Reds for Riot," *The Manila Times*, 1 February 1970.
[44] Lacaba (2003) [1982]: 98.
[45] "Armed Vigil Continues Over Greater Manila," *The Manila Times*, 4 February 1970.
[46] Lacaba (2003) [1982]: 71.

the students from the purported "insurrectionists" who had infiltrated the movement "without the students knowing it."[47] Student leaders consistently blamed
the violence either on non-student "toughies and provocateurs" – planted, it was
sometimes suggested, by Marcos himself[48] – or on police brutality.

Leading politicians mostly defended the students from Marcos' red-baiting,
rather than condemning them for destabilizing the nation's capital. Benigno
Aquino "praised the activists, saying that he and his Liberal colleagues 'felt that
our place was with the students,' and condemned police suppression of their
demonstrations."[49] Aquino and fellow Senator Salvador Laurel "directed their
legal staffs to give legal aid to the arrested students," hundreds of whom faced
sedition charges.[50] Vice President Fernando Lopez called for an investigation of
police brutality, declaring that he would "not tolerate massive and brutal police
retaliation on all the demonstrators for what is possibly the fault of a few."[51] And
when national police chief Vicente Raval implied that the four students killed on
January 30th might have been shot by other protestors, rather than by riot police,
Senator Sergio Osmeña Jr. was apoplectic: "It is the height of irresponsibility, to
say the least, for a man in Raval's position to slander the students."[52]

Given the gilded backgrounds of politicos such as Aquino, Laurel, Lopez, and
Osmeña – landed oligarchs and political dynasts of the highest pedigree – their
support for the students amid this upswing in urban violence is striking. Philippine
elite responses to the First Quarter Storm were being shaped to an extraordinary
degree by *political faction* more than by *social class*. Leading oppositionists perceived
Marcos – not the demonstrating students – as the primary threat to their interests.

Nor did they keep this opinion to themselves. "The most pro-student, anti-
Marcos newspapers and magazines were owned by oligarchs who either were
allied with opposition politicians or had been alienated by the administration."[53]
The family of Vice President Lopez, which had used its sugar fortune from
Negros to amass significant holdings in the media industry, is the most important
example. "Although most Manileños disagreed with the radicals' revolutionary
aims, the demonstrators succeeded, with the help of sympathetic media, in creating a generalized sense of instability and crisis and in *making Marcos appear
responsible* for the social ills that led to the protests."[54]

The main reason for muted elite defensiveness amid the First Quarter Storm
was the reformist, pro-democratic, and anti-imperialist agenda pronounced by
student leaders. If the demonstrations had been dominated by calls for sweeping
land reform, or any radical redistribution of wealth, oligarchs such as Aquino,
Laurel, Lopez, and Osmeña would have been in a delicate position. But student
radicals in the militant Patriotic Youth (KM) were tempered by their alliance

47 "FM Blames Reds for Riot," *The Manila Times*, 1 February 1970.
48 "80 Hurt as Youths, Cops Clash," *The Manila Times*, 27 February 1970.
49 Thompson (1995): 38.
50 "293 Face Sedition, Other Charges," *The Manila Times*, 1 February 1970.
51 "MPD Tags Red Agents, Studes Cry Brutality," *The Manila Times*, 27 January 1970.
52 "Raval Theory on 4 Victims Draws Outcry," *The Manila Times*, 6 February 1970.
53 Thompson (1995): 38.
54 Ibid. 39. Emphasis added.

with the more moderate National Union of Students of the Philippines (NUSP). Journalist Napoleon Rama lamented the urban violence, while recognizing its limited character:

[T]he Marcos Administration should consider itself lucky that the students are still demonstrating, although with some degree of violence, and have not yet decided to go underground or found a Fidel Castro or Che Guevarra and have not yet gone to the mountains from where they can mount a real revolution. . . . It's the best evidence that they still, in their hearts, believe, despite the noisy outbursts of the extremists among them, that it is still possible to wring reforms from the Establishment through processes within the framework of the system, and that resort to the ultimate measure – revolution – is not yet necessary.[55]

So long as student leaders focused their demands on issues such as the Constitutional Convention and unequal treaties with the United States, and condemned any violence following student rallies, such denials of revolutionary intent remained credible. As two student leaders scoffed in response to Marcos' branding of protestors as insurrectionists: "When were stones and bottles used to overthrow the government?"[56] In a mid-February briefing at Manila's Camp Aguinaldo, military leaders told congressional investigators that "the over-all peace and order situation was 'problematical' but *still within manageable proportions.*"[57] In sum, the First Quarter Storm lacked the revolutionary intentions that could have pressed elites to deemphasize factional interests and prioritize common class interests.

Urban Unrest (Part II): Labor Strikes and Activism

As with the Huk rebellion two decades before, this division of elite opinion was due not only to the broadly reformist credentials of the Left, but to the lack of a social alliance between urban students and any militant mass base. This meant that economic elites could rest assured that their factional flirtations with student protestors would not result in class assault. But by the early 1970s, such confidence was becoming less warranted. While students stepped up their political demands, labor unions stepped up their economic demands, making 1970–72 the most strike-prone period in Philippine history.

When reviewing strike data from the decade preceding martial law, it first appears as if the labor picture was consistently worsening.[58] The annual number of strikes more than doubled, from sixty in 1961 to 136 in 1972. The number of man-days lost also rose substantially, tripling from less than half a million in 1963 to nearly 1.5 million in 1971. The most significant increase occurred in the number of strikes threatened, via official union notification of intent to strike to the Philippine Labor Board. These grew by a factor of seven, rising from fewer than 200 notifications in 1961 to more than 1,200 in 1971.

---

[55] Napoleon G. Rama, "Have Rock, Will Demonstrate," *Philippines Free Press*, 7 March 1970.
[56] "Youths Join UP Funeral Today," *The Manila Times*, 3 February 1970.
[57] "Solons to Consult AFP on 'Revolutionary Air,'" *Daily Mirror*, 19 February 1970. Emphasis added.
[58] All strike data in this and subsequent paragraphs are from Hernan Gonzalez II, "Union Issues Spawn Strikes," *The Manila Times*, 11 September 1972.

Given these figures, would it not be correct to conclude that labor activism presented an increasing threat to elites' persons, property, and privileges? And that, in response to these trends, middle classes and communal elites might accept the cancellation of democratic procedures, military elites might set aside factional interests to act collectively behind a more dictatorial dispensation, and economic elites might countenance increased direct taxation as the price of protecting their core interests?

There is far less validity to this interpretation than one might initially suspect. To understand why, one must not simply measure the raw number of threatened and actual strikes. One must carefully gauge the perceived manageability of labor mobilization under existing, pluralist political arrangements. On this score, labor's growing propensity to *threaten* to strike was countervailed by its growing willingness to *negotiate*. Both actual and threatened strikes were on the rise; but a steeply declining percentage of strike threats were being carried out. Whereas more than 30% of strike notices culminated in actual strikes in 1961, this figure declined throughout the decade, sinking to approximately 10% by 1972. And those strikes that did take place were getting shorter. In the 1970–72 period, the average length of walkouts shrunk from twenty-seven days to eleven. The total number of man-days lost to strikes was lower in 1972 than in 1971 – hardly lending credence to Marcos' claims that martial law was necessitated in part by an increasingly unmanageable labor crisis.

Marcos' ability to leverage labor unrest into broader elite support for state-building under authoritarian rule was further compromised by his culpability in the crisis. If the revolt in Mindanao was worsening because of the Marcos government's *military* abuses, and if student unrest in Manila was stoked by the President's *political* abuses, labor activism was on the rise because of Marcos' *economic* abuses. The 1969 presidential election "acted as the catalyst for the crisis," writes Amando Doronilla. "More specifically, the election tested the capacity of the Philippine democratic system to absorb the financial stresses – one may properly call them abuses – arising from a combination of economic and fiscal policies that helped Marcos's re-election."[59]

The chain of events operated as follows.[60] First, the torrent of government funds unleashed to secure the President's electoral victory pushed the economy into fiscal free-fall. The budget deficit in 1969 more than tripled the deficit of 1968, as the government's deficit spending in that single year matched its gross deficit spending throughout the 1961–68 period. This forced Marcos into the arms of the International Monetary Fund, which made its support contingent upon the floating of the peso. When the float began in January 1970, the currency lost more than 40% of its value.

The main political fallout from this devaluation would come from a worsening of inflation, which jumped from an annual average of 4.5% during the 1960s to 14% in 1970. Price hikes "shocked the people and intensified social unrest,"[61]

[59] Doronilla (1992): 153.
[60] The following discussion and figures draw from Ibid. (156–157).
[61] Ibid. 156.

most notably labor unrest. Marcos attempted to dampen labor's anger by raising the minimum wage, but with little effect: "The majority of workers were not covered by the minimum wage law," and even those ostensibly included often failed to benefit, because "the bureaucratic enforcement machinery was inadequate" to enforce it.[62] This would not be the last occasion when Marcos was hindered from bridling mass mobilization by the weakness of the Philippine state apparatus.

Yet labor's shared anger at rising prices was not channeled into any organized demands for radical political or economic change. It remained "a haphazardly organized labor movement, rent with factional infighting."[63] Strikes tended to be brief affairs, settled by minor management concessions. Not only was the trade-union movement "very splintered," but "their demands were very economic and non-ideological."[64] Even some of the most dramatic strike actions reflect these patterns. A nine-day strike at Philippines Air Lines (PAL) centered on wage adjustments, and was terminated when employees complied with a back-to-work order from the courts.[65] A strike by 200,000 government employees extracted salary increases in just one day, allowing the civil servants to go "back to work with a smile."[66] Workers at the Philippine National Railways (PNR) struck for just twelve *hours*, until management honored its commitment to compensate for shortfalls in the employees' social-security fund.[67]

In sum, labor's increasing activism represented a notable shift from a *historical* perspective, but not from a *comparative* perspective. Marcos had more to handle on the labor front than his predecessors, but he had much less to handle than leaders in Malaysia and Indonesia during their eras of most severe urban unrest. Any attempt by Marcos to portray himself as a protector of elite interests against labor militancy was further complicated by the same issues of timing that lessened his credibility as a protector against Muslim separatists and student radicals. While some elites undoubtedly perceived martial law as a sensible way to douse these flames, many others believed that it was Marcos who had sparked these brushfires of contentious politics in the first place.

Urban Unrest (Part III): Terrorist Bombings

Marcos gained little political mileage from worker and student unrest during the early 1970s, in large part because of perceptions that the President was an instigator, not a bystander. Yet Marcos was only indirectly responsible for such urban conflict, at most. When a spate of terrorist bombings rocked Manila between August 1971 and September 1972, Marcos' opponents accused him of being not merely an instigator of violence, but its author. These bloody episodes thus reinforced factional cleavages among the Philippine elite, rather than pushing elites to unify in defense of shared class interests.

---

[62] Ibid. 159.
[63] Wurfel (1977): 15.
[64] Author interview with Amando Doronilla, Quezon City, Metro Manila, 1 November 2003.
[65] "Strike Continues at PAL," *The Manila Times*, 10 October 1970.
[66] "Pay Hike Due in Two Weeks," *Daily Mirror*, 18 November 1971.
[67] Mario Macaranas, "PNR Workers' Strike Settled," *The Manila Times*, 5 April 1972.

The first bombing was the deadliest. On August 21st, 1971, two grenades were thrown onto the stage at an election rally for the opposition Liberal party in Plaza Miranda, downtown Manila. Many opposition leaders were on stage during the explosions, which killed nine and wounded more than 80, including three Liberal senators. The crime has never been definitively solved, and remains one of the biggest "whodunits" in Philippine political memory. Nor has anyone unraveled the mystery of a series of subsequent bombings that struck strategic sites in Manila such as City Hall, the Supreme Court, and the corporate headquarters of Esso and Caltex.

For purposes of this analysis, who actually conducted these attacks is irrelevant. What matters is that pro-Marcos and anti-Marcos forces perceived these violent events in diametrically opposite ways, crystallizing the atmosphere of elite polarization – not class polarization – in which Marcos declared martial law. Assessments of the Plaza Miranda bombing in particular were shaped less by evidence than by competing perceptions of Marcos as firefighter or arsonist. As one pro-Marcos investigator into the bombing describes the tenor of the time:

Marcos was rashly and rushly blamed by his Liberal Party *contra-partidos* – led by Ninoy Aquino. . . . What Ninoy lacked by way of proof, Ninoy remedied by way of populist charm and bombast, which, for most people, was sufficient basis to damn President Marcos. In that politically charged period, no one was in any mood to await the findings of forensic experts and other investigators; the whole nation became a jury, with everyone disposed to prejudge the case on the basis of partisan logic.[68]

While rightly conveying the factional tensions of the times, this partisan analysis fails to acknowledge how Marcos' own post-bombing bumbling fostered public disbelief. Marcos cryptically declared that "a 'Marxist-Leninist-Maoist' group receiving 'active moral and material support of a foreign power'"[69] was responsible for the attack, and repeatedly promised to unveil proof. Yet he consistently failed to produce evidence to back up his accusations. Eight days after the bombing, Marcos declared that investigators had "made a breakthrough," uncovering evidence "confirming our worst fears," and promised to reveal these findings "in good time."[70] Nothing happened. Four months later, Marcos announced that the government had "outstanding. . . . surprising revelations to make," and would do so in a matter of days.[71] Again, the public was left on tenterhooks.

Meanwhile, Marcos infuriated the Liberal opposition by rebuking their wounded president's appeals to appoint an independent commission to assume control over the inquiry.[72] Fueling the factional fire, Marcos used his control over the Board of Censors to "attempt to suppress the newsreel" of the attack from being publicly aired.[73] Worst of all: "By suspending the writ of habeas corpus after the bombing, Marcos seemed to show that the opposition's warnings

[68] Guevarra (1989): 1.
[69] Eduardo Lachica, "The Bombing: Who Did It?", *The Manila Times*, 27 August 1970.
[70] Manuel Salak Jr., "FM Sees Early Solution of Case," *The Manila Times*, 29 August 1971.
[71] Manuel Salak Jr., "FM Vows to Report on Plaza Bombing," *The Manila Times*, 30 December 1971.
[72] Ibid.
[73] F.H. Magno, "Miranda Film Row Escalates," *Daily Mirror*, 28 September 1971.

of dictatorship were justified."[74] Bizarrely, Marcos defended this action by arguing that it had public support in the provinces, although not, he acknowledged, in Manila – where the bombing that purportedly necessitated the suspension of democratic privileges actually took place.[75]

This flimsy effort to pin blame on "insurrectionists" gave Marcos' opponents a golden opportunity to scoff publicly at his nightmare scenarios. In response to Marcos' claim that the bombing at Plaza Miranda "certified the existence of 'a state of rebellion,'" *The Manila Times*' Eduardo Lachica howled with disbelief. "A few ideological hotheads adept at writing Marxist tracts do not necessarily make a Maoist revolution," he editorialized. "The known Maoists. . . . are too few in number to constitute a political threat," he continued, and are more adept at "playing at revolution rather than undertaking it." Lachica concluded by highlighting an obvious inconsistency in Marcos' claims that the Liberals were secretly funding leftist radicals, and that leftist radicals had attempted to assassinate the Liberal leadership. "Why should the Liberals be bloodied when they were supposed to be in league with the rebels?"[76]

Liberal leaders then seized upon the release of a special Senate committee report – chaired by Salvador Laurel, the sharpest Nacionalista bone in Marcos' throat – that minimized "the state of subversion" in the country, just two weeks after the Plaza Miranda bombing. Liberal House leader Ramon Mitra asserted that the report "does not justify but instead places under serious question President Marcos' real reasons for suspension of the writ." Mitra's colleague, Melanio Singson, sounded a similar note, stressing that the report "only confirms the citizens' stand that no such thing as 'imminent danger' of rebellion and insurrection exists to justify suspension of the writ."[77] Again, these expressions of confidence came from politicos of enormous personal wealth, who had much to lose if a revolutionary leftist movement gathered force.

Elite skepticism regarding leftist culpability in the bombing gave way to thinly veiled accusations that Marcos himself had ordered the massacre. Three Liberal politicos – all sons of former Philippine presidents – delivered such allegations from the highest heights of the national elite. Senator Sergio Osmeña Jr., who had been clinically dead in the immediate aftermath of the bombing, raged against Marcos in his first post-attack press conference. "I pledge here and now," the Cebuano dynast fumed, "that the Nacionalista administration will pay dearly in the Visayas for the attempt made on the lives of the leaders of the Liberal party." The Plaza Miranda bombing represented a "dastardly attempt to stifle opposition and protest with grenades."[78] In a campaign rally in Palawan, Ramon Magsaysay Jr. condemned what he called "the massacres of student activists" in Manila. If Marcos would bring the perpetrators of such "massacres" to justice, Magsaysay suggested, "we may even ask the people to forgive and forget what happened in

[74] Thompson (1995): 44.
[75] Manuel Salak Jr., "FM Sees Early Solution of Case," *The Manila Times*, 29 August 1971.
[76] Eduardo Lachica, "The Bombing: Who Did It?", *The Manila Times*, 27 August 1970.
[77] "Opposition Questions FM Intent in Writ," *Daily Mirror*, 6 September 1971.
[78] "Miranda Probe Failure Deplored," *The Manila Times*, 15 October 1971.

Plaza Miranda that Black Saturday of August 21."[79] Wherever there is an offer
of forgiveness, there is also an attribution of blame.

Most dramatically of all, wounded Liberal president Gerardo Roxas delivered a
half-hour address from his hospital bed a week after the bombing. The sensational
speech was broadcast on twelve television stations and 44 radio stations. Without
accusing Marcos by name, Roxas suggested that the attack was "a professional
job," and that its perpetrator wanted to "foil the exposé" at the rally of new details
regarding several administration scandals. Roxas then asked his national audience
a series of "rhetorical questions" that he clearly wanted them to answer in their
own minds:

Why should anyone want to wipe us out that evening? Was it because of what we were
about to say? Was it because Senator Osmeña was about to present the Golden Buddha case
and Rogelio Roxas? Was it because Senator Salonga was set to expose the fake ballots plot
of the administration? Or was it because Senator Aquino was slated to make a documentary
exposé of the hidden wealth of top administration officials?[80]

Yet these accusations were not only thinly veiled; they were thinly supported.
While Marcos failed to pin the blame for the Plaza Miranda bombing on shad-
owy leftists, anti-Marcos politicos had only circumstantial evidence pinning the
blame on the President. The bombings had "the fingerprints of a military operation," and reminded journalists of Marcos' use of secret military units in the 1968
Jabidah massacre.[81] But there were no smoking guns in Manila's burning buildings. Citizens were thus left with multiple credible alternatives when drawing
their own personal judgments.

Considering that the Liberals trounced Marcos' Nacionalistas in the midterm
elections of November 1971 – the last vote before martial law – one might surmise
that the opposition had gained the upper hand in terms of public opinion. Any
conviction that Marcos was more arsonist than firefighter would have been reinforced in democracy's waning days, as Senator Aquino unveiled a purported presidential plot called "Oplan Sagittarius" before Congress. According to Aquino,
Marcos had long been laying the groundwork to declare martial law – and with
the cooperation of a handful of loyal generals, the President was ready to strike.
Marcos denied it. But one week later, after an apparent assassination attempt
on Defense Secretary Juan Ponce Enrile, Marcos did precisely what Aquino had
predicted.

Conclusion: Contested Conflict and a Weak Protection Pact
When Marcos declared martial law in September 1972, he tried to convey the
impression that he was saving the Republic from an imminent social and political
implosion. "The official justifications for martial law," as summarized by Robert
Youngblood, "focused on perceived threats to the republic from a variety of
sources, including rebellion by the Communists, secessionist demands by Muslim

79 "On the Political Front," *The Manila Times*, 12 September 1971.
80 "Roxas Talks on Bombing," *The Manila Times*, 29 August 1971.
81 McCoy (1999): 129.

dissidents, coup d'état and assassination plots by rightist oligarchs, the growth of private armies and criminal syndicates, and increased urban unrest among students, workers, and the poor."[82]

Scholars of Philippine politics have looked upon Marcos' claims with attitudes ranging from cynicism to ridicule. "Filipino democratic institutions did not break down, either in the sense of an inability to maintain order or a failure to respond to changes within the society," David Wurfel argued in 1977. "The rising political violence after 1969 was to a considerable degree the creation of Marcos himself, first in trying to get himself re-elected and then in preparing a justification for martial law."[83] Vincent Boudreau suggests that Marcos' portrayal of the communist threat "was overblown," while acknowledging that "mass (if not communist) politics had attained new national and urban expressions" by the early 1970s. "The 1971–72 political crisis was hence not a crisis for state institutions, but for their incumbents."[84]

While few seemed to believe Marcos' claims that the Philippines was suffering a crisis of state, most would have probably agreed that the polity was facing "a crisis of stagnation."[85] Revolution was hard to imagine, but political gridlock and polarized partisanship were impossible to ignore. The Liberals' resounding victory in the midterm vote in 1971 suggests the opposition's superior public standing vis-à-vis Marcos' Nacionalistas; and most observers seem to agree that Benigno Aquino would have beaten Marcos in any fair presidential fight in 1973. But most Filipinos could not have avoided feeling like the grass beneath two feuding elephants. "By further polarizing the political climate," Mark Thompson suggests, "the opposition played into Marcos' hands."[86]

Widespread disgust with partisan politicking from above, combined with widespread anxiety (if not terror) toward unrest from below, provided Marcos with a cushion of acquiescence (if not a groundswell of support) upon declaring martial law. As Carl Landé summarizes, Marcos' seizure of dictatorial powers

divided the upper and the middle classes.... But what was probably a majority of the upper and middle classes and perhaps of the lower class as well had welcomed the prospects of a period of centrally imposed order. They had watched the growth of radical political activism in the schools and the labor movement, and the wave of urban political demonstrations, with growing unease. To them the old political system, and in particular the Philippine Congress, appeared discredited.[87]

Both Jose Abueva and Lela Garner Noble use the same phrase to capture the dominant attitude among politically conscious Filipinos upon the advent of martial law: "wait and see."[88] This contrasts sharply with predominant elite attitudes

[82] Youngblood (1990): 25–26.
[83] Wurfel (1977): 5.
[84] Boudreau (2002): 548–549.
[85] Franco (2000): 133.
[86] Thompson (1995): 46.
[87] Landé (1986): 116.
[88] Noble (1986): 88; and an author's interview with Abueva, Kalayaan College, Marikina, Metro Manila, 29 October 2003.

in the face of social unrest in Malaysia and Indonesia, where the urgency of curtailing mass mobilization came to be perceived in more life-and-death terms.

Revolutionary Force Meets Military Counterforce: The PKI's Rise and Demise in Indonesia, 1959–1966

Imagine the following scene in Jakarta on May 23, 1965. The main stadium, which is not far from the presidential palace and the legislature, is overflowing with people. . . . Outside in the parking lot and nearby streets more than 100,000 are milling about. It is a sea of humans. The occasion is the forty-fifth anniversary of the founding of the PKI. Judging by the size of the crowd, the party has never been healthier. . . . Red flags and big billboards with portraits of the party's heroes, such as Karl Marx and V.I. Lenin, line the city streets. . . . Those marching to the stadium acquire the name "red ants" in popular discourse: countless in number, orderly, disciplined, and self-sacrificing but militant, and capable of stinging if disturbed. . . . This May 23 celebration is almost a replay of the May Day celebration held in the same stadium only three weeks earlier. . . . No other political party can hope to organize rallies of such scale.

John Roosa, *Pretext for Mass Murder*[89]

Within mere months of the scene depicted above, Indonesia's mighty PKI would vanish from the political stage, annihilated in a gruesome and gratuitous paroxysm of military-led mass killing. To understand the relative orderliness of the "New Order" authoritarian Leviathan that emerged in the wake of this horrific bloodshed, one must first recognize how imminently threatening the PKI appeared to Indonesian elites of virtually all stripes on the eve of its decimation. The PKI had overcome its initial postwar weakness and mushroomed into a revolutionary mass organization with an imposing presence in Indonesia's biggest cities, including its capital. The PKI was an even stronger organized force in the countryside, sparking not just class conflict but communal tensions – especially in Central and East Java, where the "atheistic" party's push for land reform clashed with the Muslim social organizations that controlled much of the property to be redistributed through PKI-led land seizures.

This assessment does not derive from any uncritical interpretation of Cold War nightmare scenarios or self-serving Suharto-era propaganda. Even the New Order's staunchest and most principled critics, such as Indonesianists Benedict Anderson and Daniel Lev, have not gainsaid the perceptions of unmanageable threat that the PKI induced among a broad cross-section of Indonesian elites. The PKI "threatened the entire social and political order," Lev wrote in 1964 – "not only the other parties, but the entire traditional elite."[90] Anderson concurs that PKI policies and tactics "were interpreted as a direct threat to the Indonesian ruling elite of which the Army, was the key active force. Many of the PKI's policies, such as land redistribution, sought to overturn rather than reform the existing social and economic order."[91] The foremost chronicler of the PKI, Rex

---

[89] Roosa (2006): 205.
[90] Quoted in Mortimer (1982: 61) and Mortimer (1974: 373).
[91] B. Anderson (1978a): 1.

Mortimer, portrays the party as "cautious and moderate" in approach through the early 1960s, affirming his analytic immunity to ideological paranoia. Yet as Mortimer summarizes the changed situation as of 1964: "There was no doubt that the Communists had built up a vast organization with formidable energies and a high degree of internal coherence," and had begun to "carry through a class campaign – and on a large scale."[92]

This section aims to establish that the PKI was a revolutionary leftist force with significant urban social power, whose meteoric rise severely exacerbated communal tensions. In short, it is the clearest-cut empirical example of unmanageable contentious class politics as defined in this book. It should thus be unsurprising that Suharto's New Order would initially rest upon a protection pact of similar breadth to Malaysia's after 1969. Yet the earlier militarization of the Indonesian polity and the subsequent annihilation of the PKI would create challenges for the Suharto regime's durability over time that would remain absent in Malaysia, as we will see in the chapters to come.

"Red Ants" Rising: PKI Mobilization in City and Countryside, 1959–1965

President Sukarno's imposition of martial law in 1957 and "Guided Democracy" in 1959 brought an end to electoral politics, but not to mass politics. No longer tamed and tempered within the moderating confines of Indonesia's multiparty parliamentary democracy, the PKI gained political momentum under the patronage and protection of Sukarno himself. The increasingly autocratic leader sought a counterbalance to what had become the most powerful institution in Indonesia in the wake of the regional rebellions of the late 1950s: the military, or ABRI.

Since it ended in unmitigated catastrophe in 1965, one can easily forget how successful Sukarno was at this balancing act during the early 1960s. ABRI was in a far stronger political position after the regional rebellions than beforehand, but it still lacked the internal cohesion necessary to make an institutional bid for power. Since Sukarno had responded to the rebellions by declaring martial law and placing control over many nationalized Dutch enterprises in ABRI's hands, the military lacked a strong incentive to carry out an immediate power-grab as well. Even as Sukarno gave the military as an institution virtually everything it wanted, he worked feverishly to foster factionalism within the armed forces, and tried to divert leading generals from Jakarta intrigues with armed campaigns against Dutch-held West New Guinea and the newly formed federation of Malaysia. As Mochtar Mas'oed depicts Sukarno's efforts to keep ABRI divided, and the growing military frustrations these machinations induced:

Attempts had been taken during the second half of the 1950s to unite the army, especially by removing civilian control. But President Sukarno was always able to prevent unification. The most frustrating setback came in 1962. In that year the President succeeded in dividing the army leadership by making General Nasution the Chief of Staff of the Armed Forces, and appointing General Ahmad Yani to replace him as the leader of the army. More importantly, he took the armed services away from Nasution's control by making

---

[92] Mortimer (1982): 278, 366, 327.

each of the top leaders of the services, the army, the navy, airforce, and police, *Panglima* (Commander-in-Chief) with operational authority independent of the Chief of Staff's control.[93]

Sukarno's moves to check and balance the power of General A.H. Nasution were especially noteworthy, as Nasution had become the leading proponent of dwi-fungsi – or ABRI's dual political and combat roles – since the regional rebellions of the late 1950s. Ironically, Sukarno's attempts to fracture the military internally would be undone by his simultaneous effort to encourage the mobilization of the PKI as an *external* check against military power. The era of Guided Democracy would be marked by the robust mobilization of the PKI and its affiliated mass organizations in both urban and rural areas, as well as the first signs of coun-termobilization by the country's conservative (especially military) elites. "By the late 1950s the PKI had a firm organized base among city workers, estate laborers, and squatters on forestry lands," notes Mortimer. "As the cast of national politics grew more authoritarian, however, this base became more vulnerable. Accordingly, the party's leaders decided to enlarge and intensify their work among the peasant population."[94]

As Gregory Luebbert has shown in the European context, efforts by urban left-ists to mobilize the rural proletariat tend to invite the coalescence of a reactionary alliance to forestall the radicalization of the countryside.[95] The PKI crossed this Rubicon by making increasingly strident demands for land redistribution in late 1963 and 1964. "By *radical* land reform, [PKI leader D.N. Aidit] meant *confis-cation* of all landlord holdings and their distribution *free* to landless and poor peasants."[96] Even as the PKI launched a wave of "unilateral actions" to seize property from landed elites, more than half of its estimated twenty million mem-bers remained located in urban areas,[97] and urban strikes and street protests remained key components of the party's arsenal of contention. The PKI thus made organizational strides and transcended the urban-rural divide to an extent that Philippine communists could scarcely imagine.

The meteoric rise of the PKI also produced an intertwining of class and com-munal tensions that had no parallel in the Philippines. "Almost from the outset, religious passions were injected into the conflict over land,"[98] particularly in the highly populous region of East Java:

An element adding heat to the religious aspect of the conflict was the fact that Moslem religious institutions often owned quite large tracts of land, and in addition frequently became the recipients of land from landlords seeking to escape the application of the reform law.... Faced with the PKI challenge, committed Moslems turned to the kjai and hadji for leadership, and these men, imbued with religious zeal and dedicated to turning

---

[93] Mas'oed (1983): 197.
[94] Mortimer (1974): 278.
[95] Luebbert (1991).
[96] Mortimer (1974): 297. Emphasis in original.
[97] Ibid. 366.
[98] Ibid. 317.

back the Communist tide, *which they saw as engulfing the country and threatening the true faith*, made the most of religious appeals in countering Communist land tactics.[99]

In short, "land reform and rent equalization threatened the rural ascendancy of ulama and haji," writes Anderson. "It was easy to fuse religious and economic grievances and to read into government policies, strongly backed by the PKI, not social reform but another savage attack on Islam."[100] Yet no group felt more threatened than ABRI. "By 1963–65, when the PKI attacked 'bureaucratic capitalists,' 'corruptors,' and 'state-swindlers,' its target was clearly the corrupt military oligarchy that dominated the advanced sectors of the Indonesian economy."[101]

As the national economy collapsed under the weight of hyperinflation, the atmosphere of intimidation created by PKI forces by 1964 could not be taken lightly:

Against this background, the PKI brought its campaign against corruptors and bureaucratic capitalists to a crescendo, mounting frequent and aggressive demonstrations and demands for retooling across the country and placarding the cities, towns, and villages with violent slogans and caricatures calling for the crushing of the people's enemies and death to corruptors. By late September the party was naming economic "criminals" (including one army captain) and demanding public executions.[102]

While economic interests probably tended to factionalize the military as much as unite it, military elites were indeed broadly unified in their opposition to any PKI effort to undermine their coercive monopoly. "Sukarno's plan to authorize PKI militias in 1963 may have roused the most ABRI anxiety," argues Vincent Boudreau. "This 'fifth force' would give the PKI the single capacity that had been ABRI's alone."[103] PKI demands that the government start arming workers and peasants enjoyed Sukarno's "tacit blessing," and by June 1965, "Sukarno urged the territorial commanders to give serious consideration to the fifth force proposal."[104] Sukarnoist commanders of the navy and air force infuriated the army leadership by endorsing the plan, and "in the following month groups of volunteers, many of them PKI organizations, began to receive weapons training at Halim air force base near Djakarta."[105]

Coup d'Etat as Coup de Grace: The October 1st Putsch as the Final Contentious Straw

ABRI-PKI conflict would reach a violent denouement in the mysterious coup of October 1, 1965. Whether the coup primarily represented an outright PKI bid for power or the bloody product of military factionalism remains a topic of

---

[99] Ibid. 318. Emphasis added.
[100] B. Anderson (1978a): 4.
[101] Ibid. 2–3.
[102] Mortimer (1974): 386–387.
[103] Boudreau (2002): 547.
[104] Mortimer (1974): 381.
[105] Ibid. 383.

historical debate.[106] What is clear is that the broad swath of groups that had come to fear and despise the PKI during the preceding years perceived the putsch as the treacherous culmination of a communist campaign to seize political power and overturn the social order.

As ever, it was the *type* more than the *extent* of revolutionary violence that would shape the breadth and concertedness of the elite response. This helps explain the paradox that the PKI-backed lightning coup was "a relatively minor event" in the amount of time it lasted and blood it shed, and yet, "[d]espite its brief lifespan, the movement had epochal effects."[107] A badly bungled revolutionary coup produced one of the century's most sweeping and enduring counterrevolutions because it brought deadly violence quite literally into the bedrooms of Indonesia's most powerful and heavily armed men, and momentarily laid claim to the nation's political center.

The coup began with the attempted abduction of seven anti-communist ABRI commanders in the Jakarta area, including A.H. Nasution, in the early morning hours of October 1st. Several hundred rebel soldiers and several thousand PKI loyalists seized Merdeka Square in downtown Jakarta, capturing the national radio station in the process. A small cabal of pro-Sukarno military leaders and PKI operatives constituted the inner sanctum of the coup group, which clearly wished to preempt a feared right-wing coup against Sukarno. The plotters also clearly hoped that Sukarno would invest his own prestige in supporting the preemptive abductions, while the PKI's "red ants" would swarm the capital and other major cities, making a right-wing counterattack impractical.

"The result was disastrous," writes historian John Roosa. "Of the seven teams, only three succeeded in apprehending the generals and bringing them back alive. Nasution escaped. Yani and two other generals were shot when they resisted." Nasution himself was badly wounded and saw his daughter killed in the assault on his home. The coup-makers thus "decided to abort their plan for presenting the generals to Sukarno," and "to have all their captives executed and their corpses concealed":[108] dumped into a well at the Halim Air Force Base on the outskirts of Jakarta, where the PKI had been provocatively training its proposed "fifth force" in the preceding months.

Without Sukarno's explicit blessing – the military-dependent president "could not support a group of junior officers who had killed off his army commanders" – the coup's military operatives quickly became "ready to cancel their badly botched operation."[109] Yet the PKI leaders in the nucleus of the coup group, including party leader D.N. Aidit, had exposed themselves to ABRI retaliation and calculated that their only hope lay in doubling their bets. With the national radio station still in rebel hands, the PKI-affiliated putschists called for the replacement

[106] For the best recent overview, see Roosa (2006: 62–81). The historical discussion to follow draws heavily on Roosa's account.
[107] Ibid. 225, 4.
[108] Ibid. 217.
[109] Ibid. 218.

of Sukarno's cabinet with a Revolutionary Council, as well as the leveling of ABRI hierarchy through the abolishment of all ranks above lieutenant-colonel.

An armed revolt in support of the coup subsequently broke out in the Central Javanese city of Yogyakarta – but nowhere else. Even in Jakarta, the mass organizational vehicles of the PKI failed to mobilize in sufficient numbers to protect the coup-makers stationed centrally – but vulnerably – in Merdeka Square. Having prioritized secrecy in the run-up to the coup, and having squandered the possible support of the PKI's primary patron, Sukarno, the party's machinery failed to function as the coup group desperately extemporized. By the evening of October 1st, the armed forces of reaction, led by General Suharto, were on the march in Jakarta. Within weeks, an anti-communist pogrom of epic proportions would be unleashed across the Indonesian archipelago.

Conclusion: Comparing Types of Contention in Authoritarian Onset

Few if any authoritarian regimes have been conceived through deadlier birth-pangs than Suharto's New Order in Indonesia. The mass killing of suspected PKI members and sympathizers marks one of the last century's greatest crimes, rivaling any other episode of state-led massacres for their indiscriminate and indefensible character.[110] The October 1st coup was, as Roosa rightly puts it, a "pretext for mass murder." Yet although the mass killings that ushered in the New Order were senseless and pointless in the extreme, a similar lack of logic cannot be ascribed to the broad elite coalition that arose in initial support of the Suharto regime. Considering the contentious circumstances in which it was founded, it should not be surprising that the new political dispensation received extremely broad and active elite support, as we shall see in the next chapter. A mere pretext of contentious class politics would have failed to secure such sweeping support for the Suharto regime from upper and middle classes.

One needs look no further than Marcos' Philippines to witness the limited centripetal pull of contentious politics as pretext. There, an increasingly autocratic elected president was broadly perceived as an instigator and even an author of urban violence, while anti-Marcos protest movements were seen by a wide range of elites to be credibly reformist, hopelessly disorganized, and devoid of any threatening claims to the Philippines' hallowed Catholic institutions. Indonesia's dictatorial birthpangs more closely resemble those of Malaysia, where an urban underclass fueled by communal outrage struck violently at supporters of Chinese-dominated leftist parties, combining class and communal conflicts in a way that no elite figure in the country could look upon with equanimity – especially given the echoes of the May 1969 violence with earlier episodes of Malay-Chinese carnage.

---

[110] For details on the obvious and deplorable American complicity and connivance in what was fundamentally a homegrown genocide, see Ibid. (188–197). For the best comparative analysis of the domestic political logics underpinning the Indonesian army's annihilation of the PKI, see Boudreau (2004, Ch. 3).

In sum, Marcos' narrative of "avant moi, le deluge" was by far the most uncon-
vincing among the three countries considered in this chapter – in part because
leftist and regional unrest did not precede Marcos' presidency at all. On the
continuum from protection rackets to protection pacts, authoritarianism in the
Philippines was most flagrantly founded upon a racket. Yet one must also appreciate the initial "flaws" in the Indonesian and Malaysian protection pacts as
they rose to power. (As noted in Chapter 1, ideal-typical protection pacts are
only approximated in real political life, never duplicated.) In Malaysia, many
Chinese perceived the ruling UMNO party to have been complicit if not explicitly supportive of the anti-Chinese riots. It is not hard to find Malaysian Chinese
who think of UMNO as a racketeer more than a legitimate protector – even
as the sincerity with which many Chinese worry aloud about renewed ethnic
unrest in the absence of a grand authoritarian ruling coalition is too unmistakable to ignore. Finally, Indonesia's anti-communist genocide ultimately proved
self-defeating for Suharto's protection pact, as his regime's tired invocation of a
PKI threat rang increasingly implausible as the years of the "red ants" faded into a
distant, post-extermination memory. It will be vital to keep the initial flaws in the
Indonesian and Malaysian protection pacts in mind as we consider the evolution
and ultimate fates of those countries' authoritarian Leviathans in Part III.

THE FOUNDATIONS AND FATES OF AUTHORITARIAN LEVIATHANS

6

Protection and Provision in Authoritarian Leviathans

Introduction

The outbreaks of contentious politics discussed in Chapter 5 marked a violent end to the postwar era of political pluralism in Malaysia, the Philippines, and Indonesia. New Southeast Asian authoritarian Leviathans were born at the height of the global "second reverse wave" of democratization, when electoral democracies – the only *real* dominoes of the Cold War era – were toppled throughout Asia, Africa, and Latin America. Like so many postcolonial countries, the Philippines restored democratic politics during the "third wave" of democratization that followed, in 1986. Indonesia's authoritarian Leviathan held on longer, surviving the end of the Cold War and enduring until 1998. In Malaysia, the UMNO-led authoritarian Leviathan remains in power to this day.

Why did authoritarian rule prove more durable in Malaysia than in Indonesia, and in Indonesia than in the Philippines?[1] This variation is best explained by variation in elite collective action, which is best explained in turn by the presence or absence of a *protection pact*: an elite coalition united by shared perceptions that a powerful authoritarian Leviathan represents a necessary bulwark against sociopolitical unrest. If elites have credible experiential grounds to associate authoritarianism with order and democracy with disorder, authoritarian rule can become so consolidated as to appear utterly permanent.

To understand this sense of authoritarian permanence, one must recognize that historical patterns of contentious politics shape more than elite attitudes and coalitions. They shape *institutions* as well. With their predilection to support the centralization of political authority, elite partners in protection pacts not only acquiesce to the imposition of open-ended authoritarianism. They also lend their support to authoritarian leaders' attempts to build a stronger state and ruling party, consolidating their regimes' grip on power. Specifically, four

---

[1] As ever, a regime's durability entails its political stability over time, not just its raw temporal duration.

sets of elites provide authoritarian regimes with the strategic resources they need
to develop a preponderant advantage in coercive, remunerative, and symbolic
power over any potential political opposition: (1) state officials, (2) economic
elites, (3) communal elites, and (4) middle classes. Party and state institutions
provide the vehicles for the orderly extraction of these elites' strategic resources
(e.g., taxes, party financing and membership, symbolic legitimation, electoral support, and coercive capacity) to take place. By contrast, where historical patterns
of contentious politics have produced no protection pact, elites remain highly
factionalized rather than broadly organized. Resources predominantly flow *away*
from the authoritarian Leviathan, not toward it. Without a strong coalitional
substructure, party, state, and regime institutions are as unstable as if they stood
upon sand.

This chapter traces the origins and evolution of authoritarian coalitions and
institutions in Malaysia, the Philippines, and Indonesia up to and until their
moments of most severe political crisis (to be examined in Chapter 7). While
Malaysia and the Philippines provide useful benchmarks of a highly stable protection pact and a highly unstable provision pact, respectively, Indonesia once again
serves as an informative intermediate case, where the authoritarian Leviathan's
defining coalitional logic gradually shifted from protection to provision – with
debilitating consequences for the Suharto regime's durability.[2]

Ordering Power via a Protection Pact: Malaysia's Strong State and Ruling Party, 1969–1997

Why not say bravely that the people of Malaysia are too immature for a workable democracy? Why not say that we need some form of authoritarian rule? We are doing that
anyway and *it looks as if we are going to do that for a very long time to come....* The racial composition of this country is such that real democratic process can promote as much ill-will
as authoritarian rule. *Authoritarian rule can at least produce a stable strong government....* We
must accept that there is not going to be a democracy in Malaysia.

                                                        Mahathir Mohamad, September 1969[3]

Only four months removed from the urban race riots of May 1969, one of
UMNO's most prominent politicians brashly proclaimed that Malaysian democracy was gone for good. Twelve years later, Mahathir Mohamad would become
Malaysia's fourth prime minister, and devote his two-plus decades in power to
proving his own prediction right. Even after Mahathir's resignation in 2003,
Malaysia's UMNO-led regime retained its hegemony over a political system that
continued to lack the fundamental individual and collective liberties that constitute and define democratic politics.

---

[2] This chapter's empirical sections are structured differently to best capture each case's distinct prevailing logic. Malaysia's powerful authoritarian institutions counsel an *institutional* approach. The
weakness of institutions in the Philippines recommends a focus on distinct *types of elites* under
authoritarianism. And Indonesia is analyzed *chronologically* to capture the Suharto regime's considerable coalitional and institutional evolution over time.

[3] Cited in Khoo (1995: 261). Emphasis added.

The Malaysian case exemplifies the importance of distinguishing between the attitudinal and institutional sources of durable authoritarianism. Even if elites perceive a declining need for authoritarian controls over time – as memories of past outbreaks of contentious politics fade – this does not mechanistically undermine the state and party institutions that underpin authoritarian rule. What we see in Malaysia is a gradual weakening of shared elite perceptions that authoritarian restrictions are essential to preserve the peaceful communal order: an attitudinal softening that has been more pronounced in the majority Malay than in the minority Chinese community. Yet Malaysia's strong state and ruling party coalition now have more than fear to sustain them – even though it was shared elite fear of communalized threats from below that made these institutions such effective vehicles for elite collective action *in the first place*. Decades of uninterrupted party-state rule have produced fixed routines, loyalties, and patterns of interaction that transcend any particular individuals' attitudes about the proper form of political order.

In this section, I aim to show that widely shared perceptions of endemic threat among Malaysian elites in the early 1970s were the vital factor giving authoritarian leaders the leverage to craft these stronger party and state institutions. These institutions ordered power for decades before the UMNO-led regime was put to its sternest test during the reformasi movement of 1998.

Ordering Power in the State: Coercive and Extractive Institutions

As we saw in Chapter 4, endemic and unmanageable threats from below inspired the construction of a strong and centralized state apparatus in Malaya in the decade following World War II. By the time of independence in 1957, the Malayan state was already noteworthy for the effectiveness of its coercive and administrative institutions. These initial processes of state-building were compounded and accelerated in the early 1970s, as the racial riots of May 1969 provided a powerful impetus for government leaders to strengthen their coercive grip and increase their fiscal demands upon the Malaysian population.[4] With economic elites, communal elites, and middle classes joining state officials in broad support of more authoritarian politics, government leaders enjoyed considerable elite acquiescence as they sought to extract the strategic resources necessary to reorder the Malaysian state.

The relative robustness of the Malaysian state begins, but by no means ends, with its coercive institutions. As Simon Barraclough argued twenty-five years ago, the government's policing powers have long been more than adequate to counter any threats to the regime as it defines them:

The physical capacity of the Malaysian Government to apply coercive measures is beyond question.... Malaysia is reputed to have one of the most efficient Special Branch forces in the region. In the event of demonstrations or acts of civil disobedience, an efficient communication system enables units of the Federal Reserve Unit (FRU) and Light Strike Force

---

[4] The May 1969 riots also occasioned an increased centralization of Malaysia's federal polity, as the country's thirteen constituent states became increasingly dependent on the strengthened political center. See Slater (2005: 283–285).

to speedily reinforce the constabulary. Should the necessity arise, the Royal Malaysian Police's para-military wing, the Special Field Force, may be called in. In the event of grave disorder, the army may be deployed, as was the case during the May 1969 communal riots.[5]

The Malaysian army underwent a major "buildup after 1969 [as] a response to racial rioting in that year," in order "to back up the government in the event of further communal conflict."[6] Yet military intervention has virtually never been necessary in the post-1969 period. Nor has the UMNO-led regime felt any need to mobilize or allow the mobilization of auxiliary, unofficial security forces to complement its own coercive power.

Malaysia's civilian police force has had precious little difficulty maintaining social stability on its own. This is partly because of its impressive internal capacity, and partly because even the regime's opponents have generally shared the regime's discomfort with disorderly political action in a context of endemic communal divisions. The regime has "justified its repressive apparatus" as being "necessary for the maintenance of order in a multicommunal society where *racial tensions could flare up and turn into violence at any moment*."[7] Such arguments have even tended to resonate among opposition leaders. "Most concede that the Special Branch has a legitimate function," even though opposition leaders have been the most frequent targets of a police force prone to "adopt a staunchly pro-regime stance."[8] This oppositionist acquiescence helps explain why "coercive acts have rarely produced dramatic or unmanageable responses," as little more than "boycotts and minor demonstrations have followed the detention of opposition figures, or the introduction of laws considered unduly coercive."[9] Even a critic of the Malaysian Leviathan's authoritarian controls such as Barraclough concludes: "Its use of coercion has, for the most part, been accepted by the general population as legitimate."[10]

In the decades since Barraclough made this argument, Malaysians have become more broadly critical of the government's coercive practices. But the UMNO-led regime was initially able to leverage this widespread attitude of acquiescence to assert state control over religious and student associations: two common sources of organized opposition to authoritarian rule. By nipping the autonomous organization of these social forces in the bud during the 1970s and 1980s, the government put itself in a stronger position to combat growing student and Islamic opposition in the late 1990s – as attitudes toward authoritarianism changed, but authoritarian institutions did not.

Tight control and close supervision of Islamic institutions date back to the colonial period, and even to before World War II. Yet government authorities tightened these practices of control and surveillance in response to outbreaks

---

[5] Barraclough (1985): 800.
[6] Crouch (1996): 134–135.
[7] Ibid. 95. Emphasis added.
[8] Barraclough (1985): 810.
[9] Ibid. 802.
[10] Ibid. 820.

of contentious politics in the 1940s, 1950s, and 1960s, and have strengthened their grip over political Islam throughout Malaysia's authoritarian era. "A vast expansion of the Federal religious bureaucracy was projected" in the early to mid-1970s.[11] Especially after Mahathir Mohamad's rise to the prime minister-ship in 1981, "the UMNO government launched an unprecedented degree of restructuring, both in scale and in scope, of Islamic institutions," writes Kikue Hamayotsu. "The government tackled the key areas of: *Shari'ah* (Islamic) courts and the judicial establishment, mosques, religious schools and *zakat* (Islamic tithe) collection, as well as religious officialdom in general and *ulama* (Islamic scholars) in particular."[12] No state institution was more vital in these processes than the Religious Affairs Department within the Prime Minister's Department: "when the Department was first established in 1968, it held a staff of 8; by 1987 this fig-ure had grown to 608. The bureaucratization of religious authority.... allowed for the control of increasing religious diversity perceived as a challenge to the Administration's authority."[13]

These state institutions provide ample capacity for coercion and control of Islamic forces. Federal overseers of Islamic practice exhibit an "ISA mentality," and a readiness to apply "[a]uthoritarian and punitive measures" against religious activists. Even when Muslim scholars and imams refrain from expressing alter-native views in the political sphere, state officials often extend their tentacles into houses of worship to nip "incorrect Islamic teachings" in the bud. "The list of criteria and features of these apparently erroneous teachings is vague and gener-alized, and could easily be misused to silence discussion and debate of the legal or religious measures introduced by the state."[14]

In much the same way that the UMNO-led regime's broad support among Muslim elites gives it leverage to crack down on Muslim oppositionists, the coali-tion's considerable backing from students prevents any wider political eruptions when the state represses student activism. Malaysia witnessed only one major outbreak of student protest between the birth of the authoritarian Leviathan and the reformasi movement in 1998:

In 1974, both prosecutions and detentions without trial were used against students and academic staff involved in mobilizing mass demonstrations.... Following extensive stu-dent demonstrations in December 1974, even tougher measures were adopted. A number of marches were dispersed by elements of the Federal Reserve Unit and Police Field Force, more than 1,000 students were arrested for illegal assembly, and a number of stu-dent leaders and academic staff were detained under the Internal Security Act.... Such stern measures, combined with subsequent legislation further restricting student political involvement, effectively ended campus-based political activism in Malaysia.[15]

Whereas state repression has tended to galvanize and unify university students against authoritarian regimes in the Philippines and Indonesia, it has fragmented

[11] Nair (1997): 31.
[12] Hamayotsu (2002): 358.
[13] Nair (1997): 34.
[14] Othman (2003): 128.
[15] Barraclough (1985): 814.

campus communities and demoralized student oppositionists in Malaysia. This is due in part to the cohesion and efficiency of Malaysia's police forces, which make coercion against student protestors both swift and certain. It is also due to widespread student acquiescence to the notion that the authoritarian Leviathan plays a necessary stabilizing role in an inherently unstable society. Malaysian students have contradicted Samuel Huntington's dictum that "[s]tudents are the universal opposition; they oppose whatever regime exists in their society."[16] Instead, Malaysian students have historically played a low-key and supportive political role in a society where "the consensus is for a strong government capable of maintaining political stability."[17] Even as we witness "a growing sense of resentment on the part of Malaysia's growing middle-class against the regime's preoccupation with restricting the realm of political participation"[18] – most dramatically expressed during the reformasi protests of the late 1990s – the UMNO-led regime's institutional advantages over actual and potential political opposition remain enormous.

This is as true of the Malaysian state's administrative institutions as its coercive institutions. We have already seen in Chapter 4 how the central Malayan government imposed progressive direct income and corporate taxes and introduced the Employees' Provident Fund (EPF) against the backdrop of contentious leftist politics in the late 1940s and early 1950s. The tight intertwining of class and communal grievances in the riots of May 1969 left Malaysia's Chinese economic elites doubly vulnerable, and doubly desperate for state assistance in defusing social conflict. This put the UMNO leadership in an extremely strong position when devising its response to the communal bloodshed. "Arguing that Malay participation in the 1969 riots had expressed merely economic deprivation and resentment of the non-Malay wealth.... UMNO declared that the way to end this explosive economic disparity was for the government to promote rapid Malay economic advancement," writes Clive Kessler. "While this had always been part of UMNO policy, it was now to be pursued with an unprecedented determination, and with vast government resources."[19]

The cornerstone of this approach was the New Economic Policy. Introduced in 1971, the NEP marked a dramatic shift in the balance of power between the (Malay-dominated) state and the (Chinese-dominated) private sector. "Malays and Malay interests (that is, government trust agencies and state enterprises) were targeted to own at least 30 per cent of the share capital of the corporate sector by 1990, from a base of less than 2 per cent in 1970."[20] To some degree, restructuring could be achieved without expropriation of Chinese firms. Yet the NEP still delivered a tremendous blow to Malaysia's Chinese bourgeois stratum. "In short, Malay economic and political ascendancy was inflicting a blow to the status and identity of the Chinese business community," argues James Jesudason. "Just like the Malays before them, the Chinese were fearing for their future in society. If, in the past, Chinese economic preponderance compensated somewhat

[16] Huntington (1991): 144.
[17] Faruqi (1995): 15.
[18] Barraclough (1985): 820.
[19] Kessler (1980): 7.
[20] Jesudason (1989): 71–72.

for their subordinate political position, now it appeared that they were losing everything."[21]

The NEP both exemplified and expanded the extractive power of the Malaysian state. Such a concerted effort to reshape the country's corporate sector would have been impossible in the Philippines, where clientelistic and dyadic relationships *between* state officials and economic elites tend to be stronger than the formally institutionalized relationships *within* the state apparatus itself. "The NEP itself was in a sense a product of Malaysia's bureaucracy,"[22] argues Natasha Hamilton-Hart. "Clearly, it was not going to be the lack of elite unity that would potentially derail the state's economic objectives,"[23] adds Jesudason. State cohesion assured the relatively efficient extraction of corporate wealth into government trusts and corporations. While corruption and favoritism have marred the *distribution* of wealth from state agencies, the bountiful assets of these agencies are a tribute to their effective *collection* in the first place.

Although Chinese businessmen lobbied intensely to shield their enterprises from state restructuring, no one in the corporate sector was untouchable. Not only were Malaysia's most powerful corporate figures forced to sell shares to state agencies and new Malay tycoons – they were forced to do so at a substantial discount. Even H.S. Lee, a co-founder of the MCA and the country's first finance minister, was not spared the axe; Lee transferred a 30% stake in his bank, Malaysia's sixth-largest, to a Malay timber magnate in 1975. "The fact that even the company of a former government minister had to restructure in favor of Malay interests showed the difficulty of large Chinese companies getting immunity from restructuring."[24]

This accumulation of corporate assets has complemented the state's fiscal power, which was substantial even before the 1969 riots kindled Leviathan's extractive appetite. Malaysia's "percentage of government revenue to national income was the highest in South-East Asia" as early as the mid-1960s.[25] Mukul Asher remarks upon the clear spike in Malaysian revenues after the 1969 crisis, and traces the increase to the growing redistributive demands of Malay popular sectors:

The tax effort indicator for Malaysia, after generally stagnating in the 1960s, showed a rapid rise in the 1970s. Indeed, its tax effort indicator is the highest among the ASEAN countries. It is more than three times that of Indonesia, if oil revenues are excluded, and almost twice that of Thailand. The main reason for this high ratio is the conscious policy of using the government sector to increase the relative share of national income going to bumiputras.[26] This policy has resulted in a very high level of government expenditure to G.D.P. (about 35 per cent in 1977), thus necessitating a corresponding rise in the tax effort as well.[27]

---

[21] Ibid. 133.
[22] Hamilton-Hart (2002): 111.
[23] Jesudason (1989): 80.
[24] Ibid. 106.
[25] Ibid. 49.
[26] Bumiputra means "sons of the soil" in Malay, reflecting Malays' claim to indigenous status.
[27] Asher (1980): 16. This revenue came largely from direct taxation, allowing state revenue to balloon even further during the economic boom that began in the mid-1980s. "The subsequent rapid

While redistributive pressures help explain why Malaysian authorities had such a strong *incentive* to increase their tax yield after 1969, they do not explain the state's *capacity* to do so. This was in part a legacy of earlier bouts of state-building, which made it easier for the bureaucracy to be "disciplined and effective when it came to such tasks as revenue-gathering and data-collecting."[28] Yet the bigger point is that state strength fundamentally depended on the ruling regime's capacity to order power from economic elites. As Syed Farid Alatas puts it: "the Malaysian state was internally strong in comparison to the Indonesian state and this is accounted for by the fact that *dominant class support was forthcoming in the former while it was absent in the latter*."[29] State power is a function not only of its own institutions, but of the broader coalitional environment in which it operates: "internal state strength implies that the state has the resources of the dominant class available to it, whether this is in the form of tax revenues, election funds or parliamentary support."[30]

The UMNO-led regime has enjoyed access to all these resources and more – while extracting power resources from groups other than Alatas' "dominant class" of economic elites. Most notably, the Employees Provident Fund (EPF) has provided an ideal institutional mechanism for the state to sink its fiscal claws into Malaysia's middle class. "The EPF has been the major source of funds for the government."[31] Like direct taxation, the EPF's origins and subsequent strengthening have followed the rhythms of contentious politics. Founded at the peak of the Emergency in 1951, the EPF grew in importance in the wake of the ethnic riots of 1969. It has played such a prominent role in Malaysian public finance because of its broad scope of coverage, its steep rates of mandatory contribution, and the administrative effectiveness with which compulsory contributions have been collected.

In terms of coverage, the EPF managed to cover 500,000 members and 12,000 employers at its inception in the early 1950s.[32] Thanks to this broad coverage, it already held ten times the assets of Malaysia's private pension funds combined by 1965, to the tune of M$160 million.[33] This was chicken feed compared to the EPF's haul after 1969, however. In 1971, "the law ceased to allow any new private provident funds to be established," and "all employees irrespective of wages and size of their establishments were covered by the EPF on a compulsory basis." This ensured that the financial savings arising from Malaysia's economic boom would accrue to the state, not just to the private sector. By 1994, the EPF was collecting compulsory contributions from 6.6 million employees and 210,000 employers, generating more than M$64 billion in reserves.[34]

economic growth resulted in significant revenue collections for the federal government, *especially from income tax on corporations and individuals*. The income tax collection increased from RM6.1 billion in 1987 to RM7.3 billion in 1989" (Herbert [1994]: 126, emphasis added).

[28] Hamilton-Hart (2002): 111.
[29] Alatas (1997): 119. Emphasis added.
[30] Ibid.
[31] Herbert (1994): 127.
[32] Salehuddin (1994): 259.
[33] Edwards (1970): 284.
[34] Salehuddin (1994): 259. At 1994 exchange rates, this amounted to about US$25 billion.

Not only was the EPF collecting contributions from 89% of the Malaysian workforce by the early 1990s.[35] Its rates of contribution from both employers and employees, along with those in Singapore next door, were "the highest in the world."[36] Starting at a 5% mandatory contribution from both employers and employees in 1952, rates were raised incrementally in 1975, 1980, and 1993 to extract 10% of paychecks from employees and 12% from employers.[37] In sum, the Malaysian state was collecting 22% of the salary of 89% of the Malaysian workforce through the EPF, in addition to the country's already high rates of direct taxation.

To be sure, societal compliance with mandatory contributions to a pension fund is less problematic than compliance with direct taxes. Such funds are ultimately remitted back to the contributors, typically with a modest return on their investment. Yet the time-lag between collection and payout is measured in decades, meaning that state authorities enjoy a large surplus of funds to play with. Nor is compliance totally unproblematic. "Administrative and compliance practices and norms, including enforcement of penalties, need to be set so as to minimize employee-employer collusion, or employer evasion."[38] In other words, state capacity is a must. "The administrative ability to collect and manage funds is a condition of such appropriation," writes Hamilton-Hart. "To enforce contributions, the EPF developed an active field inspection staff in its early years and published information on defaulting employers. The 7,236 prosecutions of employers between 1990 and 1994 suggests vigorous enforcement."[39]

As if Malaysia's NEP, EPF, and direct tax system were not enough to make the state a paragon of fiscal power, the country was also a beneficiary of the oil booms of the 1970s. Since Malaysia's extractive institutions had already been performing comparatively well for decades, this influx of discretionary funds flowed into capable administrative hands. As a result, petroleum wealth has not suppressed tax effort in other areas. For instance, non-oil corporate taxes amounted to nearly twice the haul of taxes on oil companies from 1987–94.[40] The state oil firm, Petronas, has certainly been associated with a number of financial boondoggles as it was enlisted to help bankroll Malaysia's heavy-industry drive of the late 1970s and early 1980s, as well as the UMNO-led privatization policies of the 1990s. Yet the firm has been quite professionally run, helping Petronas maintain enormous financial reserves for the past thirty years.

In sum, the Malaysian state expanded both its coercive and fiscal power in the wake of the Kuala Lumpur race riots of May 1969. The state's success was predicated on its capacity to extract resources and command compliance from economic elites, communal elites, middle classes, and officials within the state apparatus. The main beneficiary of this powerful state has been the authoritarian regime that controls it. Regime durability has been due both to the capacity of

---

[35] Hamilton-Hart (2002): 148.
[36] Asher (1994): 238.
[37] Salehuddin (1994): 259.
[38] Asher (1994): 245–246.
[39] Hamilton-Hart (2002): 148–149.
[40] Kasipillai and Shanmugam (1996): 143–144.

the state that the UMNO-led regime has commanded, and to the cohesion and robustness of the UMNO-led party coalition itself – to which we now turn.

Ordering Power in the Ruling Parties: Gathering Members, Money, and Votes

Access to political power in Malaysia has been consistently monopolized by party institutions rather than military institutions. Malaysia's prime minister is always the president of UMNO, and his cabinet always comprises leading figures in the constituent parties of the ruling Barisan Nasional (BN), or National Front – as the Alliance was renamed and reconfigured after 1969. For any Malaysian politician with national aspirations, to be expelled from a BN party is to be cast into the political wilderness.

Why has Malaysia's ruling party coalition been so immune to the sort of unbridled elite factionalism that has decimated parties and undermined authoritarian regimes throughout so much of the world? Much like the Malaysian state, Malaysia's parties have derived their strength from their historical success at the twin tasks of *extraction* and *organization*. The BN has been extraordinarily successful at recruiting members, collecting party finance, and generating votes on behalf of its member parties. Such impressive elite collective action originated in response to especially threatening and challenging types of contentious politics.

Members

Ruling parties' social power typically rests upon a broad middle-class membership. As seen in Chapter 4, the two core parties of the ruling Alliance – UMNO and the MCA – were already broad-based organizations well before the 1969 riots. They were not only strong internally; they were also tightly wedded together as a coalition. These internal and collective party strengths initially developed in direct response to the threats and challenges of leftist Chinese mass mobilization during the decade following World War II. The riots of 1969 would have a similar strengthening effect on elite collection action, both within and among the ruling coalition's member parties. As regime change converted Malaysia's ruling coalition from a democratic electoral alliance into an authoritarian protection pact, the party coalition was both broadened and tightened.

The UMNO-led coalition was broadened by incorporating former opposition parties into the government fold. With its rebirth as the BN, "[t]he former Alliance's most successful political opponents were strategically removed from the oppositionist front."[41] The BN grew to encompass both the Chinese-dominated Gerakan party, which had trounced the Alliance in Penang in the May 1969 election, and the Islam-oriented PAS, which had prevailed in Kelantan and Trengganu. UMNO leaders appointed the heads of PAS and Gerakan to front the National Operations Council's security bodies in Kelantan and Penang, respectively. Beyond offering such carrots of power-sharing, the expansion of the BN threatened opposition parties with the stick of permanent exclusion. "The choice for the leaders of opposition parties was to either join the ruling party and

---

[41] Khoo (1997): 58.

have a small amount of influence and prestige, or remain as opposition parties with their hands tied."[42] For PAS in particular, it seemed likely that with a more authoritarian system being introduced, "new political restrictions would prevent it from operating as an opposition force."[43]

Yet it was *shared* fears of endemic communal instability among Malay and Chinese elites – not oppositionists' fears of increased authoritarian repression – that best explain the decision by Gerakan and PAS to join and support the BN. When PAS leader Mohammed Asri presented the case to join the BN at the PAS General Assembly in July 1972, he told his followers that "UMNO shared similar views on the two crucial issues of security and development. *Communism and communalism represented an immediate serious threat to security, and their containment required greater national unity.*"[44] In sum, "[t]he [1969] election and its immediate aftermath led Malays to feel that non-Malays were on the verge of seizing political power, and they closed ranks to prevent this."[45]

In 1977, PAS departed the BN coalition, and returned to oppositional politics. This was because it was far harder, given PAS' base in areas with only a tiny Chinese minority, for UMNO to invoke the language of communal threat to keep the party in line.[46] Once the BN had seemingly restabilized the political order and brought Chinese communalism into check, the specter of a Chinese bid for power had dimmed. Chinese-led opposition parties remained a threat to win parliamentary constituencies in areas with large Chinese populations, however. This helps explain PAS' consistent failure to displace UMNO as the party of choice for Malay voters outside the Malay heartland.

Unlike PAS, Gerakan has stayed in the BN until the present day. Shared Chinese fears of continued Malay violence were even more palpable than shared Malay fears of a Chinese power-grab in the wake of the May 1969 riots. As Jomo K.S. writes, "it was by no means a given" that the Malay majority and Malay-dominated security forces would not seek "to systematically eliminate the non-Malays."[47] To be sure, patronage gives Gerakan a powerful reason to stay within the BN ranks as well.[48] But one cannot understand either Gerakan's readiness to join the BN in the first place, or the party's continued electoral success among voters who do not enjoy access to patronage flows, without grasping the unifying

---

[42] Jesudason (1989): 77.

[43] Kessler (1980): 8.

[44] Funston (1980): 250. Emphasis added.

[45] Ibid. 293–294.

[46] PAS was expelled from the BN when federal authorities declared emergency rule in Kelantan and forcibly displaced the PAS leadership. Yet the crisis itself was precipitated by PAS' unwillingness to follow UMNO dictates in Kelantan, exemplifying UMNO's weaker leverage in parts of Malaysia lacking large Chinese populations. See Crouch (1996: 104–106) for an overview of the PAS-UMNO split.

[47] Jomo (1990): 144.

[48] Patronage has played a larger role in keeping ruling parties in the East Malaysian states of Sabah and Sarawak – where ethnic politics is dramatically different from the peninsula's – under the BN's wing. Yet East Malaysia's parties have only been convinced that loyalty to the BN is the best way to continue securing patronage because the BN has ordered power on the peninsula so completely to begin with.

effect of the 1969 riots on the Chinese population as a whole, and the importance of lingering perceptions that such anti-Chinese violence could be rekindled if Chinese voters were once again to abandon the UMNO-led coalition.

Not only did UMNO and the MCA strengthen their position in this period by bringing new parties into the BN; they did so by building their own parties up. Most important, the riots had indicated that "an immediate imperative was the strengthening of UMNO":[49]

The return to parliamentary government saw a general move to strengthen existing political parties. Steps taken by UMNO included: constitutional changes to tighten party discipline, project a more dynamic image, and emphasize the dominant role of the party in government; strengthening the party secretariat in a bid to ensure greater efficiency; efforts to attract "intellectuals" and youths, while easing out the corrupt or ineffectual; a much freer mobilization of finance than in the past, complemented by the use of civilian bureaucracy; and a fresh attempt to create an ideological basis for the party.[50]

Such revitalization efforts may be a necessary condition for ruling party renewal, but they are far from sufficient. Party leaders must also find a receptive audience in wider society, especially among the middle classes who prove so pivotal in providing or denying their support to incumbents. On this front, UMNO's success at regenerating its public support was resounding:

The response was overwhelming. Virtually all the Bureaux numbered senior civil servants or academics among their members. Both groups also assisted the party by presenting working papers on various topics, and by other means: in early 1975 the head of the major Malay literary organization, expressing the mood of many educated Malays, declared that the present government genuinely represented the aspirations of Malaysian nationalism and hence should be fully supported.[51]

UMNO thus gained ground among Malay middle classes by swerving in a more authoritarian direction. "Disenchantment arose not merely over the outcome of the 1969 elections but with democracy itself."[52] The aftermath of the riots saw the gradual replacement of Tunku Abdul Rahman's moderate leadership with the rise of the UMNO "ultras," led by new Prime Minister Tun Abdul Razak. When the most outspoken member of this group, Mahathir Mohamad, condemned the Tunku for being so "deeply committed to the idea of Sino-Malay partnership in government,"[53] UMNO elites were slow to take Mahathir's side: "but he gained even stronger support from Malay academics and tertiary students. The latter held mass demonstrations against the Tunku and denounced his policies."[54]

---

[49] Funston (1980): 294.
[50] Ibid. 235.
[51] Ibid. 237.
[52] Goh (1971): 17.
[53] Ibid. 30.
[54] Funston (1980): 224.

The Malaysian case is noteworthy for the active support lent by urban middle classes to the authoritarian Leviathan *at its very inception*. As Goh Cheng Teik describes Malay students' response to the Mahathir-Tunku imbroglio: "This allegation of softness and weakness on the [Tunku's] part towards MCA and the Chinese gained wide currency, especially among the Malay-medium school teachers and high-school and college students."[55] A conference of Malay university students in April 1970 urged the Tun Razak-led NOC to stay in power for as long as necessary – in other words, not to restore competitive elections – until racial leveling had been achieved. When one Malay student group backed Mahathir in an anti-Tunku rally in July 1969, their protest was joined by a significant number of university lecturers.[56] When UMNO promulgated its new ideology in May 1971, it "explained that democracy as practiced in developed countries could not be followed since priority had to be given to unity and government intervention on behalf of the poor."[57] What is striking is not that UMNO made this claim, but that its authoritarian turn received such broad and boisterous elite support.

UMNO's heightened popularity after 1969 was expressed in the broadening of party membership. In quantitative terms, the party surpassed a membership of 500,000 by 1976, and surpassed the two-million-member mark by 1996.[58] These foot soldiers were "arrayed in 3,500 branches and 165 divisions" as of the mid-1990s. In qualitative terms, the party transcended its pre-1969 foundations in the "administocratic"[59] elite of aristocrats (communal elites) and civil servants (state officials), as well as schoolteachers (middle classes). UMNO made tremendous strides in recruiting the emergent Malay business class (economic elites) and Islamic activists (communal elites, again) from the onset of the BN era. The co-optation of Islamic social forces achieved its greatest success in 1982, when UMNO lured the leadership of Malaysia's Muslim youth movement, ABIM,[60] away from PAS, and incorporated the group under the UMNO umbrella.

One must not only consider the impressive breadth of UMNO's membership, but also assess the terms under which new social forces have been incorporated into the party. UMNO has not seen its protection pact replaced wholesale with a purely patronage-based provision pact. Yet it is clear that the logic of collective action qua communal self-protection has weakened among the Malay population in recent decades. Writing in 1996, James Jesudason captured the uncertainty and increasing plasticity of Malays' shared threat perceptions on the threshold of reformasi. On the one hand, Jesudason noted "real anxieties" among Malays regarding their communal status. "Clearly the efficacy of ethnic appeals has not been a simple process of manipulation by the political elite."[61] Yet among the

---

[55] Goh (1971): 30–31.
[56] Ibid. 31–32, fn. 12.
[57] Funston (1980): 238.
[58] These estimates come from Dancz (1987: 155) and Case (1996: 121).
[59] The term was coined in Jomo (1986).
[60] ABIM stands for Angkatan Belia Islam Malaysia, or the Malaysian Islamic Youth Movement.
[61] Jesudason (1996): 133.

new Malay elite, attitudes of self-confidence appeared to be gradually displacing worries about self-protection:

There are indications that ethnicity has become less salient for the Malay corporate class as its ability to accumulate becomes increasingly based on general economic growth rather than direct state sponsorship. *Even the Malay middle class has developed an instrumental attitude to the UMNO, and is showing evidence of shedding its deep ethnic attachment to the party.* As many as 400,000 of more than two million UMNO members have failed to register to vote, many of them from the rich and middle-class strata. The leaders of the UMNO have expressed bewilderment at this development, having expected the party to become even stronger as Malays became better off.[62]

Luckily for UMNO, the protection pact has been slower to erode among the Chinese population than the Malays. Even as the MCA and Gerakan acquiesced to an NEP-style system that privileges the Malays, the parties consistently out-organized and out-polled their fervently anti-NEP rivals in the DAP. This only makes sense when one realizes that the BN has been perceived by many of its supporters as the only arrangement capable of protecting the Chinese from a far graver fate. May 1969 ushered in the era of the "lowered expectations of the Chinese community."[63]

Chinese nightmare scenarios initially centered less on Malay votes than on Malay violence. The MCA had generated its social power in the 1940s and 1950s by countering violent Chinese mobilization from below, and its robustness increased as it reorganized in the early 1970s to counter violent Malay mass mobilization. In short, the MCA "began to assume a 'new look,'" as "over a very short period of time, the MCA succeeded in getting itself rejuvenated," writes Loh Kok Wah. "The familiar call for Chinese unity behind the MCA actually began to be realized."[64] Again, contentious politics lay behind increased elite collective action: "In the aftermath of the May 13 incident, the slogan of Chinese unity seemed particularly apt and appealing."[65]

Even many long-term supporters of Chinese opposition parties had become convinced by the violence that cooperation with UMNO was the sensible route. "In order to understand their preference for the MCA, we must realize that one of the lessons of May 13 was that support for the opposition parties which fared so well in the 1969 elections had only resulted in communal violence, political instability and the dissolution of Parliament; none of which had benefited the Chinese."[66] By late 1971, the spirit of the unity movement was finding expression in grassroots party-building within the MCA, as "labor seminars were organized; public service bureaux to help the illiterate apply for land, citizenship and passport were initiated; even a Hawkers' Committee and an Urban Development Committee to monitor the Kuala Lumpur Federal Territory Development plans

[62] Ibid. 156. Emphasis added.
[63] Heng (1988): 277.
[64] Loh (1982): 3.
[65] Ibid. 13.
[66] Ibid. 18.

so as to ensure that it would be fair to all sectors of the community were set up."[67] By late 1971, it was clear that the MCA was undergoing nothing less than a "spectacular rejuvenation."[68] As of 1983, the party's total membership had surpassed 500,000.[69]

The Alliance's brush with disaster in 1969 thus led to the rejuvenation of both UMNO and the MCA, along with the broadening of the party coalition into the wider BN. The ruling parties' domination in raw manpower during the post-1969 era has had a mutually reinforcing effect on their preponderance of power in two other critical areas: party finance and electoral support.

Money

Political finance loves a winner, and campaign donations in Malaysia have overwhelmingly favored UMNO and its BN partners over the opposition. During Malaysia's era of parliamentary democracy from 1957–1969, the MCA was the primary beneficiary of donations from economic elites, while UMNO became deeply dependent on MCA largesse for its funding needs. "Chinese businessmen almost exclusively made contributions to the MCA" in this period, writes Jesudason. "It was thus able to contribute a larger than proportional share to the Alliance party's coffers for electioneering and organizational purposes, compensating to some extent its weaker vote-pulling capacity in comparison to UMNO."[70]

The BN period has seen UMNO's financial machine surpass the money-making capacity of the MCA. If UMNO's initial financial weakness was directly due to "[t]he dearth of wealthy businessmen in the party,"[71] the wholesale recruitment of new Malay economic elites into UMNO during the NEP era has dramatically changed this state of affairs. The post-1969 period has seen UMNO "mobilize greater financial resources in pursuit of its goals," writes John Funston. "None of the usual pre-1969 complaints about a financial shortage were aired, and occasional reference to financial affairs in annual reports are an impressive indication of financial liquidity." UMNO is not simply living off its direct access to state funds, but is swimming in "money given by the private sector for the party's use."[72]

What is most exceptional about party finance in Malaysia is not that economic elites provide so much financing to the political leadership, but that the cohesion of that leadership allows such funds to be concentrated rather than dispersed among warring factions. As with state-building, effective party-building involves not just extraction, but *a combination of extraction and organization*. When the murky world of UMNO political finance was briefly illuminated by public accusations of corruption against the Chief Minister of Selangor state, it became

[67] Ibid. 21.
[68] Ibid. 22.
[69] Dancz (1987): 217.
[70] Jesudason (1989): 53–54.
[71] Heng (1988): 164.
[72] Funston (1980): 237–238.

apparent that political finance was benefiting UMNO as a whole, and not just individual party leaders:

Just before the UMNO General Assembly in July 1976, it was disclosed in the High Court during the corruption trial of Dato Harun Idris that since 1959 Tun Razak, first as UMNO Deputy President, then as UMNO President had been operating a "special fund" to which huge firms and industries, in the private sector, apart from local millionaires, had been contributing on a regular basis.... *The money collected was apparently used for party purposes such as election campaigns.*[73]

None of this is to say that BN leaders never strip state assets or feather their own nests. The point is that, with so many copious sources of party finance on hand, individual party members can skim off the top without putting the financial viability of their party at risk. An excellent example is Multi-Purpose Holdings (MPH), established by the MCA as its own corporate arm in 1975 "to pool Chinese economic resources."[74] As UMNO leaders pushed through regulations to sharpen the extractive bite of NEP restructuring policies on Chinese firms, the MCA took the lead in organizing elite collective action in response, via the MPH. "Such was Chinese trepidation over these legislations and agencies which increased state controls over the private sector that Chinese, particularly small and medium-sized, companies were *compelled to overlook narrow clan divisions* to participate in a 'corporatization movement.'"[75]

MPH permitted the MCA to order power from Chinese economic elites and middle classes in much the same way that the UMNO-run state uses the Employees Provident Fund (EPF) to order power on behalf of the ruling regime. "Strongly supported by the Chinese middle class and co-operatives, MPH's paid-up capital escalated from $87.2 million in 1980 to $450 million in 1982."[76] While the party gained from MPH, select MCA leaders benefited even more. By the mid-1980s, several company directors were imprisoned for siphoning millions of dollars into personal accounts.

Yet the theft of golden eggs does not kill the geese that lay them. As time has passed, MPH has been superseded by an array of semi-private, semi-public holding companies in which corporate proxies hold shares on behalf of prominent politicians.[77] The vital point remains, however, that no businessman gets rich without great connections to BN leaders, and no businessman is totally immune from the party-state's fiscal demands. Malaysia's economic boom has not diverted remunerative power from state to non-state actors, but enriched political and economic elites in tandem.

Votes

Once every four or five years, the BN puts its power preponderance over the political opposition to the test in national elections. The coalition's dominance

---

73 Chandra (1979): 127. Emphasis added.
74 Jesudason (1989): 155.
75 Gomez (1999): 183. Emphasis added.
76 Jesudason (1989): 157.
77 Gomez and Jomo (1999) is the consummate study.

in money, manpower, and machinery combines with authoritarian controls on opposition organization and media expression, as well as a highly gerrymandered electoral map, to ensure that BN victories are never in doubt. The fact that elections take place at all is more of a testament to the impenetrability of the BN's authoritarian hegemony than to its democratic credentials. If elections are a surefire win, why not hold them? As Goh Cheng Teik put it at the birth of the BN era, UMNO leaders seem inclined to support the electoral exercise only so long as it does "not hinder UMNO from enjoying and exercising a preponderance of political power."[78]

The six general elections from 1974–95 gave consistent credence to BN confidence. In terms of parliamentary seats, these six elections gave the BN an advantage over all opposition parties of 135–19 in 1974; 131–23 in 1978; 132–22 in 1982; 148–29 in 1986; 127–53 in 1990; and 162–30 in 1995. With the sole exception of the DAP's 24–22 victory in seats over MCA and Gerakan in 1986, neither Chinese nor Malay opposition parties ever outpolled their ethnic competitors in the BN.[79] Considering that "Malaysian elections have not been characterized by widespread fraudulent practices such as ballot-box stuffing or blatant physical pressure on voters,"[80] these results indicate that BN parties have consistently commanded significant social support.

This electoral might compounds the BN's domination over remunerative, coercive, and symbolic power in the Malaysian polity. Since these power sources firmly reside in *party and state institutions* rather than individual leaders enjoying charismatic or traditional authority, even the most talented and popular politicians cannot win power without working through BN parties. Factional fights repeatedly arise, to be sure; but they resemble a struggle within a swarm of mosquitoes, in which each mosquito fights to get closer to a solitary lamppost on a pitch-black night. Fights over control of BN parties are so intense precisely because to lose is to be relegated to the political darkness.

Ironically, UMNO's capacity to order power was most dramatically expressed during the party's worst experience of internal *disorder* in the mid- to late 1980s. Shrinking patronage resources during an economic recession led to increased discontent with Mahathir Mohamad's leadership, and gave rise to a dissident movement within the party to wrest the UMNO presidency (and hence the prime ministership) from his hands.[81] Critically, the dissidents did not wish to *leave* UMNO, but to *seize* it. Mahathir barely survived the challenge of former finance minister Tengku Razaleigh, winning an intra-party vote by a narrow 761–718 margin in April 1987. UMNO was thus split into Mahathir's "Team A" and Razaleigh's "Team B." The dissidents challenged the victory of Team A in court, arguing that Mahathir had received illegal votes from unregistered party branches. In a stunning decision, the court ruled that the existence of such unregistered branches not only nullified the results of the Mahathir-Razaleigh runoff, but invalidated UMNO itself as an organization.

[78] Goh (1971): 40.
[79] Numbers tabulated from Crouch (1996: 75).
[80] Ibid. 57.
[81] The following discussion draws heavily on Ibid. (118–121).

In the legal wrangling that followed, one point was abundantly clear: both factions desperately wanted to receive recognition as the "real" UMNO. Team B attempted to register itself as a new party called UMNO Malaysia, while Team A tried to gain official recognition as UMNO Baru (New UMNO). Thanks to Mahathir's control over the home ministry, only Team A was permitted to retain the gilded acronym. UMNO's sizable financial assets were thus transferred to the "new" UMNO, while Razaleigh's Team B dissidents were left in the cold.

Despite the bitterness and breadth of the factional dispute, only twelve of UMNO's 83 members in parliament defected. Nearly 49% of party members had sided with Razaleigh in his quest to become UMNO leader, but less than 15% of UMNO parliamentarians were willing to continue supporting him after he left the party. At the end of the day, all Malay politicians know that UMNO is where the votes, money, and members are. Razaleigh put as brave of a face as he could on the situation, vowing to "continue the struggle of the old UMNO" in the guise of a new party called "Semangat '46 (Spirit of '46), referring to the year of UMNO's foundation in 1946."[82] The upstart party captured only eight parliamentary seats in 1990, and a paltry six seats in 1995. Semangat '46 subsequently dissolved, and its members returned to the UMNO fold.

The fizzling of Tengku Razaleigh's challenge was by no means the first example of a highly popular and powerful politician crashing and burning after bucking or being expelled from a BN (or Alliance) party. When UMNO founder and Malay national hero Onn Jaafar bolted the party in a factional dispute in 1951, his upstart Independence of Malaya Party (IMP) was crushed by the UMNO-MCA Alliance in both the 1952 and 1955 elections – despite active British support for Onn's IMP. UMNO leaders similarly succeeded in expelling Selangor Chief Minister Harun Idris on corruption charges in 1975, and imprisoning him the following year. Although described as "an effective populist politician able to mobilize widespread support" whose "rising popularity within the party made him a potential threat" to Tun Razak's leadership, Harun was killed off politically with no serious reverberations.[83]

Factionalism within the MCA has exhibited similar dynamics. Party president Lim Chong Eu left the party in 1959 in protest over UMNO's refusal to let the MCA contest as many seats as it wished; but the MCA survived his departure with nary an electoral hiccup, and Lim returned to the ruling coalition as head of Gerakan after the 1969 riots. Similarly, the MCA suffered a nasty split in 1973 over party elites' refusal to let the popular young leaders of the "Chinese Unity Movement" ascend the party ranks. Much as Tengku Razaleigh and Harun Idris had wished to control UMNO rather than oppose it, MCA dissident leader Lim Keng Yaik insisted that "the Party was the best vehicle to achieve Chinese unity and to cooperate with the other communities, 'but that the machinery must be streamlined in order for it to function effectively.'"[84] Lim and his allies were expelled, and fifty MCA branches comprising 3,500 members bolted the party

---

[82] Ibid. 121.
[83] Crouch (1996): 100.
[84] Loh (1982): 65.

in support of Lim's group. Rather than heading into the wilderness of political opposition, the MCA dissidents joined Gerakan. This kept them within the cozy confines of the BN, in alliance with the MCA leaders who had spurned them. Despite the departure of such popular figures, the MCA still managed to crush the DAP in the 1974 election, winning nineteen seats against the DAP's nine.

This history would repeat itself during the reformasi crisis of 1998–1999, which pitted Prime Minister Mahathir Mohamad against his former deputy, Anwar Ibrahim. A highly powerful, popular, and charismatic figure within UMNO, Anwar was expelled from the party when Mahathir perceived that he was planning to challenge him. Despite Anwar's broad support within the party, almost no UMNO members sided with him after he was unwillingly cast into the political wilderness. The Malaysian party-state applied the full weight of its coercive, remunerative, and symbolic power upon the nascent protest movement that arose on behalf of Anwar individually and democratic reform more generally. State power and party robustness, the joint institutional product of decades of elite collective action within the BN's protection pact, would provide the Mahathir regime with the resources it needed to survive its greatest political crisis.

Authoritarianism without a Leviathan: Coalitional and Institutional Weakness in the Philippines, 1972–1982

Life under a regime of martial law or a Marcos military dictatorship would be little different from life under the Japanese Occupation. How many would submit to it?

Philippines Free Press, January 1971[85]

Look at the mess we were in and where we are now! Look at our nation's economic and social progress!

Ferdinand Marcos, August 1976[86]

Intensifying social conflict during the run-up to Ferdinand Marcos' declaration of martial law neither mobilized radical demands among the working class against the upper class, nor worsened communal tensions in the process. This explains why Marcos continued to face such implacable elite opposition in the days before he definitively destroyed democratic practices in the Philippines.

This relatively tepid social support for Marcos parlayed into his regime's relative incapacity to order power from four key upper groups: (1) from economic elites, tax payments and political financing; (2) from religious elites, symbolic legitimation and abstention from mobilizing their followers against authoritarian rule; (3) from middle classes, membership in the ruling party and non-participation in acts of mass mobilization; and (4) from state officials, absolute loyalty to the political regime, including a willingness to forego personal opportunities for corruption, and to deploy violence against any group threatening to overturn it. By failing to meet these objectives, the Marcos regime failed to gain a

---

[85] "Again?" 23 January 1971.
[86] Quoted in Abueva (1979: 75).

preponderance of coercive, remunerative, and symbolic power, and stood – from day one of martial law – on shaky coalitional ground.

Economic Elites

As Marcos attempted to step up revenue collection in the early days of martial law, he hoped that he enjoyed enough credibility as a protector of elite interests to generate elite compliance. Yet he possessed a tax apparatus sorely lacking in fiscal power. An IMF study estimated that during the 1966–68 period, "the actual tax ratio of the Philippines.... was about 36 percent below the expected tax ratio."[87] As of 1972, the year Marcos declared martial law, public investment in the Philippines amounted to only 2.0% of GNP: half the 4.0% figure in Kenya.[88] The Philippine state consistently managed to mobilize about 10% of GDP in internal revenue throughout the pre-martial law era, and typically collected only about 20% of that paltry total through direct taxes.

The proximate cause of this fiscal powerlessness was the steadfast refusal of the Philippine Congress to countenance any increase in direct taxes. In 1969, Marcos had managed to push through a new Omnibus Tax Code, as the deteriorating internal security situation evidently "made Congress more willing to accept extreme measures."[89] By raising corporate and luxury tax rates and introducing a new fixed tax on professionals with annual incomes exceeding six thousand pesos, Marcos laid the groundwork for a moderately more progressive tax system.

But compliance remained highly problematic, with leaders of the Chamber of Commerce and sectoral business associations decrying the new levies as "excessive," "ruinous," "oppressive," and "confiscatory."[90] Even an effort to link more progressive taxes directly to the growing problem of social unrest failed to generate compliance. To subsidize local police departments through a new "peace and order special account," Congress authorized special taxes on travel and stock transfers in late 1970. When this failed to extract the needed revenue from those Filipinos with enough resources to take vacations and own stocks, Congress reverted to its normal, regressive approach, proposing to double the tax on beer to make up the difference.[91] In sum, Marcos' efforts to exert fiscal power in this period proved more Sisyphean than Herculean, as collections of income and corporate taxes remained flat between 1969–72.

In declaring martial law, Marcos not only sought to free his regime from all democratic constraints. He also aimed to overcome the Philippine state's historical subservience to economic elites. Nowhere would his success or failure at doing so be better indicated than in the arena of fiscal politics. On paper, Marcos appears to have enjoyed considerable success in tipping the balance of power in

[87] Cited in Cheetham and Hawkins (1976: 392–393, fn. 3). As economist Edita Tan summed up the situation in 1971: "There has been a heavy reliance on indirect taxes which are inherently regressive. The progressive taxes have been ineffectively collected." Quoted in Asher and Kinantar (1986: 125).
[88] Doronilla (1992): 142–143.
[89] Author interview with Amando Doronilla, Quezon City, Metro Manila, 1 November 2003.
[90] See, for instance, "CCP Seeks to Stop 3% Tax Ordinance," *Daily Mirror*, 18 January 1969; and "Ass'n to Fight Car Tax Increase," *The Manila Times*, 17 January 1969.
[91] "Solon Proposes Liquor Tax Hike for Police Fund," *The Manila Times*, 27 January 1972.

favor of the state during the early years of martial law. Even as American military assistance tripled, and a timber boom provided his regime with "a ready source of vast, highly discretionary revenues,"[92] Marcos was in no mood to satisfice. "Tax reforms and improved tax information and administration increased the revenues sharply,"[93] Jose Abueva notes. "The dictatorship vastly improved the collection of taxes," Patricio Abinales concurs, "breaking earlier patterns of state inability to exercise this prerogative."[94] After decades in the 8–10% range, tax revenues grew from an estimated 9.7% of GNP in 1972 to 11.4% by 1974, before peaking at an estimated 11.8% of GNP in 1977.[95]

Nor was this spike in extraction limited to regressive, indirect tax measures. Both indirect *and* direct taxes increased as a share of GNP during the first five years of martial law. After ranging between 1.5 and 2.0% of GNP under Marcos' democratic administration, direct taxes shot up between approximately 3.0 and 3.5% of GNP from 1973–77. From 1973–75, direct taxes grew at a faster clip than indirect taxes. Administratively speaking, dramatically more Philippine citizens were captured in the state's revenue net: "The number of people who filed their income taxes increased four times during the first two years of martial rule."[96] It thus appears reasonable to suggest that Philippines oligarchs "experienced their most profound loss of power"[97] under Marcos in the 1970s, rather than under Magsaysay in the 1950s.

Much like Magsaysay's burst of state-building during the Huk rebellion, however, Marcos' burst of state-building in the wake of worsening urban unrest was as significant for what it was not, as for what it was. Direct taxes increased as a share of GNP *for only one year*, fiscal year 1972–73. From as early a vantage point as 1977, David Wurfel recognized that the Marcos regime had managed only a "brief upsurge" in income tax collections.[98] Why did upper groups comply with direct taxation for so short a time? "They weren't doing it out of civic virtue," Abueva wryly observes.[99] As martial law was launched:

The government mounted an extensive tax-information campaign, promising that increased revenues would go to constructive public projects and threatening severe penalties for tax delinquency. The penalties included fines, forfeiture, arrest and imprisonment, revocation of licenses and permits (which were made renewable in shorter periods), withholding of government salaries and fringe benefits, outright dismissal, and disqualification from transacting business with the government. At the same time, from 1973 to 1975 partial tax amnesties were granted on undeclared incomes and so-called "hidden wealth," and those who availed themselves of the amnesties were guaranteed immunity from any investigation or prosecution from the government.[100]

---

[92] B. Smith (2005): 446.
[93] Abueva (1979): 58.
[94] Abinales (1997): 29.
[95] Unless otherwise noted, tax data represent my own calculations, drawn from the Philippine Statistical Yearbook (National Economic Development Authority [1979]).
[96] Abueva (1979): 58.
[97] Abinales (1997): 44.
[98] Wurfel (1977).
[99] Interview with the author, Marikina, Metro Manila, 29 October 2003.
[100] Abueva (1979): 43.

In other words, the advent of authoritarian rule convinced many recalcitrant taxpayers to settle their accounts with the state before the state could settle its accounts with them. To see the significance of this amnesty factor, one must take a closer look at direct taxation in fiscal year 1972–73 – the only year when direct taxes grew faster than GNP. According to government estimates, the state collected 647 million pesos through its official income tax, or a modest increase of 12% on the previous year. Meanwhile, it collected even more revenue from its "amnesty tax" – 717 million pesos, from a baseline of zero. But Marcos could only mobilize such delinquent funds once. By 1975, "amnesty taxes" had virtually vanished, and income tax collections resumed their historically flat trajectory.

A similar logic applies to the spike in corporate tax collections. Revenues from this category nearly quintupled in only two years' time, skyrocketing from 385 million pesos to 1.0 billion pesos in 1972–73, and to 1.8 billion pesos the following fiscal year. But by 1974–75, corporate tax collections were declining, and the only source of buoyancy in state revenue was indirect taxes. Considering that Marcos was threatening to revoke the business licenses of companies that remained in arrears, and even to imprison recalcitrant captains of industry, it is hardly surprising that most corporations paid a high initial price to secure the regime's goodwill.

Marcos made his threats credible by imprisoning and expropriating some of his foremost elite enemies. Benigno Aquino and Eugenio Lopez Jr. wound up in prison, "a large part of the Lopez economic empire ended up in the hands of the Marcos family," and "numerous other family corporations" were "pressed into transferring millions of dollars worth of stocks and other evidences of ownership to the President and his representatives with only symbolic compensation."[101] Economic elites were paying a higher price for protection. But they were buying protection from Marcos, not the masses.

This strategy could only boost the state's fiscal power in the short term, because it rested on intimidation rather than institutions. Once the vast majority of economic elites had paid the initial price of protection at the outset of martial law, they returned to their usual games of hide-and-seek with the country's outmanned tax bureaucrats. Even at the peak of the state's fiscal power in the mid-1970s, the World Bank noted that "the Philippine revenue system" lacked "a strong, centralized authority in charge of revenue planning, legislation, and enforcement. The Bureau of Internal Revenue and the Bureau of Customs" worked "as fairly independent agencies," with the Finance Ministry enjoying little capacity to coordinate or monitor their efforts.[102] Rather than strengthening the tax state, Marcos personalized it: "The First Lady's favorite brother, Benjamin 'Kokoy' Romauldez, exercised de facto control of the Bureau of Customs, the General Auditing Commission, and the Bureau of Internal Revenue" during martial law.[103]

This left the Marcos regime with little institutional capacity to extract a highly strategic resource – direct taxes – from his country's cacique class. As

[101] Wurfel (1977): 11.
[102] Cheetham and Hawkins (1976): 396–397.
[103] Thompson (1995): 53.

TABLE 4. *Fiscal Power in Authoritarian Southeast Asia, 1981–1985*[104]

Cases	Revenue/GDP	Tax/GDP	Direct Tax/Total Tax
Singapore	31.0	19.6	48.0*
Malaysia	26.8	22.7	42.1#
Indonesia	21.3	20.6	65.4#
Thailand	14.5	13.1	23.6
Philippines	12.4	11.0	23.4

* Excludes property taxes; 63.1% if included
\# Excludes petroleum taxes; 48.6% in Malaysia if included, 78.1% in Indonesia if included (1978–79 and 1983–84 figures for Indonesia only).

shown in Table 4, the Philippines lagged behind its most comparable Southeast Asian neighbors in terms of fiscal power during the early 1980s, as authoritarian Leviathans in each of these cases prepared to enter the more democratic global era of the late 1980s and 1990s.

Although it is easy to ascribe Marcos' personalization of power to his "sultanistic" tendencies, I submit that his disinterest in building stronger institutions had deeper coalitional roots. When they take organizational forms, institutions provide avenues for the elites who inhabit them to act collectively. If elites are broadly unsupportive, authoritarian rulers are likely to disperse elite energies rather than concentrate them. If Marcos had constructed an independent tax bureaucracy, it might have gone too hard on his allies or too easy on his enemies, undermining his fragile basis for rule.

The logic of my argument that weak elite support can weaken a ruler's interest in building institutions is more clearly expressed by Marcos' decision, upon declaring martial law, to abolish *party* institutions altogether. If Marcos had enjoyed strong support from a broad section of elites upon declaring martial law, he presumably would have tried to develop a ruling party as an institutional bulwark for his regime. Yet Marcos had nothing to ensure elite loyalty except patronage; and unlike fear, largesse is a limited commodity. To give a contract to one businessman is to deny it to another. In the early years of martial law, any large agglomeration of elites would almost certainly have included individuals whom Marcos could not reliably buy off. Thus, he refused to create any sort of ruling party until 1978, once his patronage networks had been more firmly established.

Rather than economic elites paying the Marcos regime a high price for protection, Marcos was paying economic elites a high price for support – and destroying those who could not be bought. Unable to generate the funds for regime maintenance from within, Marcos turned to external creditors for the lifeblood of his rule:

Marcos had to increase foreign borrowing because government institutions were too corrupt to be effective revenue collectors and a tax hike would further highlight growing

[104] Asher (1989): various pages.

graft in the regime. A stagnant tax base could not finance the mounting demands on public resources by his inner circle, whose greed seemed to know no bounds.... By 1980 the Philippines' foreign indebtedness was $17.3 billion (49 percent of GNP), reaching $26.3 billion by 1985 (81.7 percent of GNP).[105]

Even these obscene levels of profligacy were not enough to secure broad political support for Marcos among economic elites. Martial law knocked his oligarchic opponents down, but not out. Marcos' "rivals like the Lopez and Aquino clans" may have been "initially impotent" under martial law, but "they nonetheless constituted an elite, fuming, opposition *from the dictatorship's inception.*"[106] Coercive tactics kept anti-regime energies scattered and suppressed throughout most of the 1970s. As his coalitional confidence increased, Marcos reconvened a sham parliament in 1978, along with sham elections to select its members, and a sham political party to contest them. Yet he lacked the social support necessary to control even the counterfeit institutions he had created. Although the Marcos regime did not collapse until February 1986, the tepidness of Marcos' support among economic elites had much deeper historical roots.

Communal Elites

Authoritarian durability rests not merely on remunerative and coercive power, but on symbolic power as well. If the direct taxation of economic elites is the surest route to gaining remunerative power, and the construction of loyal and hierarchical police and military institutions is the best way to secure coercive power, symbolic power is best gained through the active support of communal elites: leaders of ethnic or nationalist associations, and top figures in religious organizations. Such elites help regimes accrue symbolic power through their active legitimation of incumbent authorities. When communal elites fail to play a regime-supportive role, one of the key social foundations for authoritarian durability is removed.

In the Philippines, communal elites primarily mean religious elites: particularly the ranking members of the Catholic Church, to which the vast majority of the country's population gives its fealty. Since no popular mobilization was necessary to secure independence, the Philippines lacks nationalist mass organizations. This leaves the Catholic Church as the dominant institutional vehicle through which identity politics is expressed.[107] Fortunately for the state, and the regimes that have run it, the Church has ordinarily acted as a conservative force in Philippine public life. Its leaders have normally eschewed political activism, and willingly illuminated political authorities with the beatific glow of the Church's symbolic power.

From the outset of martial law, however, the Church leadership was deeply divided. This contrasts sharply with the historical experience of Malaysia and Indonesia, where religious authorities provided new authoritarian Leviathans with active and overwhelming support. Whereas mass mobilization in Malaysia

[105] Thompson (1995): 66.
[106] Boudreau (2002): 553. Emphasis added.
[107] Slater (2009): 229–230.

and Indonesia was perceived by religious authorities as an imminent threat to the institutions that provided them with their elite positions, leftist upheaval in the Philippines never called the central role of the Catholic Church in public life into question. There was thus no broadly shared threat to unify the Church in support of open-ended authoritarian rule.

Throughout the Marcos period, there existed a marked "conservative-progressive dichotomy" within the Philippine Church that shaped attitudes toward martial law.[108] Marcos had success at recruiting conservative figures to express support, especially in martial law's early days. The most conservative religious organization, the Catholic Bishops' Conference of the Philippines (CBCP), cautioned its followers "to remain calm and law-abiding" when Marcos seized autocratic power.[109] In January 1975, the archbishop of Caceres visited Marcos at Malacañang, declaring that the martial-law regime represented the "legitimate constitutional government to which every citizen is bound to render respectful allegiance." In case anyone missed his point, the archbishop went on to notify his humble listeners that "the habitual attitude of the loyal citizen is that of sympathetic faith, not that of criticality and distrust."[110]

Dictators hear this sort of rhetoric in their sweetest dreams. Yet Marcos never came close to orchestrating a united chorus of such unconditional support from Church leaders. Even the conservative CBCP was divided. By Robert Youngblood's estimates, 58% of the CBCP's bishops could have been considered conservative in orientation, meaning that "if they criticized the government at all, they did so in moderate terms, and only on matters of specific church interests." Meanwhile, 23% of CBCP bishops were classified as moderates, who "reserved the right to criticize specific injustice, while not going to the extent of attacking the legitimacy of the regime." The remaining 19% of CBCP bishops were "considered progressive and activist," and "differed from the other two groups by repeatedly speaking out against a wide array of reported governmental and military abuses as well as by condemning the Marcos regime as immoral and without legitimacy." These critical voices found echoes in other leading Catholic organizations such as the Association of Major Religious Supporters of the Philippines (AMRSP), which was "viewed as more progressive than the CBCP" and was "less inhibited about criticizing government programs and military abuses."[111]

If any single vector can be traced from these multiple streams in Church opinion, it is best captured by Manila Archbishop Jaime Cardinal Sin's depiction of church-state relations under martial law: "critical collaboration." This phrase nicely captures the relatively critical stance of the Church vis-à-vis authoritarian rule in comparative perspective, while suggesting a conceptual continuum to help us track the shift in Church attitudes toward Marcos over time. Although "there was more collaboration than criticism"[112] during the early days of martial law,

---

[108] Youngblood (1990): 74.
[109] Ibid. 172.
[110] Ibid. 173.
[111] Ibid. 72–74.
[112] Thompson (1995): 118.

criticism was never silenced, and it became much louder over time. Whatever honeymoon Marcos enjoyed with religious elites was comparatively short, and not particularly sweet.

From martial law's inception, even moderate Church leaders such as Cardinal Sin showed a willingness to challenge the Marcos regime when it contravened Church interests. In its initial coercive sweep of leftist elements, Marcos did not spare Church-based activists inspired by "liberation theology" to champion populist causes. Most notably, Church activists had been joining the Federation of Free Farmers (FFF) "in a series of sit-ins, pickets, and demonstrations from 1967 until the declaration of martial law."[113] Such activism led a Marcos administration report to declare, in a fit of ill-advised pique, that the Catholic Church had become "the single biggest obstacle to progress in the country."[114] After martial law was declared, Marcos ordered a series of military raids on Church property to weed out subversive elements. "Right from the start of martial law, a minority of bishops, religious superiors, pastors, and other church officials protested military actions on church property and against religious persons."[115]

Such protests quickly swelled. The sharpest attacks came from progressive Church organizations such as the AMRSP, whose "commitment. . . . to help the poor and to improve social justice conditions was accelerated by the declaration of martial law." At a meeting in January 1974, the AMRSP voted "to continue financial assistance to a number of people's organizations," such as the National Federation of Sugar Workers.[116] The group also "formed Task Force Detainees (TFD) in 1974 to investigate reports of torture and illegal detention."[117] With only thin and conditional support among moderates and conservatives, Marcos could not strike at such progressives without inviting rebuke from the Church leadership. After military "raids against the National Council of Churches in the Philippines (NCCP) and the Sacred Heart Novitiate in June and August 1974. . . . powerful members of the Catholic hierarchy began to speak out sharply."[118]

Church-state relations soured dramatically in November 1975, when a strike at the La Tondeña Distillery in Manila led Marcos to issue a presidential decree prohibiting all walkouts. Marcos also deported the foreign missionaries who had been assisting the workers, and prohibited further foreign involvement in labor disputes. "If they expected these pronouncements to end the matter, Marcos and his advisors must have been surprised by the reaction,"[119] as

bishops, religious orders, and lay groups protested around the country, with the support of Cardinal Sin. In late November nearly 4,000 Manila workers and their supporters held an open-air mass and rally which ended in cries of "Strike, Strike!" Then again on December 6, during the visit of President Ford to the Philippines, more than 4,000 workers and

---

[113] Youngblood (1990): 79–80.
[114] "Political War and Martial Law?" *Philippines Free Press*, 23 January 1971.
[115] Youngblood (1990): 114.
[116] Ibid. 85.
[117] Thompson (1995): 72–73.
[118] Youngblood (1990): 114.
[119] Kerkvliet (2000): xvii–xviii.

religious [sic] gathered for worship. After prayers they spontaneously decided to march on Malacañang to protest the strike ban, gathering more than 2,000 additional supporters along the way.[120]

More than a decade before Cardinal Sin became famous for helping lead the "People's Power" movement that toppled the Marcos regime, he had already begun to enunciate a critical role for the Church. As he expressed the wide-ranging nature of his political concerns in an interview with the *Far Eastern Economic Review* in December 1976:

I am afraid of the future. I have always conveyed this fear. *The security of the country is based on the Constitution.* The Constitution should be above the President. At the moment he controls the Constitution. He says it is the people who change the Constitution, but I don't believe the people know what is happening.[121]

Nor were early protests against the regime's political abuses limited to progressive and moderate Church elements. The conservative head of the CBCP responded to the deportation of foreign missionaries by insisting that "the Catholic hierarchy would 'do everything within its power' to see that foreign priests were not denied due process.'"[122] By 1977, David Wurfel could write, quite presciently, that "the Catholic Church has provided the most effective leadership for mass discontent against the martial law regime. It is today the most significant non-governmental linkage between the elite and masses in the country, and only a small portion of its potential has at yet been utilized."[123]

Recognizing that he had no hope of turning the Church into a harmonious choir of legitimation, Marcos attempted to ensure that it remained a political cacophony, too divided to threaten his position. He wielded his power to tax like a Sword of Damocles, threatening to impose levies on Church organizations that refused to toe the administration line. Before declaring martial law, Marcos had tried, but failed, to impose new taxes on profitable Church properties.[124] This all changed once Marcos had no more parliament to haggle with:

Church-owned school property was made taxable for the first time in 1973 by PD 76. Then a "stay of execution" was given until the end of 1974 (PD 261). During 1975 and early 1976 church and other private schools were given month-by-month stays, forcing some influential Catholic educators to approach Malacañang in supplication and thus weaken the independent stance advocated by other churchmen.[125]

Once again, we see Marcos *employing selective intimidation rather than building stronger institutions* to manage his relations with societal elites. Like economic elites, religious elites had no compelling reason to give Marcos open-ended support, given the manageability of contentious politics in the pre-martial-law era. The President thus aimed to forestall rather than foster their collective action.

[120] Wurfel (1977): 16.
[121] Abueva (1979): 71. Emphasis added.
[122] Youngblood (1990): 113.
[123] Wurfel (1977): 17.
[124] "Tax Eyed on Religious Properties," *The Manila Times*, 5 August 1969.
[125] Wurfel (1977): 18.

Marcos' failure to elaborate effective institutions for controlling religious elites provides another useful window on the personalization of his regime. Once again, Marcos' apparent disinterest in building institutions reflected not simply his "sultanistic" personality, but weak underlying coalitional support. Even the attempts by Ferdinand and Imelda Marcos to construct a personality cult through grotesque practices of "self-exaltation"[126] resulted not simply from their monstrous vanity. Rather, such efforts can be seen as second-best means of generating symbolic power for a regime that received precious little active legitimation from communal elites.

A comparative perspective again proves useful. Ruling elites in Malaysia have defended their legitimacy by reminding their subjects of their effective *institutional* responses to historical episodes of social unrest. Communal elites have generally complied in echoing these ruling elites' version of events. Thus, even leaders with little patience for elite consultation such as Mahathir Mohamad have personalized power without being forced to construct personality cults.[127] But Marcos had a less compelling tale to tell, and less support from the Church in telling it. He was thus relegated to lying about his *personal* military record to bolster his legitimacy. When this heroic background was proven to be a fabrication, it served as another nail in the coffin for his dying regime.[128]

Middle Classes

Marcos' initial support among the Philippines' middle class was even softer than his support among economic and religious elites. To some degree, this reflected the general difficulty authoritarian regimes face in gaining support among middle sectors of the population (e.g., students, professionals, small businesspeople). Too numerous to buy off with targeted patronage, such groups are difficult to incorporate into provision pacts. Yet their class separation from popular sectors and broadly shared interest in political stability make them excellent potential recruits for protection pacts. In Indonesia and Malaysia, such groups provided considerable support to new authoritarian Leviathans in the shadow of highly threatening and challenging episodes of contentious politics.

Once again, the Philippines looks dramatically different. Granted, the regime enjoyed somewhat of a honeymoon among urban groups weary of the unrest and instability that presaged martial law. Marcos attracted some support from "a wider urban bourgeoisie and petty-bourgeois constituency: middle-level civil servants, doctors, nurses, teachers, businessmen, shopkeepers, and so on," that was "both anti-oligarchy and anti-popular in orientation."[129] David Wurfel gauged the extent and intensity of such support by dividing the Philippine population into four groups.[130] After setting aside the 3–4% of the population Wurfel estimated

---

[126] Ibid. 54.
[127] Slater (2003).
[128] On Marcos' military record and its public discrediting, see McCoy (1993: Ch. 5).
[129] B. Anderson (1998) [1988]: 212.
[130] The following paragraphs draw directly from Wurfel (1977: 12–13).

to be "regime participants" who supported Marcos out of direct self-interest, and the 50% he categorized as apolitical "unsophisticated subjects," Wurfel classified the remaining 45% as "sophisticated subjects" (30%) and "opposition participants" (15%). By Wurfel's reckoning, most middle-class Filipinos belonged to one of the latter two categories.

The 15% of the population depicted as "opposition participants," in Wurfel's terms, "refuse to grant legitimacy to the regime and do not even acquiesce verbally," although as of 1977, only "a small minority have engaged in any kind of organized or public protest." While such oppositionists were prevented from mobilizing against Marcos by the threat of coercion alone, "sophisticated subjects" tended to "find sufficient economic benefit under the present regime to acquiesce." But by the same token, this estimated 30% of the population "do not believe that the regime rules by legal or moral right." This cross-class group with a large middle-class segment thus belonged to a provision pact, but not a protection pact. "Even in this group," Wurfel predicted, "acquiescence will dwindle if economic prospects do not improve."

Middle-class acquiescence to martial law was more tenuous from the outset than middle-class support for authoritarian regimes in Indonesia and Malaysia. Nowhere is this contrast more striking than in the case of the student population at elite universities. Whereas such students in these other cases were initially broadly supportive of new authoritarian Leviathans, Philippine students were practically unanimous in condemning Marcos' imposition of martial law.[131] Rather than rallying behind the new regime, "the moderate wing of the 1960s student movement" was generally "radicalized by mounting government repression and social inequality under martial law."[132]

As moderate students became more radical, radical students became more violent. This "radical intelligentsia, largely of bourgeois and petty-bourgeois urban origins, and typically graduates of the University of the Philippines," began to play leading roles in the Communist Party of the Philippines (CPP) and the New People's Army (NPA).[133] Whereas these two groups had only formed a loose alliance of small numbers before 1972, the CPP/NPA became a tighter movement with a larger mass following under martial law. Marcos had inadvertently acted as "the best recruiter for the Communists" and "enabled Filipino communism also to achieve a national presence that it never was able to accomplish before."[134]

If such patterns of contentious politics had arisen *before* Marcos declared martial law, he might have had more success at constructing a protection pact to buttress his rule. But even those who did not blame Marcos for worsening the security situation could scarcely have believed that his regime had *improved* it.

---

[131] This comparative conclusion draws on an interview with Joel Rocamora, Quezon City, Metro Manila, 27 October 2003.

[132] Thompson (1995): 8.

[133] B. Anderson (1998) [1988]: 211.

[134] Abinales (1997): 49, fn. 60.

"This is a state that, at its weakest, was able to maintain social peace and stability and keep the upper hand over its adversaries," Patricio Abinales argues. "In its authoritarian form, in contrast, this state stimulated formidable opposition,"[135] and increasingly violent opposition at that.

Marcos not only failed to contain violent radicalism on the middle class' leftist fringe. He also failed to build institutions to channel more moderate middle-class opinion in his favor. Most crucially, Marcos made only a belated and half-hearted attempt to organize social support through any sort of political party. Whereas authoritarian rulers in Malaysia and Indonesia made strategic use of party institutions to incorporate the middle class, Marcos let his existing party apparatus evaporate. "Rather than build the Nacionalista into a coalition-maintaining organization that could provide predictable access to the center of political power, he focused instead on forging individual ties to personal friends and select members of the military and bureaucracy, essentially a transition from clientelism to sultanism."[136]

Marcos did not simply let his party wither because he had sultanistic proclivities. He did so because he was well aware – considering the highly contested nature of his seizure of dictatorial power – that the party was as likely to serve as an effective institutional conduit for elite opposition as support. Recognizing the need to establish some sort of institutionalized backing, Marcos organized new "citizens' assemblies" at the village (barangay) level,[137] and mobilized mostly impoverished, out-of-school youth to serve in barangay councils.[138] Educated middle-class youth were too strong in their oppositional stance to be candidates for such incorporation, so Marcos handled them with coercion alone: "informers reporting to military intelligence are found in large numbers on all college and university campuses."[139]

Although Marcos' thin elite support made it extremely risky to build a new party from scratch, he eventually decided that the risk was worth taking. To enhance his legitimacy both at home and abroad, Marcos called for new elections in April 1978, and founded a new political party – the KBL (Kilusang Bagong Lipunan, or New Society Movement) – to contest them. While Marcos correctly calculated that the renewal of electoral politics would revitalize the support of his American benefactors, he was overconfident if he assumed that elections could bolster his flimsy legitimacy at home. His high-stakes gamble in founding the KBL proved to be a bad bet in every sense. On the one hand, the party "never amounted to much more than a collection of Marcos' favored cronies."[140] The KBL "wasn't even an organization," argues Jose Abueva.[141] "Its function as an election list more than a political organization was a symptom of Marcos'

[135] Abinales (2000): 5–6.
[136] B. Smith (2005): 447.
[137] Franco (2000): 158.
[138] Wurfel (1977): 19.
[139] Ibid.
[140] B. Smith (2005): 447.
[141] Author's Interview, Kalayaan College, Marikina Metro Manila, 29 October 2003.

continued aversion to party building," Jason Brownlee notes. "The KBL's policies and resources were those of Ferdinand Marcos."[142]

Those resources were far from sufficient to buy off the Philippine middle class. The KBL thus remained too socially hollow to provide the Marcos regime with meaningful institutional support. Equally troubling for Marcos, the KBL *did* succeed in providing a vehicle for elite collective action – but not of the sort Marcos would have preferred. "[T]he KBL accomplished little more in the late 1970s than to catalyze the beginnings of an opposition coalition."[143] With no protection pact at his disposal, Marcos' patronage machine provided insufficient centripetal force to bring and hold together any broad coalition of middle-class groups.

State Officials

The fate of authoritarian Leviathans ultimately rests on whether employees of the state obey the political leadership's commands. When state officials undermine public authority from within, a regime loses the primary foundation for its rule. Patterns of contentious politics in the Philippines before 1972 not only provided Marcos with weak support in society at large, but within the state apparatus itself.

This was most importantly witnessed in the Philippine military, which ultimately would not use collective force against Marcos' opponents to keep the aging and ailing dictator in power. This was the proximate cause of Marcos' fall. But before asking why the military failed to crush "People Power" in 1986, we must ask why Marcos came to rely so completely on the military for his self-preservation in the first place. In short, Marcos became so dependent on the military because he failed to build any civilian institutions to complement or counterbalance it. We have already seen that Marcos built no robust political apparatus, such as a strong ruling party, to check military influence. Marcos also failed to elaborate an effective administrative apparatus that might have quelled opposition through a more effective mix of co-optation and coercion.

As we saw earlier in the case of taxation, Marcos' centralization of power was achieved through intensified intimidation rather than new institutions. Marcos initially talked a tough line on corruption, demanding "*disiplina*"[144] from his civil service. Yet the reality of reform fell dramatically short of the rhetoric. Marcos "was more interested in centralizing patronage resources than in centralizing administrative structures."[145] The most significant administrative restructuring proved to be Marcos' creation of a new Ministry of Ecology and Human Settlements, run like a shadow state by his wife Imelda. Similarly, the most significant restructuring of local government served to incorporate all the fragmented local authorities near the capital into a single political unit, Metro Manila, under the authority of a single mayor: Imelda Marcos. And Marcos entrusted

---

[142] Brownlee (2007): 116.
[143] B. Smith (2005): 448.
[144] Abueva (1979): 35.
[145] Hutchcroft (2000): 300.

Imelda's brother – a notorious smuggler of guns and cigarettes[146] – to oversee the Philippines' revenue-collection agencies.[147] Marcos reorganized "the whole economy," argues Ricardo Manapat, "into different fiefs managed by relatives and cronies who regularly shared their earnings with the dictator."[148] Rather than a tax state, Marcos was building a shakedown state.

Such unabashed graft and cronyism at the top translated into continued venality in the state's lower administration. "Though corrupt practices did indeed diminish sharply in the first months after the declaration of martial law, when fear of the consequences of misdeeds was still high, old ways quickly returned."[149] This undermined Marcos' attempt to increase societal compliance with taxation, and left him with little capacity to deliver the benefits of development to his supporters and potential opponents. Time and time again, as Ledivina Carino argued in a 1976 manuscript on the Philippine bureaucracy, "something breaks down at the level of implementation."[150]

Marcos could not convert the bureaucracy into a sharpened instrument for governance with coercion alone. Nor could he convert it into a wellspring of political loyalty through patronage alone. Not that he failed to try. By establishing new state-owned enterprises, Marcos provided government employment to over 130,000 Philippine citizens by 1984 – a growth of 226% from 1975. "During the same period, the entire government civil service experienced a 145 per cent increase, from 533,284 in 1975 to 1,310,789 in 1984."[151] The reintroduction of elections in 1978 led Marcos to shower this burgeoning civil service with cash. In short, "the regime dispersed large sums of 'pork barrel' money to *barangay* officials for local infrastructure projects, such as road and bridge construction," and "improved the KBL's chances by increasing the salaries and benefits of government employees, including public school teachers."[152] Rather than mobilizing civil servants into a mass political party, Marcos tried to secure their support with the scattershot provision of largesse.

All this money bought Marcos precious little love from his administration. "Even the lower middle classes directly nurtured by the state, such as the huge numbers of public school teachers and other civil servants, have not developed any strong sense of professional or institutional loyalty to the state, making them more open to oppositionist activities against the state itself," Temario Rivera argues. Anti-Marcos sentiment ran especially strong among teachers – a group his regime was targeting most carefully with patronage, and which has long served as the middle-class bedrock of UMNO in Malaysia. "Among the civil servants, public school teachers at varying levels proved to be the most responsive to the

---

[146] McCoy (1999): 153.
[147] Thompson (1995): 53.
[148] Quoted in McCoy (1993: 18).
[149] Wurfel (1977): 10.
[150] Cited in Abueva (1979: 54).
[151] Rivera (2001): 238.
[152] Youngblood (1990): 60, 58.

anti-dictatorship struggle, and a number of both aboveground and clandestine militant organizations emerged from their ranks."[153]

With no strong state or party at his beck and call, Marcos had little choice but to rely on the military. Much like Magsaysay twenty years before, Marcos failed miserably at reshaping the state's administrative apparatus, but enjoyed clear successes at tightening his grip over the state's *coercive* apparatus. To some degree, this took the form of organizational restructuring, including the centralization of the national police force and the installation of military "development officers" in rural provinces. Again like Magsaysay, Marcos implemented this plan to counteract rural insurgency. "Not coincidentally, all the regions where the top post in charge of regional economic development was entrusted to a military man were considered major strongholds of the CPP-NPA."[154] This causal linkage from rural rebellion to low-level state-building is similarly traced by Abinales, who argues that "this projection of national power in suppressing an insurgency.... reflected the unprecedented building of the Philippine state."[155]

Yet military forces had only been restructured to channel Marcos' commands downward, not to mobilize the military's political support upward. This would have required the creation of a political party with considerable military membership, akin to Indonesia's Golkar (as we will see later in this chapter). But Marcos was loath to take the political risk inherent in fostering any such elite collective action. Marcos instead banked on money politics to keep the armed forces happy. "Before declaring martial law, Marcos increased the size of the armed forces from 45,000 to 60,000 and more than doubled their budget." He also "reshuffled military commanders.... to make sure he had their absolute loyalty." The dozen officers who helped Marcos plan the imposition of martial law became known as "the Rolex Twelve,"[156] for reasons that should be self-evident.

After seizing dictatorial power, Marcos tried to spread the largesse more widely. The police doubled in size, and the military nearly tripled its troop strength. Military salaries "jumped by 150 percent immediately after the imposing of martial law and increased by another 100 percent for some ranks in 1976."[157] On the whole, "national defense outlays rose from 13.4 to 21.8 per cent of the total" between 1972 and 1975 – a remarkable figure, given that the Philippines' external defense was guaranteed by the Americans. Troops received "inducements such as subsidized commissaries and housing,"[158] in a country where welfare provisions are practically nonexistent.

These were table scraps in comparison to the patronage Marcos provided to these soldiers' commanding officers. The President provided new "opportunities for high-ranking officers to be appointed to boards of directors of government

---

[153] Rivera (2001): 233, 238.
[154] Franco (2000): 160.
[155] Abinales (1997): 32.
[156] Thompson (1995): 47.
[157] Youngblood (1990): 43, 44–45.
[158] Wurfel (1977): 25.

corporations," notes Wurfel. "For instance, the privately owned Jacinto Iron and Steel Sheets Corporation (sequestered by presidential order soon after the declaration of martial law) is now run entirely by the military. Furthermore, the President has closed his eyes to growing corruption among the military, symbolized by colonels and their wives driving Mercedes-Benz automobiles."[159] Calling the Philippine military one of the few "real beneficiaries of the regime," Benedict Anderson notes Marcos' use of "favored officers to manage properties confiscated from his enemies, public corporations, townships, and so forth. The upper-echelon officers came to live in a style to which only the oligarchy had hitherto been accustomed."[160]

There were two fundamental problems with this strategy for controlling the military, however. First, there were only so many Rolexes, Mercedes-Benzes, and corporate directorships to go around. Given the Philippine state's lack of fiscal power, this high-priced political strategy was certain to leave many military officers feeling relatively deprived. It also siphoned scarce revenues from the state's administrative agencies, "causing intense dissatisfaction in the civilian bureaucracy,"[161] where support for Marcos was shaky to begin with. But the biggest problem with Marcos' approach was his undermining of military unity and morale, as the institution lost its remaining professional integrity amid the rampant politicization of the officer corps. "The armed forces were no longer the servant of the state under martial law, but the bastion of a particular regime."[162]

From his inauguration in December 1965, Marcos had a divisive effect on the military with his blatant practice of regionalist cronyism and favoritism. "Indeed, in the seven years before martial law, Marcos groomed a hierarchy bound to him by strong personal ties – old classmates from the U.P. cadet corps, blood relatives, and fellow Ilocanos, the northern Luzon ethnic group known for being clannish."[163] The nerve center of this personalization agenda was the Presidential Security Command (PSC). Even before martial law, disgruntled officers observed that the PSC's commander, Marcos' cousin Fabian Ver, was turning the institution into "Marcos's one big private army."[164] The Jabidah massacre in 1968 made the existence of clandestine units under Marcos' command a matter of public knowledge. By the late 1960s, "Marcos seemed to be building a 'parallel command,' promoting loyalists and creating covert-action units outside the formal hierarchy."[165] But these tendencies dramatically worsened once Marcos could dispense with all mechanisms of democratic accountability:

After martial law in 1972, the PSC expanded into a multiservice force of seven thousand men, with tanks, helicopters, and patrol ships. In the regime's fourth year, Ver opened "Camp 1" in his home province to train loyal Ilocano soldiers for the palace. He also

---

[159] Ibid.
[160] B. Anderson (1998) [1988]: 215–216.
[161] Wurfel (1977): 25.
[162] McCoy (1999): 191–192.
[163] Ibid. 28.
[164] Quote by General Victor Osias, former Marcos chief of staff (Ibid. 123).
[165] Ibid. 29.

awarded his sons key postings in his command as they grew old enough to join the military.... As concurrent head of the National Intelligence and Security Agency (NISA), Ver transformed it from a small analysis unit into a dreaded secret police that controlled the currency black market, gambling, smuggling, and safe houses for torture-interrogation. Beyond the palace, Ver began influencing postings within the armed forces to such an extent that "discipline began to disintegrate" and the "president lost control over the military."[166]

The key point is not that Marcos lacked military support throughout his rule. It is that the support he enjoyed derived almost entirely from the instrumental calculations of individual officers, rather than any shared conviction that the Marcos regime represented a necessary bulwark against political instability. As such, military support was highly vulnerable to any disruption in patronage networks, and highly prone to producing factional effects, given the impossibility of satisfying all officers' material wants. Throughout the martial law period, "the military appeared to remain split at the top, undisciplined at the bottom."[167]

The Philippine military's debilitation through factionalism and personalization comes into sharp relief when one considers the impact of regional rebellions on military cohesion in comparative perspective. In Indonesia and Burma, such conflicts arose before these countries' militaries had been significantly sullied by civilian elites' patronage and politicization. Regional rebellions had a powerful unifying effect on both the Burmese and Indonesian armed forces, inducing political militarization and enhancing authoritarian durability in both cases. While no less *corrupt* than the Philippine military, these militaries have been far more *cohesive.*

Regional rebellion in the southern islands of Mindanao and Sulu had a dramatically different effect on the Philippine armed forces. While counterinsurgency experience apparently made soldiers in the field more loyal to each other, it did not make soldiers more supportive of the regime that put them in harm's way. This is because counterinsurgency took place "in the context of the cronyism and lack of professionalism of the top loyalist Marcos generals."[168] It is illustrative that Gregorio "Gringo" Honasan, a leading military conspirator against Marcos in the mid-1980s, credits his experience in Mindanao for making his cohorts feel "closer.... than brothers."[169] By deepening horizontal, factional loyalties, the bloody war in Mindanao ironically exacerbated Marcos' considerable challenge in securing the political allegiance of his military.

Marcos personalized the military for the same reason that he dissolved his existing political party and steered clear of any major attempt to reorganize the bureaucracy. Pre-1972 patterns of contentious politics had not provided him with enough credibility as a protector to build a coalition on that basis. Any institutions Marcos created or allowed to survive could easily be transformed into vehicles for organized opposition. He thus aimed to build a coalition through patronage

---

[166] Ibid. 226.
[167] Noble (1986): 111.
[168] Rivera (2001): 237.
[169] McCoy (1999): 203.

alone. Given the Philippine state's limited fiscal power (due in part to his own fear of letting a non-family member run the tax bureaucracy), this was an uphill battle from the start. It would be an exaggeration to say that the Marcos regime was doomed from its inception; but it would be even more problematic to suggest that Marcos launched his authoritarian Leviathan from anywhere near as strong a coalitional position as his counterparts in Malaysia and – as we will now see – Indonesia.

From Protection Pact to the Personalization of Power: Suharto's Shrinking Coalition in Indonesia, 1966–1995

Due to the farsightedness and firm tactical action of General Suharto he has been able to create an atmosphere of security and calm, and heavy is this task, for the Sukarno regime has left behind a hideous Augean stable, which ought to be cleaned. Stability in the political and economic field is most imperative! Hence, all funds and forces available are aimed towards the achievement of this stability.

> *General Suharto: Man of Destiny* Indonesian Ministry of Information, 1966[170]

It is a point of considerable consensus among Indonesia specialists that shared desires for protection against communist mobilization best explain the strength and breadth of elite collective action at the Suharto regime's onset. "Anti-communism provided a basic ideological reference point from which the Army was able to organize a diverse coalition of anti-left wing groups," argues Rob Goodfellow. "This alliance had one common denominator. It shared a mutual desire to see an end to the political and economic upheaval for which the PKI was held solely responsible."[171] Benedict Anderson concurs: "The coalition that united behind General Suharto.... was highly diverse, united only in its fear and hatred of the Indonesian Communist Party."[172] Edward Aspinall argues that the bloody coup attributed to the PKI in late 1965 "provided the trigger for the coalescence of the 'New Order coalition,'"[173] which Mochtar Mas'oed describes as "a coalition of all religious groups, students and intellectuals.... Generally, it was a grand alliance of those groups long harassed by the aggressive Indonesian Communist Party."[174]

At its outset, then, Indonesia's New Order approximated the coalitional breadth and logic of Malaysia's UMNO-led protection pact. Yet by the time of its demise in the late 1990s, Suharto's patronage-driven regime and shrunken coalition had come in many ways to resemble the Marcos regime more than the Mahathir regime – as captured in the popular Indonesian pun that Suharto had become "exactly like Marcos."[175] Unlike the Malaysian and Philippine cases,

---

[170] Quoted in Goodfellow (1995: 2).
[171] Cited in Ibid. v.
[172] B. Anderson (1978a): 2.
[173] Aspinall (1996): 216.
[174] Mas'oed (1983): 25, 26.
[175] In Indonesian, the pun arises from the New Order's abbreviation of the 1966 letter transfer-
      ring power from Sukarno to Suharto (Surat Perintah Sebelas Maret, or Directive Letter of

Indonesia's authoritarian Leviathan underwent significant coalitional *evolution* – or involution – over time.

This section aims to explain both the intermediate strength and the shifting character of Indonesia's authoritarian coalition and institutions. First, I show how the political militarization that had followed regional rebellions in the late 1950s placed soldiers rather than civilians atop the anti-PKI protection pact of the mid- to late 1960s. Party and administrative institutions remained on a short leash, as military elites balked at building civilian institutions that could equal the military's political power. Second, while the PKI presented an unmanageable threat to elite privileges and property, it did not produce the kind of *endemic* perceived threat that has helped sustain attitudinal support for authoritarian politics in Malaysia. By completely annihilating the PKI during its seizure of power, the Indonesian military ironically deprived itself of the kind of endemic social threat that can make authoritarianism close to impregnable.

As his coalition's protection logic vanished, Suharto sought increasingly to forestall elite collective action instead of fostering it. Much like Marcos, Suharto tried to disperse rather than concentrate elite political energies as his coalition withered. This was a far more complicated political task for Suharto than Marcos, considering the complex institutional setting in which Suharto saw his protection pact erode. With a powerful military, a relatively robust ruling party, and a highly organized Islamic political sphere already in place as of the mid-1970s, Suharto could not personalize power by simply ignoring institutions, as Marcos had – instead, he needed to *balance* them.[176] By pitting military and civilian institutions against each other, however, Suharto gradually factionalized and weakened the relatively impressive and cohesive organizational weapons that had initially been at his political disposal.

Origins: Military Domination with Civilian Backing, 1966–1973

Elite support for military rule in Indonesia was initially forthcoming from civilian state officials, communal elites, economic elites, and middle classes – the same broad groups that have backstopped party domination in Malaysia. Anderson's depiction of the initial New Order coalition closely resembles the typology of elites that guides this book. "The most important elements in it were the following, each with its own reasons for anti-communist animus," he details: "(1) The bulk of the senior officers of the Indonesian army; (2) The devout Islamic community, both urban and rural; (3) Protestant and Catholic minorities; (4) A small indigenous entrepreneurial, professional and bureaucratic middle class; (5) A Westernized intelligentsia, partly professional, partly academic, and partly artistic."[177]

Since Sukarno remained in formal control for nearly six months after the 1965 coup, the first tasks for ABRI's civilian allies were to join the attack on the PKI

March 11th) as "Supersemar." Anti-Suharto wags rephrased the abbreviation as "sudah persis seperti Marcos," or, loosely, "He's become exactly like Marcos."

[176] Slater (2010).

[177] B. Anderson (1978a): 2.

and to pressure Sukarno to step down. In both tasks, communal elites – especially Islamic organizations – played leading roles. "The followers of the main Islamic organizations provided the bulk of the masses in the demonstrations in Jakarta and other cities, and Islamic youth participated directly in the eradication of the Left in rural areas."[178] The carnage reached genocidal proportions as "Muslim organizations sacralized the campaign, calling it a holy war or *jihad*."[179] Religious fervor was not merely an epiphenomenal element of class-motivated massacres. "The PKI's executioners in 1965–66 were largely teenage boys and youths without established property interests but with strong religious convictions,"[180] Anderson insists. "[I]n East Java and Bali where, in proportion to the population, the death toll appears to have been heaviest," Rex Mortimer adds, "communal tensions exacerbated by the land reform conflicts of 1964–65 and other political feuds go far to explain the scale of the slaughter."[181]

The intertwining of class and communal conflict in Sukarno's fall and Suharto's rise was thus unmistakable. This explains why elite support for the New Order was by no means limited to the soldiers and Islamic groups who conducted the massacres. While ABRI's Muslim allies were the coalition's main shock troops, "[t]he second source of support was what can be described, for want of a better term, as the secular-oriented urban middle classes."[182] Most interesting from a comparative perspective, students were part and parcel of the initial New Order coalition, much like in Malaysia but very unlike in the Philippines: "rather than facing down a rebellious student movement (as Marcos had done) Suharto drew important support from student demonstrations in 1965," notes Vincent Boudreau. "In the process he acquired street legitimacy essential to his consolidation of New Order Indonesia."[183]

It is difficult to overstate the role of Indonesian students in Suharto's rise – and, as we will see, in Suharto's fall as well. With their recognized historical role in the revolutionary struggle against the Dutch, students in Indonesia are no typical middle-class constituency. They enjoy enduring nationalist credentials, allowing them to assume the political centrality and leadership role of communal elites in times of crisis. And students indeed proved pivotal in anti-Sukarno and anti-PKI urban demonstrations. "The coalition of student organizations was very effective in mobilizing popular support for the army and the Orde Baru [New Order]," argues Mas'oed. "Soon thereafter, the efforts to form action fronts mushroomed to include all fields such as high school students, teachers, university graduates, youth, women, labor, and several more."[184]

Such wide-ranging social support for the New Order is better explained by shared threat perceptions than by shared material interests. Consider the

---

[178] Aspinall (1996): 216.
[179] Hefner (2000): 16.
[180] B. Anderson (1978a): 3. Indonesia's small but influential Catholic minority also "violently opposed communism on religious grounds" (Ibid. 4).
[181] Mortimer (1974): 390.
[182] Aspinall (1996): 216.
[183] Boudreau (1999): 6.
[184] Mas'oed (1983): 73.

acquiescence with which severe price hikes during the New Order's early days were met:

> The state railway increased its rate five-fold, while the postal service raised its rate 17 times. These were accompanied by increases in the prices of electricity, water, and bus fares. And most important of all, the price of petroleum was increased eight times. These increases seemed to be justified and acceptable to every group in the New Order coalition. In contrast to the price increases in 1965 that aroused mass demonstration, that ultimately led to the demise of the Old Order, there was no such protest following the price increases of early 1967.[185]

Support for the Suharto-led attack on the PKI and toppling of Sukarno emanated from the state as much as from society. Most important, impressive unity of purpose was displayed within the military. Given Sukarno's longstanding efforts to factionalize ABRI and promote personal loyalists and leftist officers to key posts, this was no foregone conclusion. Only the severity of the PKI threat, as it had gathered force with the "red ants" and culminated with the bloody coup of 1965, can explain this impressive counterrevolutionary solidarity. The successive pressures of regional and leftist unrest had transformed the Indonesian military from a fragmented post-guerrilla warfare force into a formidable power center. Suharto gradually accomplished both the coordination of ABRI forces and the consolidation of his personal position atop this increasingly centralized military apparatus from 1966–70.[186] "Suharto stood for the reassertion of military hierarchy, and commanded widespread support among senior officers."[187] Evidence for this support could be seen in the fact that – quite unlike Marcos – Suharto was able to *cut* military budgets as he reordered ABRI's command structure.[188]

Last but not least, the New Order could count civil servants among its core coalitional backers – particularly the powerful Ministry of Home Affairs. Throughout the state apparatus, bureaucrats celebrated the opportunity to free their ministries of the rampant party infiltration of the Sukarno years. The Suharto regime's exceptional early stability could thus be located in a "historic consensus between civilian experts and army officers that lies at the heart of the New Order."[189]

Yet there were also chinks in the New Order's coalitional and institutional armor from the very outset. This distinguished Indonesia from Malaysia-style domination as well as Philippine-style fragmentation. First, Indonesia's ethnic Chinese economic elites did not have compelling reason to see military rule as conducive to their collective protection. The PKI had targeted military and landed wealth more than Chinese wealth, because ABRI and its Muslim landowning allies were political rivals in a way that the Chinese, with less than 3% of Indonesia's total population, were not.

---

[185] Ibid. 162.
[186] Crouch (1978).
[187] Anderson (1978a): 3.
[188] Booth (1997): 298.
[189] Emmerson (1978): 105.

The PKI also had purportedly sought to equip its paramilitary "fifth force" with arms from the Chinese mainland. This made anti-communist forces more inclined to attack Chinese interests than protect them. In the bloody days following the alleged PKI coup, "amidst reports that the Chinese Embassy had refused to lower its flag for the funeral of the six generals and rumors that China had played a part in the coup plot, the razzia [violent raids] extended to the shops, homes, and persons of Indonesians of Chinese descent."[190] The New Order would cater to racist sentiments by introducing restrictions on Chinese Indonesians' ethnic expression that knew no parallel in Malaysia. This incorporated them into a protection *racket* as much as a protection pact. The Suharto regime's alleged culpability in exacerbating communal cleavages and stirring up communal discord would be a recurrent theme over the subsequent decades, giving a somewhat hollow ring to its claims to be an effective protector against ethnic unrest.

The terms under which Indonesian students and intellectuals initially supported the Suharto regime were an additional signal of coalitional trouble. The New Order coalition was bound together by a "common enemy"[191] in the PKI, not by shared regime preferences. Military and bureaucratic elites were generally eager for Suharto to replace Sukarno's Guided Democracy with something entirely guided and not remotely democratic. Yet many students, Islamic politicians, and anti-communist intellectuals backed the New Order in the "hopeful expectation" that it would prove *less* authoritarian than its predecessor. Sukarno's final years had been marked by disregard for the rule of law and burgeoning restrictions on expression and dissent. This produced an ironic situation in which "[s]tudent activists and proponents of democratization generally supported the central role of the armed forces in politics," because they "saw the military as a potential agent of democratization and modernization."[192] Hence at least some Indonesian elites actively backed Suharto's takeover in the misplaced hope that he would deepen democracy, not destroy it.

The rhythms of electoral and contentious politics could not help but produce divided opinions as to whether the PKI's meteoric rise had been attributable to too *much* or too *little* democratic competition. The PKI had managed only a fourth-place finish in the free and fair national elections of 1955, capturing 16% of the vote at a time when its political program remained relatively moderate. Only after electoral pressures for moderation were lifted in 1959 did the PKI become so radical and so powerful at the grassroots. Anderson describes "the extraordinary mass politicization and mobilization of the Guided Democracy era" as a "largely unanticipated consequence of *intense party competition without elections*."[193] Indonesia's New Order commenced with a paradox: recent traumas

---

[190] Mortimer (1974): 389.
[191] This and the following quote are from an interview with Burhan Magenda, an editor of the influential student paper *Harian KAMI* from 1966–74, as well as a Cornell-trained political scientist and current member of Indonesia's parliament (July 16, 2004).
[192] Ramage (1995): 129.
[193] B. Anderson (1996): 30. Emphasis added.

had induced an acute "antipathy to party politics"[194] among a wide range of elites, but they had not produced the kind of direct linkage from electoral competition to ethnic conflict witnessed in Malaysia.

Nor had those traumas clearly signified an endemic rather than episodic mass threat. While Malaysia's ethnic divisions remained palpable after 1969, Indonesia's PKI was violently erased from Indonesia's political map after 1965. "[T]hese killings fundamentally reshaped the dimensions of social power by *decisively eliminating* any organized Indonesian resistance to Suharto's New Order regime from the outset."[195] The communist threat had become *unmanageable* absent counter-revolutionary elite collective action, but this did not mean that it would remain an *endemic* threat after the pogrom was complete. "'Crisis legitimacy' and 'role expansion' were used to justify military involvement in politics at the first stage of the New Order, but they were highly vulnerable to changed circumstances when the crisis had passed."[196] As Marcus Mietzner depicts the incomplete and impermanent incorporation of Indonesia's diverse Islamic forces as allied collective actors into the New Order's initial protection pact:

It was only by 1967 that Islamic leaders began to realize that their support for the army had not only resulted in the collapse of Sukarno's pro-communist regime, but also in the creation of another authoritarian polity with equally strong reservations towards political Islam.... *With the PKI destroyed, the single most important bond of solidarity between Islamic organizations had vanished*, and their diverging interests began to dominate the political attitudes within the *umat* once again.[197]

The dominant role of the military in Indonesia's authoritarian coalition represented a final "birth defect" in comparison to Malaysia's party-led protection pact. This would be expressed in ABRI's unwillingness to countenance the construction of autonomous party and state institutions that might ultimately usurp it as the preeminent power in Indonesian politics. "Having gained control of the government for themselves, the army leaders had no intention of handing power over to the political parties," writes Harold Crouch. "The emergence of the army to a position of unchallenged domination of the government had been welcomed enthusiastically by a small section of civilian political opinion and accepted as an unavoidable reality by most of the rest."[198]

Given the broad elite support with which the New Order was inaugurated, Suharto and his associates enjoyed an extraordinary opportunity to build stronger state and party institutions as civilian scaffolding for military rule. They did so to a greater degree than the Marcos regime in the Philippines, but to a lesser extent than UMNO's Malaysian authoritarian Leviathan. The intermediate strength of the Indonesian tax state is immediately suggested by deep historiographical disagreements among county experts as to the New Order's fiscal power. Scholars such as Benjamin Smith note "an immense spike in revenues" after 1966, thanks

[194] Emmerson (1978): 105.
[195] Boudreau (1999): 5. Emphasis in original.
[196] Honna (2003): 55.
[197] Mietzner (2009): 80. Emphasis added.
[198] Crouch (1978): 245.

to "the immediate efforts of the New Order regime to rebuild the state's extractive capacity," and stress that "non-oil taxes remained a significant share of total government revenues" even after the OPEC oil boom of the mid-1970s.[199] Others concur with Richard Tanter's depiction of the Suharto regime as a system of "rentier militarism" in which, thanks to bounteous quantities of petroleum revenues and foreign aid, "the state has not been required to entertain the political compromises that would be entailed in a domestic revenue base."[200]

In the final analysis, no one could reasonably dispute that the New Order exhibited greater fiscal power during the period from 1966–73 than the Sukarno government had ever exhibited. Yet state-building was hindered from the outset by the domination of coercive over administrative institutions. Civil servants were more actively supportive of the Suharto regime than state officials in the Philippines – but as political allies, they could never be as reliable as military officers. Thus from Jakarta to the farthest provinces, "[o]fficers were recruited to toughen up the bureaucracy with an exoskeleton of military command." Even in agencies where civilians held top postings, ABRI personnel would be assigned as their ostensible subordinates, "enabling officers to play watchdog roles 'underseeing' civilian ministers." The ubiquity of military appointees to provincial governorships inspired a local joke: "Under colonialism, we had a governor-general; now that we're independent, we have general-governors."[201]

Military dominance of the bureaucracy chronically geared public authority toward purposes of surveillance and control, rather than the kind of critical and complicated administrative tasks typically undertaken by civilian officials (e.g., direct income taxation, land reform, professional economic planning).[202] For all its territorial and infrastructural reach, Indonesia's authoritarian Leviathan was never rooted in the kind of professionalized bureaucracy that tends to characterize state apparatuses that are more civilianized than militarized or personalized. "The New Order.... brought profound changes to the nature of state organizations" as "the reach of state organizations expanded as never before into the countryside; and the state apparatus developed a degree of cohesion and order," Natasha Hamilton-Hart argues. "[B]ut it was a coherence that only minimally resembled rationalized bureaucratic forms, even in supposedly technocratic organizations such as the central bank."[203]

Military power also militated against any regime effort to concentrate authority in a civilian ruling party. While "New Order militants" urged a thoroughgoing militarization of the polity, Suharto's many bureaucratic and societal allies sought an active stake in the regime they had helped to forge. To marginalize the militants and incorporate civilian supporters, Suharto and his closest allies revised

[199] B. Smith (2007): 94. See also Emmerson (1978), Liddle (1996), Mas'oed (1983), and MacIntyre (1990).

[200] Tanter (1990): 53, 69. Similar tones are sounded by Hamilton-Hart (2002), Winters (1996), and Robison (1986).

[201] Cited in Emmerson (1978): 83, 102, 103.

[202] For studies on complex administrative tasks as an influence on state-building, with Southeast Asian empirics, see Doner (2009) and Doner, Ritchie, and Slater (2005).

[203] Hamilton-Hart (2002): 45, 29.

Indonesia's system of party politics in a manner intended to consolidate, not complicate military domination. Rather than working through an existing party or creating a party from scratch, the Suharto regime retooled a diverse assortment of preexisting "functional groups" (golongan karya, or Golkar[204]) into the New Order's quasi-civilian political wing. Such functional groups had mushroomed under Guided Democracy, first among PKI supporters with Sukarno's blessing and then, in direct counterrevolutionary response, among anti-PKI forces with military backing. Military elites had led an effort in late 1964 to reorganize these anti-PKI Golkar into a new secretariat, which "in effect [became] the army's political party."[205] As Julian Boileau describes the role of the revolutionary PKI in facilitating elite collective action via the birth of this counterrevolutionary military-civilian alliance:

> Throughout 1964 the political situation was becoming increasingly destabilized. The PKI dominance of political life. . . . grew progressively greater. The civilian and military elements involved with functional groups decided that a more coordinated attempt to counter the PKI was needed. . . . As a result it was agreed to form a coordinating secretariat of functional groups. . . . It was hoped that establishing a semblance of unity amongst the diverse functional groups would reduce the PKI's ability to capitalize on the divisions among them.[206]

This initial counterrevolutionary elite collective action would only tighten after the military seized power and began coercing and co-opting all state employees into the Golkar fold. Working closely with fellow generals Ali Murtopo and Amir Machmud (nicknamed "the bulldozer"), Suharto compelled the consolidation of more than two hundred Golkar affiliates into just seven, in preparation to contest and – in local parlance – "success" the 1971 elections. Rather than building an autonomous ruling party that might upstage the military, the Suharto regime deployed a quasi-party long dominated by the military itself. A creature of state more than society, Golkar provided a useful political outlet for the New Order's many non-military supporters, especially but not exclusively in the bureaucracy. Civil servants were forbidden from maintaining party memberships and forced to declare "monoloyalty" to Golkar.

In and of itself, Golkar proved to be a relatively formidable political apparatus. It was especially successful at generating support among state officials; but it also mobilized considerable electoral support among the population at large, capturing 63% of the national vote in the relatively competitive (if far from free and fair) 1971 election.[207] Yet Golkar never enjoyed considerable success at bringing Indonesia's primary Islamic and nationalist organizations into the party fold. If Suharto had worked quickly to reshape party politics in the immediate wake of the 1965 coup – when his protection pact was still in place – he might have had more success in making Golkar a wider political umbrella encompassing society as well

---

[204] The organization was called Sekber Golkar, or the Golkar secretariat, until after the 1971 elections, but I use the term Golkar throughout to avoid confusion.
[205] Boileau (1983): 44.
[206] Ibid. 45.
[207] Slater (2008a): 263–266.

as the state. Yet ABRI's preexisting preeminence and deep aversion to party politics made any such robust party formation process unthinkable. Suharto waited until the early 1970s to construct a new party system, by which time it would have required far more coercion to bring old groups like the PNI, NU, and Muhammadiyah under Golkar's direct control. Instead, Suharto pushed existing Islamic groups to join the regime-created PPP and pressed existing nationalist groups to join its new nationalist party fabrication, the PDI.[208] This was a second-best solution that would give Indonesian communal elites more room to maneuver as the New Order's protective logic progressively dwindled.

As a creature of the military, Golkar not only relied heavily on coercion and compulsory membership for its support from below – it also confronted resistance to its development from *above* among ABRI elites unwilling to see the New Order's ruling party gain more power than its ruling military. Golkar failed to organize wide-ranging elite collective action through a single peak institution, as strong ruling parties typically do. With a cohesive, politicized, and centralized military already in place and in power, party formation served instead to *bifurcate* political elites into separate institutions.

This institutional bifurcation might not have exacerbated factionalism if the New Order had enjoyed steadfast coalitional backing. Yet the complete annihilation of the PKI left the Suharto regime with less leverage than its Malaysian counterparts when seeking to command resources and support. As memories of the PKI faded and the New Order coalition constricted, leading actors within Suharto's ruling institutions became less politically acquiescent and reliable. His response was to undermine the cohesion and autonomy of military, party, and state institutions, treating them as potential rivals to be checked instead of allies to be trusted. Indonesia's authoritarian Leviathan gradually became more fragmented and distracted by factional considerations, and less able to order social power.

Involution: Coalitional Withering and Institutional Balancing, 1974–1994
Different scholars emphasize different benchmarks in the decline of the New Order coalition – but no one questions that the coalition shriveled over time. In a prescient 1978 analysis, Benedict Anderson argued that, by 1971,

> the first clear signs of the disintegration of the anti-communist coalition became visible. In a very simple way, *the government weakened its own support by its complete success in destroying the organized left in 1965–66....* By 1971, the "communist menace" had begun to recede into memory, and government legitimacy derived solely from this source was becoming tenuous.... *With the decline of the vividness and plausibility of the "communist threat," the prime cement of the 1965 coalition necessarily grew brittle.*[209]

Anderson jumped the gun in predicting the New Order's impending demise; but he correctly identified the rapid expiration of its protection pact, as the Suharto regime had come to rest almost entirely on a combination of provision and

---

[208] PPP stands for Partai Persatuan Pembangunan (United Development Party), and PDI stands for Partai Demokrasi Indonesia (Indonesian Democratic Party).

[209] B. Anderson (1978a): 6–7. Emphasis added.

coercion. The relative durability of authoritarianism in Indonesia vis-à-vis the Philippines is thus better explained by institutional than attitudinal mechanisms of reproduction. Indonesia's New Order was relatively effective when extracting resources, purveying patronage, and deploying coercion because it had built relatively strong state and party institutions between the mid-1960s and the early 1970s – *when its protection pact was still in place.*[210] Yet the declining attitudinal salience of anti-communism would have a corrosive effect on elite collective action within and between Indonesia's key political institutions.

The earliest major sign of coalitional withering and institutional fragmentation arose with the so-called Malari Affair in January 1974. Troubles began in 1973 with growing student agitation over economic corruption and mismanagement, as well as "rising protests by PPP (the then newly formed Islamic party) and other leading Muslim organizations and individuals against the government's promotion of a new marriage law" that "would remove marriage, divorce, and the entire realm of family law from the religious court system."[211] This rising unrest reflected growing sentiments that the New Order was becoming less attentive to the array of Islamic and student allies who had helped usher the regime to power.

The major lightning rod was General Ali Murtopo. "Suharto's right-hand man" served as Interior Minister and as commander of Opsus,[212] a secretive military unit founded by Suharto in 1968. Not only did Murtopo have stronger ties to Christian than Muslim constituencies. He also seemed to "want to use Golkar as his own power base,"[213] proposing to transform it into a cadre party independent of military control. This raised the ire of General Soemitro, who had strong ties to Islamic groups deriving in part from their collaboration against the PKI. While Murtopo commanded Opsus, Soemitro led ABRI's Operational Command for the Restoration of Security and Order (Kopkamtib), the institution founded by Suharto in the wake of the 1965 coup, serving as the heart of the New Order military ever since. Soemitro raised eyebrows in late 1973 when he "began a series of visits to major university campuses" and publicly called "for 'two-way communications' between the government and the people," John Bresnan reports. "Many thought at the time that Soemitro's highly publicized visits to the campuses represented an independent move to challenge the members of Soeharto's inner circle"[214] – most obviously Murtopo.

These factional tensions helped spark a violent eruption of student protests and urban riots in January 1974. The so-called Malari disaster[215] resulted in the death of approximately a dozen people and the arrest and injury of hundreds

---

[210] In his discussion of Islamic groups, Mietzner (2009: 86) suggests a similar early trajectory for the New Order as the one proposed here. "The massive threat of the PKI towards the religio-political privileges of both the traditionalist and modernist communities legitimized, in the eyes of Muslim leaders, temporary praetorian rule. When Islamic groups realized that the armed forces had no intention of handing back power to civilian actors, the authoritarian regime was already deeply entrenched in the political system."

[211] Sidel (2006): 107.

[212] Opsus was short for Operasi Khusus, or Special Operations.

[213] Suryadinata (1989): 145.

[214] Bresnan (1993): 139, 144.

[215] "Malari" is short for Malapetaka Lima Belas Januari, or the January 15th Disaster.

more, as well as the destruction and looting of hundreds of Jakarta buildings. In political terms, the violent events shattered Suharto's confidence in his support among student and Islamic groups, as well as their perceived military patrons. "Implicated in the student protests and, by association, the Malari riots, Soemitro was forced to resign his post."[216] Suharto also cracked down hard on the student media, especially those of an Islamic bent, further sacrificing his support in Islamic circles. As John Sidel has argued, Malari was a violent expression of worsening coalitional friction. "This series of events reflected – and in considerable measure exacerbated – a set of growing tensions between rival factions, and between conflicting institutional, social, and religious elements, within the New Order regime."[217] Beyond the hazy confines of palace intrigue, Malari also indexed the deepening disenchantment of those student activists who had never accepted military dictatorship as anything more than a temporary and necessary evil to combat the communist threat and stabilize a turbulent economy and society. Such students displayed

a sense of invincibility arising from the moral force of their ideas. They were also impelled by a sense of urgency, by the conviction that time was running out, that the country was heading for autocracy. Undoubtedly they hoped to spark a series of events that, if not capable of bringing down the government altogether, would at least put a brake on the growth of presidential power.[218]

Yet Malari would produce precisely the opposite result. Soemitro was replaced as Kopkamtib head by a Suharto loyalist lacking Soemitro's revolutionary credentials and autonomous political base: Catholic general Benny Moerdani. This was the most important in a series of personalizing blows leveled against collective military leadership. Since Soemitro had been the most powerful obstacle to an expanded political role for Golkar, his fall from grace also helped Golkar make modest gains vis-à-vis ABRI, if mostly through the growing clout of a single loyalist, Ali Murtopo. Golkar's total number of field secretaries expanded from five to eleven after 1973. Seven of those eleven "were Ali Murtopo's men." Murtopo tried to leverage his enhanced power over Golkar with calls in 1974 for a "dynamic balance between the civilians and ABRI"[219] rather than the kind of military hegemony that had characterized the New Order during its initial years.

Golkar nevertheless remained a far weaker institution than ABRI, largely because ABRI elites still dominated Golkar's upper reaches. "The military was the dominant political force within Golkar"[220] between the 1971 and 1977 elections. Yet Golkar's initial power disadvantage ironically proved advantageous over time, as Suharto saw it as a weaker and more malleable ally than ABRI, and hence worthy of presidential favor. Organized support from a strengthened and civilianized Golkar could help protect Suharto against the kind of military disloyalty that had seemingly erupted with Malari.

---

[216] Sidel (2006): 109.

[217] Ibid. 108.

[218] Bresnan (1993): 142.

[219] Suryadinata (1989): 59 fn. 30, and 39.

[220] Ibid. 84.

Suharto's decision to seek a third presidential term in the 1977 elections accelerated ongoing processes of regime personalization and coalitional decay. Public criticisms of Suharto increased from within ABRI, even as voices in Golkar and wider society increasingly denounced ABRI's domination of the state apparatus. While Golkar romped to another manufactured landslide victory in the 1977 vote, growing social discontent at Suharto's narrowing base produced rising support for the Islamic PPP, which scored outright victories in the province of Aceh and in Jakarta itself. Electoral opposition was followed by contentious opposition, as the early months of 1978 preceding Suharto's re-inauguration witnessed a more organized upsurge of urban middle-class protest than the rather riotous unrest of the Malari period.

As his protection pact evaporated, Suharto tightened his personal grip on key authoritarian institutions. Initially this took the form of a strengthened alliance with Ali Murtopo and other personal allies within ABRI:

Shortly after his re-election, Suharto announced a new Cabinet. Far from representing an attempt to widen his shrunken political base, it bore all the characteristics of a regime under siege. It contained far more generals than its predecessor, and these generals were all members of the old palace clique. What new faces emerged were mainly creatures of General Ali Murtopo's intelligence apparatus.... For the first time in Indonesia's history the ministry of religion (an old Muslim bailiwick) was given to a general.[221]

Even as he showered ABRI with prime appointments with one hand, Suharto began reducing Golkar's dependence on the military with the other. At its 1978 congress following Suharto's re-election:

The Golkar leadership introduced a policy which stated that the military officers on active duty would not be permitted to hold office in Golkar.... It was also stated by the Golkar leadership that in the future, the chairmanship of Golkar supervisors' councils at the provincial and district levels would not be held automatically by local military commanders. Some Golkar leaders interpreted this as a sign of the "civilianization" process. Interestingly, this civilianization process was accompanied by the greater role played by President Suharto in Golkar.[222]

This creeping personalization of the Suharto regime was neither an unintended consequence of Golkar's growing status, nor a simple result of the president's "sultanistic" tendencies. Like Marcos, Suharto became disinclined to foster strong and autonomous authoritarian institutions as soon as he lacked a protection pact to keep leading actors in those institutions in check. Civilianization served to balance Suharto's potential rivals in ABRI – not to build an autonomous ruling party. Golkar was gaining state resources and positions, but only by trading its subservience to the military for subservience to Suharto. Another UMNO it plainly was not.

The political shocks of 1977 and 1978 were also followed by Suharto's invigorated efforts to steer the national economic product toward his own hands and those of his very closest allies. "Far from being a creature of the military high

[221] Anderson (1978): 16.
[222] Suryadinata (1989): 99–100.

command, the Presidency in Indonesia became a center of power with its own momentum."[223] All state banks were mandated in 1978 to give 8% of their profits to new presidential foundations (yayasan), which would provide Suharto with bounteous sources of discretionary finance in the decades to come. Much as Golkar was no UMNO, Indonesia's yayasans were no Malaysian EPF. Siphoned and distributed in haphazard patrimonial fashion, Suharto's yayasan funds were more often deployed selectively for the business boondoggles of factional allies than strategically for purposes of viable and financially sustainable development projects.

Yet the Suharto regime's *intermediate* willingness to accept technocratic constraints on freewheeling economic spending – more than in the Philippines, but less than in Malaysia – underscores Indonesia's positioning as an intermediate case. "Soeharto continued to employ a talented team of economic technocrats to guide macro-economic policy while at the same time ploughing back a significant part of the oil funds into heavy industrial development," Harold Crouch reminds us. "It needs to be emphasized, however, that Soeharto never allowed the technocrats' quest for efficiency to seriously undermine the patronage network on which – together with his control over the instruments of coercion – Soeharto's political power rested."[224] Whereas Malaysian leaders have generally taken care to ensure that patronage flows would not disrupt macroeconomic stability, Suharto generally exhibited greater concern that macroeconomic considerations might disrupt his vital patronage flows[225] – if not the same kind of wanton disregard for macroeconomic stability exhibited by the completely patronage-driven Marcos regime.

Indonesia's drift from militarization toward personalization could also be seen in the replacement of Murtopo with Sudharmono as the president's right-hand man. Sudharmono lacked Murtopo's autonomous base in ABRI: "Although Sudharmono was a retired general, he had not been accepted by the military establishment as a full member," Leo Suryadinata explains. "Unlike most of the military leaders who were field generals, Sudharmono was a staff general without battle experience. His power base had been in the bureaucracy rather than in the military per se."[226] In sum, Indonesian politics after 1978 would be characterized by increasing ambiguity as to whether Golkar or ABRI enjoyed the upper hand as Suharto's primary political vehicle, alongside decreasing uncertainty that Suharto was the only real driver of elite politics.

Institutional balancing and political personalization were logical if Machiavellian responses by Suharto to the vanishing of his protection pact. Without an endemic PKI threat to serve as coalitional cement, and in response to the PPP's electoral gains and subsequent mass protests in 1978, Suharto began to criticize any and all critical groups for defying Pancasila – the vague, consensual

---

[223] Robison and Hadiz (2004): 48.
[224] Crouch (2001): 147, 148.
[225] My gratitude to Sofia Fenner for helping me convey this critical comparative point.
[226] Suryadinata (1989): 138.

national ideology first introduced by Sukarno in the 1940s to bridle ideological and religious conflict. During a speech to military commanders in May 1980, Suharto condemned the PPP as "anti-Pancasila" and declared that "because of the presence of anti-Pancasila forces, ABRI would be forced to choose a partner and a friend who fully supported Pancasila. It was clear that he was referring to Golkar."[227] A dissident group led by retired generals including ABRI founder A.H. Nasution emerged in response to Suharto's abuse of Pancasila and apparent intention to convert ABRI into a bodyguard for Golkar and himself. Although the so-called Petition of Fifty failed to gain political traction, their public dissent signified the deepening alienation between the professional military and the Suharto clique.

Rather than yielding to military concerns on Golkar's growing independence, Suharto moved the New Order ever closer to *a party-military balance that denied effective decision-making power to party and military institutions alike.* Sudharmono captured the chairmanship of Golkar unopposed in 1983, and during his five-year tenure, "the Suharto government.... succeeded in reorganizing Golkar and transforming it into a kind of 'cadre party.' This was aimed at making the organization a more effective political movement under Suharto's personal control."[228] Suharto and his wife fittingly became Golkar's first individual cadres in 1984.

Suharto's apparent institutional gains masked deeper coalitional losses. In the same year when Golkar became a cadre party, the New Order suffered a series of major and lasting blows to its support in the Islamic community. If the protests of 1978 marked Suharto's declining backing from students, the military's massacre of several hundred Muslim protestors in the Tanjung Priok section of Jakarta in 1984 signaled a similar bellwether in the New Order's relations with political Islam. ABRI Commander Benny Moerdani, a Catholic, was widely blamed for the killings, and "the 'Tanjung Priok Incident'.... came to signify the marginalization and abuse of Indonesia's poor Islamic majority at the hands of an oppressive – and ostensibly Christian-led–regime."[229] Having once depended on ABRI to protect them from the PKI, Indonesia's urban Islamic elites increasingly came to see the military as an unwanted rival and oppressor, instead of a necessary protector.

Less dramatically but just as ominously, the New Order experienced growing political separation in the mid-1980s from Indonesia's largest Islamic mass organizations: the Nahdlatul Ulama, or NU, and Muhammadiyah.[230] In the wake of Suharto's decision to force all social and political organizations to accept Pancasila (and hence not Islam) as their sole ideological foundation, new NU leader Abdurrahman Wahid pulled the organization out of formal politics altogether, pledging to focus the NU on spiritual matters alone. This wounded the PPP in the short term, since the party had embraced Pancasila at Suharto's behest and depended on the NU rank-and-file for much of its electoral support. Yet

---

[227] Ibid. 109.
[228] Ibid. 123.
[229] Sidel (2006): 56.
[230] Nahdlatul Ulama can be translated as the Council of Islamic Scholars.

in the long term, the NU's withdrawal from Indonesia's authoritarian political structures gave the wily Wahid more room to maneuver, allowing him to become a leading (if quixotically inconsistent) critic of the Suharto regime throughout the New Order's final decade. NU's political autonomy was mirrored by that of Muhammadiyah, which similarly "withdrew" from politics to focus its energies on its followers' "moral regeneration."[231] With Islamic groups becoming less wedded to New Order institutions, the military, Golkar, and Suharto became the only three actors that counted in Indonesia's authoritarian Leviathan.

Golkar's growing social base worsened tensions with ABRI in the run-up to the 1987 elections. Suharto added fuel to the fire, not only by picking a Golkar figure rather than an ABRI man as vice-president for the first time, but by choosing Sudharmono, Suharto's point-man in Golkar's expansion. Meanwhile, Moerdani's star as ABRI commander was on the decline. For his sins of opposing Suharto's appointment of Sudharmono as vice-president and "complaining about the unrestrained greed of his children" – but not for committing atrocities at Tanjong Priok – Moerdani "was shunted upstairs to the less powerful post of defense minister," and eventually "removed from the cabinet entirely."[232] His institutional power base, Kopkamtib, was disbanded. Suharto's sacking of Moerdani in 1988 was "a defining moment, because from that time on he never delegated a significant amount of power to any senior armed forces officer."[233]

The year 1988 was not only a defining moment in terms of the personalization of regime power. It also saw the last nail being driven into the coffin of Suharto's original protection pact, as anti-communism became a weapon in intra-elite, factional disputes for the first time. Furious at Sudharmono's vice-presidential nomination in March, Moerdani deployed the communist bogey to further fracture rather than unify Indonesia's political elite. "Kopkamtib was mobilized to identify 'communist penetration' in the Sudharmono-led Golkar," Jun Honna relates. "During the period between the March MPR session and the Golkar election in October, an intensive campaign was conducted to discredit Sudharmono by alleging his involvement in the activities of communist organizations in the late 1940s. . . . Soeharto's September decision to abolish Kopkamtib was made under these circumstances."[234] From 1988 on, Indonesian elites had far more reason to fear being *accused* of communism than being *attacked* by communists. The New Order regime's slide from protection pact into pure provision pact appeared complete.

The 1990s saw Suharto channel ever more resources to an ever smaller circle of allies. In economic terms, Suharto famously became obsessed with helping his children amass untold personal fortunes. By the mid-1990s, the Suharto family had become "by far the most powerful economic dynasty in the country."[235] In

---

[231] Madrid (1999): 20.
[232] Schwarz (1994): 146.
[233] Liddle (1999): 105.
[234] Honna (2003): 113.
[235] Schwarz (1994): 141.

political terms, Suharto's main shift came with the founding in 1990 of a new organization of Islamic elites, ICMI,[236] as a counterweight to the increasingly unreliable military and a regimist replacement for Indonesia's autonomous Islamic mass organizations, the NU and Muhammadiyah. Suharto only favored ICMI through the leadership of one of his closest allies, lifetime friend B.J. Habibie. As Adam Schwarz situated ICMI's political role in historical perspective: "Much like Sukarno once looked to the communists to counteract unhappy army officers, Soeharto now looks to Muslims to play the same balancing role."[237] Such transparently Machiavellian machinations could only serve to wed an especially opportunistic subset of communal elites to the Suharto regime, and to do so in the most crass, instrumental, and precarious of ways.

More a provider of balance than a source of authority, ICMI suffered the same basic plight that had always afflicted Golkar. Even in the 1990s, Golkar's station remained to balance ABRI rather than to influence Suharto. The autocratic potentialities of institutional balance were displayed when ABRI nominated General Try Sutrisno to replace Golkar's Sudharmono as vice-president for Suharto's sixth term in 1992. Suharto accepted the suggestion, even though most analysts believed that he preferred his main loyalist, Habibie. But he made ABRI pay for its impudence. "When Suharto announced his cabinet in March 1993, only a few ministers had senior military backgrounds," as it "included more Suharto loyalists and associates of Habibie."[238]

Old-guard ABRI nationalists thus had increasing reason to feel politically side-lined, and growing incentives to explore new routes to political influence. Deteriorating relations between Suharto and ABRI spilled over into party politics. The early 1990s saw the Sukarnoist phoenix rising from the nationalist ashes – with apparent if covert backing from nationalist factions in the military, especially networks linked to ousted General Benny Moerdani. In 1993, Sukarno's daughter Megawati Sukarnoputri "became the center of an almost hysterical campaign" to take control of the PDI, launching her candidacy with a pamphlet entitled "I Have Unfurled the Flag!"[239] Suharto relented to nationalist pressure and allowed Megawati to seize control of the PDI, even as he stepped up his personalization and Islamicization of ABRI to punish his nationalist rivals and critics. The replacement of Edi Sudradjat with Feisal Tanjung as ABRI commander purged an old Moerdani ally and promoted a Habibie favorite. "Edi's sudden replacement was only the most dramatic incident in a broad and accelerating change in the ABRI leadership that through 1993–94 saw many important 'discontented' ABRI officers being moved from senior posts," Edward Aspinall argues. When Suharto's son-in-law Prabowo Subianto secured a major strategic posting in 1995 after "becoming the youngest officer to attain the rank of major general,"[240] Suharto's

[236] Ikatan Cendekiawan Muslim Indonesia, or Indonesian Association of Muslim Intellectuals.
[237] Schwarz (1994): 176.
[238] Aspinall (2005): 44.
[239] Ibid. 145, 156.
[240] Ibid. 46.

personalization of power was essentially complete. As one Indonesian brigadier-general summed up ABRI's political marginalization by 1995:

ABRI is no longer dominant; it is no longer even involved in decision making. It is only Suharto who makes the decisions. ABRI is simply the implementer of what the government decides.... Now it can do nothing, and ABRI recognizes it is no more than the fire brigade.[241]

Suharto had thus squandered the New Order's original image as an expression of military cohesion and power, ruling as a credible protector of a broad social coalition. This made it increasingly unclear whether ABRI would continue to perceive Suharto's regime as worth defending. The big question thus became whether any organized challenge to Suharto could emerge, and put his increasingly factionalized ruling apparatus to the repressive test. As in the Philippines, it would be communal elites and urban middle classes – no longer bound to authoritarian rule in a protection pact – who would take the lead. It would be the relative lack of oppositional activity among similarly situated elite groups in Malaysia – combined with the steadfast willingness of state personnel to crush opposition with force – that would doom that country's own reformasi movement in 1998 to a brutal defeat.

[241] Roekmini Koesomo Astoeti, quoted in Ibid. 54.

7

Contentious Politics and the Struggle for Democratization

Introduction

One of the central messages of this book has been that patterns of contentious politics profoundly shape the *initial foundations* of authoritarian Leviathans. Contentious politics also profoundly shapes authoritarian Leviathans' *ultimate fates*, when political crises call their continuing survival into question. When swarms of ordinary people team up with pivotal sets of elites to challenge an authoritarian regime in the streets of a capital city, a seemingly stable dictatorship can fall victim to a "democratic revolution"[1] in what superficially appears to be a stunningly short span of time.

To be sure, democratic revolutions are neither necessary nor sufficient for a democratic transition to take place. Democratization can occur through an authoritarian regime's electoral defeat or internal splintering, both of which are made more likely by severe economic crisis – and democratic uprisings are as likely to end in authoritarian crackdowns as democratic transitions. Yet the emergence of a cross-class urban protest movement, willing to risk repression by confronting a dictatorship's coercive apparatus at a polity's geographic and symbolic center, serves as the most powerful stimulant for an authoritarian retreat. Even when a dictatorship suffers a shocking defeat at the polls or devastating defections from its inner ranks, it can take massive cross-class democratic mobilization to push a wobbly regime over the political precipice. In fact, it is often the rise of such a movement that makes a dictatorship lose an election or suffer worsening dissension among ruling elites in the first place.

By definition, a cross-class democratization movement requires elite involvement. *As sudden as democratic revolutions may appear, the complex constellations of elite politics that determine their emergence and fate are shaped over long periods of time.* Previous chapters have shown how elite politics in Indonesia, Malaysia, and the Philippines had been structured by the enduring and evolving coalitional and institutional strengths and weaknesses of those countries' authoritarian

---

[1] Thompson (2004). See Slater (2009: 204, fn. 2) for further conceptual discussion.

Leviathans. This chapter analyzes the fate of these regimes when they came to confront their most severe political and economic crises. In all three cases, an economic downturn and oppositional upturn put authoritarian coalitions and institutions to their sternest test. These regimes' capacity to withstand these seemingly sudden challenges depended directly on how well they had managed to order power from state and societal elites throughout the preceding decades.

As ever, elite collective action was of the essence. Authoritarian durability would rest upon the capacity of party, military, and state institutions to extract and organize critical political resources from economic elites, communal elites, middle classes, and state officials themselves. Having consistently failed to order power through authoritarian institutions, the Philippine regime's resilience proved minimal. Having consistently succeeded at ordering power through its powerful party-state, the Malaysian regime's resilience proved remarkable. Having gradually decayed from a relatively institutionalized arrangement into a highly factionalized and personalized system of rule, Indonesia's regime was again something of an intermediate case, whose resilience had become deeply compromised and highly uncertain.

Patterns of elite collective action during extraordinary times would look surprisingly similar to patterns during ordinary times. In the Philippines, Marcos would be felled by an alliance led by elite actors who had either opposed him or extracted a high price for their political support throughout the martial-law era. In Indonesia, Suharto's maltreatment of the military, squandering of state revenue to elite cronies, and failure to organize reliable support from middle classes or communal elites would seal his political fate. In both cases, *the severity of economic crisis was more a consequence than a cause of coalitional and institutional frailty*. In the contrasting case of Malaysia, the Mahathir regime would survive its leanest days on stores of coercive, remunerative, and symbolic power accrued over three decades of politically stable and economically successful BN rule. Elite attitudes toward regime change in all three cases would be shaped by one factor above all others: whether the authoritarian Leviathan was perceived as a legitimate protector, making elites more secure from the threat of renewed mass unrest – or as a violent racketeer, attacking rather than protecting elites to keep them in line.

While all types of elites had important roles to play in democratic mobilization, this chapter stresses the pivotal role played by *communal elites*. Contrary to conventional claims that anti-authoritarian protest arises from class-based economic grievances, Southeast Asian cases exemplify how religious and nationalist sentiments and solidarities can provide the emotive thrust and cross-class appeal necessary for such collective acts of high-risk political opposition to emerge and succeed.[2]

End Game in the Philippines: From Aquino's Assassination to People Power, 1983–1986

Since the Marcos dictatorship rose to power in active confrontation with a wide range of economic elites, it was fitting that the political crisis that brought Marcos

---

[2] Slater (2009).

down would be triggered by his hostile relations with the Philippine oligarchy. Since Marcos had long been targeted for criticism by leading elements in the Catholic Church, it was equally fitting that communal elites assumed a leading oppositional stance as the crisis worsened. And since Marcos never enjoyed the steadfast support of a cohesive coercive apparatus, it should come as no surprise that factionalism within the Armed Forces of the Philippines would sound the death knell for his politically bankrupt regime in February 1986.

The Philippines' democratization drama unfolded in three main acts of cross-class mobilization. The first groundswell arose in direct response to the assassination of opposition leader Benigno Aquino upon his return to Manila from exile, in August 1983:

165 rallies, marches, and other demonstrations took place between August 21 and September 30, 1983. The largest was Aquino's funeral procession in Manila, which took eleven hours and was attended by an estimated 2 million people. Protest demonstrations continued into the following year, with more than 100 held between October 1983 and February 1984. The biggest of these was the 120-kilometer "Tarlac to Tarmac" run (from Aquino's home province to the international airport where he was murdered), attended by an estimated five hundred thousand people.[3]

As important as the demonstrations' massive size was "the involvement of the upper and middle classes."[4] As Temario Rivera notes: "during the twilight years of the authoritarian regime, some of the most vivid open protests erupted in the very centers of high commerce and finance involving the professionals, white collar workers, and the anti-crony personalities."[5] Although Marcos' economic mismanagement and jaw-dropping venality had long provided ample grounds for societal grievance, it would be Marcos' assassination of his factional archenemy that would serve as "the catalyst that forced hitherto reluctant groups among the middle class into more direct action."[6]

While the middle class provided much of the biomass for protests, economic elites provided funding, and religious elites provided inspiration. "Filipino-Chinese business leaders began secretly contributing money to the opposition," writes Mark Thompson. "The large crowds that anti-Marcos executives could mobilize and the substantial financial assistance that they could provide made them crucial to the success of the traditional opposition."[7] Meanwhile, the Church's response to the assassination was deeply critical, and far from collaborative. In Dennis Shoesmith's terms, this signaled "that the assassination marked a shift in the moral and even the supernatural order: that the regime had lost all moral authority."[8] No less a communal elite than Manila Archbishop Jaime Cardinal Sin expressed as much in his funeral homily for Aquino, tearfully proclaiming that "our people.... wait, no longer as timid and scattered sheep, but as

---

[3] Thompson (1995): 116.
[4] Ibid.
[5] Rivera (2001): 238–239.
[6] Barry (2006): 166.
[7] Thompson (1995): 120.
[8] Cited in Ibid. 117.

men and women purified and strengthened by a profound communal grief that has made them one."[9]

Even as the commander of an exceedingly weak authoritarian Leviathan, Marcos still had far more guns and money at his disposal than the opposition. But money alone was proving insufficient to keep all those guns loyal. Even before Aquino's assassination, two of the nation's top three military officers, Juan Ponce Enrile and Fidel Ramos, had threatened to resign over the "maladministration of the military" by the hydra's third head: Fabian Ver, of Marcos' Presidential Security Command (PSC). Ver was then widely blamed for arranging Aquino's murder, intensifying "the Ilocano intramurals" rattling the military's highest echelons.[10] "Enrile, to show that he was not involved in the killing, met with the Aquino family and other oppositionists when they came to claim the former senator's body," notes Thompson. "The young officers serving in Enrile's security force intensified their organizing among other low-level officers disillusioned by mounting corruption in the military,"[11] speeding their efforts to build a Reform the Armed Forces Movement (RAM). This factionalism had produced operational incapacity by the mid-1980s, as "the Ver-Ramos stand-off" left the armed forces "immobilized by the intensity of factional struggle."[12]

With his symbolic power in eclipse and his coercive power on the fritz, Marcos calculated that his advantage in remunerative power might permit him to stabilize his regime through national elections, which could be bought or rigged as needed. His electoral gamble also stemmed from confidence that his opponents – mostly a factionalized assortment of business oligarchs – would never agree on a single candidate to challenge him. What Marcos failed to appreciate was the awesome political potential of the mass religious and nationalist upheaval that had followed the moral shock of Aquino's 1983 assassination. Elections spurred the second major bout of cross-class mobilization presaging Marcos' fall, as the President's opponents gathered forces to compete in the February 1986 vote.

First, economic elites needed to set aside factional concerns and choose a single candidate to oppose Marcos. Aquino's widow Corazon was a poignant choice. Opposition oligarchs then mobilized an estimated $6 million to finance the campaigns of anti-Marcos candidates. In rural areas especially, "the Laurels and other powerful opposition clans were able to counteract the KBL's financial advantage with their own family-based political machines."[13] Given Marcos' readiness to raid the national treasury to buy an electoral win, economic elites lacked the funds necessary to win the day with money alone. "In the cities, the moral appeals of the opposition overcame the patronage advantage of the ruling party."[14]

This moral advantage derived in no small part from cross-class outrage over the assassination of Aquino, "for which the Marcoses were widely believed to

9 Cited in Ileto (1985): 12.
10 McCoy (1999): 228.
11 Thompson (1995): 120–121.
12 Wurfel (1985): 235.
13 Thompson (1995): 129.
14 Ibid. 130.

be responsible."[15] As vital as this shared sense of outrage was the willingness of activists among the middle class and religious organizations to build an institution to ensure that outrage could be effectively expressed. Specifically, the National Citizens Movement for Free Elections (NAMFREL) managed to mobilize 500,000 volunteers to monitor the polling in 85 percent of all national precincts in the February 1986 vote.[16] This "contributed to the large turnout of voters on election day."[17]

NAMFREL represented a clear institutional expression of the Catholic Church's commitment to restoring Philippine democracy. The group "established a 'marine corps' made up of priests and nuns, because they were less likely to be harmed than laypersons." Furthermore, "Sin and the Catholic hierarchy praised NAMFREL in pastoral letters and provided it with institutional support," Thompson notes. "Parish priests and nuns were often the leaders of local NAMFREL chapters."[18] This Church support was vital, helping to "provide NAMFREL with a mantle of legitimacy that helped undermine attempts by the regime and boycotters to discredit the organization as a tool of the United States."[19]

Not only did the Church play a leading role in ensuring a competitive vote – it also helped ensure that Marcos could not steal a win through fraud. NAMFREL enjoyed significant credibility when it claimed, after Marcos' assertion of victory, that Aquino was the rightful winner. More dramatically, the CBCP, the most conservative of all Philippine Church institutions, "denounced the polls as 'unparalleled in the fraudulence of their conduct.'"[20] Such statements gave Aquino momentum as she sought to force Marcos to accept defeat. "Aquino launched the Tagumpay ng Bayan (triumph of the people) civil disobedience campaign on February 16, 1986, when an estimated 2 million gathered at Luneta Park in downtown Manila to hear her condemn the regime."[21]

To this point, the military had played only a backstage role in the unfolding drama. Before the vote, the Reform the Armed Forces Movement (RAM) "urged the armed forces to remain neutral in the elections,"[22] rather than throwing their coercive weight behind Marcos and his KBL. Opposition politicians had in fact been meeting with RAM officers for nearly a year.[23] After Marcos claimed victory, one of his long-time military opponents "led over a hundred PMA [Philippine Military Academy] alumni in a call for nonviolent protest."[24] Marcos was taking no chances, as "about a third of the AFP's combat forces were allocated to presidential security while growing numbers of communist guerrillas roamed

---

[15] Haggard and Kaufman (1995): 56.
[16] Thompson (1995): 148.
[17] Youngblood (1990): 198.
[18] Thompson (1995): 148, 127.
[19] Youngblood (1990): 198.
[20] Thompson (1995): 151–152.
[21] Ibid. 154.
[22] Ibid. 149.
[23] Thompson (1995): 121.
[24] McCoy (1999): 158.

the countryside unopposed."[25] The autocrat was failing to act as a protector of anyone besides himself.

Political gridlock was broken when the RAM launched a coup on February 22nd, seizing two military bases on opposite sides of Manila's massive thoroughfare, Edificio de los Santos Avenue (EDSA). As Marcos' tanks prepared to roll up EDSA to crush the revolt, anti-Marcos forces sprang into action. First, Corazon Aquino's brother-in-law, "who was in close contact with [RAM leader Fidel] Ramos, impulsively implored on Radio Veritas for civilians to protect the rebels."[26] Little happened, however, until Cardinal Sin himself received a desperate phone call from the wife of the second co-leader of the coup, Juan Ponce Enrile. Sin went on Radio Veritas and uttered the following fateful words: "I call the people to come out from their houses and to protect our friends, the soldiers."

It was time to mobilize. "As phones rang across the city, political networks, primed by the recent elections, reacted quickly," writes Alfred McCoy. "A crowd of some fifty thousand people gathered within hours at the gates of Camp Aguinaldo," where Ramos' and Enrile's troops were holed up. The throng swelled to approximately 500,000 by the following morning.[27] Priests and nuns led the way, many of whom brought crucifixes and statues of the Virgin Mary for people to hold because, as one nun said, the "people will need symbols to rally around."[28]

That this forward religious presence was fundamental to the size and scope of cross-class mobilization is suggested by Michael Pinches' ethnography of Manila slum-dwellers who participated in People Power. "Some said they responded directly to the call of Cardinal Sin, and a great many said they would not have gone had it not been for this directive and the large presence of nuns and priests."[29] The Church not only led the way in inspiring the revolt; it also helped keep it organized. Bryan Johnson reports that when Radio Veritas briefly went off the air during the uprising, the protestors became like a "fleet of taxicabs without any central dispatcher."[30] But radio contact was quickly restored, and the multitude remained unified.

In short, People Power "galvanized the participation of the people from all walks of life, rich and poor alike."[31] This made it more politically difficult for Marcos' troops to open fire when they finally reached the military camps. The critical moment came when Marine General Artemio Tadiar's tanks arrived at Camp Aguinaldo, with orders to ram through the people to crush the mutiny:

But in front of Tadiar were thousands kneeling in the path of his tanks, nuns in white habits reciting the rosary, children in the firing line. His uncle's voice pleaded with him

[25] Ibid. 227.
[26] Thompson (1995): 157.
[27] McCoy (1999): 246.
[28] Thompson (1995): 160.
[29] Pinches (1991): 172.
[30] Quoted in Thompson (1995: 159).
[31] Rivera (2001): 239.

over the radio to turn back. His bishop's voice came next, saying "We're all Filipinos." His former PMA superintendent, General Manuel Flores, urged him not to kill "classmates and fellow alumni."[32]

General Tadiar turned his tanks around. The crowd grew to more than a million. Images of democratic mobilization led by "ubiquitous priests and nuns"[33] ultimately "pushed the wavering Reagan administration to recognize that the situation was untenable."[34] Marcos fled to Hawaii, where his American benefactors provided him a secure exile from justice, if not disgrace.

It would be a grave disservice, however, to attribute Philippine democratization to foreign intervention. "Ultimately," McCoy concludes, "it was the refusal of the officer corps to fire on the rebels and their supporters that assured the triumph of people power."[35] And it was the high-risk mobilization of a particularly broad constellation of social forces that made it so difficult for those troops to follow Marcos' orders. The Philippine experience thus affirms that "democratization, more likely than not, requires alliances among people from different class backgrounds."[36] The absence of an elite protection pact was thus a precondition for the Philippines' democratic revolution. As we will see in the next section, the triumph of Indonesian *reformasi* similarly depended on the evaporation of the Suharto's regime's founding protection pact, and the cross-class opposition and elite defections that this long-term coalitional involution had allowed.

Ridding the Nation of a Racketeer: Elite Opposition and Democratic Mobilization in Indonesia, 1996–1998

Indonesia's New Order was inaugurated with far broader and stronger elite support than Marcos' self-styled New Society, facilitating the construction of far more robust and cohesive authoritarian institutions in Indonesia than in the Philippines. Yet as we have seen, the Suharto regime's coalitional foundations decayed over time, as its protective purpose vanished and elites became entirely consumed with struggles for factional advantage rather than collective self-defense. One can only understand the malfunctioning of what had once been relatively functional authoritarian institutions by the mid- to late 1990s by appreciating how this coalitional rot had essentially hollowed those institutions out. As I argued in this book's opening pages: *When elites do not act collectively, authoritarian institutions do not function effectively.*

The New Order was thus badly weakened even before the financial crisis that ostensibly forced Suharto to resign in May 1998. In fact, the depths of the economic collapse were closely intertwined with the declining performance and

[32] McCoy (1999): 249.
[33] Rivera (2001): 239.
[34] Haggard and Kaufman (1995): 67.
[35] McCoy (1999): 223.
[36] Kerkvliet (2000): xix.

coherence of Indonesia's authoritarian institutions. As Harold Crouch argued after Suharto's resignation, Indonesia's economic implosion

was clearly the precipitating factor in the political changes that occurred in 1998. However, it is remarkable that Indonesia was the only country to experience a change in political regime as a result of the Asian Financial Crisis... Mahathir actually tightened his grip in Malaysia. The replacement of the Soeharto regime, therefore, was not due simply to the regional crisis but to *its own internal structures which inhibited it from coping with the challenge*... [P]olitical scientists were well aware of these features and wrote about them extensively, but we had become reluctant to predict that the regime would fall as a result of them.[37]

One can profitably portray Suharto's fall in 1998 as a failure of state, party, and military institutions to order power in his regime's favor. The New Order state had long become more distributive than extractive in fiscal terms, squandering rather than accruing the remunerative power necessary to hold together what had degenerated into a pure provision pact. Tempering factionalism at the highest levels increasingly required the provision of outlandishly uneconomic monopoly concessions to ever fewer core Suharto supporters. Without a powerful extractive Leviathan to sustainably finance new economic activities, state-linked banks were impressed into giving ever larger loans for bigger and bolder boondoggles. Short-term portfolio capital flooded in from overseas throughout the 1990s, banking on Suharto's autocratic writ to protect highly leveraged crony capital. The fact that the Indonesian economy suffered so mightily from the "Asian contagion" was less a function of the severity of the international downturn itself, and more a product of Indonesia's lack of acquired immunity against the disease of financial panic and subsequent capital flight.

Nowhere was this more evident than in Indonesia's failure to impose capital controls to cope with the consequences of the country's colossal financial hemorrhage. The core problem was not bad policy choice, coalitional constraints,[38] or IMF conditionality – it was the Indonesian Leviathan's administrative incapacity to carry out capital controls at all. "Even in the absence of conditionality," Natasha Hamilton-Hart argues, *"capital controls would not have been a viable policy option, for, unlike Malaysia, Indonesia did not have the organizational resources to implement them."*[39] The Suharto regime was helpless in the face of monetary meltdown not only because of the Indonesian private sector's history of reckless financial investments – it was helpless because of its own historical failure to make adequate *institutional* investments.

This was as true of party institutions as state institutions. As we saw in the previous chapter, Golkar had long failed to incorporate critical nationalist and Islamic

---

[37] Crouch (2001): 149. Emphasis added.

[38] For a sophisticated alternative argument that Malaysia imposed capital controls but Indonesia did not because of coalitional considerations, and that these economic adjustment measures determined regime outcomes, see Pepinsky (2008).

[39] Hamilton-Hart (2002): 160. Emphasis added. Thanks also to former Malaysian Central Bank official Din Merican for his insights on the institutional requisites of capital controls (author interview in Kuala Lumpur, March 2008).

social forces into its organizational ambit. By the mid-1990s, Suharto would face increasing criticism and opposition from these politically autonomous communal elites. Suharto's attempt to develop ICMI into a new, regimist organization of Islamic elites throughout the 1990s could never create a credible Islamic counterweight to historically rooted mass organizations such as NU and Muhammadiyah. Instead, Suharto's tactical favoring of ICMI served to sharpen NU leader Abdurrahman Wahid's public criticisms; surround himself with opportunistic elites more concerned with advancing political Islam than serving Suharto; position ICMI leader B.J. Habibie as a potential alternative focus for Islamists' political loyalty; and further alienate military officers who saw the New Order's historical mission in strictly non-sectarian terms.[40] None of these were favorable outcomes for Suharto – but given the impossibility of generating more steadfast elite support from communal elites without a protection pact, the aging autocrat could only hang onto power through divide-and-rule tactics and the co-optation of growing numbers of politically unreliable opportunists.[41]

While Suharto's energetic patronage of ICMI served more to worsen relations with nationalist elites than to secure uncritical support from Islamic elites, his cultivation of Golkar served less to organize social support than to bifurcate the regime along civil-military lines. Golkar's failure to order elite politics was not merely a matter of failing to incorporate communal elites and middle classes, but of failing to bridle factionalism within the regime itself. The "stronger" Golkar got, the worse friction became between Golkar and ABRI. By helping to divorce ABRI from the actual exercise of political power, "Golkarization" reduced ABRI's stake in protecting Suharto from overthrow.

This would lead to the final malfunctioning of New Order military institutions, alongside the similar breakdown in state and party institutions. Once Suharto placed upstart son-in-law Prabowo Subianto in command of key military units in Jakarta, ABRI had become personalized like never before. Suharto's divide-and-conquer tactics were a rational approach to avoiding a possible coup, as "military officers had become increasingly unhappy with the way in which Soeharto used them for his own political purposes." A coup against Suharto remained unlikely as long as ABRI elites "were too divided among themselves – partly as a result of his clever manipulation of military appointments."[42]

Yet a divided military is only conducive to a dictator's survival when levels of social protest are very low. By 1996, this was no longer the case. As in the Philippines, the rise of cross-class anti-authoritarian protest in Indonesia was not initially sparked by economic grievances, but by the regime's use of lethal violence to thwart a widely revered opposition figure. Concerned that Megawati Sukarnoputri was crafting an opposition alliance with NU leader Abdurrahman Wahid and planning to contest the 1997 presidential election, Suharto engineered

---

[40] The best source on such ICMI-related political dynamics is Hefner (2000).
[41] For more on the concept of opportunists as distinguished from insurrectionaries as agents of political change, see Mahoney and Thelen (2010); for a detailed application to Indonesia's New Order, see Slater (2010).
[42] Crouch (2001): 150, 151.

Megawati's downfall as PDI leader at a kangaroo party congress in the North
Sumatran capital of Medan in June 1996. Back in Jakarta, Megawati and her
passionate supporters within the PDI refused to accept the result:

> In Jakarta, Megawati gave a speech before a large crowd, warning them not to be overcome
> by emotion, but also telling them, "Today, let us show the people of Jakarta, the nation,
> that we should uphold democracy." Some twenty thousand people then marched through
> Jakarta's central business district, cheered on by construction workers and at least some of
> the office workers on the streets. Eventually the demonstrators made their way to Merdeka
> Square, where troops assaulted them in front of a contingent of reporters.... In following
> weeks, a wave of protests gathered pace around the country, culminating on July 27 with
> the most destructive and widespread rioting Jakarta had seen, at least since the Malari
> affair, twenty-two years earlier.[43]

What triggered the shift from peaceful urban protests to violent urban riots was
the regime's assault on the PDI's Jakarta headquarters, which Megawati's backers had been refusing to vacate. The assault ousted Megawati's supporters, but
public outrage subsequently exploded with the destruction of dozens of downtown buildings. Intriguingly, New Order elites seized the apparent opportunity
to paint their opponents as PKI-style revolutionaries and the regime as a necessary protector. "Regime leaders from Suharto down immediately launched a
fevered propaganda offensive, reviving the communist specter in a way not seen
since the 1970s. They accused those responsible of being communists who had
aimed to overthrow the government," Edward Aspinall details. Regime propagan-
dists targeted the leftist, labor-linked People's Democratic Party (Partai Rakyat
Demokrasi, or PRD), "denouncing it as a reincarnation of the PKI." Yet with
no protection pact in place, such propaganda was simply not credible. Hence
"the regime made little headway in imposing its version of the July 27 affair. *In
a post-Cold War world, and with Indonesia's own conflicts of 1965 a distant memory,
warnings of communist infiltration had lost their power to convince.*"[44]

Only when one understands the long-term evaporation of the New Order's
protection pact and related weakening of its authoritarian institutions can one
properly comprehend the role of the Asian financial crisis in bringing the Suharto
regime down. To be sure, Indonesia's financial collapse exacerbated elite tensions
by shrinking the patronage pie. Yet the deeper point is that *the Suharto regime
no longer had anything besides patronage to generate elite support.* Furthermore, the
factional and institutional frictions the crisis exposed had been decades in the
making. Most important, the New Order had failed either to sustain ABRI or
to construct Golkar as a peak institutional vehicle for managing elite politics.
The manifold factional cleavages that Suharto had produced with his divide-
and-conquer tactics foreclosed the possibility that elites might perceive the crisis
as a positive-sum game in which the survival of the regime was paramount, rather
than a zero-sum game in which each faction needed to struggle desperately to
secure the biggest possible piece of the shrinking pie of national revenue. And one

---

[43] Aspinall (2005): 178.
[44] Ibid. 191, 192. Emphasis added.

can only understand the scale of Indonesia's economic downturn by considering the ragged condition of the New Order's administrative state institutions at the time the global financial panic commenced.

In the final analysis, the emergence and success of the reformasi protests in 1998 are better explained by politics than economics. For starters, the New Order's durability had been undermined even before the economic crisis by shifts in attitudinal, coalitional, and institutional factors: especially the vanished PKI threat, growing criticism from communal elites, and worsening factionalization within the military. Any argument centering on economic factors would also need to explain *why there was such a notable delay between the crash and the explosion of protest*. When the national currency plummeted to one-seventh of its former value in January 1998, "[t]he initial societal response was muted." In class terms, "[t]he urban working class was badly affected by the job losses but anyway lacked strong organization, so that through 1998 it played little role as an organized political force. The initial middle-class reaction was panic," as witnessed in a "rush on supermarkets in Jakarta and other towns" – not collective claims on government institutions. Mass upheaval in early 1998 looked very little like a democratic uprising, as "a series of small-scale riots [took] place in a number of towns and cities around Indonesia," usually in "the form of attacks on Chinese-owned shops or department stores, with looting and destruction of goods."[45]

In Indonesia as in the Philippines, it would require the leadership of elites with widely recognized nationalist and religious credentials to channel cross-class outrage into cross-class democratic mobilization. Much as politicized youth groups had blazed a contentious path for fellow citizens during the nationalist struggle against the Dutch,[46] university students seized the initiative in early 1998 in Indonesia's urban centers. "For months, in fact, students were the only ones confronting Suharto and the Indonesian military."[47] In her ethnography of student activists in the Javanese city of Yogyakarta, which witnessed some of the largest anti-Suharto demonstrations, Robin Madrid directly observed the role of nationalist identifications in driving student protest. "It does not take an observer long to. . . . discover that the students have a heightened and strong sense of historical mission. When I was doing my research in the mid-1990s, activist students of all persuasions spoke as much of the proud role students had played in the independence movement and in the downfall of Sukarno as they did of political problems in modern-day Indonesia." Students perceived themselves as "the bearers of an almost mythic tradition of student activism (they saw themselves as a group with a special responsibility to protect the nation)." And nationalist and religious sentiments intertwined, as "[t]he majority of students who organized the student demonstrations belonged to Islamic organizations."[48]

Student-led protests were also emboldened by the implicit moral sanction and, at times, the explicit moral support of a widening range of religious and

---

[45] Sidel (1998): 184.
[46] Anderson (1972) is the classic work on Indonesia's revolutionary nationalist youth.
[47] Madrid (1999): 17.
[48] Ibid. 21, 17.

nationalist elites. Thanks to Muhammadiyah's institutional autonomy from New Order control, its leader, Amien Rais, was able to serve as "the most outspoken critic of the government," and his efforts to organize student activists played an important role in "enlivening the movement."[49] Moral support from other communal elites was more subtle but by no means insignificant. NU leader Wahid behaved in bafflingly inconsistent ways throughout the crisis – in part to protect his mass organization from Suharto's machinations; in part because of NU's historical rivalry with Muhammadiyah and more recent tensions with ICMI;[50] and in part because he suffered a debilitating stroke in January 1998. Yet his longstanding dissident stance was well known and continued to find occasional public expression, as well as to inspire his loyal Islamic charges, as seen in March 1998 when "NU's youth organizations were demonstrating in front of the Armed Forces Headquarters and demanded that Suharto not be reappointed."[51] No openly contentious moves were forthcoming from Megawati, whose political caution and aloofness made her poorly suited for movement leadership – yet her iconic status as Sukarno's daughter and victimhood status in the wake of her ham-fisted removal as PDI leader made her an evocative focal point for collective outrage as protests gathered steam.

Student protestors were also steeled by growing calls for political reform among military and bureaucratic elites. As ever in Indonesian politics, such encouragement was offered behind the scenes more often than in the open. "Expressions of support among the political elite, tacit as well as explicit, clearly encouraged students not to relent even in an atmosphere where the kidnapping and torture of known activists by the military had become well known," argue Richard Robison and Vedi Hadiz. "Similarly, encouragement from former Soeharto associates and ministers such as Ali Sadikin, Kemal Idris, Emil Salim, Subroto, Sarwono Kusumaatmadja and Edi Sudrajat – discarded by Soeharto at one time or another – also buoyed student activists."[52]

Indonesian students' elite backing and nationalist self-understandings inspired ongoing high-risk confrontations with Suharto's troops. When deadly military violence against student protestors took place, it represented the splintering rather than the solidarity of ABRI as a political force. "In the late afternoon of May 12, after hours of protests in and around Jakarta's elite Trisakti University, security forces opened fire and shot dead six students, wounding many more," writes Sidel. "The killings, suspected to be the premeditated handiwork of military elements led by Lt. Gen. Prabowo, generated widespread public outrage. On May 13, thousands joined a burial ceremony for the slain students, bringing crowds to the streets." The shootings were also followed by riots that "were unprecedented in their scope, violence, and impact."[53] It is noteworthy that urban unrest worsened in direct response to the political shock of military

---

49 Ibid. 20, 24.
50 Bush (2009).
51 Mietzner (1998): 190, 191.
52 Robison and Hadiz (2004): 167.
53 Sidel (1998): 188.

violence against students – not the economic shock of skyrocketing prices.[54] Politics rather than economics was driving Indonesia's regime crisis.

More important, *it was the regime rather than the masses that appeared to be driving the violence.* From the beginning of the financial crisis, leading officials including Suharto himself had been scapegoating ethnic Chinese businessmen for the rupiah's freefall. When a bomb mysteriously went off in Jakarta in January 1998, an official investigation headed by a close ally of Prabowo tried to link the explosion to prominent Chinese businessman Sofyan Wanandi, who had criticized Suharto's handling of the crisis and refused to participate in Suharto's quixotic "Love the Rupiah" campaign.[55] Implausibly, investigators tried to link the super-wealthy Wanandi to the "communist" PRD in the bombing. Subsequent acts of violence against Chinese property and Christian houses of worship similarly bore the evident imprint of regime racketeering rather than unbridled unrest. "Reports that some riots were started by outsiders who arrived in trucks or motorcycle convoys led some local and foreign journalists to conclude that many of these incidents had in fact been staged by elements within the regime."[56]

Hence when the post-Trisakti mobs began to target Chinese businesses and, horrifically, defenseless Chinese women, public suspicions immediately fell upon Prabowo and Suharto. Anthropologist James Siegel, in Jakarta at the time, reported his ethnic Chinese informants' perceptions of the tragic events:

> The victims were furious; *they felt betrayed by the police, the army, and the government who had failed to protect them and who, indeed, they were sure instigated the riots.* Though to say "the government" instigated the riots would be too broad. Elements within the army, they were sure, had done it. "They came in trucks and some had on [military] boots." I heard this sentence more than once in just these words in several sections of the city . . . [B]efore the local people arrived, others were already there, also arriving in trucks. In Glodok these early visitors had large crowbars they used to pry up the metal shutters of the shops. They then told the locals, mainly male youths, to help themselves to the goods. These military types then themselves spread gasoline and set the place afire. Of the 1,100 people reported killed during the events of May 13 and 14, most of them are said to have been looters who died in these fires.[57]

It thus appeared that Prabowo and perhaps Suharto were setting off urban sectarian violence to create a pretext for declaring martial law, and to regain elite support for the New Order by seeming to act once again as an elite protector. Yet in the absence of a protection pact, such violence only alienates the elites that an authoritarian regime needs on its side. "Even if intended to confirm the need for order and stability, and by consequence elicit support for the government, especially among the middle class and propertied, the violence also sent other messages," Robison and Hadiz argue. "If the riots were an attempt to channel public anger through religious and racial conduits and thus divert attention from

---

[54] The removal of subsidies that "hiked gasoline prices by 70 percent, diesel by 60 percent, and kerosene by 25 percent literally overnight" had taken place back on May 4 (Ibid. 189).

[55] Ibid. 182.

[56] Ibid. 184.

[57] Siegel (1998): 81. Emphasis added.

the regime, this clearly backfired. The outbreak of violence was only to strengthen the perception that the regime – so focused on maintaining order in its official rhetoric – was indeed quickly unraveling."[58] Aspinall concurs:

A key claim to legitimacy of Soeharto's New Order had been that only it could prevent a return to the political chaos and disorder of the 1960s. After the escalating unrest through 1998, and especially after the 13–14 May riots, this claim was utterly discredited.... This played an important role in motivating middle class support for Soeharto's removal. It also clearly had an impact on even those members of the political elite which had most strongly supported Soeharto in the past.[59]

With communal elites and middle classes emboldened in their opposition to Suharto, and the military fragmented over whether to defend him, democratic mobilization snowballed. Hundreds of thousands of protestors turned out in major university cities such as Bandung and Yogyakarta, even as fears of a "Tiananmen" scenario loomed large.[60] Amien Rais, whose "role was especially crucial in mobilizing students for peaceful protests and demands for democratization,"[61] called for a "million-personal rally" at the National Monument in downtown Jakarta. Military officials led by ABRI Commander Wiranto – Prabowo's main rival – convinced Rais to cancel it. Yet they permitted a student-led throng estimated at 100,000 to occupy the national parliament building.[62] Military officers seemed unwilling to use overwhelming force to protect a dictator who had long sought to divide them, while Golkar politicians resigned from the cabinet in droves to position themselves for a political future without the dictator who had long sought to dominate them. A regime born in a remarkable upsurge of elite collective action was destroyed by an equally remarkable wave of elite collective defection. Suharto was left with no choice but to resign.

Once again, cross-class protest – made possible by deep elite fragmentation – had stimulated a democratic transition. Urban protest activity had swelled beyond the community of student activists, as "former officials of the regime, yuppie professionals, housewives, workers and urban slum dwellers, were all to be involved in protest action against Suharto."[63] The authoritarian end-game in Indonesia would not witness the same levels of open elite transgression that accompanied Marcos' fall in the Philippines – Indonesia remains, as ever, an intermediate case. Yet Suharto's contentious fall more closely resembled the cross-class democratic revolution in the Philippines[64] than the violent crackdown by cohesive institutions of state coercion that was about to unfold in Malaysia.

---

[58] Robison and Hadiz (2004): 170.
[59] Aspinall (2006): 139.
[60] Ibid. 236.
[61] Cheng and Brown (2006): 28.
[62] Madrid (1999): 27. Wiranto also opposed Suharto's proposal to establish a Kopkamtib-style security command in the wake of the riots of May 13–14 (Mietzner [2009]: 130–131), vividly signaling the dramatically different political meaning of mass violence in the mid- to late 1990s from that of the mid-to late 1960s.
[63] Robison and Hadiz (2004): 167.
[64] On the many important contrasts between the Indonesian and Philippine movements, however, see Boudreau (1999).

The End Game that Wasn't: Crisis and Crackdown in Malaysia, 1997–1999

For all its remarkable political stability throughout four decades of independence and a quarter century of UMNO/BN rule, Malaysia suddenly seemed ripe for a democratic transition by 1998. The Malaysian economy was suffering a crisis of unprecedented proportions; long-serving Prime Minister Mahathir Mohamad had become increasingly perceived as despotic and incompetent;[65] and Indonesia's dramatic authoritarian collapse in May raised the prospect of spillover to its ostensibly more liberal, pluralist Malaysian neighbor. Economic collapse, political personalization, and international diffusion are hypothesized to facilitate democratic revolutions in general, but this would not be the case in Malaysia. The late 1990s would not witness a sudden triumph of people power, but the continuing triumph of ordered power.

The Asian financial crisis had devastated the Malaysian economy by late 1997. The Malaysian ringgit lost more than 50% of its value and the Kuala Lumpur Stock Exchange lost more than 60% of its capitalization (amounting to twice the size of Malaysia's annual GDP), leaving the bourse "littered with penny stocks."[66] Even worse for Mahathir, his own missteps were widely blamed for the severity of the downturn. He initially responded to falling asset prices by unleashing a vitriolic tirade against foreign portfolio investors and currency traders. Such "blame-the-speculators pronouncements propelled the ringgit to new depths."[67] As the economy plummeted, even UMNO members began to criticize Mahathir's mismanagement. "People are getting fed up with his constant attack on foreigners," said one UMNO official. "It's beginning to hurt us."[68] By March, *Asiaweek* reported that "Mahathir finds his legacy in limbo, his country in jeopardy, and his backers in retreat."[69]

Mahathir may have been playing his hand quite badly – but the bigger point is that he had inherited a strong hand. Thanks to the Malaysian state's fiscal power, public debt remained at manageable levels, and much of the private sector's gargantuan debt was owed to domestic rather than foreign institutions. This was in marked contrast to Indonesia, where relative fiscal powerlessness had left state authorities much more heavily indebted, and private business far more leveraged internationally as the rupiah wilted against the dollar. Malaysia "managed to stave off an Indonesian-style crisis only because, unlike much of Asia, the bulk of its debt is in local currency."[70] Thanks to these stronger fundamentals, Malaysian authorities kept interest rates lower than in neighboring countries throughout the crisis – Indonesia's rates were more than three times higher than Malaysia's

---

[65] On Mahathir's personalization of power during the 1988–98 period, see Slater (2003).
[66] Eddie Toh, "Mahathir: Worst Not Over But There Won't Be Racial Riots," *Business Times* (Singapore), 15 July 1998.
[67] Santha Oorjithan, "Don't Rock the Boat," *Asiaweek*, 20 February 1998.
[68] Quoted in Murray Hiebert, "Tactical Victory," *FEER*, 2 July 1998.
[69] Jim Erickson and Assif Shameen, "Mounting Pressure," *Asiaweek*, 27 March 1998.
[70] Salil Tripathi, "Savings at Risk," *FEER*, 30 April 1998.

by late April[71] – and used domestic funds rather than IMF monies to buy out the banking sector's enormous overhang of dud loans.

In short, the Asian financial crisis delivered a similarly powerful punch in Malaysia as in Indonesia, but the Malaysian private sector enjoyed access to a much stronger state to cushion the blow. Malaysia's authoritarian Leviathan entered the crisis with a cornucopia of funding sources that had gotten ever more bountiful over the preceding decades. The most important were the well-managed state oil company, Petronas, and the state provident fund, the EPF. Each had accumulated more reserves than the central bank when the crisis hit – approximately US$25 billion for Petronas,[72] and US$34 billion for the EPF.[73] As corporate debt skyrocketed, economic elites looked to these funds – and the BN officials pulling the purse-strings – for their financial salvation. As a comedy troupe in Kuala Lumpur lampooned the lobbying of Malaysian corporate leaders: "we don't want the IMF. All we need is the EPF."[74]

Corporate bailouts proved controversial, however. Disagreements over the proper amount of public support for insolvent firms worsened the friction between Mahathir and his deputy, Anwar Ibrahim. While Anwar publicly expressed concern that bailouts should not compromise foreign investor confidence or squander the savings of EPF contributors, Mahathir remained committed to avoiding Schumpeterian creative destruction. Tensions worsened in March when Petronas, under Mahathir's control, announced that one of its subsidiaries was buying Konsortium Perkapalan Berhad (KPB), a heavily indebted shipping concern. The deal would use US$220 million in state funds to wipe out the personal debts of KPB's chief executive – Mirzan Mahathir, the prime minister's oldest son. When Anwar insisted upon an independent audit of KPB's value, he aggravated worries in Mahathir's inner circle that Anwar might not be a reliable champion should he capture power.

After Suharto resigned in May under a hailstorm of cries against "corruption, cronyism, and nepotism," Mahathir became more defensive about his regime's financial support for well-connected firms. He recognized that the bailout issue threatened to catalyze middle-class opposition, since government largesse could only go so far. "If a person is a satay seller," Mahathir bristled, "surely we can't award him the Bakun dam project."[75] As UMNO's June general assembly approached, Anwar was forced to decide whether to make a bid for the UMNO presidency, or to defend his boss against growing criticism. If there was ever a time when Mahathir was vulnerable, this was it.

Yet as the historical lesson of Onn Jaafar, Harun Idris, and Tengku Razaleigh had shown, expulsion from UMNO meant instant political marginalization, even for Malaysia's most popular politicians. Anwar thus tread cautiously.

---

71 Shamsul Akmar and Wan Hamidi Hamid, "Tight Enough," *The Star*, 30 April 1998.
72 Choong Tet Sieu and Arjuna Ranawana, "Filling Up at Petronas," *Asiaweek*, 13 November 1998.
73 Salil Tripathi, "Savings at Risk," *FEER*, 30 April 1998. The EPF reserves alone amounted to 55% of Malaysia's annual GDP.
74 Ibid.
75 Quoted in Wan Hamidi Hamid, "Foreign Ploy," *The Star*, 27 June 1998.

He encouraged his ally Ahmad Zahid Hamidi, the leader of UMNO's powerful youth wing, to "raise the issue of nepotism and cronyism in a way that indirectly challenged Mahathir's leadership."[76] Mahathir and his allies responded force-fully, "releasing a list of names which showed that Anwar's relatives and close associates, including Zahid, had also benefited substantially from privatized state contracts and special share allocations."[77] Zahid backpedaled: "We do not want anyone to doubt our loyalty to the party leadership or the country."[78] Anwar was equally conciliatory. Party unity was of "paramount importance," he insisted. "We have only one leader and skipper, our Prime Minister Dr. Mahathir."[79]

Anwar's abortive challenge exemplified the perils of confronting the leadership of Malaysia's authoritarian Leviathan – even for the second-most powerful man in the country. The only possible route to Malaysia's political summit was through UMNO, yet to challenge the UMNO president was to court expulsion from UMNO. As one senior party official put it on the eve of the June assembly: "If he challenges Mahathir, Anwar is dead. If he doesn't challenge Mahathir next year and in 2002, he's dead too."[80] With all the institutional weapons of the party-state in Mahathir's hands, Anwar calculated that his best option was to bide his time, hoping to remain the prime minister's chosen successor.

Despite Anwar's protestations of loyalty, "Mahathir's distrust of his protégé became irreversible."[81] The trick for Mahathir was to dispose of his deputy with-out sending financial markets into a tailspin, since Anwar was viewed interna-tionally as the only leading government figure committed to economic reforms. Mahathir found the solution in a one-two punch: on September 1st, he imposed capital controls and fixed the value of the national currency, making it impossible for foreign investors to repatriate their capital or speculate against the ringgit. This was a viable strategy in Malaysia – unlike Indonesia – because the state had the institutional capacity to administer capital controls effectively, as well as the fiscal power to fund the immense cost of economic recovery from within. With capital controls in place, Mahathir had Anwar expelled, first from the cabinet, and then from UMNO – ostensibly on the grounds that he was a homosexual, and had abused his power to stonewall a police inquiry into his private life.

Thus was the battle between Mahathir and Anwar officially joined. Yet it was far from a fair fight. Anwar's disadvantage was not individual, but institutional. "Anwar is popular on the ground," argued Jomo K.S., "but organizationally he is weak."[82] This organizational weakness can be explained precisely in terms of the party and state institutions that have been the primary focus of this book. These institutions had successfully ordered power from state officials, economic

---

[76] Hwang (2003): 302.
[77] Ibid.
[78] Quoted in V. Chandrasekaran, "Zahid: We're Not Hitting Out at Anyone," *The Star*, 13 June 1998.
[79] "Unite Behind Mahathir, Anwar Tells Umno Members," *The Star*, 22 June 1998.
[80] Quoted in Jim Erickson, "Little Room at the Top," *Asiaweek*, 19 June 1998.
[81] Hwang (2003): 302.
[82] Quoted in Choong Tet Sieu and Arjuna Ranawana, "A Case of Order and Disorder," *Asiaweek*, 16 October 1998.

elites, communal elites, and middle classes for more than half a century. As we will now see, the Malaysian party-state continued to extract resources and compliance from these elite groups as Anwar launched the most serious opposition reform movement the BN had ever faced.

The extraordinary cohesion of UMNO and the BN left Anwar virtually friendless at the elite level. Only three out of forty members of UMNO's supreme council spoke in Anwar's defense when Mahathir demanded his expulsion.[83] "The president of the party opened the meeting by suggesting that I have to be expelled from the party before giving me the floor," Anwar explained. "What do you expect the supreme council members to do? If they disagree, they will be expelled too."[84] A floor vote in parliament then delivered unanimous BN backbencher support for Anwar's dismissal.[85] With any dreams of defeating Mahathir from within the system dashed, Anwar had no choice but to look to his grassroots base to save him from political destruction. Yet since UMNO and the BN command the state apparatus, the ruling parties' blanket support for Mahathir meant that Malaysia's powerful coercive and administrative institutions would work in tandem to keep Anwar's opposition movement in check. Anwar's problem was not merely that the Malaysian state has a battery of coercive regulations against public speech and assembly on its books – it was that Malaysia's ruling elites would act collectively in throwing the authoritarian book at him from the moment he was expelled from UMNO.

Anwar's only hope was that he might generate sufficient cross-class urban protest to raise the costs of repression and engender new splits within the Mahathir regime. Yet he faced enormous structural difficulties in attracting and mobilizing support from the kinds of communal elites and middle-class groups who had driven democratic uprisings in the Philippines and Indonesia. To be sure, Anwar had cut his teeth as an Islamic youth activist and enjoyed his strongest support among educated and politically engaged urban Malays. His passionate following in such circles was on display from the outset of reformasi, when Anwar held nightly political rallies in the backyard of his family home in Kuala Lumpur to evade authoritarian restrictions against public assemblies. While drawing thousands of enthusiastic supporters from across Malaysia's ethnic spectrum – as Anwar acknowledged on at least one occasion by opening his remarks with successive greetings in Malay, Mandarin, and Tamil, to the raucous delight of the crowd – the bulk of his "visitors" were Muslim and Malay. Chants of "Allah'u Akbar" loudly punctuated the more ecumenical cries of "Reformasi" and "Long Live Anwar."[86] As in Indonesia and the Philippines, religious solidarities were being invoked and embraced to mobilize cross-class support in Malaysia's struggle for democratic reform.

---

[83] S. Jayasankaran, "Protege to Pariah," *FEER*, 17 September 1998.

[84] Quoted in Eddie Toh, "Anwar Not Ruling Out Switching to Opposition Party PAS," *Business Times* (Singapore), 5 September 1998.

[85] "Backbenchers Reaffirm Support for Dr M," *The Star*, 15 September 1998.

[86] Author's personal observations from a rally at Anwar's home, September 1998.

Yet shared religion could not serve as the same sort of cross-class coalitional cement in Malaysia as in Indonesia and the Philippines. For one thing, the Malaysian state's longstanding tight control over Islamic practice and organization meant that mosques could not become "free spaces" for oppositionists. This became clear as soon as Anwar attempted to move reformasi out of the confines of his backyard and into the wider public sphere. After Anwar addressed supporters after Friday prayers at a mosque in the Kampung Baru section of KL, UMNO's information chief ominously intoned: "Misuse of mosques can confuse the people particularly during the present economic and political situation."[87] The Prime Minister's Religious Affairs Department quickly ordered mosque authorities to deny Anwar the use of their sound systems after Friday prayers.[88] And in a direct response to Anwar's effort to drum up support among Muslim associations, Pusat Islam, "the government's religious watchdog," announced that it was investigating the activities of 55 religious groups, and that police leaders would do their "own assessment on the danger of such teachings."[89]

With state authorities so ready, willing, and able to intervene in Islamic affairs, even those Muslim associations most favorably inclined toward Anwar's struggle adopted a low oppositional profile. ABIM publicly expressed its concern that Anwar receive a fair hearing rather than any desire for regime or leadership change.[90] The leader of opposition party PAS initially insisted that Anwar need not launch a struggle for reform at all, since PAS was already leading one.[91] Most devastating of all in symbolic terms was the consistent and continuing lack of critical engagement in politics by Malaysia's collaborative sultans – the country's consummate communal elites – who since colonial times had enjoyed "status and influence at the expense of autonomous Muslim associational activity," underscoring the "enduring pattern of state control over Islam in Malaysia." This is why, in 1998 as before, "Malaysia's mostly state-sponsored Islamic institutions have failed to provide either the spiritual leadership or the institutional infrastructure associated with civil religions and political oppositions elsewhere"[92] – especially but not exclusively the Philippines.

Anwar faced similar structural constraints in mobilizing support among more secularly oriented urban middle classes and state officials. UMNO's information chief sought to preempt campus protest among Anwar's many young supporters, publicly urging university administrators to impart the "correct information" about Anwar's sacking to students to prevent them from becoming "tools" of his movement.[93] Students did not play a Philippine- or Indonesia-style opposition

---

[87] "Yusof: Don't Misuse Mosques," *The Star*, 6 September 1998.
[88] "I Will Keep on Fighting: Anwar," *Business Times* (Singapore), 12 September 1998.
[89] "Watch on 55 Religious Groups," *The Star*, 18 September 1998.
[90] See "Give Anwar Fair Hearing, Says Abim President," *The Star*, 14 September 1998. Similar caution marked the statement of support for Anwar from the Association of Malaysian Islamic Scholars. "Ulamak Group Backs Anwar," *The Star*, 15 September 1998.
[91] "Nik Aziz: No Need for New Reform Movement, Just Join PAS," *The Star*, 7 September 1998.
[92] Hedman (2001): 938–939.
[93] "Yusof: Don't Misuse Mosques," *The Star*, 6 September 1998.

role in large measure because joining protests entailed facing not just repression, but ruination. Education Minister Najib Abdul Razak repeatedly reminded students that the Universities and Colleges Act prohibited students from political participation, under penalty of expulsion: in short, "they cannot get involved."[94] Najib's deputy, Fong Chan Onn, made sure that Chinese students received the message as clearly as Malays: "Students are to refrain from participating in Anwar's movement or show any kind of support for him."[95] Given the Malaysian state's infrastructural capacity to monitor and regulate student activism, such comments were not mere threats, but promises. The government's chief secretary made it clear that state personnel could expect to be arrested for participating in rallies as well. "Although we have yet to determine whether Anwar's reform movement is political or not," he warned, "civil servants better be on the alert."[96]

When Anwar commenced a "road show" to drum up backing outside the capital city, it became immediately obvious that these were no idle threats. An estimated 10,000 supporters turned out in a suburb of KL to see Anwar speak at an institute run by a pro-reformasi Islamic scholar; but the police shut down the gathering before Anwar could even appear.[97] Before a subsequent rally in Malacca, authorities padlocked and cut the electricity to the assembly hall where Anwar had planned to speak, and announced on the radio that the meeting was forbidden.[98] Anwar attracted crowds numbered in the low thousands at protest rallies in the states of Penang, Kedah, Negri Sembilan, Johor, Trengganu, and Selangor in the two weeks following his expulsion from UMNO. In response, the national police's deputy commander announced that anyone caught distributing reproductions of Anwar's speeches would be arrested and imprisoned under the Printing Presses and Publications Act,[99] complicating Anwar's efforts to make his case for political reform to a broader cross-class audience.

The continuing grip of UMNO over Malay politics was poignantly displayed when Anwar threatened to mobilize a full-blown democratic revolution for the first time. Speaking on September 19th before an audience estimated at 10,000, Anwar directly challenged Mahathir's leadership: "Do you want to resign now," he thundered, "or do you want to end up like Suharto and Marcos?"[100] What was most striking was not *what* Anwar said, but *where* he said it. In a final desperate nod to the party that was purging and pursuing him, Anwar demanded Mahathir's resignation in Batu Pahat, Johor – the same town where Onn Jaafar had founded UMNO in the wake and on the site of Malaya's worst communal bloodshed in 1946. No matter how harshly UMNO had rejected him, Anwar could not simply ignore or overturn the party's historical centrality. He thus felt pressed,

94 "Stay Clear of Movement, Students Told," *The Star*, 19 September 1998.
95 Ibid.
96 "Don't Get Involved in Politics, Govt Staff Warned," *The Star*, 13 September 1998.
97 "Anwar's Gathering in Bangi Cancelled on Police Directive," *Malaysia General News*, 11 September 1998. Accessed through Lexis-Nexis.
98 Assif Shameen and Sangwon Suh, "Reaching Critical Mass," *Asiaweek*, 25 September 1998.
99 "Action Against Anwar for Speech in Kajang," *The Star*, 18 September 1998.
100 Quoted in Eddie Toh and Ruth Wong, "Anwar Arrested After Day of High Drama," *Business Times* (Singapore), 21 September 1998.

ironically, to deliver his strongest call for people power at the birthplace of ordered power.

Authoritarian regimes cannot be overturned by protests numbering in the low thousands at a polity's geographic periphery, however. Democratic revolutions require the mobilization of many thousands at a polity's geographic center. Hence Anwar brought his "road show" back to KL on September 20th. His planned appearance at KL's Independence Square was thwarted by the preemptive presence of ten truckloads of riot police. Diverted to the nearby National Mosque, Anwar addressed a large crowd of supporters after Friday prayers. The throng then marched to Independence Square – swelling to approximately 30,000 protestors en route – hoping to hear Anwar denounce the Mahathir regime at the symbolic heart of the Malaysian polity. Police threats of a crackdown evidently convinced Anwar not to attend the rally, however. When an estimated 5,000 protesters split from the crowd and marched toward the prime minister's residence to demand Mahathir's resignation, they confronted another phalanx of riot police, who attacked the protestors with tear gas and water cannon.[101] Meanwhile, a police special operations unit forcibly entered Anwar's residence, taking him into custody under the ISA, where he would be blindfolded and brutally beaten by the inspector-general of police. Although Anwar's public support from elites was clearly minimal, the government took no chances, immediately detaining UMNO Youth leader Zahid and four ABIM leaders under the ISA as well. The dragnet spread from there, jailing a total of sixteen Anwar supporters under ISA restrictions by the end of September.

Solitary confinement did the trick in puncturing Anwar's paper-thin layer of open elite support. Even Zahid promised to support Mahathir after barely a week in detention, declaring that "I have never been and will not be involved in the reformation movement."[102] The leader of a major Muslim students' association held out a bit longer; but after his two-week detention under the ISA, he echoed Zahid in "categorically" denying any connection to reformasi.[103] For most of Anwar's elite supporters, the extreme measure of ISA detention proved unnecessary for evoking expressions of renewed loyalty to the ruling party. One of Anwar's oldest supporters in UMNO, Ibrahim Saad, explained that while he had indeed visited Anwar at his home during the interregnum between his dismissal from the cabinet and his sacking from UMNO, "when the majority agreed to the sacking, I respected their decision and supported it. Leaders may come and go and I may even be out tomorrow but the party will remain till the very end."[104] As in previous UMNO leadership struggles, the most valuable currency was not personal popularity, but institutional position. "The party hierarchy is very strong," said Chandra Muzaffar. "And in the end, what the rank-and-file understand is

---

[101] All crowd estimates in this paragraph are from Reuters News Service, as cited in "Malaysia Police Clash With Anwar Supporters," *Business Times* (Singapore), 21 September 1998.

[102] Quoted in "Umno Youth Chief Quits Post, Severs Ties With Reform Group," *Business Times* (Singapore), 3 October 1998.

[103] Quoted in "Student Leader Amidi Freed After Two Weeks' Detention," *The Star*, 5 October 1998.

[104] Quoted in Derrick Vinesh, "Ibrahim Reiterates Loyalty to Umno," *The Star*, 28 September 1998.

power."[105] It is the effective ordering of power that makes it so easy to detect, and so difficult to defy.

The swiftness and thoroughness with which coercive institutions suppressed the demonstrations following Anwar's arrest made it impossible for protests to gain momentum. The Malaysian police acted as "fearsome defenders of executive prerogatives" throughout the crisis.[106] Just days after beating Anwar unconscious with his bare hands, the inspector-general of police coolly traced his force's capacity to quell reformasi to its long operational experience with mass contention. "From our experience in the '50s and '60s," he told reporters, "we know what we are dealing with."[107] The message was not lost on Anwar's supporters. As one protestor explained his group's quickness to disperse as the ubiquitous batons, tear gas cannisters, and water cannon laced with skin-burning chemicals approached: "It's not that we are scared, but we are fighting for reform and we can't do that if every one of us gets arrested."[108] With no realistic hope that the police might refrain from using force or split into factions, the groundswell of urban opposition could not reach critical mass.

This is not to say that the Mahathir regime was only saved from collapse by its cohesive coercive institutions. The Malaysian government could draw on the significant capacity of its administrative institutions, as well as its significant stores of symbolic power, to stifle support for the opposition in the first place. Of particular symbolic importance was the positioning of the Malay sultans squarely within the UMNO-led protection pact, sharing the historical apprehension of fellow Malaysian elites that mass political mobilization could undermine stability and their own status. When an estimated 10,000 protestors marched to the National Palace in KL in mid-October, imploring the King[109] to intervene on Anwar's behalf, their pleas fell on deaf ears. Police units cracked down with sufficient force to send thirty-five of the King's subjects to local hospitals, and hundreds more to local jails.[110] Unlike in Indonesia and the Philippines, no support from Malaysia's top religious leaders for political reform was forthcoming.

The BN regime's edge over its opposition was attitudinal as well as institutional. In a society where mass mobilization has historically been associated with communal instability, authoritarian rulers have an easier time using scare tactics to dissuade average citizens from joining or supporting street protests. Mahathir's backers played on Malaysians' historical fears by persistently exaggerating both the communalism of the movement and the violence of the protests.[111] The pro-government press repeatedly referred to protestors as "rioters," even though the police consistently used force first, and demonstrations remained peaceful whenever authorities left the protestors to their own devices. Anwar took great pains

---

[105] Quoted in Nisid Hajari, "Out of the Bottle," *Time International*, 5 October 1998.

[106] Case (2001): 45.

[107] Quoted in "Police Outlaw All 'Reformation Meetings,'" *The Star*, 23 September 1998.

[108] "Protesters Flee Police But Vow to Fight on," *Business Times* (Singapore), 22 September 1998.

[109] Malaysia's king is selected from among its eleven sultans, on a rotating basis.

[110] "Civil Servants Among Demonstrators in Custody," *The Star*, 20 October 1998.

[111] For an especially egregious example, see Wong Chun Wai, "Mob Violence Is Not the Way," *The Star*, 23 September 1998.

to stress the non-communal nature of his reform movement, meeting with DAP leader Lim Kit Siang and addressing a rally on behalf of DAP deputy head Lim Guan Eng, who had been imprisoned for publicizing a Malay girl's statutory rape accusation against Malacca's chief minister. "It must be a multiracial effort," Anwar insisted. "If not, we will not win."[112] Education Minister Najib wasted no time in portraying Anwar's links to the DAP as anti-Malay, given historical tensions dating back to Lee Kuan Yew's "Malaysian Malaysia" proposals: "The act of supporting the DAP, which is rejected by the Malays for its struggle, is unacceptable and unforgivable."[113] Of course, BN leaders simultaneously accused Anwar of Malay communalism to Chinese audiences, highlighting his ties to PAS.

In portraying reformasi as violent and communalist, Malaysian authorities had more than history on their side – they had the contemporary specter of communal violence in neighboring Indonesia to aggravate nervous souls. For reasons of shared language as much as shared political intentions, Malaysian oppositionists had adopted the same "reformasi" slogan used by the anti-Suharto movement. But Indonesia's democratic transition and aftermath had been marred by anti-Chinese violence, providing the BN with a golden opportunity to remind Chinese Malaysians of their insecure communal position. "[S]upporters of Mahathir depicted the anti-Chinese violence from Indonesia as a threat to the success of the Malaysian state in maintaining social and political order," write Ariel Heryanto and Sumit Mandal. "Images and reports were reproduced in the mass media that tended to intimidate the general public by hinting at the chaos the *Reformasi* movement would lead to in Malaysia if Malaysians followed the example of Indonesians by taking to the streets."[114]

The BN's scare campaign was by no means limited to hints. When pressed to defend his decision to incarcerate Anwar, Mahathir replied: "It was clear he was working up emotions the way it was done in Indonesia, where the people rioted daily in order to overthrow the government."[115] Mahathir again played the race card in an interview with five Chinese-language dailies: "I worry that the power of UMNO will be weakened and the moderate political parties will be swept away." He insisted that the BN was uniquely capable of "taking overall control to maintain racial harmony," ignoring the reformasi movement's cross-communal character.[116] More shamelessly, Information Minister Mohamed Rahmat argued after an outbreak of communal bloodshed in Jakarta in November 1998 that the violence was the work of reformasi protestors, even though such protests had ceased with Suharto's resignation six months before. "The movement has now turned to ethnic violence, including burning houses of worship," Rahmat declared. "Is this the kind of movement we want to support?"[117] The

---

[112] Quoted in "Anwar Encouraged by Show of Support at Talks," *The Star*, 18 September 1998.

[113] "Najib Slams Anwar for Supporting DAP," *Business Times* (Singapore), 21 September 1998.

[114] Heryanto and Mandal (2003): 10.

[115] Quoted in Leslie Lopez, "Malaysia Leader Defends Arrest of Anwar," *Asian Wall Street Journal*, 23 September 1998.

[116] Both quotes are from David Liebhold, "Malaysia's Chinese May Hold Key to Mahathir's Fate," *Time International*, 16 November 1998.

[117] Quoted in "Mohamed Links Gore to Latest Jakarta Unrest," *Straits Times*, 25 November 1998.

attitude expressed by one Indian Muslim shopkeeper captured a common sentiment among opponents of reformasi, which I heard in various guises on dozens
of occasions in the KL area in late 1998: "Look at Indonesia. As long as we can
survive, we are grateful."[118]

The rhetoric and reality of riots intimidated Chinese Malaysians most of all.
So long as "Chinese Malaysians were forced to contemplate the fearful implications for Malaysia of the racialized atrocities in neighboring Indonesia," it was
unsurprising that "citizens of Chinese descent were not as politically active as
those in Indonesia in challenging authoritarianism in the streets."[119] Anthony
Loke, a Chinese student leader at the time of the protests and now an elected
parliamentarian for the DAP, agrees that the BN's manipulation of Indonesian
unrest dampened Chinese support for reformasi: "You saw it every night on
television: a few minutes of footage from Indonesia, showing burning cars and
burning buildings." Such tactics help explain why pro-BN Chinese voters "look
at the Philippines and Indonesia, and think Malaysia is heaven."[120]

Indonesian violence exacerbated Chinese Malaysians' fears of communal
unrest, but it by no means created it. For more than thirty years, Chinese
Malaysians have been told, and often tell themselves: "Politics is not your cup
of tea." Loke attributes this depoliticization to Malaysia's legacy of racial unrest.
"Since 1969, for the Chinese, staying out of politics has become a norm." When
asked whether his fellow Chinese students were deterred from participating in
reformasi protests primarily by the threat from above (state repression) or by the
threat from below (Malay communalism), Loke scarcely hesitates: "The big fear
is from the bottom up."[121] In light of the certainty and severity of government
reprisals meted out to students who actively oppose the BN regime, this is powerful testimony to the lingering fear of ethnic unrest afflicting Malaysia's Chinese
community as of the late 1990s.

Such fears helped keep Chinese voters wedded to the BN in the general elections of November 1999 – the end-point of the end-game of authoritarianism that
was not to be. Chinese support compensated for UMNO's loss of ground among
Malay voters, who increasingly turned to PAS and Keadilan, the new multiracial
party led on behalf of Anwar by his wife during what would prove to be Anwar's
six-year prison term. While UMNO lost twenty of its 92 parliamentary seats, and
relinquished the state of Trengganu to PAS in a rout, support for the MCA and
Gerakan stayed firm. The BN retained its two-thirds majority with ease, in spite
of the severity of the recent economic crisis and the plummeting popularity of
Mahathir. The BN's weaker performance in the 1999 vote can be almost entirely
ascribed to Malay anger at Mahathir over his handling of the Anwar affair, and
not to any structural weakening of the BN. Internal UMNO polls before the elections suggested that up to 80% of Malay state officials disapproved of Mahathir's

---

[118] Quoted in Chen May Yee, "Economic, Political Woes Erode Support for Mahathir," *Asian Wall Street Journal*, 21 September 1998.
[119] Heryanto and Mandal (2003): 8, 9.
[120] Interview with the author, Kuala Lumpur, 16 February 2004.
[121] Ibid.

handling of the country's economic and political crises,[122] as many of UMNO's bedrock supporters in the civil service "came to view Mahathir as repugnant" after his brutal dismissal of his popular former deputy.[123]

Malay voters felt freer than Chinese voters to reject the BN in 1999 – especially in states with overwhelming Malay majorities – because historical Malay fears of Chinese political domination have all but evaporated. According to a leading oppositionist, Tian Chua, such fears have weakened among Malays only recently. In explaining Malay trepidation toward the electoral alliance of Tengku Razaleigh's Semangat '46 with the DAP in 1990, Chua argues that "the Malays still had not graduated from the fear that Lim Kit Siang would become Prime Minister."[124] Yet Chua perceived little Malay anxiety about Chinese political intentions while playing a leading role in organizing the reformasi protests of the late 1990s.

The protection pact remained strong among Chinese voters, however. When asked why reformasi failed to gain as much support among Chinese as Malays, despite economic policies systematically favoring the latter over the former, Chua replied: "The Chinese fear that if they rock the boat, they will be punished." In terms of the argument presented here, Chinese support for the BN stems more from ethnic protection than from economic provision. "The BN gets maximum support from minimum concessions" among Chinese voters, says Chua. "*It's fear that holds it together.*"[125]

In sum, Malaysian oppositionists failed to generate the sort of sustained urban groundswell of cross-class protest that helped topple authoritarian regimes in the Philippines and Indonesia. In comparative perspective, Malaysian democratic mobilization was "limited, ephemeral, and unsuccessful."[126] This was because the movement had virtually no elite backing whatsoever – most crucially from communal elites, who remained firmly in the maw of Malaysia's cohesive and capable authoritarian Leviathan. Mahathir's claims to be acting as a protector of broad elite interests against the threat of renewed communal instability proved far more credible than similar cries of "après moi, le deluge" from Marcos and Suharto – especially among Malaysia's sizable ethnic Chinese population. Even a massive economic crisis could not shift Malaysian elites from a stance of authoritarian acquiescence to one of democratic action against a regime showing no hint of buckling from within.

Epilogue: Mahathir's Resignation, Anwar's Release, and Reformasi's Rebirth, 2003–2008

Skies got only brighter for the BN as the millennium turned. When Mahathir stepped down as prime minister and UMNO president in October 2003, a popular ruling party was freed from the grip of an autocratic and widely feared leader. The

---

[122] Weiss (2006): 273, fn. 37.
[123] Case (2001): 50.
[124] Interview with the author, Kuala Lumpur, 16 February 2004.
[125] Ibid.
[126] Hedman (2001): 951.

anti-Mahathir protest vote that shook UMNO in 1999 vanished in the elections of March 2004, delivering a landslide victory to BN parties across the board. The BN's vote share leaped from 56.5% to 64.4%, and its edge in parliamentary seats swelled from 147–42 to 198–20. UMNO was the biggest winner, boosting its total seats from 71 to 109. PAS lost twenty of its 27 seats while Keadilan, the party of reformasi, was nearly annihilated as Anwar languished in prison, retaining only one of the seven seats it had won in 1999.

As ever, elite collective action underpinned regime durability. An especially telling example came when the imam at Kuala Lumpur's national mosque not only refrained from giving moral support to Anwar's wife, Wan Azizah Wan Ismail, when she assumed leadership of Keadilan from her imprisoned husband and contested a parliamentary seat – he *directly opposed her* as UMNO's candidate. The contrast with Indonesia and, especially, the Philippines – where religious leaders rallied behind opposition leaders victimized by regime coercion – was profound. Wan Azizah prevailed, remaining the lone Keadilan representative in parliament; but she was only confirmed as the winner after a series of recounts. It thus seemed after the March 2004 elections that Keadilan – the sole institutional descendant of the reformasi movement – was as close to defunct as an opposition party can get.

The Chinese-led DAP fared better than its Malay-led counterparts, boosting its seat total from ten to twelve – yet the MCA and Gerakan fared better still. Continuing Chinese support for BN parties reflected lingering concerns with ethnic security. The terrorist attacks of September 11th, 2001, were a godsend for the BN's protection pact, especially when PAS misread the political winds and blamed the attacks on American foreign policy. To the limited extent that the DAP gained ground, it was due to the party's shunning of its alliance with PAS, which had cost it dearly in the 1999 vote. Communal fearmongering remained rampant in the campaign, as seen in the festooning of Chinese neighborhoods in KL with pro-MCA posters transposing the DAP symbol (a rocket) against the symbol of PAS (the moon).[127]

Chinese communal anxiety had transformed in the years following the reformasi protests, but not vanished. "In 1998, the Chinese were afraid of riots," Tian Chua told me in 2004. "Now, they're afraid of an Islamic state," which PAS claims it would implement if it ever seized national power – which it plainly cannot.[128] With Chinese political power no longer a concern and the protection pact essentially expired in the Malay community, Malay voters were free to choose UMNO over PAS on the basis of more quotidian factors such as economic policy and the clean reputation of new prime minister Abdullah Badawi, rather than any lingering concerns with Malay needs for ethnic protection.

---

[127] Author's personal observation, Kuala Lumpur, March 2004. For more subnational evidence of the lingering role of communal protection in sustaining BN rule, consider that, with PAS making "deep inroads into the rural heartland and Chinese voters recoiling in turn toward the government, UMNO has resorted to ever more intricate forms of gerrymandering, *now diluting many heavily Malay districts with ethnic Chinese*" (Case [2006]: 102, emphasis added).

[128] On PAS's incapacity and even disinclination to pursue national power, see Slater (2004).

Ironically, then, *UMNO secured its strongest electoral result just as its strongest justification for Malay support was evaporating*. This critical attitudinal shift had been foreshadowed a quarter century before, when Chandra Muzaffar offered a counterfactual scenario whereby the Malay middle class might shed its "unquestioning loyalty" to UMNO:

> Suppose the non-Malay component of the citizenry was small and the country largely Malay, it would not have been possible to evoke the idea of a non-Malay threat.... In such a situation, a Malay elite would find it difficult to pose as the protector of the community against an external threat. It is conceivable that, without this fear of a non-Malay challenge, internal differences within the community arising from sheer competition for power would have manifested themselves more easily.[129]

This is no longer a hypothetical scenario. Demographic shifts have swollen the Malay majority, and no Chinese political organization holds even remote hopes of capturing the political pinnacle. Even when Chandra presented this "counterfactual" in the late 1970s, he might have recognized that he was already describing politics in certain parts of Malaysia quite accurately. In Malay heartland states such as Kelantan and Trengganu, UMNO never succeeded in constructing a protection pact. UMNO has been forced to compete for those states in the way that most electoral authoritarian governments do – providing patronage from the center when they win, and denying such patronage when they lose.[130] Yet ruling through patronage alone produces elite foes as well as friends, and saps the fiscal resources that an authoritarian Leviathan needs to maintain support in a "post-protective" era.

A worsening of factionalism within UMNO and other BN parties in the wake of its 2004 electoral landslide provides a partial explanation for the BN's shocking reversal of fortune in the March 2008 elections. For the first time since 1969, UMNO and its partners failed to capture a two-thirds majority of parliamentary seats. The BN's national vote plummeted from 64.4% to 51.2%, UMNO lost thirty of its 109 seats, and its major Chinese and Indian partners each surrendered more than half of their total seats to the opposition. PAS recouped most of its losses from 2004, bouncing back from seven seats to 23. But the spectacular opposition gains came from the DAP, which converted its 31–12 seat deficit vis-à-vis the MCA into a stunning 28–15 edge; and Keadilan, which came back from the political dead to capture 31 seats and become the largest party in opposition, just four years after it was a series of recounts away from having no seats in the national parliament. The states of Penang (DAP), Selangor (Keadilan), and Kedah (PAS) fell into opposition hands for the first time, while PAS easily recaptured Terengganu and maintained its grip on Kelantan.

While any single election result can only be adequately explained with reference to contingent as well as structural factors, the opposition's dramatic gains in 2008 are better explained by tectonic shifts in Malaysia's political context than in

---

[129] Chandra (1979): 153.

[130] Most notoriously, the federal government denied the state government in Trengganu its customary share of petroleum revenues after the state fell to PAS in the 1999 election.

its economic context. In the final fiscal quarter before the 2008 election, Malaysia had the fastest economic growth (7.3%) and the lowest inflation (2.7%) in Southeast Asia, while unemployment remained minimal at 3.1%.[131] The economy had been far worse in 1999, when the BN had fared far better. What had diminished between 2004 and 2008 was not Malaysians' level of well-being, but the levels of *coercion* the regime was using to repress opposition forces, and the levels of *confidence* elites felt that the BN was a surer protector of Malaysia's communal order than the multiethnic opposition alliance.

One cannot possibly explain Keadilan's political rebirth without appreciating the reduction in state repression the party faced after the 2004 vote. Most important, Anwar's release from prison after a federal court overturned his sodomy conviction in September 2004 permitted him to play the kind of active leadership role in 2008 that he could not in 1999 or 2004. The Mahathir government had also detained five other Keadilan leaders under the ISA from June 2001 until June 2003, and prevented several of these oppositionists from contesting in the 2004 election because their legal cases were still in process. 2008 thus marked the first occasion when Malaysian voters could witness a largely unmolested electoral campaign by a truly ecumenical opposition party.

Anwar's star power and the regime's apparent complacency about his party's prospects allowed opposition rallies to swell to unprecedented sizes under the police's watchful eyes. "It used to be that ceramahs [rallies] could only be a few hundred people, and they had to point their speakers inward," notes Chinese media executive Leong Khee Seong. "These were not just ceramah. There were as many as 50,000 people."[132] Anwar cleverly invoked the revisionist account of 1969 to reassure a massive crowd near KL that a vote for reform did not equal a vote for chaos, promising that the opposition would defend the people if UMNO – as in 1969, implicitly – responded to an electoral setback by unleashing communal violence.[133]

If Chinese voters had become much more inclined to perceive UMNO as a racketeer instead of a legitimate protector by 2008, UMNO had only itself to blame. As factionalism within the party intensified during the fat days following the 2004 landslide, ethnic outbidding increased. The most flagrant example came when UMNO Youth head Hishamuddin Hussein – the grandson of party founder Onn Jaafar and the son of former Prime Minister Hussein Onn – provocatively brandished a ceremonial keris dagger at the nationally televised UMNO General Assembly in June 2006. Rather than backing down in the face of widespread criticism for the move, Hishamuddin went even further at the 2007 assembly, not merely waving a keris but receiving it from his underlings in an elaborate formal ceremony.

In the interviews I conducted in KL in late March 2008, Hishamuddin's menacing symbolism was portrayed as a watershed in Malaysian ethnic politics. One

---

[131] "Economic and Financial Indicators," *The Economist*, 22 March 2008, 101–102.
[132] Interview with the author, KL, 27 March 2008.
[133] Thanks to Lee Hock Guan of the Institute for Southeast Asian Studies in Singapore for relating his experience at this rally.

wealthy ethnic Chinese woman went so far as to call it "the straw that broke the camel's back" among Chinese voters.[134] In the heavily Chinese cities of Ipoh and Penang, the DAP emblazoned campaign posters with an image of Hishamuddin waving the keris.[135] While UMNO appeared more arrogant and chauvinist after its 2004 victory, PAS' electoral drubbing pushed it in the opposite direction, making the opposition coalition a safer bet for non-Islamist voters. "After their defeat in 2004," Leong Khee Seong relates, "PAS became much more moderate, and stopped talking so much about the Islamic state."[136] As journalist Assif Shameen argues, the lesson of the 2008 election is that "the ghost of 1969 is dead and buried."[137] Or, in the terminology of this book, Malaysia's protection pact may now be a thing of the past, with the attitudinal mechanism of reproduction – endemic perceptions of mass threat – no longer sustaining authoritarian rule.

At this point, however, it seems more prudent to portray the BN's protection pact as dormant, not dead. Unforeseeable violent events could restore non-Malays' historical sense that the BN is a necessary protector against Malay and Islamic radicalism. Chauvinistic public remarks by Chinese oppositionists could again rally Malays behind the UMNO standard. And even if elite attitudes have indeed irreversibly shifted, it remains a long and difficult road from attitudinal change to institutional change. Malaysia's authoritarian institutions remain strong, and a full-blown return to the highly coercive ways of the Mahathir days can by no means be ruled out – indeed, the renewed judicial harassment of Anwar Ibrahim and the reimprisonment of Tian Chua since Najib Razak[138] replaced Abdullah Badawi as prime minister in 2009 suggest that such a return to highly coercive authoritarianism is already under way. After so many decades of ordering power, Malaysia's ruling elites will not become so disordered as to permit democratization easily.

---

[134] Confidential interview with the author, KL, March 2008.
[135] Thanks to Zainon bin Ahmad, publisher of *The Sun* newspaper in KL, for his insights on Hishamuddin's actions and the resulting political fallout.
[136] Interview with the author, KL, 27 March 2008.
[137] Interview with the author, Singapore, 23 March 2008.
[138] This new prime minister is the son of Tun Abdul Razak, Malaysia's second prime minister, who presided over the country's authoritarian turn after May 1969.

PART IV

EXTENDING THE ARGUMENTS

8

Congruent Cases in Southeast Asia

Parts II and III of this book explored how the ebbs and flows of contentious politics after the Second World War shaped authoritarian coalitions and institutions in Malaysia, the Philippines, and Indonesia. Whether authoritarian Leviathans would successfully resist pressures for democratization on the "back end" depended deeply on whether patterns of contentious politics facilitated elite collective action and the construction of powerful state and regime institutions on the "front end." For all their undeniable quirks and particularities, each of these cases could fruitfully be conceived as an instantiation of a more general counterrevolutionary political trajectory: *domination* in Malaysia, *fragmentation* in the Philippines, and *militarization* in Indonesia.

This chapter widens the empirical scope, comparing four additional Southeast Asian cases with the three traced above. First, Singapore presents a case of domination that exhibits considerable congruence with Malaysia. Thailand and South Vietnam serve as cases of fragmentation in which party, state, and military institutions displayed incapacity and incoherence broadly congruent with the Philippine case. Finally, Burma provides an additional case – indeed, a paradigmatic case – of militarization, exhibiting noteworthy parallels with the political and institutional trajectory traveled by postcolonial Indonesia.

To summarize my findings at the outset: In Singapore, mass mobilization with an urban and communal impact between 1945 and 1965 gave rise to considerable elite collective action and the strongest authoritarian Leviathan in all of Southeast Asia. In Thailand and South Vietnam, as in the Philippines, class conflict proved far more difficult to manage after the inauguration of an authoritarian Leviathan than beforehand, and never exacerbated communal tensions – thus failing to unify elites into broad protection pacts. Once again, *the type and timing* of contentious politics prove more politically consequential than its raw intensity: Thailand and South Vietnam are polar opposites on the continuum from mild to intense internal conflict, yet produced similarly weak authoritarian Leviathans. Finally, Burma saw elite coalitions and political institutions shaped by regional rebellions rather than leftist unrest in the aftermath of World War II. Separatist pressures exerted a centripetal political effect on the military, while the relative manageability of the leftist threat provided other elites with little imperative to support open-ended authoritarian rule. Burma's authoritarian Leviathan thus lacked the elite social support necessary to build a strong central state or ruling party – yet the thoroughgoing militarization of both state and regime yielded one of the world's most long-lasting and lamentable dictatorships.

In sum, in these four congruent cases as much as in this book's three primary cases, variation in contentious politics preceding the birth of authoritarian Leviathans provides the best explanation for variation in those Leviathans' capacity to cement and sustain elite collective action, and to order power over time. This variation in ordering power best explains variation in the durability of Southeast Asia's authoritarian regimes.

Singapore's Domination Trajectory

Even more than in Malaysia, politics in Singapore exhibits astonishing regularity and predictability. "[T]racking Singapore politics is like observing a shiny new washing machine at work," local academic and journalist Cherian George has observed. "You may marvel momentarily at its smooth, silent operation, its reliability and its cleansing power, but staring at it is not exactly the most thrilling of pastimes."[1] Such enduring political stability is the product of consistent elite collective action, expressed through highly cohesive, effective, and extractive state and party institutions. With elites so thoroughly ordered in support of the ruling People's Action Party (PAP) and the state it has commanded since independence in 1965, opposition forces have proven incapable not only of overturning PAP authoritarianism, but of generating an organized challenge in the first place. The PAP has been "extraordinarily unified since the party's formation in the 1950s," writes William Case. "The lack of factional conflict within the ruling party has given little opportunity for the emergence of a strong opposition."[2]

A strong state and ruling party emerged in Singapore for much the same reason they emerged in Malaysia, but failed to emerge in the Philippines. As in Malaysia, contemporary elite stability in Singapore is a legacy of historical patterns of mass instability. The two countries' historical experience with unmanageable class contention shares broad similarities – most obviously from 1963–65, when the two political units were briefly and combustibly merged. If anything, urban strife with intertwined class and communal implications was even more explosive in Singapore between 1945 and 1965, when Singapore's expulsion from the Malaysian federation terminated its era of pluralist party politics. Hard as it is to fathom now, Singapore was long considered "the traditional center for communist activity in the region."[3] As a direct consequence, Singapore's counterrevolutionary political development has witnessed state-building that has surpassed and

---

[1] George (2000): 10.
[2] Case (2002): 20.
[3] Stubbs (1988): 231.

party robustness and regime durability that have rivaled its Malaysian counter-part.[4]

Contentious Origins of Party-State Domination in Singapore, 1945–1965
As the most predominantly Chinese city in Southeast Asia, Singapore suffered the harshest effects of Japan's military occupation, commencing with a genocidal "purification by elimination" campaign. More than 70,000 Chinese were detained in concentration camps, including "leading bankers, merchants, and community and political leaders." While "the bulk of the detainees were transported by lorries to rural areas to be executed," others were forced to serve as political informers.[5] The Japanese thus left Chinese elites as sitting ducks when they suddenly surrendered in August 1945, and withdrew most of their forces across the causeway to Johor. "This meant that the security of Singapore was left to a small police force and a few Kempeitai officers," writes Cheah Boon Kheng, "with disastrous consequences for public order":

> As soon as they learnt that the Japanese troops were withdrawing from the Singapore city center, the MPAJA guerrillas from the mainland of Johor state crossed over to Singapore.... Thus began what [Japanese civilian official Mamoru] Shinozaki described as "a second period of terror and confusion for Singapore" (the first being the Japanese occupation on 15 February 1942). Those local collaborators able to do so fled to Hong Kong. *Some gave themselves up to the police, feeling safer in prison than outside.*[6]

With even more intensity than in neighboring Malaya, Chinese leftists in Singapore converted their energies from postwar reprisals into labor militancy. For more than three weeks in December 1945, the city was effectively paralyzed. "Hospital attendants, taxi and bus drivers, engineering mechanics, telecommunications employees, municipal, brewery, and rubber factory workers were all on strike at some stage of the month."[7] And Singapore's labor conditions worsened appreciably over the subsequent eighteen months, even more dramatically than in Malaya:

> In the year following 1 April 1946 there was a total of 713,000 man-days lost as a result of strikes in the Malayan Union, or nearly two days per employee, and in Singapore the extraordinary total of 1,173,000 man-days or over ten days per employee. Virtually every type of worker in Singapore was involved in a strike at some stage of the year and many were involved in more than one. Huge financial losses were suffered by both workers and employers and at the peak of the various strike waves public services were disrupted and Singapore business brought almost to a standstill.[8]

As in Malaya, British authorities in Singapore responded to labor radicalism with considerable state-building efforts, anchored by the imposition of direct income

---

[4] For an argument that the pressures of external threat and resource scarcity, combined with those presented by social conflict, explain why Singapore became more of a developmental state than Malaysia in its ability to pursue economic upgrading, see Doner, Ritchie, and Slater (2005).

[5] Cheah (1983): 22.

[6] Ibid. 140. Emphasis added.

[7] Stenson (1970): 65.

[8] Ibid. 105.

taxes in December 1947. This entailed a dramatic shift in fiscal strategy in a city where more than 78% of revenues derived from indirect customs levies, and less than 5% was generated by direct taxes of any sort. Despite the political and administrative difficulties involved – and the natural temptation for an entrepôt to continue depending on trade and transit taxes instead – Singapore's governor insisted that the move was necessary to extend public services to the highly mobilized labor population:

From the Singapore point of view there is absolutely no doubt that we must meet the legitimate demands of the people for new schools, better hospital facilities, housing schemes for the masses and social welfare. All these cost money, and one of the ways in which we can get it is by the income tax....That is what we want to achieve, but we will not be able to achieve it without extra revenue.[9]

When Singapore's governor joined his Malayan counterpart in vetoing the Legislative Council's rejection of income tax, his willingness to stand up to economic elites gained political capital for the British among labor. The Singapore Government and Municipal Labor Union (SGMLU) – which had been threatening on the eve of the vote to launch a general strike – issued a statement "hailing with gratitude" over the imposition of income tax, proclaiming that the move "augurs well for the social future of this island-colony."[10] By contrast, business elites were publicly apoplectic, as seen in the "bitter and almost hysterical attack upon the concept of income tax" launched by peak employers' associations in Singapore as well as Malaya throughout late 1947. Yet business was beckoning Leviathan as well as berating it – only months before, the Singapore Association had been "demanding firm measures to control labor, which had been 'allowed to get completely out of hand.'"[11]

Besides political capital, the shift produced tangible capital for the British-run state; direct taxes leaped from 4.6% of total revenue in 1947 to 36.5% of revenues in 1948.[12] The continuing leftist threat gave the colonial Leviathan added impetus and leverage to sink its fiscal teeth ever deeper into economic elites' swelling profits. When British companies in Singapore and Malaya paid especially large dividends to investors in December 1949, "[t]he Governor of Singapore pointed out that, 'it must be obvious that success against Communism in Malaya and the continuance of such exploitation on behalf of the United Kingdom interests are mutually exclusive.' Corporate tax rates in both Singapore and Malaya were quickly increased."[13]

Singapore was spared the violence of the Malayan Emergency from 1948–57. But the island continued to suffer intense class and communal conflict – and with much greater and graver urban impact than Malaya during the same period. Singapore's Malay community showed it was capable of violent mass mobilization when it felt threatened, as the Maria Hertogh riots of 1950 erupted when British courts returned an adopted Muslim teenage girl to her Christian

 9 Quoted in "Gimson on Need for Income Tax in Singapore," *Straits Times*, 17 October 1947.
10 Quoted in "Unionists Pleased With Tax," *Straits Times*, 6 December 1947.
11 Stenson (1970): 174, 156.
12 Stubbs (1988): 83.
13 Ibid.

biological parents, annulling her recent Islamic marriage. "The Singapore-based Utusan Melayu, Melayu Raya and Dawn trumpeted 'Islam in danger'" and one local Muslim leader "called for a holy war" to prevent the girl's forced conversion and separation from her Muslim family. "[R]ioting broke out in the vicinity of the Supreme Court and spread to the area of the Sultan Mosque. The violence lasted 48 hours and during it 18 people were killed (nine by the rioters and nine by the police or military), 173 were injured and nearly 200 vehicles were damaged or destroyed. Most of the casualties were Europeans or Eurasians"[14] – suggesting that no one in Singapore had sufficient status to be spared.

The Maria Hertogh riots seemed to signify the "complete collapse and demoralization of the police."[15] Official investigations into the police response to the riots concluded that "the Malay rank and file, whose sympathies lay with the rioters, had stood idly by in the face of mob violence." This strengthened the hand of the British defense minister, Emmanuel Shinwell, who even before the riots "had been a vigorous spokesman of the services' viewpoint and a critic of the apparent reluctance of the civil authorities in Malaya to shoulder responsibilities in the campaign against insurgency." The urban bloodshed spurred Shinwell to call for "drastic steps" to "be sure that our Colonial Administration and Police Forces everywhere are really efficient and adequate."[16] One such step was the introduction of compulsory national service registration for all Singaporean males – most important from a British and Chinese perspective, *non-Muslim* males – in 1952. Another involved the stepped-up use of Special Branch forces to detain and deport leftist and communalist activists of multiple stripes. A total of 254 activists were deported between 1948 and 1953.[17]

Chinese communalism remained a chronic concern as well, as seen in Chinese-educated students' demands for equal treatment vis-à-vis their English-educated counterparts: "the student groups were able to mount a series of demonstrations, some of which became full-blown riots," Richard Stubbs reports. "At times, notably in November 1956, the Singapore Government's ability to maintain order was severely tested."[18] Yet it was ongoing labor militancy that gave Singaporean elites of all stripes the most cause for concern. To gauge the comparative strength of Singaporean labor, it is useful to recall that in Malaya, leftist insurgency only shifted from the cities to the jungle fringes in 1948 because the colonial state succeeded at rousting the Malayan Left from its base in the urban labor movement. In Singapore, by contrast, organized labor had proved too strong to defeat. Urban strikes thus ceased in Malaya, but continued in Singapore, after 1948. During the mid-1950s, labor militancy became violently intertwined with student communalism:

In 1955 946,354 man-days were lost because of strikes, or approximately 2.15 per man employed, the highest since 1946. Many of the strikes were successful, gaining for workers concessions similar to those of the forties.... *British officials and employers also became*

---

[14] Stockwell (1986): 330.
[15] White (1996): 108.
[16] Quoted in Stockwell (1986: 331, 332).
[17] Wade (2007): 8.
[18] Stubbs (1988): 229.

thoroughly alarmed when strikes became associated with militant Chinese economic-cultural-political agitation originating in the Chinese-language high schools and erupted in scenes of violence, notably during the Hock Lee Bus strike of 1955.[19]

This upswing in contentious class and communal politics sparked new state-building and party formation efforts. In terms of state-building, British authorities responded to the worsening of mass unrest in Singapore in 1955 in the same way as they had done in Malaya at the worst point of the Emergency in 1951 – by implementing a compulsory savings scheme, known as the Central Provident Fund (CPF). Like the EPF in Malaysia, Singapore's CPF has ensured that the preponderance of national savings remains in public rather than private hands, complementing the fiscal power of a highly extractive tax state. Such fiscal power would not necessarily have fostered the long-term survival of an authoritarian regime in Singapore, however, unless a unified ruling party could emerge to seize the state that was so abundant in revenue. As of the mid-1950s, Singaporean elites had become ordered into relationships involving considerable economic extraction, but not political organization.

As in Malaya in the mid- to late 1940s, radical mass mobilization would help inspire elite collective action via political party formation in Singapore in the mid- to late 1950s. Considering that the Singaporean Left was extremely strong at the grassroots level, with its domination over the labor and student move-ments, pro-British elites found themselves at a disadvantage. When Lee Kuan Yew returned to Singapore from his studies in England in the early 1950s, and began his foray into local politics, he "was shocked" to discover that the Left had "such a phenomenal mass base."[20] With independence looming, Lee and his anti-communist allies needed to act collectively to ensure that the balance of forces would not favor the radical Left when the transition came.

When the PAP was founded in November 1954, it "drew blessings from diverse sources" at the elite level.[21] Clearly nervous that Singapore's mixture of Chinese communism and communalism could destabilize Malaya's own fragile communal bargain – since it was "the pro-Communist groups who were most successful in manipulating and focusing the chauvinism of Singapore's Chinese and who were most likely to have come to power on the basis of these emotional ties"[22] – the leaders of both UMNO and the MCA crossed the causeway to address the PAP's inaugural meeting. Although the British played a low profile in the PAP's forma-tion, it is unthinkable that Malayan political elites would have actively blessed the new Singaporean party without British encouragement. Abetting the emergence of the PAP "meant making empire the whipping boy of radical nationalists" to some degree; but the power of the Singaporean Left made the British "happy to trade colonial rule for Communist rout."[23]

---

[19] Ibid. 245. Emphasis added.
[20] Comments by Chua Beng-Huat at a public talk, "Interpreting Strands of Political Culture in Singapore," Asia Research Institute, National University of Singapore, 2 March 2004.
[21] Bellows (1970): 136, en. 1.
[22] Ibid. 13.
[23] Keay (1997): 317, 318.

British elites would work closely with PAP elites to quell labor radicalism between the mid-1950s and the early 1960s. It was a daunting and delicate political task. Led by English-speaking elites, the PAP had no electoral base in a city of Chinese-speaking masses. "The Communists were so well organized and placed in such key positions that it would have been impossible to compete against them."[24] The PAP thus forged a marriage of convenience with leftist elements, helping it win 43 of 51 parliamentary seats in the 1959 elections that ushered in Singaporean self-rule. Yet the PAP's anti-communist elites remained outnumbered by its pro-communist masses: "The head was in constant danger of being ingested by the body."[25] British and Singaporean authorities thus precipitated the party's breakup in 1961 by using Emergency-style security laws to crack down on radical unionists. The leftist Socialist Front (Barisan Socialis) bolted the PAP, leaving the party with a slim 26–25 advantage in parliament.

In institutional terms, the split was a disaster for the PAP. "Control of nearly all branches slipped from the PAP into Barisan hands," says Thomas Bellows. "The remnants of the party organization in 1961 could not realistically be described even as skeletal."[26] But in coalitional terms, the PAP commanded the wide-ranging support of a protection pact at the elite level. This was most obvious within the PAP itself, where non-communists had retooled party procedures back in 1957 to ensure their stranglehold on the Central Executive Committee. This hard core of anti-communist elite cadres was hardened further by the jolting experience of the 1961 split. These PAP elites could also enlist the support of the Singaporean state, dominated by anti-communist civil servants, in draining popular support from the Barisan. PAP leader Lee Kuan Yew had long been appealing for a joint effort of party and state institutions to counter the appeal of communism. As he warned the assembled bureaucrats at the opening of the Civil Service Political Study Center in August 1959: "Let us never forget that the communists are only too ready to offer the people more drastic alternatives in social revolution than the democratic system of Government."[27] Against the backdrop of a decade-plus of endemic urban tension and recurrent urban conflict, such rhetoric had far greater credibility and wider resonance in Singapore than in Thailand or the Philippines in a similar period.

By crafting "a coalition between political leadership and the civilian bureaucracy,"[28] the PAP accessed Leviathan's coercive and remunerative powers. Systematic coercion was the bluntest instrument in the party-state's arsenal, most fearsomely deployed when twenty-four Barisan leaders and more than a hundred leftist activists were detained in "Operation Cold Store" in February 1963. Such naked repression did not spark any elite backlash because of shared elite trepidation about the power of the Left, particularly in a society divided by deep

[24] Bellows (1970): 20.
[25] Ibid. 21.
[26] Ibid. 28.
[27] Quoted in Chan (1976: 22).
[28] Khong (1995): 115.

communal cleavages. Lee had leveraged communal anxieties in his forging of a broad anti-communist coalition during a series of radio broadcasts in 1962: "The Malay-speaking, Tamil-speaking and the English-speaking groups are quite certain that [Barisan founder] Lim Chin Siong and his Communist friends are up to no good, and consider that they should be put away and not allowed to do mischief."[29] Lee had more than his own rhetorical skills working in his favor as he made this pitch – he had nearly two decades of shared experience with the destabilizing consequences of radical leftist and communalist mobilization to tie Singaporean elites to the emerging PAP-led protection pact.

With a well-organized state apparatus willingly serving as "a close handmaiden of the party,"[30] the PAP could survive without a strong grassroots party apparatus. Its first test in mobilizing support came in the general elections of September 1963, held just days after Singapore's incorporation into the new federation of Malaysia. As discussed in Chapter 5, the merger had been inspired by mutual fears of Singapore voting its way into communist hands if the city were not incorporated into the safely counterrevolutionary, Malay-dominated federation. Lee continued to leverage threat perceptions on the campaign trail, taunting his opponents: "Vote for chaos and anarchy – vote for the *Barisan Socialis*."[31] Singaporean voters rallied behind the government, delivering 37 of 51 seats to the PAP. Whatever party persuasion had not accomplished, state coercion had. As PAP chairman Toh Chin Chye matter-of-factly explained the role of repression in his party's landslide victory over the Barisan in the 1963 vote: "The General Elections were held after Operation Cold Store, when their leaders were all in jail. That was the way it was."[32] With their use of illiberal coercion unpunished by Singapore's voters, PAP leaders quickly ordered more rounds of arrests and deportations, decimating the Barisan's oppositional prospects even further.

Just two weeks after the PAP's electoral triumph, Indonesia's leftist government declared a policy of Konfrontasi against Malaysia. The two-year campaign proved utterly inept in military terms; but it gave Singaporeans' fears of communism and communalism a new lease on life. More important, Singapore suffered chronic social tensions and multiple outbreaks of social conflict during its merger with Malaysia from 1963–65 (as discussed in Chapter 5). At Singapore's moment of independence in August 1965, "anti-Chinese sentiments among the Malays were gathering momentum"[33] – a threat that the island's expulsion from Malaysia allayed, but by no means eliminated. This gave the PAP leadership considerable leverage to pursue new state-building efforts, while much tighter restrictions on political association made the system more authoritarian than beforehand. Singapore and Malaysia had parted ways, but their authoritarian Leviathans ironically converged on a strikingly similar pathway of durable political domination.

---

[29] Quoted in Chua (1995: 14).
[30] Chan (1976): 224.
[31] Lau (2003): 45.
[32] Quoted in Ibid. 30.
[33] Alatas (1997): 135.

Singapore's Durable Authoritarian Leviathan, 1965–

At its onset in 1965, the PAP's authoritarian Leviathan rested upon a protection pact – or what Cho-Oon Khong calls an "initial agreement that gave the leadership the political authority to act," which "originally derived from beliefs and considerations that predate its economic achievements." Any argument that elite quiescence in Singapore rests purely on the PAP's impressive economic performance must reckon with the historical fact that *the quiescence preceded the performance*. Perceptions of endemic and unmanageable mass threat were at the heart of this founding elite pact. "[T]he political leadership was initially accorded legitimacy contingent on its restoring order to a turbulent society and polity,"[34] Khong argues. By parlaying its initial coalitional strength into revamped state and party institutions, Singapore's leaders ordered the power necessary to build not only a high-growth economy, but a high-durability regime.

The core of Singaporean state-building since 1965 has been the continued and enhanced mobilization of revenue through the tax system and the CPF. Although "the departmental structure of the bureaucracy changed very little" after independence, "[g]overnment revenues escalated.... from 16 percent of GDP in the first half of the 1960s to 29 percent in the second half of the 1980s."[35] Mandatory employee and employer CPF contribution rates reached a combined 20% by the late 1960s, helping the Singaporean state secure "a growing and dependable source of domestic loan finance" and "build up a substantial level of external reserve balances."[36] As in Malaysia, the regime in Singapore has used compulsory contributions to its highly efficient national provident fund to lessen its financial dependence abroad, and to cultivate political quiescence within.

At the heart of the PAP's initial campaign for quiescence were two key institutions: Citizens' Consultative Committees (CCCs) and the Housing Development Board (HDB). First conceived in 1963 and first implemented in 1965, the CCCs were "motivated by two major considerations – the need to fight the communists effectively, and the need to establish a linkage between the people and the Government."[37] By recruiting local neighborhood leaders to front these new grassroots state institutions, which were vaguely (and rather ominously) entrusted to "promote good citizenship amongst the people of Singapore," PAP leaders incorporated middle classes into the evolving authoritarian power structure.[38] "The medium and small businessmen, the merchants, and the shop-keepers were the main sources of CCC leadership," Chan Heng Chee writes. "Also included in the CCC were the leaders of trade guilds and associations of the predominant economic groupings in the constituency."[39] The CCCs helped underpin

[34] Khong (1995): 110, 109.
[35] Hamilton-Hart (2002): 80, 147.
[36] Edwards (1970): 63. By 1991, mandatory contribution rates had reached a combined 40% (Asher [1994]: 238).
[37] Chan (1976): 133.
[38] Ibid. 136. Lest one doubt the CCCs' authoritarian pedigree, it is notable that Lee Kuan Yew drew inspiration for the CCCs from the local-level surveillance units of Japanese occupation forces during World War II (Ibid. 134).
[39] Ibid. 149, 153.

a broader coalitional arrangement in which the authoritarian Leviathan prioritized the extraction and organization of elite support over the distribution of elite
patronage:

> The leadership began its rule by seizing the initiative, setting out its own political vision,
> and enforcing cooperation from, if not indeed coercing, all other social groups. *It did not
> allow itself to be restricted by striking accommodations with critical social elites.…* The regime
> may be characterized as inclusionary in the sense that various elites were co-opted by the
> political leadership to form a governing coalition and therefore attached themselves to
> the institutional structure of the state. *But in this attachment they lost their own independent
> identity even as their aims coalesced with those of the political leadership.*[40]

Even the HDB was a political exercise in extraction and organization before it
could become an economic avenue for resource distribution. Founded in 1959 to
provide affordable rental properties for Singapore's badly overcrowded masses,
the HDB was retooled in the late 1960s to provide affordable homeownership
opportunities for Singaporean middle classes. Yet the HDB's primary purpose
has always been political: to serve as "an instrument by which to maintain the
ideological hegemony of the PAP and incorporate the popular sectors in the
state apparatus."[41] As Chua Beng-Huat depicts the historical role of the HDB
in shifting social power away from civic groups and toward the Singaporean
Leviathan:

> The public housing programme benefited the populace but also simultaneously trans-
> formed them into dependants of the state. Community organizing efforts in the high-rise,
> high-density housing estates are carried out in turn by government-sponsored agencies,
> controlled through the Prime Minister's Office. Historically, the negligence and inactivity
> of the colonial regime had produced a rich network of voluntary organizations, consti-
> tutive of a strong civil society, which carried out many such social welfare activities. In
> contrast, the penetration of the PAP government/state progressively reduced not only the
> power but also the initiatives of these voluntary associations in community affairs.[42]

One must thus understand the HDB as an institutional exertion of the state's
formidable ordering power, not simply as a policy of regime provision. Nor can
one divorce the PAP *regime's* ability to house approximately 85% of the city's
population from the Singaporean *state's* capacity to order power. This was witnessed, first and foremost, with the "effective enforcement of compulsory land-
acquisition policies"[43] such as the "draconian"[44] Land Acquisition Act of 1966,
which "authorized the HDB to acquire, through compulsion, any private land for
its development programs" at below-market prices. The upshot is that the Singaporean state came to own "almost 80 percent of the entire landmass."[45] In 1968,

---

[40] Khong (1995): 116, 117. Emphasis added.
[41] Park (1998): 283.
[42] Chua (1995): 19. Since these displaced civic associations were often organized along ethnoreligious lines, the HDB's rise has undermined the position of ethnically based communal elites in
  authoritarian Singapore as well.
[43] Park (1998): 285.
[44] Chua (1995): 130.
[45] Park (1998): 285.

the PAP began permitting Singaporeans to withdraw a portion of their CPF savings to purchase HDB condominiums at subsidized interest rates. This cleverly married the state's ultimate institution for fiscal extraction with the regime's ultimate institution for welfare provision.[46] 1968 also saw the PAP win a monopoly of parliamentary seats in national elections, thanks to the Barisan Socialis' understandable but self-defeating decision to boycott the authoritarian election process.

In the four-plus decades since the PAP-led authoritarian Leviathan cast it into the political wilderness, the Singaporean opposition has found it impossible to recover. The PAP won every single parliamentary seat in the elections of 1968, 1972, 1976, and 1980. Small chinks in the PAP's electoral armor appeared for the first time in the early 1980s – precisely when *historical threat perceptions began to fade*. When the PAP finally lost a single parliamentary seat in a 1981 by-election, it was seen by some as "a demonstration that from then on not only was opposition possible but that it would not inevitably break the nation's will and ability to survive; a threat commonly touted by the PAP." When the PAP lost two out of 79 seats in 1984, declining security concerns were a critical background factor. "There was an increasing proportion of the electorate who had no experience or memory of the turbulence and economic difficulties of the 1950s and 1960s," argues Chua Beng-Huat. "With social and economic stability and a declining threat of communism, the tight social discipline of a paternalistic/authoritarian regime which the first generation of PAP leadership had been able to impose became increasingly unacceptable to the citizenry."[47] Yet ongoing legal and political intimidation of oppositionists helped ensure that the PAP would not even face *an opponent* in more than half of Singapore's districts until 2006. The opposition finally fielded enough candidates in 2006 to force the PAP to wait until election day to declare victory, yet only captured two of 84 seats.

The chronic absence of any significant contentious or electoral challenge to PAP domination bespeaks the chronic quiescence of Singapore's middle classes, communal elites, economic elites, and state officials. Given the historical absence of any intense nationalist struggle, as well as the deep demographic divisions separating the city-state's religious communities, it is hard to imagine how communal elites could ever play a Philippine- or Indonesia-style democratizing role in Singapore.[48] Local businessmen are often portrayed as dissatisfied with the PAP's favoritism toward foreign multinationals and state-owned firms; yet they surrendered their capacity to play an oppositional role early on, when acquiescing to the imposition of authoritarian rule for purposes of class protection: "The irony of their position is that *in their desire for stability they had originally supported the bureaucratic-authoritarian state*."[49] While middle classes are almost certainly

---

[46] Ibid.

[47] Chua (1995): 174.

[48] For a discussion of how long-term patterns of political development and demographic change have deprived Singapore (and Vietnam) of politically salient and autonomous communal elites, see Slater (2009).

[49] Khong (1995): 119. Emphasis added. Khong rightly describes the Singaporean bourgeoisie as "a declining immigrant commercial order whose assets have dissipated away," making it "increasingly unlikely that they could ever provide a focal point for a possible alternative political grouping in the future" (Ibid. 119, 120).

becoming more attitudinally open to supporting opposition candidates, the social weakness of communal and economic elites – combined with the PAP-led state's cohesive practices of social control – leaves Singaporean voters without many viable opposition candidates to support.

The strength of the Singaporean state is not a straightforward product of external threat, and the durability of the PAP's domination cannot be adequately explained in terms of the regime's success at delivering the economic goods. Significant state-building took place *before* Singapore's singular experience with external aggression from 1963–65. The state that emerged from that bout of violence was different from its immediate predecessor in degree, but not in kind. Political violence during those years made state-building easier in the years that followed; yet this violence was far more internal than external in character, and represented the sort of *urban and communal threat from below* that has been the focus of this book. Similar types of internal conflict fostered considerable party-building and state-building efforts in the mid- to late 1950s, when no hint of geopolitical vulnerability was yet in the air. Even today, Singapore's "insecurity" derives more from shared Chinese perceptions that the sizable Malay minority might press for the island's reintegration into Malaysia than from any military threat from neighboring countries.

As in Malaysia, strong party and state institutions have underpinned regime durability in Singapore. This combined institutional strength derives from the authoritarian party-state's coalitional foundation in a protection pact among political, economic, and societal elites. Again like in Malaysia, but unlike in Indonesia, the Singaporean authoritarian Leviathan's founding promise to preserve order and security has been a promise consistently kept. Economic performance has *supplemented* but not *supplanted* this basic logic of authoritarian persistence. "[T]he PAP sought to base its legitimacy, *first, on the establishment of political order*," Khong reminds us, "and, second, on its commitment to securing the welfare of its citizenry."[50] Even after forty years of communal peace, the enduring presence of a large Malay-Muslim minority looms ominously in the Singaporean political imagination – especially as acts of Islamist terrorism in Southeast Asia and around the world capture increasing media attention.

While the institutional foundations of Singaporean authoritarianism churn along undisturbed (like Cherian George's metaphorical washing machine), its attitudinal foundations may certainly fade. Yet the destiny of demography in a deeply divided and historically contentious society still seems to prevent them from vanishing altogether. At the level of political attitudes, one might say that "[t]he problem lies in determining whether people believe that authoritarian practices are essential to maintaining order and are in the general interest of society (as we have suggested was the case in the initial period of PAP rule) or whether that belief has been superseded by a suspicion that authoritarian practices have been imposed by political leaders to ensure their hold on power."[51] Yet attitudes are shaped by historical experience and evidence, not just by "suspicions" that the coast might finally be clear for democracy and political order to coincide. This

50 Khong (1995): 114. Emphasis added.
51 Ibid. 123.

is especially so when a highly organized and cohesive authoritarian Leviathan offers consistent and credible reminders of a turbulent pre-regime past. In the final analysis, the durability of Singapore's authoritarian Leviathan is not simply a function of contemporary attitudes – it is a function of a preponderant regime power advantage generated by decades of ordering power.

Thailand's Fragmentation Trajectory

While postcolonial Singapore has experienced virtually no elite factionalism, postwar Thailand has experienced virtually nothing but. Postwar Thai leaders inherited one of the strongest administrative Leviathans in all of Southeast Asia, yet endemic factionalism has chronically prevented them from expanding the extractive power of the postwar state. Nor has elite collective action ever been effectively channeled through regime institutions such as a robust ruling party or a cohesive ruling military. Lacking the state and regime institutions necessary to extract power resources and organize political support, Thailand's successive military regimes have proven incapable of forestalling recurrent cross-class pressures for democratization. As in the Philippines, we see a weak state, a factionalized military, weak parties, and wobbly dictatorships in Thailand. Whereas political institutions remained chronically weak in the Philippines because of the *type and timing* of contentious politics, similar outcomes in Thailand occurred because of the virtual *absence* of mass contention during the years following World War II.

Thailand's Weak Left and Weakened Leviathan, 1945–1958

It is a point of consensus among comparative students of Southeast Asian rebellions that, as Harold Crouch puts it, "It was only in Thailand that a strong communist movement failed to develop."[52] This can be explained largely by the country's success at avoiding the massive disruption of elite control that accompanied Japan's military occupation of Southeast Asia. "Japanese troops were stationed in Thailand not as an occupation force, but as friendly allies,"[53] due to Prime Minister Phibun Songkhram's capitulation to demands that Thai territory be made available for Japan's incursions into neighboring Burma and Malaya.

Political continuity at the elite level spared Thailand the sort of leftist eruption that we have already seen following Japan's surrender in Malaya, the Philippines, and Singapore. The main political effect of Japan's quasi-occupation of Thailand was a worsening of conflict between *factions*, not classes or communal groups. Even before the war, Thai politics had become increasingly defined by the bitter rivalry between Field Marshal Phibun and civilian economist Pridi Banomyong, his erstwhile partner in the bloodless overthrow of the absolute monarchy in 1932. As the King's regent, Pridi refused to back Phibun's decision to ally

---

[52] Crouch (1985): 38. For similar assessments of the Thai Left as relatively weak in regional perspective, see Goodwin (2001), Hedman (2001), K. Jackson (1985), B. Anderson (1978b), and Osborne (1970).

[53] Wilson (1962): 20.

with Japan, organizing a resistance group known as the Free Thais. The group enjoyed considerable support among anti-Japanese and anti-Phibun elites, but mobilized little mass membership, and did not engage in anti-Japanese military operations. The Free Thais received armaments from Allied forces in the waning months of the war, however, allowing Pridi's supporters to rival the pro-Phibun Thai military in firepower after Japan surrendered. As Kasian Tejapira describes Thailand's rapid postwar descent into factional violence:

Political violence in the postwar decade took two major forms: private murders of personal political opponents within the ruling circles by state power holders and armed putsches. The growth and spread of political violence was caused by the ready availability of leftover firearms from the war and easy access to them through both official and black market channels. Of particular relevance were the substantial firearms delivered by the Allies for anti-Japanese purposes near the end of the war, which, in the possession of the Free Thai Movement, facilitated its emergence as a rival of the Royal Thai Army.[54]

Violent elite factionalism raged after 1945 in large measure because there was no organized threat from below pressing Thai elites to work collectively for common class interests. A central labor federation emerged as the war drew to a close, "but it was doubtful whether the active members numbered more than a few hundred," writes Victor Purcell. In short, "*it attained nothing like the same scale as the Malayan General Labor Union, and there was little industrial unrest in Bangkok.*"[55] Some observers suggest that the workers' federation was clandestinely created from above by Pridi as a weapon against Phibun.[56] Like Benigno Aquino's tactical support for leftist rebels in the Philippines in the early 1970s, Pridi's effort to organize urban workers for his own purposes signifies both the weakness of the Left and the salience of factional cleavages in postwar Thailand.

With elites so deeply divided along factional lines, Thai political institutions failed to function throughout the 1945–58 period – precisely when Malaya and Singapore's state and party institutions were undergoing some of their most dramatic development. With Phibun disgraced by his wartime collaboration, a pro-Pridi civilian government assumed power; but it quickly offended military sensibilities by attempting to reduce troop levels, and lost the support of its royalist allies when the King was mysteriously assassinated in June 1946. "Thereafter the burden of criticism against Pridi turned from corruption and partisanship to regicide."[57] In the same year when Malay elites collectively rallied behind their monarchs with the founding of UMNO, Thai elites became hopelessly splintered as their own monarch was assassinated in anti-Pridi forces' apparent pursuit of factional advantage.

Intra-elite violence became endemic. A military coup in November 1947 replaced Pridi as prime minister with a royalist politician. This was quickly followed by another coup in April 1948, returning Phibun to the political apex of what was once again an unabashed military regime. Arising in the absence of

---

54 Kasian (2001): 77.
55 Purcell (1965): 158. Emphasis added.
56 For instance, see Thak (1979: 71, fn. 34).
57 Wilson (1962): 24.

any tangible leftist threat, the pro-Phibun coups in 1947 and 1948 were nothing more than factional power-grabs. The impetus for military rule was not to prevent democratic practices from strengthening the radical Left – the Thai parliament contained precisely one pro-communist member[58] – but to crush Pridi's faction. "The period from 1948 to the end of 1951 was one of extraordinary instability even for Thailand," as "a variety of groups and cliques were maneuvering for advantage."[59]

Most ominously, the military became deeply divided. October 1948 saw the imprisonment of army officers who had opposed the latest coup. Four months later, "a revolt broke out in the middle of Bangkok in which it is understood the marines were supporting a comeback by Pridi," says David Wilson. "The revolt failed and was followed by a purge, the equal of which had never been seen in Thailand. A number of officials and politicians were shot under mysterious circumstances."[60] This would pale in comparison to the intra-elite violence that erupted in June 1951. Marine and naval officers kidnapped Phibun in a coup attempt that set off "three days of heavy fighting"[61] with pro-Phibun forces in the army and air force. The battle ended when the army scuttled and sank the navy's largest ship in the Chao Phraya River.

With the core coercive institutions of the Thai state so divided and debilitated, it should come as no surprise that its administrative institutions floundered as well. Direct tax collections remained at the same level in the decade after 1945 as in the decade before,[62] even as British restrictions on Thailand's collection of rice export taxes (as reparation for its wartime alliance with Japan) presented added pressures to find new sources of revenue. Instead of stepping up direct tax collection, Thai authorities "recalled all one-thousand baht notes," then "allowed public gambling" and "resorted to the sale of gold bullion."[63] More administratively challenging levies were politically unthinkable so long as the state was literally at war with itself. Factional strife prevented the coup-makers from party-building as well as state-building:

After the military coup of 1947, the Coup Group attempted to play party politics by forming its own party which invariably involved a coalition of various parliamentary factions. It was difficult for the military leaders to generate genuine solidarity within its political machinery and internal squabbles became a source of headaches for the ruling military elite. Their attempts to play party politics also cost them heavily, for bribery became a major instrument for control. The 1947 Coup Group's Sahaphak or United Front Party proved costly to run as well as frustrating to keep intact. Thus the Silent or Radio Coup of 1951 was staged in an attempt to get rid of "troublesome" MP's who demanded more privileges and more money.[64]

---

[58] Darling (1971): 238.
[59] Wilson (1962): 25.
[60] Ibid. 26.
[61] Ibid.
[62] Chai-Anan (1971): 46.
[63] Thak (1979): 18–19.
[64] Ibid. 146–147.

It was with this coup in 1951 that Phibun began perfecting a new approach to raising revenue – using the bogey of communism to extract aid from the United States. The Americans had grudgingly recognized Phibun's return to power in 1948, despite his fascist past, as a check against communism. Yet Thailand was seen as a vital American ally because of the *weakness* rather than the *strength* of its radical Left. "Thailand, relatively free from any viable communist force was naturally seen as a possible stronghold against the spreading 'communist menace.'"[65] Leftists had gained no appreciable strength during the 1948–51 period. Yet "[a] month before the 1951 coup, Phibun had gravely informed a somewhat skeptical parliament that the police had unearthed a communist plot to overthrow his government."[66] Thai communists were "an obscure petty nuisance" in the decade from 1948–57, but their strength was "willfully misrepresented and manipulated by the Phibun government."[67]

Phibun's McCarthyite tactics played well in Washington, but they did little to help him consolidate elite support at home. With Pridi eliminated as a political factor after the failed "Manhattan Rebellion" in 1951, the main factional cleavage shifted from army vs. navy to military vs. police. Military commander Sarit Thanarat and police chief Phao Siyanon "became the heads of separate clique structures based in different institutions."[68] At the same time when police and military commanders in Malaya were receiving unprecedented new funding by virtue of the enormous tax hauls accompanying the Korean War commodity boom, their Thai counterparts were relegated to more covert forms of financing. While Phao "used his control of the local opium trade to finance his political machine,"[69] Sarit mobilized revenue for his faction through his control over the lottery bureau. Given the lack of leftist mobilization in this period, Thai elites faced no direct peril from this shortage of funding for the country's core coercive institutions. A new anti-communist *law* was passed in 1952, but military and police *institutions* were not revamped as in Malaya. The contrast was vividly displayed when the Phibun regime took advantage of the new anti-communist law by "arresting *a few leftist politicians* who were members of *a peace movement*."[70]

With more reliable political support forthcoming from his American backers than from his fellow Thai elites, Phibun tried in 1955 to shore up his position in the same way Ferdinand Marcos would respond to his similarly tenuous position thirty years later – by calling for elections. His goal was to "obtain a popular mandate so as to enhance his authority in relation to Phao and Sarit."[71] Yet Phibun (again, like Marcos) had no robust party apparatus to channel support in his direction. His military government had formed a party called Seri Manangasila to organize elite support; but it was fractured at the top, with bitter rivals Phibun, Phao, and Sarit as its three leaders, and could only attract elite members with promises of patronage rather than protection. Thus "the Coup Group

[65] Ibid. 78.
[66] Ibid. 78–79.
[67] Kasian (2001): 127.
[68] Wilson (1962): 29.
[69] Thak (1979): 197.
[70] Morell and Chai-Anan (1991): 80. Emphasis added.
[71] Prudhisan (1992): 43.

had to spend large sums of political patronage to keep this group together" and "indulged in illegal and corrupt tactics to find funds to keep party members happy and used repressive methods to clamp down on opposition factions in parliament."[72]

Party-building was a losing battle for the "triumvirate military regime" because it "sought to broaden public support at a time of rising discontent with corruption and authoritarian rule."[73] The Phibun regime's lack of support among Thailand's state employees is especially glaring in comparative perspective. "That these civil servants were seen as politically independent of the state is evident," writes James Ockey, "first in the strong support they had demonstrated for Pridi, even after he was removed from power, and secondly, in that Phibun sought to gain loyalty by conducting psychological warfare among bureaucrats as early as 1952."[74] State employees would become a critical and willing constituency for authoritarian ruling parties in Malaysia, Singapore, and Indonesia, but not in Thailand: "The civil service was dragooned into party work."[75]

The February 1957 elections signaled the lack of elite support for military rule. Seri Manangasila won the most seats, "but it aroused widespread hostility because of numerous election irregularities."[76] As in the Philippines in 1986, a stolen election in Thailand in 1957 triggered urban middle-class protests and a military coup in support of the protestors. The coup was led by army commander Sarit, whom Phibun had given emergency powers to crack down on post-election protests. But Sarit stabbed Phibun in the back, condemning electoral fraud at a protest at Bangkok's elite Chulalongkorn University and promising not to use his emergency powers to stop students' anti-Phibun actions. His calculation was utterly factional: "one of the main reasons which motivated Field Marshal Sarit to stage the coup...was because he had been discharged from his post as chairman of the State Lottery monopoly."[77] As with Suharto's coup in Indonesia a decade later, middle-class protesters in Thailand viewed Sarit's coup through unrealistically democratic lenses. Sarit was broadly viewed as "a 'savior' statesman who wanted only to purify the system by getting rid of its corrupt members." His "coup of September 1957 was a popular one."[78]

With democratic sentiment fueling his rise, Sarit attempted to give his new regime democratic moorings. He created another new political party, Sahaphum, to contest new national elections in December 1957. The elections were clean, but Sahaphum could not manage a decisive victory, winning only a handful more seats than the opposition Democrats and fewer overall than political independents. "In the major cities, the Sahaphum candidates were routed."[79] Sarit thus scrapped Sahaphum and founded yet *another* party, Chatsangkhomniyom, to contest local elections in March 1958. This time pro-Sarit forces lost outright, as the

[72] Thak (1979): 147.
[73] Darling (1971): 233.
[74] Ockey (2002): 117.
[75] Wilson (1962): 31.
[76] Ibid.
[77] Chai-Anan (1971): 67.
[78] Thak (1979): 123.
[79] Ibid. 133.

Democrats won 13 of 22 contested seats: "Especially in Bangkok and Thonburi, the government party was soundly defeated despite heavy campaigning by military leaders."[80] Having won 8 of 9 seats in Bangkok in the December 1957 vote, the opposition Democrats swept all 12 of Bangkok's seats in March 1958. "The victory of the Democrats can be explained by the fact that the voters in Bangkok remained opposed to the military regime."[81]

With no fear of mass unrest tying them to a pro-military party, urban Thais overwhelmingly favored Sarit's civilian opponents when given a chance to do so. As in the mid- to late 1940s, whatever strength urban labor possessed in the mid- to late 1950s was by virtue of tactical elite sponsorship rather than its own mobilizational powers. Like Pridi before him, Phao created a Free Labor Association in 1954, and Phibun pushed a liberalized Labor Act in 1956 because "the Phibun government was confident that it could control a broader labor movement," and hoped – in vain – that labor would back his Seri Manangkasila party.[82]

The chronic weakness of the Thai Left made it difficult for Sarit's new government to order power through state institutions as well. Even modest and regressive tax proposals proved to be non-starters among a non-threatened elite:

The budget for fiscal year 1958 was another stumbling block for the weakening government. The government-proposed budget showed a deficit of over 2,200 million baht. In an attempt to balance this deficit, the government proposed to raise taxes on certain commodities such as gasoline, cement, and other imported goods. This led to heavy criticism from the press and the opposition parties, as well as from certain quarters within the Chatsangkhomniyom itself.[83]

Patently unable to organize elite support using democratic methods, Sarit tried to construct an authoritarian Leviathan instead, seizing absolute power in another coup in October 1958. Yet without any radical threat from below justifying his dictatorial move, Sarit could not generate elite support by providing class protection. Thai democracy had not produced the kind of widespread fear of unmanageable class and communal conflict that would arise under pluralist conditions in Malaysia and Singapore; it had produced only the sort of widespread disgust with elite corruption and abuses that would be witnessed in the Philippines.

Thailand's Fragmented Authoritarian Leviathan, 1958–1973

With no protection pact at Sarit's disposal, "one of his major overriding concerns was the search for a long-term legitimizing program."[84] The strategy he adopted was half economic, half symbolic. In economic terms, Sarit emphasized distribution over extraction, as "the immediate needs of the public were to be achieved regardless of cost."[85] The lack of emphasis on extraction from elites in Thailand's National Economic Development Plan (NEDP) of 1961 stands in

[80] Ibid. 138.
[81] Suchit (1996): 85.
[82] Morell and Chai-Anan (1991): 183.
[83] Thak (1979): 138–139.
[84] Ibid. 255.
[85] Ibid. 149.

striking contrast to Malaysia's NEP ten years later. Even as the Bangkok city government was "ordered to abolish certain taxes, license fees, and charges for official services," the national government initiated a vast array of new spending programs, ranging from electricity subsidies to tuition reductions to free health care for the needy to cheap credit (and a reduced workweek to boot) for civil servants.[86]

Whereas new authoritarian Leviathans in Malaysia, Singapore, and Indonesia demanded and secured fresh sacrifices from economic elites, Sarit ushered in an era that would be dominated less by Leviathan than by laissez-faire. "To obtain the support of the elite and businessmen in the cities, industry and the private sector were left alone and government assistance was provided when needed."[87] The Sarit era was one when "the businessmen could be said to have gained increased leverage over the bureaucrats"[88] – a phrase no one would use to describe state-business relations in Singapore circa 1965, Indonesia circa 1966, or Malaysia circa 1969. Progressive taxes were assiduously avoided as "the basic corporation [sic] of government revenue remained relatively unchanged. The government depended heavily on indirect taxes," notes Chai-Anan Samudavanija. "Revenue receipts from income taxes increased slightly and by 1969 constituted only 12 per cent of total tax revenue. The Thai government did not embark upon any great tax increases during this period but preferred to use deficit financing for the economic development of the country."[89] The economy boomed, but the Thai state did not reap the kind of revenue benefits seen in Malaysia and Singapore – with important implications for the durability of authoritarian rule.

Neither Sarit nor his military successors (after his death from cirrhosis in 1963) made any concerted effort to bolster the administrative institutions of the state. Whereas Singaporean authorities established a Civil Service College to socialize party and state officials into a common project, Sarit's new Defense College aimed "to link military and civilian elites, *largely on military terms*."[90] With no administratively challenging leftist insurgency to confront, military leaders had no incentive to defer to their civilian counterparts. Even after rebels from the Communist Party of Thailand (CPT) began clashing with government forces in the far northeastern reaches of Thai territory in August 1965, the insurgency was far too remote and rural to alter the political calculations of Bangkok elites. To the extent that the CPT revolt inspired more state intervention in the countryside, it was perceived – like the Philippines' Huk rebellion – as a job that could be handled with military institutions alone. And like Magsaysay, Sarit managed only to concentrate control over military and police institutions into his own hands, not to revamp them into more capable coercive organizations.

Without broad elite backing, Sarit lacked the coalitional foundations to build either an effective ruling party or a stronger administrative state. Running the Chatsangkhomniyom party had shown Sarit how difficult and expensive it was

---

[86] Ibid. 149, 187.
[87] Ibid. 232.
[88] Prudhisan (1992): 55.
[89] Chai-Anan (1971): 46.
[90] Thak (1979): 289. Emphasis added.

to organize elite support in the absence of a protection pact: "he had spent more than fourteen million baht already on the party and all he got in return were headaches."[91] Sarit disbanded the party in 1959 – much as Marcos disbanded his Nacionalistas in 1972 – and gave his regime a veneer of constitutionality by convening a completely appointive parliament instead. By selecting an assembly of 170 military and police officers and only fifty civilians, Sarit signaled his lack of confidence in his political support beyond the state's coercive apparatus – a lack of confidence more pronounced than that of Suharto in Indonesia a decade later, whose initial protection pact made it easier for him to attract civilian and electoral support. These appointed Thai parliamentarians had to be organized on the basis of provision rather than protection, as Sarit "used his control over the appointment of members of the Assembly to extend patronage as payment for services rendered or for future support."[92]

Besides rampant and unsustainable levels of patronage, Sarit tried to compensate for his weak state and regime institutions with a heavy dose of symbolism, tying his regime as tightly as possible to the Thai monarchy. The King was indebted to Sarit for toppling Phibun, who had led the overthrow of the absolute monarchy in 1932 and ruled with disregard for the constitutional monarchy ever since. He thus embraced Sarit's authoritarian Leviathan to snuff out his primary elite rival – not to suppress radical politics.

The distinction is vital. With no endemic need for military protection, the Thai monarchy retained considerable freedom for maneuver in its marriage of convenience with military rulers. This was in contrast to Malaysia, where Malay sultans allied with UMNO in a marriage of *desperation* rather than convenience. This left Malaysia's monarchy as something of a spent political force, dependent on the protection of the ruling party in a way that had no parallel in Thailand.

Thailand's authoritarian Leviathan era (1958–1973) thus saw military rulers serving the needs of the monarchy more than the other way around. Desperate to borrow the legitimacy of Thailand's unrivaled object of nationalist and religious affection, Sarit and his successors allowed the monarchy to take on state-like qualities of its own. Rather than controlling the King's purse strings, military rulers relied on the monarchy "as an institution for receiving private contributions for charity work," notes Thak Chaloemtiarana. "At the king's discretion and with the government's acquiescence, these funds were channeled to public programs, enhancing their popularity in the process."[93] The King not only assumed "the role of legitimizer of political power" and "symbolic focus of national unity," but that of a "'broker' for transferring funds from the private sector to the state treasury" as well. "Sarit made it possible for the monarchy to grow strong enough to play an independent role after his death."[94]

In sum, Sarit had only managed to "institutionalize the granting of favors,"[95] not the extraction of resources or support. His successors thus inherited a state

[91] Ibid. 137.
[92] Ibid. 283.
[93] Ibid. 311.
[94] Ibid. 334.
[95] Prudhisan (1992): 52–53.

with little fiscal power, a military with little cohesion or capacity, and no party apparatus whatsoever. In the absence of effective authoritarian institutions, "[t]he departure of the autocratic patron with a strong personality meant that clique rivalries surfaced once more."[96]

The decade following Sarit's death (1963–1973) witnessed a resurgence of the military factionalism that had characterized the decade preceding his rise to power. A new triumvirate of military leaders emerged, paralleling the Phibun-Phao-Sarit triumvirate of yore. Field Marshal Thanom Kittikachorn was primus inter pares, with Field Marshal Praphat Charusathien and General Krit Sivara perched in second and third position. Since all three men had gained power through elite intrigues – collectively backing Sarit's coups in 1957 and 1958 – it is hardly surprising that they tried to retain power in similar fashion. Although they "shared certain viewpoints, their personal rivalries and competing ambitions caused friction."[97]

This fragmented military regime proved unable to manage growing elite demands for democratic reform in the late 1960s and early 1970s. In early 1968, the King responded to increasing student demands for political liberalization by telling an audience at Bangkok's Thammasat University that he expected the Thanom regime to promulgate a new constitution and call national elections within the year. Facing such pressure from its primary legitimizer, the regime complied by early 1969. When a pro-government candidate claimed that the King fully supported the new political party that Thanom had hurriedly organized for the elections, the King denied any such endorsement, informing another audience of university students "that if he went to the polls he would not vote along party lines."[98] He went on to criticize the military's violent suppression of communists in northern Thailand, as well as its tendency to characterize all political dissent as communist. By calling "the use of force self-defeating in the long run," the King rejected the military's claim that authoritarian measures were necessary to keep Thailand safe from communism. By publicly chiding the ruling generals that "they must learn to listen to the people,"[99] he gave the trend toward liberalization momentum.

Like Phibun's elections in 1957, Thanom's elections in 1969 failed to rally social support for military rule. The pro-government United Thai People's Party (UTPP) captured only 75 of 219 seats, while the opposition Democrats won 57 and political independents won 72.[100] In the absence of any imminent threat from below, the "highly fragmented" and "faction-ridden" UTPP had nothing but patronage to keep elites in line.[101] Yet the inherent difficulty of winning urban middle-class electoral support with patronage alone was amply displayed, as the UTPP proved "most unpopular in the Bangkok metropolitan area where it has dispensed the largest amount of public resources."[102] Even UTPP

---

[96] Ibid. 56.
[97] Morell and Chai-Anan (1991): 51.
[98] Ibid. 66–67.
[99] Ibid. 68–69.
[100] Darling (1971): 231.
[101] Chai-Anan (1971): 239–240.
[102] Darling (1971): 240.

parliamentarians could not be induced by massive financial benefits to act in collective support of the Thanom regime's policy agenda, as "members of the government party" came "to divide among themselves on some important issues such as the Tax Increase Bill in July 1970."[103]

Thanom responded to his frustrating inability to organize elite support in Sarit-like fashion, with yet another coup in November 1971. "It was uncanny to witness Thanom's replay of the Sarit coups of 1957 and 1958 all at once."[104] A primary rationale appeared to be the shared desire of Thanom and Praphat to smooth the political rise of the former's son and the latter's son-in-law, Lieu-tenant Colonel Narong Kittikachorn. Predictably – and eerily foreshadowing reactions to Suharto's promotion of his own son-in-law to a top military com-mand in Indonesia a quarter century later – this "unprecedented specter of dynas-tic succession" was "unwelcomed by the military high command"[105] and quickly "created serious tensions within the army."[106] This personalistic turn was not simply the result of Thanom's and Praphat's venality – a trait that afflicted pre-vious Thai military rulers in similar measure – but their sensible calculation that their coalition had crumbled to the point that no one outside their immediate inner circle could be trusted. As Prudhisan Jumbala summarizes the 1971 coup: "This contraction of the ruling circle was a last ditch attempt to salvage the Sarit system gone sour."[107]

The coup was unsympathetically received across the board. When Thanom tried to paint his power-grab in anti-communist terms to a group of civil servants, "the knowledgeable sections of the *prachachon* which included former MP's, stu-dents, teachers, and those who had been closely following events since 1969 were frankly skeptical of Thanom's explanation that the country faced grave internal and external dangers and that the throne was in jeopardy."[108] The King gave no sign that he perceived the coup as necessary to protect his position: "Noticeably, royal pardon was not forthcoming for the 1971 coup action," in contrast to ear-lier coups. "In retrospect, it appears that by 1972 the King was taken with the idea that military-bureaucratic power should be countervailed by extrabureau-cratic forces."[109] Such an idea has never taken hold among communal elites in Malaysia but echoes the support for democratization offered by communal elites in the Philippines in the waning days of the Marcos regime.

Authoritarianism would collapse in October 1973 as a combined result of divi-sions in the military, opposition from urban middle classes, and withdrawal of sup-port from Thailand's communal elite extraordinaire, the King. The "end game" began when thirteen students were arrested at Bangkok's Democracy Monu-ment for handing out leaflets demanding a return to constitutional rule. "The

---

[103] Chai-Anan (1971): 239–240.
[104] Thak (1979): 345.
[105] Prudhisan (1992): 62.
[106] Thak (1979): 346.
[107] Prudhisan (1992): 61.
[108] Thak (1979): 347.
[109] Prudhisan (1992): 62–63.

government announced that the police had uncovered a communist plot to over-throw the administration, and the thirteen were charged with treason."[110] The claims lacked credibility – especially since just five months before, students had "discredited regime claims that an Army helicopter crash happened on an anti-communist mission by exposing that it was actually used by military officers close to Narong in a pleasure hunt in a National Reserve."[111] The regime's accusa-tions of communist treachery were "met with widespread public skepticism and anger."[112]

Broad public support for the detained students triggered the mobilization of "a flood of students, well-dressed urbanites of the middle classes, and some lower class workers and unemployed to demand their release."[113] As Thak describes both the massive and cross-class character of the protests: "The occasion drew from two hundred to five hundred thousand participants, from junior bureaucrats down to common vendors."[114] Public support was overwhelming behind the scenes as well as in the streets: "The middle class made its presence felt in 1973 by rendering moral and financial support to the student-led uprising against the military."[115]

Well-organized regimes with loyal coercive apparatuses can often withstand such massive democratic uprisings – but as we have seen, Thailand's fragmented military government was never such a regime. As protests swelled, "General Krit Sivara, army commander-in-chief, began to adopt a position independent of the Thanom-Praphat group. This split prevented those who advocated use of strong measures, particularly Colonel Narong, from staging a major attack on the demonstrators. General Krit's intervention rendered further military suppression untenable."[116]

Not that Thanom and his backers failed to try. Indeed, "the government ordered in troops complete with combat gear backed by tanks and helicopters to suppress the demonstrators." But the regime "lost the backing of the key First division which had been historically vital in the seizure and maintenance of power since 1947" and which was commanded by a factional rival of Narong's.[117] (The parallels with Suharto's "end game" – particularly the role of the Wiranto-Prabowo factional split – are again striking.) Given the Thai monarchy's con-sistent refusal to give blanket approval to Thanom or his associates, "it was not at all surprising for the king to intervene to end the bloodshed and order Thanom and Praphat into exile. Lacking the king's support, the armed forces fell from power."[118] The King's decision reflected public sentiment: "soldier and

[110] Morell and Chai-Anan (1991): 147.
[111] Prudhisan (1992): 64.
[112] Morell and Chai-Anan (1991): 147.
[113] Prudhisan (1992): 65.
[114] Thak (1979): 348.
[115] Anek (1996): 209.
[116] Morell and Chai-Anan (1991): 147–148.
[117] Thak (1979): 348.
[118] Morell and Chai-Anan (1991): 69.

police brutality. . . . angered and consolidated public opinion in demanding that Thanom, Praphat, and Narong be arrested and brought to trial for murder."[119]

Beyond Thailand's Age of Authoritarian Leviathans, 1973–1992

October 1973 did not signal the eternal triumph of Thai democracy, but it did sound the death knell for Thai authoritarian Leviathans. The military reclaimed political power on the heels of a violent right-wing backlash against urban leftists in October 1976; yet "in less than a year Thailand was back on the road to democracy," since "the educated middle classes accepted military guardianship only as a means to stop democratic vices but not as an alternative government."[120]

The same could be said for the King and many elements in the military. They had seen Thai communism gain strength *after* the military takeover in 1958, and witnessed a similar radicalization effect *after* democratic procedures were abolished in 1976. Leftist parties had been trounced in the democratic elections of January 1975 and April 1976, while the big victors were parties led by emergent economic elites. Meanwhile, the authoritarian backlash of 1976 had shown that "repression, instead of stemming the tide of insurgency, fueled it."[121] The liberalizing regimes of Kriangsak Chomanan (1977–1980) and Prem Tinsulanonda (1980–1988) were broadly guided by a historical recognition "that *past dictatorships have been conducive to continuously increasing communist strength; and. . . . that the only real way to gain victory over the communists was through establishing a democratic political system.*"[122]

In sum, the rhythms of contentious politics and regime politics in Thailand more closely resembled those of the Philippines than those of Malaysia or Singapore. Competitive elections strengthened economic elites at the expense of radical leftists, whereas dictatorship largely accomplished the reverse. Democracy had proven frustrating in Thailand – not frightening. This is why General Suchinda Krapayoon enjoyed broad elite acquiescence when forcibly replacing a corrupt elected government with a more technocratic variety in February 1991, but sparked a cross-class democratic revolution when trying to preserve power for himself in May 1992. Suchinda's coup was basically a replay of Thanom's coup in November 1971. And the public reaction it elicited – the mobilization of cross-class urban protests, the fragmentation of the military, and the democratic intervention of the King – was basically "a replay of October 1973."[123]

South Vietnam's Fragmentation Trajectory

If counterrevolutionary political institutions were shaped by the raw intensity rather than the type and timing of contentious politics, Thailand and South Vietnam would have developed the most *dissimilar* pair of authoritarian Leviathans in Southeast Asia after World War II. No government in the region

---

[119] Thak (1979): 348.
[120] Anek (1996): 218, 219.
[121] Prudhisan (1992): 90.
[122] Ibid. 93. Emphasis added.
[123] Girling (1996): 22.

confronted a weaker communist movement than Thailand's, and none ultimately battled a stronger one than South Vietnam's. Yet the two countries' authoritarian Leviathans traveled markedly *similar* trajectories of endemic factionalism, institutional fragmentation, and regime instability in the three decades following World War II.

Once again, the critical factor is *the type* of contentious class politics that erupted between 1945 and the birth of an authoritarian Leviathan. In South Vietnam's case, open-ended military rule was installed quite early, with General Ngo Dinh Diem's seizure and consolidation of power in 1954–55. Although it is hard to imagine in retrospect, the decade following World War II did not present South Vietnamese elites with the kind of physically threatening and administratively challenging patterns of mass mobilization that characterized the same time-period in Malaya and Singapore. Not only did Vietnamese communists have a weak urban presence before 1955 – they were also immensely stronger in the northern than in the southern half of the country. And in part by virtue of Vietnam's relative ethnic homogeneity and lack of politicized communal cleavages, the Viet Minh proved capable of mobilizing cross-class support by emphasizing their nationalist credentials rather than their communist agenda. Only after the Tet Offensive in 1968 unleashed massive leftist violence in southern urban centers do we witness even a modest – and fatally belated – increase in collective action among South Vietnamese elites.

Like Thailand and the Philippines, South Vietnam did not witness the emergence of a broad elite coalition or effective political institutions during the decades following World War II. When the American-backed military regime collapsed in April 1975, it fell at the hands of communist revolutionaries rather than democratic reformists; and when the regime collapsed, the entire South Vietnamese state collapsed along with it. My framework cannot explain why Vietnamese communists proved capable of outright military victory, unlike their counterparts in Thailand and the Philippines – but it does offer an explanation for why South Vietnamese political institutions were as weak and fragmented as in these neighboring countries, making some sort of regime transition virtually inevitable in the face of concerted cross-class opposition.

South Vietnam's Nationalist Revolution and Fragmented Counterrevolution, 1945–1954

Long before the Japanese entered the picture in 1941, the French governed Vietnam with far more vigor in the south than in the north. This allowed French authorities to destroy the first seedlings of communist organization in the south; "the ICP [Indochinese Communist Party] suffered a great setback with the failed rebellion in southern Vietnam in 1940," notes Tuong Vu; "all central committee members were either arrested or executed by the French."[124] By ruling through Vichy French collaborators from 1941 until early 1945, Japanese occupiers avoided the political disruptions that created dramatic new opportunities for leftist mobilization elsewhere in Southeast Asia. Only when Japan turned against its erstwhile French allies in March 1945, seizing direct power, did the Viet Minh

---

[124] Vu (2004): 189.

resistance movement experience explosive growth in numbers and significance. "The Viet Minh obtained weapons and ammunition from French troops fleeing to China and, given the general breakdown of political authority after March, was able to establish 'People's Revolutionary Committees' in many towns and villages, *particularly in northern Vietnam.*"[125]

To be sure, Japan's sudden surrender in August 1945 produced a chaotic interregnum, reminiscent of Malaya's, in both the northern and southern portions of the country. Like the MPAJA, the Viet Minh was the only approximation of political organization in Vietnam until European forces could reestablish control. But the brief period of Viet Minh ascendance in August and September 1945 was experienced very differently in different parts of the country. In northern and central Vietnam, the Viet Minh enjoyed an enormous advantage, allowing it to seize the cities of Hanoi and Hue, and establish effective local control. But in the south, the lack of preexisting Viet Minh or ICP organization (especially in urban centers) meant these groups were only part of "a coalition of nationalist forces in capturing Saigon."[126] Lacking strong local organizations, the Vietnamese Left had no capacity to establish even fleeting control over Saigon:

> The Communists as well were in a weaker position than in the North; *there had been no opportunity to consolidate their scattered nuclei in the countryside.*... The Communists had no disciplined organization either.... Even in Saigon the Communists' reservoir of strength was the mobs who came on to the streets to celebrate, with looting and violence, the end of the Japanese (and French) occupation. Tran Van Giau, who represented the Vietminh and the Indochina Communist Party, tried with limited success to discipline these mobs through the cadres of what survived of the youth movement.[127]

These organizations' self-proclaimed temporary "administration" in Saigon was nothing of the sort. It "lacked the discipline and leadership of its Hanoi sponsor" and "could scarcely claim even de facto status."[128] The French had Saigon firmly in hand by late September. The same could not be said of the province of Tonkin, Hanoi's province, where the Viet Minh could not be budged. An uneasy truce in Tonkin broke down in November 1946 when the French "indiscriminately shelled the city of Haiphong, killing six thousand Vietnamese by their own estimates."[129] The First Indochinese War (1946–1954) was underway.

The war against the French was overwhelmingly rural and predominantly northern. "Comparatively speaking, the South Vietnamese cities and provincial centers were less subject to Communist administrative and political networks due to the French presence."[130] Rather than fighting to seize Saigon, "[t]he task assigned to the Communist organization in the South was therefore unspectacularly to second the main effort to 'liberate' Tonkin."[131] Although the Viet Minh

[125] Goodwin (2001): 92. Emphasis added.
[126] Ibid. 93.
[127] Duncanson (1968): 159. Emphasis added.
[128] Keay (1997): 280.
[129] Ibid.
[130] Lem (1971): 199.
[131] Duncanson (1968): 179.

retained considerable strength in rural areas of the south, this presented no imminent bodily threat to southern Vietnam's powerful rural elites, as "most of the big landlords were absentee owners, having fled to the cities" when the war against the French commenced.[132]

The remoteness of the guerrilla conflict bred overconfidence in the ability of the French-backed Bao Dai government to prevail. In early 1952, the *Far Eastern Economic Review* editorialized that, from the communists' perspective, "it would look as if the time were approaching when.... the whole venture must be written off as a failure."[133] In precisely the same article in which they lambasted British authorities for losing the Malayan Emergency through lack of political will, the editors of *FEER* noted "an improvement in Indo-China" as "the military tide has begun to turn," optimistically echoing French hopes "that 1952 will be the last year of this long and costly conflict."[134]

While the location of mass mobilization from 1946–54 was primarily rural and northern, the ideology driving mass mobilization was primarily nationalism – not communism. The Viet Minh's effort to forge a cross-class coalition against foreign imperialism dated back to the eve of Japanese occupation. As invasion loomed, the ICP leadership "withdrew the slogan 'To confiscate landlords' land and distribute it to the tillers' and by May 1941 the theme of 'national liberation' held the center of the stage."[135] The outbreak of conflict against the French in 1946 only heightened the movement's need (and capacity) to attract broad, national support. Tuong Vu describes the Viet Minh in this period as "a united front with its membership incorporating all social classes." When Ho Chi Minh initially captured power in Hanoi in September 1945, his fifteen-member cabinet included eight non-communist members. His Vietnamese Communist Party (VCP) would remain "a party full of middle peasants and urban bourgeois" well into the 1950s.[136] This cross-class membership was intimately connected to the Party's toned-down ideological approach. "Until 1953, the Viet Minh adhered to a 'national liberation' program that explicitly deemphasized class struggle," writes Jeff Goodwin. "[T]he Viet Minh focused its agrarian program on modest rent and interest reductions so as not to alienate rich peasants and even 'patriotic landlords,' who played a surprisingly large role in the movement."[137]

In sum, mass mobilization from 1946–54 was far more rural than urban, far more nationalist than communist (or communalist), and far more northern than southern. It should therefore not be surprising that the threat from below inspired no significant collective action among southern elites. This is clearly witnessed in the area of taxation. The Vietnamese state proved unable to extract revenue in a reliable manner, even during the Korean War commodity boom that proved so lucrative for public authorities in Malaya. This was attributable to corruption

[132] Dacy (1986): 4.
[133] "Hesitations in Strategy for Asia," *Far Eastern Economic Review*, 31 January 1952.
[134] "1951 and the Conflicts of Asia," *Far Eastern Economic Review*, 27 December 1951.
[135] Goodwin (2001): 91.
[136] Vu (2004): 173, 179, 189.
[137] Goodwin (2001): 110.

among bureaucrats and delinquency among elite taxpayers, not to the disruptions of civil war:

> More serious was the financial aftermath of the war: the new state had started its life in 1950[138] with no loan charges on its budget, but also with negligible cash reserves with the banks. *The collection of direct taxes had become so erratic – as much on the excuse of insecurity as because of the reality of it – that even the Municipality of Saigon had to be subsidized by the central Government* to the extent of 25 per cent of its expenditure in 1954, while the profits tax in Cochinchina actually brought to account (not necessarily the amount collected, still less that which was due) fell, inversely to the soaring of profits, from 160 million piastres in 1952 to only 6 million in 1953.[139]

Saigon was comparatively unthreatened and untaxed. Without taxing the country's main center of wealth, French colonial officials and their Vietnamese partners lacked the resources to govern the southern countryside by the time the First Indochinese War ended in 1954. "It is impossible to arrive at an accurate statistical assessment of the condition of the country at the moment of the ceasefire," writes Dennis Duncanson. "For a decade the cracked apparatus of government had been papered over at many points by the recording of statistics that were not necessarily measured on the ground."[140] So long as southern Vietnam remained far removed from the front lines of Viet Minh insurgency, there was little imperative to repair the cracks. "The physical scars of war were not conspicuous" in the South, even as late as 1954 – "the principal fighting had been in the North."[141]

South Vietnam's Fragmented Authoritarian Leviathan, 1955–1968

One might suspect that the trouncing of French forces on the (far northern) battlefields of Dien Bien Phu in May 1954 would have punctured southern Vietnamese elites' sense of physical remove from the communist threat. Yet if anything, the partitioning of the country into a communist North and anticommunist South had the opposite effect. Although analysts disagree on precisely when the Second Indochinese War pitting North against South began, the consensus appears to be that conflict ceased from 1954 until 1958 at the earliest, or 1960 at the latest. Smarting from its casualty toll at Dien Bien Phu, the Hanoi regime "bided its time"[142] in the years immediately following the Geneva Accords. The Viet Cong guerrilla movement in the South was not even formed until 1960. While rural areas suffered some scattered attacks before then, "the seriousness of the developing situation was discounted or underestimated by both the South Vietnamese Government and the United States."[143] Disorganized leftist violence exhibited little elite impact, as "neither the government of South

---

[138] Vietnam had a "new state" as of 1950 in the sense that the French ostensibly transferred sovereignty to a government led by former monarch Bao Dai.
[139] Duncanson (1968): 205.
[140] Ibid. 204.
[141] Ibid. 205.
[142] Osborne (1965): 4.
[143] Ibid. 5.

Vietnam nor that of the United States seems to have been much concerned by it up to 1959."[144] One scholar goes so far as to say that American officials felt "the insurgent problem was over after the Geneva Agreements."[145] Even when elite threat perceptions eventually intensified, "the assumption [was] that the chief threat to the Diem regime would be in the form of military invasion from the north,"[146] not the kind of unmanageable insurgency from within that might have pressured elites to reorder Leviathan in order to manage it.

Such perceptions would have fateful consequences for South Vietnam's political institutions. It was during this breathing space from active internal conflict in the mid-1950s that the Ngo Dinh Diem regime was born and its key institutions founded. With no active leftist insurgency to confront or out-organize – even in rural areas – Diem had neither the incentive nor the capacity to build strong state and party institutions to buttress his rule. Foreshadowing the highly personalistic regimes soon to be founded in Thailand and the Philippines against backdrops of manageable mass politics, Diem sought to secure his position by constructing a "father image" and generating a "personality cult," grounded in a pseudo-ideology he called "personalism."[147] Having risen to power with "neither widespread acclaim nor any party organization," the new president cultivated a narrow clique whose only source of cohesion was that it was "dedicated to the maintenance of Diem in office." Rather than seeking to organize elites beyond his limited faction, the Diem clique "eliminated, neutralized, or at least kept under discreet surveillance individuals who were not so tied."[148] The fragmentation of South Vietnam's rivalrous elites meant that Diem would have been unable to build a strong elite coalition even if he had made the attempt: "the previous conduct and present jockeying for advantage which absorbed the energies of most of those rivals did not betoken any useful, or even willing, response had the gesture been made."[149]

In the absence of elite collective action, party and state institutions were debilitated from the onset of Diem's authoritarian Leviathan. Even the basic coercive institutions of the state remained unreformed. A team of American advisers came to Saigon in 1955, "[p]ointing out the connection between Communist subversion and the lack of a nationally-organized rural police force," and "urg[ing] forcefully the retraining of the civil guard as rural police."[150] With communist insurgency in abeyance and the South's landlord population safely ensconced in Saigon, Diem ignored their recommendations. Policing the South Vietnamese Left entailed increasing incarceration, not improving institutions. As of 1960, "between 15,000 and 20,000 Communists and active sympathizers had been detained by the government in 'political re-education centers' since 1954."[151]

---

[144] Dacy (1986): 7.
[145] Lem (1971): 175, fn. 98.
[146] Osborne (1965): 7, fn. 18.
[147] Ibid. 205–206.
[148] Duncanson (1968): 218.
[149] Ibid. 219.
[150] Lem (1971): 180, fn. 10.
[151] Scigliano (1960): 336.

The military provided Diem with factional balance more than infrastructural power. Diem's tendency to favor fellow Roman Catholics was especially blatant in his military appointments: they made up only about 10% of South Vietnam's population, but more than 50% of the military's officer corps.[152] The perceived externality of the communist threat also meant that the Diem regime had no compelling rationale to deploy military institutions to step up governance in the countryside, in Thai or Philippine fashion. Instead, "the emphasis was put on training and equipping the Armed Forces for conventional capability against an invasion from the North." As late as the early 1970s, one Vietnamese scholar would note that the military's "suitability for guerrilla fighting has been very limited."[153]

Administrative institutions fared even worse under Diem. One of the new president's first moves was to permit "exceptional entrance and promotion" into the civil service, overturning a system of recruitment and advancement based on "strict rules of merit as assessed by the objective criteria of formal degree and success in examination."[154] This provided Diem with a small circle of loyalists, but also served "to undermine the morale and competence of the bureaucracy."[155] Diem undermined state capacity even further through his "increasing appointment of military men to key positions requiring high administrative skills."[156] The regime's lack of commitment to doing the hard political work of reshaping the state was rather comically expressed in its proclamation of a "Week of Diligence in the Administrative Services" in August 1955.[157]

As in the Philippines, the South Vietnamese bureaucracy was left prostrate to a powerful class of landed elites. Far from being pressed to pay new direct taxes when the First Indochinese War ended in 1954, "ex-landlords sent their agents, *usually government officials*, to collect their rents."[158] Such collections of back rent had helped spark the Huk rebellion in the Philippines in the late 1940s and exhibited a similar incendiary effect on rural insurgency in South Vietnam. The Diem regime announced new land reform policies in 1955, "but without strict enforcement they proved to be ineffective."[159] The Malayan example inspired American and South Vietnamese elites to commence a "strategic hamlet" policy in 1961, in direct response to the Viet Cong's emergence. Yet as with land reform, the policy was marred by "poor implementation" and a "lack of coordination."[160] The consistent pattern of governance under Diem proved to be the promulgation of policy without the elaboration of necessary institutions. It was thus "at the implementation rather than at the conceptualization stage that the administration's performance seems wanting."[161]

[152] Lem (1971): 133.
[153] Ibid. 236.
[154] Ibid. 311.
[155] Ibid. 313.
[156] Ibid. 315.
[157] Ibid. 307.
[158] Dacy (1986): 4. Emphasis added.
[159] Ibid.
[160] Lem (1971): 242–243.
[161] Ibid. 247.

Having seized and exercised power through "intrigue, nepotism, simony, public humbug, and private intimidation,"[162] Diem was ultimately hoist by his own petard, assassinated in a military coup in November 1963. Unlike the coup in Indonesia in 1965, South Vietnam's coup in 1963 did not represent a unified military's response to increasingly threatening and challenging patterns of contentious politics. The impetus for the coup was not the mounting strength of the Viet Cong – whose attacks, even in rural areas, would not significantly increase until 1965 – but "mounting dissatisfaction with [the Diem] family's monopoly of power."[163]

Diem's fall thus provided no new basis for elite collective action and political order. Instead, the 1963 coup ushered in a decade of "revolving-door military juntas."[164] From 1963–65 alone, "the government changed hands six times."[165] These "military interventions in politics reflected a continuing power struggle within the officer corps for control of the army rather than the government."[166] Unable to consolidate power internally, these regimes were unable to project power beyond their narrow ruling circle. "Rather than create more power, successive juntas and regimes have sought to limit the little that existed," wrote Allan Goodman. "By relying upon the military officer corps as the base of its support and power and by clearly favoring only Catholic organizations, the Saigon government has been unable to mobilize non-communist political forces and.... compete with the Viet Cong."[167] This was most clearly expressed in successive military leaders' failure to create any sort of counterrevolutionary nationalist party to organize elites and channel mass support.

Purely rural rebellion did not suffice to unite elites behind any state-building efforts either. "Even when the 1963 coup d'etat overthrew Diem, the civil service changed little." With the military so factionalized, coup rumors would repeatedly arise, debilitating the implementation of government initiatives: "programs in the countryside are virtually held at a standstill awaiting the outcome of the expected province chief and corps commander purges."[168] American pressure on Saigon to decentralize authority after Diem's assassination ignored the common-sense notion that "before power could be decentralized it had to be created."[169] Leviathan's weakness was both expressed and exacerbated by its fiscal incapacity. South Vietnam's tax revenues hovered between 9.5% and 10% of GDP from 1956–72, and were collected regressively, consisting mainly of "a small tax on production, along with excise taxes on beer, soft drinks, cigarettes, and gasoline."[170] On the eve of the Tet offensive, the Saigon tax state hit rock bottom: "Tax collections almost ceased during 1967–68."[171]

---

162 Duncanson (1968): 225.
163 Keay (1997): 350.
164 Goodman (1973): 96.
165 Keay (1997): 351.
166 Goodman (1973): 95.
167 Ibid. 94.
168 Ibid. 104.
169 Ibid. vii.
170 Dacy (1986): 233, 10.
171 Goodman (1973): 105.

South Vietnam's fiscal powerlessness is typically attributed to the dampening effects of American aid on the need to collect taxes locally. "The word used most frequently to describe the amount of aid was 'massive.'"[172] While this might help explain the weakness of the tax state specifically, it is hard to see how foreign aid would have caused the continuing fragmentation and ineffectiveness of both coercive and administrative state institutions more generally. This fragmentation was due to the rural (and external) character of the communist threat, which failed (as in the Philippines and Thailand) to energize elites into acting collectively in self-defense.

State-Building vs. Path-Dependence after the Tet Offensive, 1968–1974

Further evidence for this argument comes from variation within South Vietnam over time. When the Viet Cong finally penetrated urban areas in the South with its deadly Tet offensive commencing in January 1968 – "the Communist forces unleashed major attacks against all major cities and towns in South Vietnam" over a period of several months[173] – contentious class politics became more directly threatening to elite persons and property, and obviously unmanageable with non-state forms of rural social control alone. As this book's theoretical framework would suggest, such a dramatic shift in the *type* of contentious politics produced added pressures for elite collective action in self-defense – even as the belated *timing* of the contentious shift complicated the authoritarian Leviathan's efforts to leverage worsening elite threat perceptions to its advantage. One indication of increased elite collective action came with the intensified interaction between bureaucratic officials and legislative deputies in governing the countryside:

> The Tet offensive provided province chiefs inclined toward the establishment of working relations with the first clear example of its worth. Subsequent attacks such as occurred in May 1968 and the winter and spring of 1969 saw the further development of deputy-province chief cooperation.... While in large measure *it appeared to be the crises that the war produced which helped to cement effective working relations* between the deputy and the province chief, interviews with both revealed that working relationships were viewed as part of a philosophy of government that each had in mind as they pursued their functions, but *there had been little incentive in the past to put it into practice.*[174]

Among South Vietnamese parliamentarians themselves, there emerged after Tet "a trend in Vietnamese politics that has been notably lacking in the past: the beginning of political coalescence."[175] A major theme of Allan Goodman's study of South Vietnamese elites is the tempering of elite factionalism produced by a worsening threat from below. "*In 1967 political leaders interviewed tended to feel that their enemies were principally each other; in 1969, they had come to view their principal opponent as the Viet Cong.* There were perceptible signs within long-factionalized organizations of progress toward resolution of factionalism

[172] Dacy (1986): 20.
[173] Ibid. 12.
[174] Goodman (1973): 219–220. Emphasis added.
[175] Ibid. 251.

and initiation of efforts to redefine the relationship between political groups and the population."[176]

This broadened elite support provided more fertile ground for state-building. In purely military terms, the Saigon government "went to full mobilization and just about doubled the size of its armed forces from 1968 to 1972."[177] More important than such raw growth was the improved coordination of coercive institutions. Most (in)famously, July 1968 saw the introduction of the Phoenix Program by executive decree. "The program, a national project to coordinate the efforts of the military and the civilian intelligence agencies in eliminating the Viet Cong infrastructure, was fully implemented in the wake of the Tet offensive of 1968 after years of American requests for such a program."[178] This marked the badly belated execution of longstanding plans to govern the countryside more vigorously: "The eighth or ninth of such projects," wrote Frances Fitzgerald, "the Phoenix program had the originality to centralize all intelligence and all powers of execution in the person of a single army or police officer in each district and province headquarters."[179] From a comparative perspective, such an approach was hardly original, but mirrored Malaya's counterinsurgency strategy of decades before. This was witnessed in Saigon's post-Tet revamping of police institutions as well, as "a 1971 proposed reorganization of the police force of pre-Communist (South) Vietnam was based on the Malay(si)an model."[180]

In terms of the state's administrative institutions, the Saigon government tried to step up tax extraction – albeit regressively – when it "put into effect an 'austerity tax' in October 1969."[181] More impressively, General Nguyen Van Thieu confronted South Vietnam's "traditional power structure" by implementing a surprisingly confiscatory land reform policy in 1970. As Douglas Dacy describes "the major socioeconomic reform" in "the entire history of the nation":

This Land-to-the-Tillers program transferred about 1.2 million hectares of land to almost 1 million tenants by the time of South Vietnam's defeat in 1975. Unlike the Diem program, this reform made no demand that peasants pay for the land they received. Rather, the government assumed the burden of reimbursing the landlords, paying them 20 percent in cash and the rest in government bonds that carried a 10 percent return. Given the delayed payment schedules implied in the swap of land for government bonds and the negative real interest rate, it is doubtful that landlords received full market value for their land. Thus, *there was some measure of confiscation attendant to the land reform, and this program furnishes another example of the government's ability to act when necessary against entrenched groups.*[182]

Yet the legacies of elite factionalism and state weakness from the Diem period proved too stubborn to overcome. Diem's undermining of the state's Weberian

---

[176] Ibid. 254. Emphasis added.
[177] Dacy (1986): 13.
[178] Goodman (1973): 224.
[179] Cited in Ibid. 225.
[180] Zakaria (1976): 57.
[181] Dacy (1986): 13.
[182] Ibid. 15. Emphasis added.

characteristics in pursuit of narrow political ends exhibited nasty path-dependent consequences. When discussing post-Tet proposals to restore practices of competitive recruitment and promotion in the civil service, Lem Troang Hoang pessimistically concluded that "these measures could at best bring the situation back to the level of 1954."[183] Having inherited such weak state institutions, post-Tet military leaders had little infrastructural power with which to implement their increasingly bold policy initiatives. The aforementioned Phoenix Program proved a disaster on the ground, as the lack of state capacity to monitor provincial counterinsurgency operations led to tremendous arbitrariness and abuse[184] – thus fueling rather than dampening mass support for the Viet Cong.

Even if land reform improved the Saigon Leviathan's rural positioning, it proved to be the right reform at the wrong time. The great irony of the Tet offensive was that "the ranks of the Viet Cong were severely thinned by the fierce fighting that took place," and hence "the character of the resistance movement changed radically, moving more and more to northern (alien) control and reduced effectiveness."[185] While the government's perception of the communist threat as basically external had led it to eschew internal state-building efforts before Tet, its belated recognition of the Viet Cong's strength led it to intensify its practices of rural governance afterward. But "[g]uerrillas indigenous to South Vietnam ceased being the major offensive threat to the GVN after 1968," notes Karl Jackson; "the Government of Vietnam's successful land-to-the-tiller program did not save it from destruction," since "although land reform may have contributed to declining communist recruitment in the South Vietnamese countryside, it did not, in and of itself, make South Vietnam capable of defending itself."[186]

Weak preexisting institutions also hindered efforts by post-Tet governments in Saigon to expand their fiscal power. As American aid plummeted, "the Vietnamese government made its first move in seventeen years to seriously alter its domestic tax structure by putting into effect a value-added tax in 1973," reports Dacy. "This is just another example of.... the increasing audacity of the GVN to govern."[187] Yet the regressive character of such taxation shows either the limits of the regime's audacity in confronting economic elites, or the impracticality of constructing a tax apparatus powerful enough to collect direct taxes from scratch. South Vietnam's final years were thus characterized by a frantic search for fiscal shortcuts – as underlined by its novel attempt at petroleum exploration in the South China Sea from 1973–75.[188]

In the final analysis, the vital point is that Vietnamese communists only penetrated urban areas in the South nearly fifteen years after the onset of Diem's authoritarian Leviathan. The *type* of contentious politics became more conducive to sparking elite collective action after Tet, but the *timing* was all wrong. As in

[183] Lem (1971): 315.
[184] Goodman (1973): 226.
[185] Dacy (1986): 12.
[186] Jackson (1985): 45, fn. 8, and 14.
[187] Dacy (1986): 18.
[188] Ibid.

Thailand and the Philippines, it was as reasonable for elites to conclude that dictatorship had exacerbated mass violence as it was to conclude that continued dictatorship was necessary to protect their persons and property. The Viet Cong's ability to appeal to nationalist rather than communalist sentiments in South Vietnam's ethnically homogenous polity only dampened elite toleration for authoritarian rule further. "Noticeably missing from the Viet Cong appeal is any Communist call for denunciation of families, pooling of land ownership, attacks on religion, and similar Communist revolutionary themes widely purveyed in the North," wrote Lem. "Instead, anti-colonialism, landlordism, and feudalism have been recurrent symbols used in the North as well as in the South."[189]

Anti-military attitudes in South Vietnam were especially pronounced among students and religious elites. As of 1971, Lem reported that "students overtly prefer an elected civilian leadership" and "tend to think the Viet Cong are first nationalist-oriented Vietnamese and only secondarily misguided conspirators."[190] Lem concluded further that most Catholic and Buddhist figures "openly oppose any military rule and demand that the government be managed by civilians representing all segments of the population."[191] Even anti-communist religious elites did not necessarily translate their anti-communism into support for continued dictatorship. As the leader of a Buddhist organization who also served as a legislative deputy said in an interview in 1969: "The principal problem that we as Buddhists face is the reconstruction of our communities that have been ravaged by the war, by the Viet Cong, *and by the repressive policies of the Thieu government.*"[192]

Having failed to organize elite support and extract elite resources since the onset of the Diem regime, South Vietnam's military leaders would lack coalitional and institutional strength throughout their war effort. This would prevent them not only from rescuing their regime, but from salvaging the South Vietnamese state.

Burma's Militarization Trajectory

Like single-party regimes, military regimes vary in their internal cohesion and social support, with profound consequences for their durability. As we have just seen, Thailand's and South Vietnam's military regimes chronically suffered from internal fragmentation and an inability to order power from elite groups. Rampant factionalism meant that "the military" rarely resembled a unitary actor. Hence *fragmentation* better captures their counterrevolutionary political trajectories than *militarization*. Chronic political fragmentation left the Thai and South Vietnamese authoritarian Leviathans – like their fragmented Philippine counterpart – without the coalitional or institutional foundations necessary to forestall cross-class mobilization seeking their overthrow.

---

[189] Lem (1971): 250.
[190] Ibid. 144.
[191] Ibid. 136.
[192] Goodman (1973): 254. Emphasis added.

By contrast, Burma's authoritarian Leviathan is best described as *militarized rather than fragmented* since its seizure of power in 1962. The military regime's enduring capacity to avoid devastating internal schisms has allowed it to repeatedly parry its determined cross-class opposition – even as it has failed to build the kind of robust and extractive state and party institutions that have made authoritarian rule so much more stable and effective in Malaysia and Singapore than in Burma. To make sense of this distinctive political trajectory, one must recognize Burma's lack of congruence with this book's cases of domination and fragmentation, as well as its considerable congruence with this book's other case of militarization: Indonesia.

As we saw in Chapter 3, Burma's broad political congruence with Indonesia commenced in the prewar era, when the two colonies experienced the most invidious practices of territorial divide-and-conquer in all of Southeast Asia. The Japanese interregnum flipped these territorialized ethnic hierarchies on their head, setting the stage for regional rather than leftist rebellions to unsettle the political landscape in World War II's wake. Yet Burma's and Indonesia's trajectories of contentious politics and elite collective action were only *imperfectly* congruent. Subtle cross-case differences will prove as illuminating as the stark cross-case similarities in tracing and explaining Burma's distinctly tragic historical trajectory of authoritarian politics.

Given the considerable complexity of the Burmese case – particularly in its initial types of contentious politics after 1945 – it bears summarizing my core argument at the outset. The radical Left was weaker in postwar Burma than in Malaya or Singapore, partly because of its own internal schisms, and partly because of its subsumption within an overwhelmingly popular, cross-class nationalist movement. Far more potent were rebellions seeking to escape the state rather than capture it. Armed separatism erupted long before the military (or tatmadaw) seized open-ended authoritarian power from elected civilian leaders in 1962, exhibiting a powerful unifying effect on the military; but the remoteness of mass violence gave other elites in Rangoon little incentive to acquiesce to military rule on the military's terms. The result has been a highly cohesive military regime that has persevered through the coercion of its opponents, rather than the crafting of an institutionalized coalition bridging the civil-military divide.

These arguments resonate with Mary Callahan's overarching insight regarding the path-dependent effects of postwar rebellions on the Burmese state and regime: "the nature and conduct of warfare in the years surrounding the transfer of power from a colonial to a postcolonial regime determined how much power the military would wield in the array of organizations that would constitute the postcolonial state for decades to come." Callahan sees Burma's path to militarization, along with Indonesia's, as being shaped by the simultaneity of civil war with "the arrival of global warfare threatening the state's claims over domestic territory."[193] By contrast, I argue that *distinguishing between regionalist and leftist rebellions* best explains why Indonesian military rule enjoyed so much more public support than its Burmese counterpart, as well as why neither Malaya nor

---

[193] Callahan (2004): 10, 11.

the Philippines traveled a militarization trajectory in the wake of domestic insurgency. Meanwhile, distinguishing the manageable demands for regional autonomy in Indonesia from the more unmanageable demands for outright secession in Burma provides a new perspective on why the Burmese military has proven more allergic to democratization than the Indonesian military.[194]

From Nationalist to Separatist Rebellion in Burma, 1945–1962

The Japanese occupation of Burma spawned the kind of powerful nationalist movement that we have seen in Indonesia and Vietnam, rather than the kind of powerful communist movement seen in Malaya and Singapore. Unlike Malaya, where a singular, unrivaled MCP emerged from the ashes of war, Burma saw a severe split within its communist ranks during the Japanese period. The more radical group was Thakin Soe's "Red Flag" communists, which represented a "skeletal underground" during the war, in which "individual communists flailed around Upper and Lower Burma trying to undermine the Japanese campaign."[195] This group ultimately split from Burma's vanguard nationalist organization, the Anti-Fascist People's Freedom League (AFPFL), in March 1946. "They tried to organize strikes, picketing, paddy looting, and even minor revolts in some districts," writes U Maung Maung. "However, as the Red Flag group was a very small faction of the main Communist Party, their activities constituted only minority splinter actions and all petered out within days of the start of the campaign."[196]

While the "Red Flag" communists were extremely radical but weakly mobilized, the "White Flag" communists were more mobilized but less radical. They were led by Thakin Than Tun, the brother-in-law of the leader of the AFPFL and Burma's future nationalist icon nonpareil, Aung San. From his failure to join a communist party cell before the war, to his service as a cabinet minister in the collaborationist wartime government, to his angling for a cabinet portfolio after Burmese independence, Than Tun's modus operandi was that he "played a cautious political game."[197] This helps explain why, "[t]hroughout the 1945–1949 period.... leaders inside the army did not consider Communist Party followers inside or outside the tatmadaw to be real threats to the future sovereignty of independent Burma." Their "concern was mainly with the power of the rightists, especially the Karens who had worked with the British throughout the colonial and wartime period."[198]

Burmese elites' sanguine attitudes toward the communist threat were due not only to the marginality of the Red Flag faction and the moderation of the White Flag group. The bigger point is that Burmese communists were *"effectively contained by non-Communist nationalists."*[199] As in Vietnam and Indonesia,

---

[194] Differentiating among types of leftist rebellion also helps explain the considerable variation in state-building outcomes between Malaysia and the Philippines, which Callahan's framework cannot adequately capture.

[195] Ibid. 73.

[196] Badgley (1974): 244.

[197] Maung Maung (1990): 153.

[198] Callahan (2004): 121.

[199] Goodwin (2001): 122–123. Emphasis added.

the refusal by colonialists to engage in serious negotiations on terms for eventual independence had a combustive effect on Burmese nationalism. In all three cases, European intransigence made nationalism a more salient basis for postwar mobilization than communism per se.

Burmese communists thus initially sought to maximize their clout by working within the AFPFL's cross-class nationalist movement. Upon its founding in August 1944, the AFPFL sought not only to incorporate all socialist and communist factions, but to eliminate their preexisting identities: "no separate political parties were to be active during the period of struggle for independence; unity within the single main organization was to be the primary means of achieving independence."[200] This stricture was only mildly loosened upon Japan's surrender in August 1945, when the AFPFL Supreme Council agreed that "various organizations could maintain their individual identities yet work together in a single, unified program to gain independence under the banner of the AFPFL."[201] The united front strategy paid immediate dividends, as mass support for the AFPFL erupted in Rangoon at rallies immediately following the Supreme Council's "Nethurein Conference" in August 1945:

> This was the AFPFL's first such meeting. . . . The signs of its importance were unmistakable: most of the shops, especially Burmese shops, were closed for the day to let people attend, so that the bazaars were practically empty. Burmese buses and pony cart associations organized voluntary transportation for people from distant quarters of the town. The Royal Lakes area around the cinema hall was full of people sitting on mats; various Rangoon associations and student groups came to the meeting in processions, carrying banners and boards with nationalistic slogans.[202]

It is instructive to consider the contrasts between the nearly simultaneous mass rallies marking the birth of Burma's AFPFL and Malaya's UMNO. Both events witnessed a passionate cross-class rejection of proposals contained in a postwar British White Paper. But while UMNO elites urged the British to work *with them* in pursuing their *communalist* ambitions, AFPFL elites demanded a British *surrender* to their *nationalist* ambitions. Collective action between British and Malay elites was fostered by a powerful, shared threat from below: the Chinese-dominated MCP. Without a powerful and autonomous communist movement serving as a common enemy to unite British and Burmese elites, there was no prospect for the kind of elite collective action seen in Malaya to emerge in Burma.

Postwar collective action in Burma thus included communists and excluded colonialists – the opposite of Malaya's coalitional constellation. This united front strategy was brilliantly conceived and executed. The AFPFL's consistent emphasis on national liberation rather than radical redistribution allowed it to generate considerable support among conservative elites – stymieing British plans to counter the AFPFL by "returning the old, pre-war politicians to the mainstream

---

[200] Maung Maung (1990): 179–180.
[201] Ibid. 180.
[202] Ibid. 181. Although I have not seen figures estimating the turnout at the Nethurein rally, subsequent AFPFL gatherings in Rangoon in January 1946 attracted an estimated 300,000 to 400,000 supporters (Ibid. 203).

of politics."[203] Meanwhile, the AFPFL's incorporation of communist elements gave it more muscle to destabilize British rule.

Events between August and October of 1946 displayed the AFPFL's nimbleness at both exploiting and tempering the power of the Burmese Left. On the one hand, Aung San responded to criticism from White Flag elements by promoting their leader to be the AFPFL's general secretary. Just two days later, AFPFL leaders "held a very successful conference on food problems with the business community, including representatives of the Indian and Chinese Chambers of Commerce."[204] The AFPFL's communist wing then stepped up its strike activity, badly disrupting the economy for several months. This was precisely what was needed to push the British to the bargaining table. "The AFPFL insisted that the problems were the inevitable outcome of the policies being pursued in accordance with the White Paper," writes U Maung Maung. "[E]ven if this strike were settled, more of the same nature would occur 'unless a National Government as demanded by the AFPFL since the meeting of the Nethurein in August 1945 is at the helm of affairs in Burma.'"[205] Urban strike activity in postwar Burma thus expressed radical *nationalism*, whereas labor unrest in Malaya and Singapore expressed radical *leftism*. Far from feeling threatened by such contentious labor politics, "the nationalists kept things moving with a combination of mass demonstrations and strikes."[206]

As diplomatic negotiations and labor unrest intensified in tandem in late September 1946, Aung San insisted that only the AFPFL could restore social stability. After meeting with striking organizations and explaining that the AFPFL's goal was "to gain full financial control so that they would be able to improve the workers' terms of service," Aung San proclaimed that "he could solve the problem of the strikes."[207] His confidence was backed up by pro-AFPFL rallies around the country, which mobilized "University students, labor unions, women's organizations, school pupils, trades organizations, the Socialist Party, the Communist Party, the road, water, and rail transport organizations, and all kinds of other associations including social and racial groups such as the Indian Community and the Burma Chinese Community"[208] in collective opposition to British rule. Just two days after the British finally invited the AFPFL into an interim government in preparation for eventual independence, Aung San "met and negotiated with each group of strikers, and came to settlement terms with almost all of them."[209]

This effective and collective pressure on British authorities set the stage for the Aung San–Attlee Agreement of January 1947, paving the way for Burmese independence in January 1948. The AFPFL confirmed its mass appeal in the general elections of April 1947, securing more than 95% of the votes. Yet as soon as the British had signaled their intention to withdraw, *there was no longer any*

---

[203] Maung Maung (1990): 188.
[204] Ibid. 226.
[205] Ibid. 235.
[206] Boudreau (2002): 543.
[207] Maung Maung (1990): 242, 241.
[208] Ibid. 242.
[209] Ibid.

common enemy pressing the AFPFL's diverse factions to act collectively. Contrary to the
Huntingtonian argument that intense struggles for independence give nationalist
movements an edge in creating cohesive ruling parties, the AFPFL supports
this book's argument that nationalist parties have little basis for sustaining elite
collective action in a postcolonial setting. Elite factionalism would rear its ugly
head even before Burmese sovereignty was secured – in July 1947, Aung San and
several of his associates were gunned down by militias apparently acting at the
behest of one of his main elite rivals.

Even more than Thailand, Burma was debilitated by violent elite factionalism
in the late 1940s. Although Aung San's assassination exacerbated factional strife,
it did not create it; after all, his own violent demise was inseparable from the
upsurge in factionalism that accompanied and followed the Aung San–Attlee
Agreement. Indeed, "assassination would remain an important form of political
action for years to come."[210] More critically for the argument here, the explosion
of unrest throughout the Burmese polity upon the British withdrawal in January
1948 was a product of this elite factionalism, not the kind of autonomous mass
unrest that can induce counterrevolutionary elite collective action in response.
"The leftist and separatist insurgencies that commenced soon after independence
descended from the postoccupation elite struggles in Rangoon."[211]

Separatist movements would prove more unmanageable than their leftist
counterparts, and hence more consequential for the long-term development of
Burmese institutions. Whereas Malayan communists pressed British authorities
to reorder the urban state apparatus with their concerted postwar strike campaign
– and only fled to the jungle fringes under terrific coercive and administrative
duress – Burmese communists were more inclined to pursue the rural, Maoist
route to power. When Burmese authorities ordered the arrest of Communist
Party of Burma (CPB) leaders after a protest rally in Rangoon in March 1948, "all
the CPB leaders. . . . left Rangoon and [took] refuge in rural areas."[212] No state-
building was necessary to uproot the CPB from the urban sphere – "for ideological
reasons the CPB has paid little or no attention to struggles in urban areas."[213]

The regionalist rebellion of the Karen National Union (KNU) and its military wing, the Karen National Defense Organization (KNDO), would have much
greater political reverberations. "[I]t has always been more concerned with the
ethnic right of self determination than with the overthrow of the government in
Rangoon," writes Martin Smith. "But this is not to underestimate the considerable challenge the KNU continued to pose. Of all the insurgent movements his
government faced, [Burma's first prime minister] U Nu described the KNU as
the most 'formidable.'"[214] Yet by threatening Burma's territorial integrity more
than the personal safety of Burma's urban elites, this separatist rebellion has not
exhibited any powerful unifying effect beyond the confines of the tatmadaw.

[210] Callahan (2004): 109.
[211] Ibid. 118. Emphasis added.
[212] Lintner (1990): 14.
[213] Ibid.
[214] M. Smith (1991): 137.

Quite interestingly in light of this book's theoretical arguments, however, the Karen insurgency briefly inspired more wide-ranging elite collective action in late 1948 and early 1949, *when it came perilously close to Rangoon.* The KNDO seized control of three cities near the capital, and forced Prime Minister U Nu to cede "control of the strategically important Twante Canal, which leads from Rangoon port to the Irrawaddy River."[215] KNU leaders then demanded an independent state "that would include.... a number of contiguous Lower Burma districts. If established, it would have surrounded Rangoon." Since the KNU and the KNDO were perceived as stooges of the British, this was perceived as an offensive more than a defensive maneuver, as "the Burmese-language press depicted this initiative as part of a greater plot to wipe out the Union government."

As in Malaya, the proximity of highly mobilized communal rivals to the center of power in Burma sparked a lessening of elite factionalism and an increase in elite collective action. U Nu gave General Ne Win total control over the state's beleaguered coercive institutions, naming him "Supreme Commander of All Defense Forces and Police Forces." All high-ranking Karen officers were purged, prompting massive defections among the military's rank-and-file in the short run, but solidifying ethnic Burman control over the tatmadaw for the long term. As racial violence erupted in and around Rangoon, defensive collective action emerged among Burman urbanites. "Burmans who lived in Karen-majority neighborhoods lost patience with the government's ability to protect them," Callahan notes. "They started collecting arms, posting vigilantes, and erecting road blocks of their own all around Rangoon. Buddhist organizations in Rangoon and Burmese-language newspapers sponsored public meetings to call on the government to disarm KNDO forces throughout the country."[216]

Yet this perceived Karen threat in the Rangoon area only proved to be *episodic* rather than endemic. The tatmadaw proved capable of defending the capital with its "patched-together forces,"[217] and the reinvigorated coercive apparatus under Ne Win's leadership rousted the Karen rebels from all their urban strongholds by early 1950.[218] *Neither leftist nor separatist rebels would menace the Rangoon area again.* This provided societal elites with no lasting rationale for supporting the concentration of authoritarian powers in a centralized state. But the tatmadaw's reorganization and successful field campaigns in 1949–50 had produced a far more unified coercive apparatus, and the endemic character of separatist violence along Burma's vast and ungoverned frontiers would motivate tatmadaw leaders to privilege their own institutional and political interests, with or without broader elite support.

Even during the parliamentary period of the 1950s, state-building would be almost entirely a military affair. While ongoing counterinsurgency operations gave the tatmadaw an imperative to consolidate and project power, there was no organized threat from below pressing civilian institutions such as the AFPFL

---

[215] This and all subsequent cites in this paragraph are from Callahan (2004: 132).
[216] Ibid. 133.
[217] Ibid.
[218] For details, see M. Smith (1991: 139–140).

or the administrative bureaucracy to do the same. In sum, "[t]he Burma army experienced a veritable explosion of institution building in the mid-1950s," while "improvements in civilian bureaucratic capacities did not keep pace with the transformation of the army."[219]

The chronic unmanageability of regional rebellions would provide the impetus for the tatmadaw not just to revamp its segments of the state, but to assume control of the regime. "In 1958, at the request of Prime Minister U Nu, the military chief General Ne Win temporarily took over power to suppress minority insurgency and restore order so that national elections could be held in 1960."[220] While the AFPFL reeled from its split into two parties, "the army wasted no time in shuffling officers into every major ministry and department of the government."[221] Although the 1958–60 period was officially a time of caretaker military rule, the generals' will to power was already unmistakable. "The tatmadaw's reading of Burma's first decade of postcolonial rule was that elected political leaders could not be trusted with holding the Union together."[222]

This concern was not widely shared in society, however. Like Sarit Thanarat in Thailand in 1957, Ne Win gained societal good will in Burma in 1960 by presiding over a democratic national election. Yet as in Thailand, *the results of the election did not show broad support for military involvement in politics.* The military-backed party was defeated by the new party vehicle of its nemesis, U Nu, who secured victory by extolling Buddhist piety rather than law and order. "U Nu's Pry-daungzu party won the 1960 elections on an antimilitary platform," Chao-Tzang Yawnghwe notes. "Its rival, the stable AFPFL, which voters saw as backed by the military, was overwhelmingly defeated."[223] Despite this lack of broader elite support, Ne Win was confident that continuing separatist unrest could help generate unified military support for another coup: "a military takeover, he argued, was the only way to prevent Burma from disintegrating," writes Jalal Alamgir. "National unity was posed as the foremost problem facing multiethnic Burma. *And it was not just sheer rhetoric – it did have a plausible ring of truth to it.*"[224]

It would of course be naïve to suggest that Ne Win's "definitive coup of March 1962" was motivated entirely by concerns with separatism.[225] From a comparative perspective, the critical point is that such shared operational concerns proved essential in maintaining the tatmadaw's institutional cohesion as it seized political power – a move that often splits soldiers into "political" and "professional" wings. Since the coup took place without the sort of wide-ranging elite backing that characterized authoritarian backlashes in Indonesia in 1965 and Malaysia in 1969, cohesion within the military itself was of exceeding importance. And "[t]his was a coup that bore the stamp of a unified, bureaucratized military," observes Callahan.

---

[219] Callahan (2004): 175, 18. For extensive details on these processes, see Chapters 6 and 7 in Ibid.
[220] Alamgir (1997): 338.
[221] Callahan (2004): 191.
[222] Ibid. 190.
[223] Yawnghwe (1995): 186.
[224] Alamgir (1997): 339. Emphasis added. Also see Chirot (1994, Ch. 9).
[225] Ibid. 202.

"This unity may well explain why this coup brought civilian rule to such a definitive end."[226]

Burma's Enduring Militarization and Recurrent Crackdowns, 1962–

It is hard to imagine what besides the tatmadaw's institutional cohesion could explain the incredible longevity of military rule in Burma since 1962. Beyond the military, the regime has no effective political institutions supporting it. State-building has been eschewed, confirming the general proposition that it does not "seem possible for military leadership to set about constructing a civil bureaucracy as a mirror image of itself," as Bernard Silberman argues. "To do so would be to create another relatively autonomous institution with great powers."[227] Unable to collect revenue or conduct other administrative tasks effectively, Burma is Southeast Asia's "broken-backed state."[228]

Nor has the tatmadaw shown any interest in crafting a genuine ruling party. The Burma Socialist Program Party (BSPP) became a cloak for military rule in the early 1970s but was then discarded, garment-like, when massive protests confirmed the unpopularity of the regime in the late 1980s.[229] Even before 1988, the BSPP "was not supreme. It was hollow: unempowered to operate as a ruling party."[230] While party weakness helped debilitate *fragmented* authoritarian Leviathans in the Philippines, South Vietnam, and Thailand, the case of Indonesia suggests that under *militarized* conditions, party formation can factionalize rather than harmonize elite politics. By keeping the military squarely positioned at the center of their authoritarian Leviathan, Burma's rulers ensured that generals and officers had a more unambiguous self-interest in crushing cross-class dissent and preserving authoritarian rule than their Indonesian counterparts.

Burma's weak civilian institutions originated in the tatmadaw's weak civilian support. From its outset, the regime has confronted economic elites, communal elites, and middle classes with extreme repression. Most famously, Burma's military rulers have maintained an extremely hostile stance toward university students.[231] When students launched protests in June 1962 against Ne Win's coup, troops opened fire, then detonated the Rangoon University's hallowed student union building with hundreds of students inside. The violent crackdown on a constituency usually honored as nationalist heroes "sent shock waves across the country, drove students and other dissidents into hiding, and irredeemably changed politics."[232] Thus "[f]rom 1962," Vincent Boudreau argues, "Burmese protesters more or less understood that demonstrations courted bloodshed"[233];

---

[226] Ibid. 203. Emphasis added.

[227] Silberman (1993): 423.

[228] K. Jackson (1985): 20.

[229] The BSPP was officially founded in 1962, but it was only in 1972 that Ne Win ostensibly resigned from the military to "civilianize" tatmadaw rule.

[230] Yawnghwe (1995): 187.

[231] For a discussion of military-student conflict as an ongoing struggle to claim Aung San's nationalist authority in postcolonial Burma, see Slater (2009: 239–245).

[232] Boudreau (2002): 546.

[233] Ibid. 544.

yet "resentment against the repressive military-socialist regime grew and festered, periodically bursting out in the open in the form of urban uprisings (1962, 1963, 1964, 1965, 1966, 1967, 1970, 1974, 1975, 1976, and so on)."[234] While such repression has obviously deepened the animosity between students and soldiers in Burma, the vital point is that the tatmadaw never had any compelling reason to work with students because students never had any compelling reason to accept military rule.

Ne Win consistently perceived businessmen as enemies rather than allies of his regime as well. Although it is easily forgotten, Burma had a vibrant private sector in urban areas before 1962, which could have served as a regime partner in an authoritarian protection pact – especially considering its ethnic composition. But it was the state, not the Left, that would turn violently against this class of middleman minorities:

> Prior to the military takeover, the nascent capitalist class in Burma was composed mostly of Chinese and Indian merchants, centered around Rangoon and other ports. The authoritarian government coupled anticapitalist ideology with fiercely nationalist rhetoric in order to wipe out this expatriate merchant class.... As it destroyed entrepreneurship in society, it also reduced significantly the potential for economic challenges against authoritarianism. Up to 300,000 settled Indians and Pakistanis were estimated to have left the country by 1965.[235]

The tatmadaw's relations with Buddhist elites have been similarly hostile, and perhaps even more confrontational than the Marcos regime's relations with the Catholic Church in the Philippines:

> The sangha (i.e., the Buddhist clergy), has played a central role in organizing opposition to the regime.... Immediately after seizing power, the Revolutionary Council asked all monks to register with the government, which they refused to do. The Buddha Sasana Council, a large religious organization, was dissolved in 1962. On numerous occasions soldiers have fired upon demonstrations by monks. They have invaded monasteries and pagodas to cleanse the clergy of "political" elements. In October 1990, for instance, over three hundred monks were arrested during a violent crackdown on the clergy; most are still in detention.[236]

It should thus be evident that Burmese military rulers did not suddenly lose their coalitional support during the political crises from 1988–90 that brought their regime such global notoriety. They suffered from an abject lack of social backing since the onset of the tatmadaw regime in 1962. The patterns of protest that emerged in 1988 were perfectly consistent with patterns of opposition throughout the life of the regime – university students and Buddhist monks assumed the lead, with urban middle classes offering moral and logistical support. The thoroughgoing unpopularity of military rule was proven at the ballot box as well as in the streets. The opposition National League for Democracy (NLD) crushed

---

[234] Yawnghwe (1995): 188.
[235] Alamgir (1997): 339.
[236] Ibid. 344.

military-backed candidates in the May 1990 vote, capturing 492 seats, compared to just 10 seats for the incumbents.

If historical themes were being repeated in Burmese patterns of political opposition, they were also being repeated in the tatmadaw's methods of maintaining power. Most obviously, the political crisis of 1988–90 saw the regime fall back on its tried-and-true tactics of brute force, with the massacre of thousands of street protestors. More subtly, the tatmadaw redeployed the old bogey of regional secessionism, not so much to discredit the political opposition (which it could not hope to accomplish), but to remind potential defectors *within the military* of the continuing operational importance of internal cohesion. In this respect, the NLD's charismatic leader played into the military leadership's hands when she began campaigning in 1989:

Aung San Suu Kyi began touring the country and crossing the boundary between the mostly pacified center and the insurgency-prone frontier areas.... Appearing at times in ethnic-minority apparel – a Karen *htamein* (sarong) or a Shan *khamauk* (conical peasant hat) – she captured the attention of populations long-ignored by politicians in the pacified central regions. Perhaps most evocative was her party's decision to use a drawing of that Shan khamauk as the ballot pictogram indicating a candidate's membership in the NLD. The symbolism of the *khamauk* connecting Aung San Suu Kyi to populations beyond the center was lost on no one.... SLORC viewed Aung San Suu Kyi's experiment in interethnic coalition building as a significant threat to the military's power and to Burma's continued existence as a unitary state.[237]

Once again, the point is not that the tatmadaw's will to power can be reduced to its members' concerns with Burma's territorial integrity. The point is that credible shared perceptions of endemic regional instability provide military rulers with a weapon for restoring internal cohesion that most military regimes lack – and that regional unrest was essential in helping tatmadaw leaders craft elite collective action *in the first place*.

To be sure, by pursuing foreign investment and armistices with separatists since 1990, Burmese generals have come to depend more on patronage, and less on lingering attitudes of shared threat, in preserving military rule. Most analysts seem to suspect that increases in external funds will bolster the regime's durability, since the tatmadaw has strategically targeted investments toward "minerals, oil, and gas – natural resources that the state can claim and control easily."[238] Yet the analysis here suggests that the growth in available patronage resources might spark elite factionalism more than it cements elite loyalty. Again to invoke Silberman:

Once military leaders begin the process of engaging in the patronage game themselves, they become increasingly subject to demands from both civil and military society. Once giving way to this process, military leadership is bound in the end to lose the capacity to present itself as public in character. *It is also bound to end by encouraging bitter factionalism within the military.*[239]

---

[237] Callahan (2004): 214.
[238] Alamgir (1997): 346.
[239] Silberman (1993): 423. Emphasis added.

For the regime to maintain its cohesion in the face of continued implacable social opposition, it can be expected to have more success if it continues to rest more upon "war fighters" than "financial generals." Even as the latter type gains ground, "[m]ost of today's senior officers were promoted based on their performances on these frontier battlefields."[240] "For these generals, the students shouting 'de-mo-ca-ra-cy' in the sports center can be no more accommodated or ignored than the well-armed insurgent armies that the tatmadaw has fought and imagined itself fighting since its inception."[241]

[240] Callahan (2004): 210.
[241] Ibid. 3. For more on the tatmadaw's recurrent crackdowns on urban protests, including a brief discussion of the tragic (and tragically familiar) crackdown of 2007, see Slater (2009).

9

The Consequences of Contention

Contentious Politics as a Causal Variable

How does war shape domestic politics?.... [T]his question should be central in comparative research, but it is not.

Gregory Kasza[1]

In its multiple guises and forms, contentious politics has long been a shared obsession in the sister subfields of comparative politics and political sociology.[2] Yet scholars almost uniformly treat contentious collective events such as civil wars, strikes, riots, protests, electoral violence, insurgencies, and revolutions as outcomes to be explained – not as forces that help explain political outcomes in their own right. What Kasza wrote more than a decade ago about researchers' neglect of warfare as a motor of politics holds doubly true when we consider the literature on contentious politics more broadly. Contentious politics receives far more attention as a *product* than as a *producer* of political phenomena.

This book has offered a theoretical framework for studying the politics that contentious politics produces. It has hopefully shown that a steadfast focus on contentious politics as a causal variable can bear surprisingly diverse analytic fruit. In ordinary times, to be sure, elites command the political process. No theory of politics can ignore the fact that, even in the healthiest and most representative democracies, elected politicians and appointed bureaucrats enjoy considerable day-to-day latitude in how they conduct a nation's political business. Yet politics in ordinary times is profoundly shaped by the legacies of politics in extraordinary times. Wherever the masses have made their collective and contentious presence felt on the national political stage, ruling elites cannot easily ignore the vivid lessons of that past experience for how they govern in the present.

---

[1] Kasza (1996): 355.
[2] McAdam, Tarrow, and Tilly (1997) coined the umbrella term *contentious politics* in a bold attempt to unify a wide plethora of existing but scattered theoretical literatures.

By treating elite collective action as the keystone of political order, and by treating variation in contentious politics as the best predictor of variation in elite collective action, this book has systematically linked the mass politics of extraordinary times with the elitist politics of ordinary times. In the context of postwar Southeast Asia, this has counseled a consistent analytic focus on authoritarian regimes and the state, party, and military institutions that – to wildly varying degrees – underpin them. Yet as broad as this book's institutional focus has been, its overarching argument is broader than the specific institutions that have been under the microscope. Simply put, it is that *contentious politics is the most powerful driver of political development.* In developing and presenting this argument, one of my underlying theoretical purposes has been to advance a research agenda on *the varied political effects of various types of contentious politics.*

Contentious politics lies at the heart of political development because it powerfully and persistently shapes how political alliances and rivalries will be defined. At its core, politics is not about individuals pursuing material gains, or internally cohesive economic classes pursuing shared wealth.[3] It is about factions striving and struggling for political power, advantage, and survival. Collective action is only liable to broaden beyond the narrow and parochial politics of faction when collective definitions of a shared "other" expand. There are many ways that such collective action may unfold: labor unions emerge as employers become perceived as shared exploiters and oppressors; nationalist movements blossom as foreign powers acquire the visage of a people's enemy, overlord, or menace; and revolutions explode as tyrannical regimes unleash indiscriminate violence against citizens of multiple stripes.[4] Collective action is never easy, of course – but imminent shared threats are far more likely to make it emerge than the always uncertain prospect of shared future material gains.

Not all kinds of collective action are equally likely to endure once established, however. Cross-class revolutionary coalitions against patrimonial autocrats or foreign occupiers tend to strain and splinter once the common enemy has been vanquished. Labor unions struggle to sustain solidarity when left unprotected against market pressures to compete rather than cooperate.[5] And even the most fervently felt nationalism can only induce a collective conviction that collective action is desirable – it cannot determine what shape or form that collective action should take. (Nationalism can tell us who we are, but not what we should do.) For collective action to endure, mechanisms of reproduction must be in place. As I have argued throughout, the critical mechanisms of reproduction are (1) institutional and (2) attitudinal.

Elite collective action is more likely to sustain itself through institutional and attitudinal mechanisms of reproduction than the other types of collective action just discussed. In attitudinal terms, elites have their common desire to preserve

---

3 For the most influential recent works portraying political development as the product of struggle between materially driven and internally coherent economic classes, see Boix (2003) and Acemoglu and Robison (2006).

4 Goodwin (2001).

5 Western (1997).

their own elite status as a potential source of enduring collective action – *but only if contentious events led them to perceive themselves more as fellow elites than as factional enemies to begin with*. If attitudinal fears of endemic contention eventually fade, the institutional mechanism of reproduction becomes paramount. Where unmanageable types of contentious politics led elites to act collectively through party, military, or state institutions as a way of surviving those extraordinary times, elite collective action at least has institutional momentum – no minor historical force, that – on its side. In settings where unmanageable contentious class politics gave the commanders of an authoritarian Leviathan the impetus and leverage to extract power resources such as tax revenue from fellow elites, the ruling regime's power advantage over any potential opposition can become so vast as to make a collective political challenge virtually unthinkable.

It is all too easy to lose sight of the contentious origins of elite collective action once the peaceability that comes with elite collective action has been secured. It is similarly easy to look at an enduringly stable authoritarian system and draw ahistoric, static conclusions: the regime is delivering the economic goods; political power is being widely and predictably shared; elites have no incentive to defect; citizens have no reason to bite the hand that feeds them.

As static snapshots, such arguments are not so much incorrect as woefully insufficient. If this book has tried to convey anything, it is that the kind of authoritarian domination we witness in Singapore and Malaysia has been the product of long-term, dynamic processes. We cannot understand how these dominant authoritarian Leviathans became so politically predictable and so institutionally capable of targeting and channeling benefits to the supportive and the quiescent (as well as punishments to the non-compliant) unless we appreciate the causal impact of contentious politics *before* these regimes on elite collective action *under* these regimes. Where contentious class politics before the rise of authoritarian Leviathans assumed less immediately threatening and administratively challenging forms, political systems marked by fragmentation rather than domination emerged, as in the Philippines, South Vietnam, and Thailand. And where regionalist contention presented a more immediate and unmanageable threat than leftist contention in the wake of World War II, as in Burma and Indonesia, military elites felt driven to act collectively before their civilian counterparts, ushering in a trajectory best depicted as one of political militarization.

The approach that this book adopts and advises is both resolutely political and emphatically historical. It is a peculiar irony of the literature on democratization that works embracing the power of politics tend to downplay the power of history, and vice versa. Class-oriented democratization theorists in the tradition of Barrington Moore succeeded brilliantly in bringing history into the causal narrative, but only by treating politics as largely derivative of greater socioeconomic forces. "Transitologists" in the tradition of Dankwart Rustow, Guillermo O'Donnell, and Philippe Schmitter brought politics back into the study of democratization with a vengeance, but sacrificed history in the bargain.[6] If two of the defining features of the state-society approach to comparative politics are that it

---

[6] Moore (1966); Rustow (1970); O'Donnell and Schmitter (1986).

(1) embraces the primacy of politics and (2) takes historical causation seriously,[7] then this book offers one of surprisingly few concerted efforts to deploy the analytic tools of the state-society perspective to the comparative politics of authoritarianism and democratization.[8]

Beyond arguing that history matters in a causal sense, however, this book has tried to specify exactly *what* in history has mattered *most*. In shaping the divergent long-term development of political systems, nothing has mattered so much as variation in patterns of contentious politics. It is right to pinpoint the resolution of factional disputes during a ruling party's founding days as having a lasting influence on its internal cohesion, but we must also ask what factors systematically tame elite factionalism. The intensity of opposition at such historical moments surely influences subsequent party robustness, but we must also recognize the starkly divergent logics of elite-led vs. mass-led opposition, as well as the greater likelihood for counterrevolutionary than revolutionary collective action to endure. It is also crucial to escape the Huntingtonian trap of focusing our analytic attentions on ruling parties alone, and to inquire into how authoritarian regimes' founding struggles shape the cohesiveness and capacity of military and state institutions as well, through their causal effect on elite collective action.[9]

As we look beyond postwar Southeast Asia, therefore, it may prove fruitful to maintain a firm theoretical focus on the legacies of contentious politics for institutional development. Exactly how well this framework "travels" is not a question that can be adequately resolved in this single chapter. Assessing the causal influence of contentious politics on state and regime institutions in Southeast Asia requires sensitivity to local historical contexts. Only by examining specific cases at close range is it possible to determine whether contentious politics was indeed perceived as endemic and unmanageable by a wide range of political, social, and economic elites, and indeed exhibited its posited causal effects on resultant political coalitions and institutions.

It would primarily be a task for experts of other regions and time periods to assess the portability of *Ordering Power* to their regions and eras of interest.

---

7 Kohli (2002): 89–90. Historical causation does not simply entail the causal analysis of historical cases, as in the "analytic narratives" approach (Bates et al. [1997]). Such studies are typically very rigorous, but they also tend to be somewhat static. Whereas analytic narratives are committed to the rigorous causal analysis of long-*ago* history, the state-society perspective presumes that adequate causal analysis requires systematic attention to long-*run* history.

8 Brownlee (2007), B. Smith (2007), and Waldner (2008) are the best recent examples of regime studies that give both politics and history their rightful due. Mahoney (2001), Luebbert (1991), and Collier and Collier (1991) were important harbingers of a more resolutely political approach to regime development, while remaining more closely wedded to the class paradigm than these more recent works. With its stress on violent political conflict and resultant forms of revenue extraction as the prime shapers of early modern European regimes, Downing (1992) perhaps foreshadows this book's approach to democratization and authoritarianism more than any other work.

9 On the initial resolution of factionalism, see Brownlee (2007). On the intensity of founding struggles, see B. Smith (2007), echoing Huntington (1970). While both of these works stress the role of ruling parties, Smith also considers state power an influence on authoritarian durability. Neither work aims or purports to explain the varied durability of military regimes.

Although there is some reason to hope that cross-sectional datasets might effectively capture the critical distinctions between urban vs. rural, class vs. non-class, and communal vs. non-communal conflict that this book has offered,[10] it would be difficult for any such dataset to capture distinctions in elite threat perceptions – and elite threat perceptions are the causal motor of this book. As in Southeast Asia, divergent trajectories of political development outside Southeast Asia have most likely been shaped by subtle variation, and not just by stark (and readily measurable) variation, in patterns of contentious politics.

The greatest potential for quantitative testing exists on my distinction *between* leftist and regional rebellions, which is more straightforward to code than variation *among* leftist rebellions. In my preliminary collaboration with a colleague on this question, we have found that regional rebellions are *more than four times as likely* to give rise to a militarized authoritarian regime as other kinds of conflict, including external war – offering intriguing initial confirmation of this book's hypothesis on the contentious origins of political militarization.[11] Nevertheless, the difficulties of precisely coding authoritarian institutions and precisely timing the onset of regional rebellions make any such quantitative finding uncertain, if highly suggestive. Even the most robust finding of this sort can only complement the kind of careful, qualitative historical analysis that will be necessary to assess my central arguments beyond the postwar Southeast Asian setting. Thankfully, leading political scientists and historical sociologists have looked quite carefully at the kinds of contentious politics that immediately preceded state and regime formation in other world regions, permitting a preliminary assessment of my causal framework's portability – or to be more precise, its transferability.[12]

Ordering Power beyond Southeast Asia

Since my framework was developed in direct dialogue with Michael Hechter and William Brustein's work on state formation in early modern Europe, that continent makes a fair place to start. Three decades after these authors critiqued the "unwarranted emphasis on the exogenous determinants of initial state formation in western European history,"[13] and pointed to threats from below as driving the expansion of state power in feudal zones of present-day France and England, the European state-building literature remains fixated on external rather than internal conflicts. This "bellicist" literature has been impressively refined

---

[10] See Thies (2004, inter alia) for the best existing effort at such an enterprise. His finding that internal conflicts only give rise to higher tax collections when they are ethnic in character lends initial support to my argument that communal tensions can facilitate state-building; and his finding that only *enduring* international rivalries have such an effect mirrors my logic on the need for *endemic* internal threats for state-building to occur.

[11] Slater and Haid (2008).

[12] Lincoln and Guba (1985) suggest that the out-of-sample validity of qualitative findings can be captured by their transferability to other specific contexts, not just by their statistical significance. An argument can thus be said to exhibit external validity so long as it applies *elsewhere*, not just when it applies *generally*.

[13] Hechter and Brustein (1980): 1063.

and rethought in recent works by Thomas Ertman and Philip Gorski[14] – but they have done so by questioning and qualifying the causal effect of geopolitical conflicts, not by inquiring into the effects of internal strife on state formation. Despite the fact that Charles Tilly defines "statemaking" as the process of "attacking and checking competitors and challengers *within* the territory claimed by the state,"[15] and portrays state-building as a process of bringing internal groups under its protective ambit, Europeanists (including Tilly himself) do not seem to have considered whether *variation* in such processes of extending state protection might help explain initial divergence in the infrastructural power of European Leviathans.

Our grasp on the origins of the European state could benefit from a deeper consideration of how internal conflicts might have shaped elite collective action. Marxist works by scholars such as Perry Anderson helpfully place alliances between political and economic elites against rising popular challengers at the heart of their analyses.[16] But again, a Marxist approach is not very useful for explaining variation, insofar as it generally takes class conflict as endemic by definition; treats ethnic, religious, and nationalist identifications as epiphenomenal; and considers Leviathan's leaders the handmaidens of the bourgeoisie. Had this book commenced with such assumptions, all of the critical causal variation it uncovered in the types of contentious politics and resultant power balances between state elites and other elites would have remained invisible.

Is there reason to think that the kind of internalist/bellicist model presented here might find empirical support in Europe? Initial corroborative evidence can be gleaned from Anthony Marx's comparative analysis of early modern England, France, and Spain. Although Marx's ultimate goal is to explain *nation*-building, his causal narrative begins with detailed attention to *state*-building in Europe's most powerful early polities. Rather like the Southeast Asian states depicted here, these Leviathans initially accrued and consolidated power by leveraging and manipulating preexisting communal tensions, through what Marx calls "the logic of exclusionary cohesion."[17] Jews and Moors in Spain, Huguenots in France, and perceived papist plotters in England were useful as widely perceived internal enemies against whom absolutist monarchs could justify their expanded and centralized powers. Reformation in England, Counter-Reformation in France, and Reconquest in Spain allowed the state to amass tremendous new sources of revenue and greatly increased policing and social regulatory powers in the 15th and 16th centuries. External conflicts would subsequently permit even greater state aggrandizement, but Marx convincingly demonstrates that "the imperative to resolve *internal* discord was *more* determinant"[18] of initial state efforts to leverage religious hatreds for its own purposes. Although I have conceptual qualms with

[14] Ertman (1997); Gorski (2003).
[15] Tilly (1992): 96. Emphasis added.
[16] P. Anderson (1979).
[17] Marx (2003): 24.
[18] Ibid. 79. Emphasis added.

Marx's portrayal of such divide-and-conquer Realpolitik as "nation-building,"[19] we are in lockstep in viewing internal tensions and conflicts as potentially conducive to the expansion of the state's coercive and administrative capacities.

Early modern Europe's internal religious conflicts seemingly spawned more deeply absolutist regimes as well as more deeply penetrative states. In terms of state power, "the war of all against all [was] an ever-looming threat," Gorski has argued, and "Leviathan's embrace was, for some, an attractive perspective, offering safety and security." As I have argued throughout this book, such embraces of desperation not only tend to generate Leviathans, but authoritarianism. "Prussian absolutism was born, first and foremost, out of confessional conflict,"[20] Gorski notes. One witnesses communal and contentious origins of authoritarian protection pacts in Prussia's neighbors as well:

> Confessional conflict between a Catholic crown and the Protestant estates also contributed to the weakening of representative government and the expansion of monarchical authority in Bavaria. And many French historians now regard the Wars of Religion as a – or *the* – crucial turning point in the dismantling of the Estates General and the assertion of absolute sovereignty in that country. In each of these cases, the monarch's role as defender of the faith enabled him to rally Catholic members of the privileged classes behind a program of monarchical absolutism as the best defense against heresy.[21]

This book sounds a clarion call for political scientists and sociologists to think more systematically about how such polity-shaping historical conflicts were directed at enemies *within*, not just without. As Europe's earliest example of absolutist state-building through the repression of internal minorities and the proclaimed protection of a religious majority, Spain makes an especially informative case to consider. As Marx has argued, the Spanish Inquisition "became a tool for building centralized state authority" and "a source of further revenue collection." As in Indonesia, Malaysia, and Singapore in the decades following World War II, processes of ordering power in fifteenth-century Spain arose in the wake of unmanageable internal conflicts:

> To stabilize and consolidate power *and to contain civil wars and regional conflicts*, the monarchs "accepted an alliance with social forces" embedded in the Inquisition. For instance, in Castile "the appearance of the inquisitors was made possible because Isabella's supporters in the civil wars imposed their authority on the local elite." *Where internal discord was high and central authority low*, the Inquisition would become most active and feared, meeting what was seen as "national emergency." Indeed, *there was a recurring coincidence of Inquisition with "attempts to gain political control after the chaos of the civil wars."*[22]

---

[19] This book has treated nation-building as a process of attempting to unify rather than further divide a polity's diverse population. What Marx depicts in early modern Europe might be more precisely portrayed as nativism than nationalism.

[20] Gorski (2003): 166, xi.

[21] Ibid. 159.

[22] Marx (2003): 83. Emphasis added.

Hechter and Brustein thus see powerful theoretical reverberations in the Spanish case, exemplifying the potential for communal as well as class conflict to forge elite coalitions in favor of state-building:

Class divisions were not the only kind of political divisions that could promote state formation, as they largely did in the feudal parts of France and England. Cultural differences within a population could serve the same end. Thus, there is little doubt that state formation in the Iberian peninsula was fostered by the Reconquista directed against an internal enemy, the Moors. The common element in both types of examples is that group formation, and consequent organization, among actors in a given category is made possible by the recognition that each can either gain substantially, or preserve his position, by the subjection of an enemy within.[23]

Whereas Hechter and Brustein conclude that class and communal conflicts can be functional equivalents, this book has argued and attempted to demonstrate that an *intertwining* of these types of contentious politics is especially likely to make elite collective action arise and endure. The relative weakness of popular sectors in early modern Spain vis-à-vis England and France might help explain why Spanish state-building was so attenuated and aborted in comparative terms. An additional explanation offered by Marx dovetails almost perfectly with the causal logic offered here. As in Indonesia, but unlike in Malaysia and Singapore (or England or France), the Spanish crown's total demolition of its enemy within through wholesale expulsion meant the internal threat would not prove *endemic*.[24] Sensibly arguing that "antagonism against any group no longer present is less likely to be binding," Marx suggests that nation-state formation in Spain was less successful than in England or France because "unlike elsewhere, no other heretical group remained in Spain to become the new target of exclusion that might further bind the populace."[25] Although my emphasis is on the binding of elites and Marx's is on the links between elites and the masses, our causal logics are intriguingly parallel.

When considering this book's implications for twentieth-century European regimes, Spain again provides an exceptionally useful case to consider. No dictatorship swam more successfully against Western Europe's post-World War II democratic tide than Francisco Franco's (1936–1975). As in Southeast Asia's most durable authoritarian regimes, Spain's dictatorship was born as a counterrevolutionary coalition against leftist forces (and, to a lesser extent, regional separatists), who had been making impressive political gains under pluralist conditions. Civil war would wed Catholic elites especially tightly to Franco's protection pact, as "the church, with its priests and nuns slaughtered, had no alternative but to

---

[23] Hechter and Brustein (1980): 1085–1086.
[24] The Spanish example thus underscores the point that the endemic character of a contentious threat is ultimately not *only* a product of the type of contention, but of the type of state violence it elicits in response. Further research should thus attend not only to why some types of conflict are perceived by elites to be more threatening and challenging than others, but to why the state is more likely to pursue strategies of total annihilation or wholesale expulsion of groups perceived as threatening in some cases than others. Many thanks to Jason Seawright for raising this important point.
[25] Marx (2003): 86.

support Franco," Raymond Carr has written; "it was the duty of Catholics to support a regime that had saved the church from destruction."[26] With a broad but military-led elite coalition resembling Suharto's in Indonesia, Franco would personalize power through similar tactics, "balancing against each other the main groups supporting the regime. These were the army, the Church, monarchists, industrialists, financiers, and the nearest Spain came to a fascist movement – the Falange."[27] Yet Franco never elevated any party to a status approximating the military's, keeping the military's stake in regime survival unambiguous – perhaps helping to explain why, unlike Suharto, Franco would remain in power until his death.

Durable military rule has been a relative rarity in the postcolonial world. Yet in those places where militaries have proven most consistently politicized and cohesive, thus presenting a constant specter of praetorianism, histories of regional rebellion appear to explain at least part of the story. As noted above, quantitative analysis suggests that regional rebellions are indeed far more likely to give rise to military-backed regimes than are other types of conflict.

One can find qualitative evidence for such causal processes in cases such as Pakistan, where the original declaration of martial law in October 1957 occurred *one day* after the Khan of Kalat proclaimed his region's intention to secede. Secessionist movements and sentiments in East Pakistan and Baluchistan similarly coincided with the military's growing role in politics in the late 1960s and 1970s, culminating in another coup in 1977. Although tensions with India over Kashmir are often invoked as a major reason for political militarization in Pakistan, the analysis here suggests that shared civilian-military concerns over that hot-button nationalist issue might have eased the military's *removal* from power on so many occasions. Speaking more broadly, eruptions of violent conflicts in separatist zones of countries as far-flung as Russia, Turkey, and Nigeria – as well as Indonesia, the Philippines, and Thailand in the Southeast Asian context – appear more likely than any other factor to bring the military back into active politics in a unified manner. Unless civilian authorities can reassure military leaders that they will attack regionalist insurgencies in ways commensurate with military preferences (as appears to be the case in contemporary Russia, Sri Lanka, and Turkey, for example), civilian politics will be especially vulnerable to military overthrow.

The kind of domination trajectory this book has explored in Malaysia and Singapore has been nearly as rare in the postcolonial world as the kind of militarization trajectory traveled by Burma and Indonesia. Yet once again, we can find enough parallel examples to suggest that these cases are not sui generis, and that this book's deductive logic indeed captures a generalizable causal dynamic.

In sub-Saharan Africa, enduring party-state domination originally emerged as a counterrevolutionary response to organized mass challengers in South Africa and Botswana.[28] While Evan Lieberman convincingly stresses the causal

---

[26] Carr (1981): 28, 29.

[27] Lee (1987): 256.

[28] My discussion of these cases draws on insights offered by my coauthor in Slater and N. Smith (2009).

significance of racial cleavage formation in the initial development of the South African tax state, his historical narrative also shows how closely state-building and party formation followed the rhythms of contentious class and communal politics. "White workers.... organized a highly disruptive political challenge in the early decades of the twentieth century, including important strikes in 1913 and 1914," Lieberman notes. "Strike activity culminated with the exceptionally violent Rand Revolt of 1922 – which amounted to a small-scale civil war, in which over 1.3 million man-days were lost to strike activity." Black resistance emerged in this same period with the founding of the predecessor to the leftist African National Congress (ANC) in 1912, and "the formation of such resistance probably aided white political elites in translating beliefs of racial supremacy into political solidarity."[29]

As in Malaya and Singapore decades later, South African authorities would respond to severe labor unrest against a backdrop of severe communal tensions with determined efforts to incorporate and control labor through strengthened party and state institutions, and to extract more income tax revenue from threatened economic elites. Contentious politics not only helped ensure the *tightness* of the coalition linking white political and economic elites; it helped ensure that the *terms* of coalescence would see Leviathan ordering power *from* societal elites instead of gradually squandering power *to* them, as is typical in polities with more fragmented elites.

Such patterns of political domination would only be reinforced in South Africa's highly contentious postwar period. An upsurge of black labor militancy in the 1940s helped induce the founding of formal apartheid under the dominant grip of the ruling National Party in 1948; and as the increasingly radical ANC gathered strength, especially in the wake of the massacre of black protestors in Sharpesville in 1960, anti-communism became the key justification for continued direct tax collection. "We were fighting a war in those days," a leading South African economist told Lieberman, "and we had to pay for this war to keep the Communists out, and the good citizens didn't mind paying for that."[30] That a communist takeover would also have meant a *black* takeover presumably made white economic elites even more acceptant of Leviathan's impressive and progressive fiscal grasp. Only as white elites increasingly perceived that apartheid was strengthening black revolutionaries, posing a deeper existential threat to their security than the prospect of full black voting rights, did the South African protection pact splinter and democratization occur.[31]

Events in postwar South Africa would have powerful knock-on effects in neighboring Bechuanaland – as Botswana was known before independence in 1966. Like Malaysia and Singapore, Botswana's peaceable postcolonial politics belies its turbulent days of decolonization. As multiple scholars have recognized, this turbulence began in the wake of South Africa's pro-apartheid National Party's

---

[29] Lieberman (2003): 93, 95.
[30] Quoted in Ibid. 159.
[31] Wood (2000).

victory in the 1948 elections. The typical logic is that since this precluded Bechuanaland's incorporation into its racist southern neighbor, British officialdom was pressed to rework the circuitries of the weak colonial state in preparation for the fragile protectorate's independence.[32] Yet impending decolonization never proved sufficient to spark major British state-building efforts elsewhere, and the same would be true in Bechuanaland, which experienced much less impressive state-building than occurred in Malaya or Singapore at the same juncture.

What *did* happen was an influx of black South African refugees – many of them anti-apartheid activists – who embedded themselves among the urban poor and founded the Bechuanaland People's Party (BPP) in 1960. The BPP advocated radical social and political reforms, the expulsion of white settlers, and the limiting of chiefly power.[33] This created an obvious threat to the indigenous chiefs as well as the colonial administrators and economic elites allied with them. Much as in Malaya, non-chiefly elites who had collaborated with the British responded to an organized leftist threat by forming a countervailing party, the Bechuanaland Democratic Party (BDP), in 1962. The BPP would eventually weaken and become a historical footnote, and never represented the kind of powerful urban labor movement that sparked state-building in late colonial Malaya or Singapore. Yet as of the early 1960s, the BPP appeared to hold a significant advantage over the fledgling BDP. As one colonial official described the situation as of 1962:

The People's Party had the advantage of being the first off the mark, having made considerable progress in capturing the main townships on the line of rail and gaining a foothold in rural areas.... They were radical, forceful and articulate.... They enjoyed the advantage which came from attack.... In these circumstances it was by no means clear that the Democratic Party would be able to arrest a snowballing movement of opinion towards the People's Party.[34]

Given the overt hostility of the BPP, the chiefs' only option was to support the moderate BDP, even though this meant wider powersharing than the chiefs preferred. The effect was an imposing electoral machine linking rural and urban elites threatened by the BPP. This elite coalition carried the BDP to a resounding victory, taking 28 of 31 parliamentary seats in Botswana's first elections in 1966. In every election since, the BDP has retained an absolute majority of the popular vote and the large majority of parliamentary seats, consistently proving "able to maintain internal discipline."[35] While diamond and cattle wealth has certainly helped *sustain* elite collective action (and mitigated the need for a more extractive state), it was the BPP's credible threat to overturn the conservative political order that *initially* brought such a wide range of elites so securely into the BDP fold.

---

[32] Lange (2009: Ch. 7) provides a sophisticated account of this sort. Intriguingly, Lange also provides evidence that intense class contention with communal reverberations helped spark state-building efforts in colonial Mauritius (Ch. 4) and Guyana (Ch. 6) through dynamics that accord rather closely with the causal framework offered here.

[33] Sillery (1974): 156.

[34] Fawcus (2000): 90.

[35] Leith (2005): 33.

At first glance, the relative rarity of such cases of counterrevolutionary domination might be interpreted as a sign of my causal framework's empirical weakness or theoretical insignificance. Yet my goal in this book has not been simply to explain authoritarian domination – it has been to explain variation among counterrevolutionary trajectories of domination, fragmentation, and militarization. *Protection pacts are especially durable, not especially typical.* My causal framework has been constructed on the premise that fragmentation is the natural state of politics, as narrow factionalism trumps broader forms of collective action in ordinary times. As such, we should expect to see fragmentation far more often than domination and militarization. Stripped bare of all nuance and context, Figure 4 is what my causal framework looks like.

The most obvious message of this diagram is that nearly all counterrevolutionary roads lead to elite fragmentation.[36] This appears to be borne out by the empirical record. Counterrevolutionary authoritarian regimes were once as ubiquitous in Latin America as in Southeast Asia; but nearly across the board, these regimes failed to undertake significant state-building or party formation, and crumbled as cross-class democratic dissent gained strength in the 1980s. As central a political role as militaries have played throughout most of the region, they have exhibited a relatively weak will to power – a pattern consistent with the fact that Latin America has experienced very few regional or separatist rebellions in the postwar era.

To be sure, the Left gained unmistakable mobilizational power in countries such as Argentina, Brazil, and Chile during the Cold War, culminating in the rise of counterrevolutionary authoritarian Leviathans in the 1960s and 1970s. Yet as Nancy Bermeo has meticulously shown, even in these extremely contentious cases, electoral politics tended to temper rather than increase the power of the radical Left, making an eventual return to democracy more palatable for economic elites.[37] Nor did the Left tend to exacerbate communal tensions in the overwhelmingly Catholic region before the democratic 1990s. "While ethnic-based movements have a long history of organizing, protesting, and mobilizing in Africa, Asia, and parts of Europe, there has been no comparable pattern of ethnic-based organizing in contemporary Latin America, until recently," Deborah Yashar has argued. "Indeed, the cultural pluralism literature often identified Latin America as the exception, the region where ethnic political debates, mobilization, and conflict did not occur."[38] If counterrevolutionary elite collective action is liable to arise anywhere in Latin America today, it is where we witness "the rise of *ethno*populism,"[39] as in Bolivia and Ecuador,

---

[36] An additional message is that, by paying greater attention to varieties of class conflict than regionalist conflict, this book has provided a far more nuanced explanation for the contentious origins of political domination than militarization. See Slater and Haid (2008) for an initial attempt at theorizing and assessing regional rebellions and political militarization beyond the Southeast Asian context.

[37] Bermeo (2003).

[38] Yashar (2005): 3–4.

[39] Madrid (2008). Emphasis added.

FIGURE 4. Contentious Politics and Counterrevolutionary Trajectories

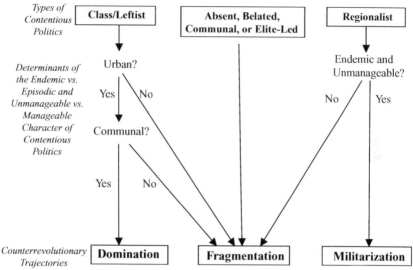

and not the rise of populism alone, as in the region's relatively non-indigenous polities.

As Yashar's invocation of Latin America's ethnic exceptionalism implies, the most endemically violent countries in postcolonial regions such as sub-Saharan Africa and the Middle East have not lacked protection pacts because of any lack of communal conflict. Rather, it is the weakness of *leftist or class mobilization* that better explains these cases' overarching propensity for political factionalism and fragmentation. All the ethnic conflict in the world will not likely induce elite collective action unless the threat can be credibly perceived to have emanated autonomously from below, as in Malaysia and Singapore. Even when ethnic conflict strikes at the urban heart of a polity, rendering all elites physically unsafe – as in Lebanon from the late 1950s through the late 1980s, for example – it will tend to worsen mutual animosity *among* elites *across* communal divides unless violent mobilization also entails significant class-based redistributive claims. Nowhere has this lesson been as tragic as in post-Saddam Iraq, where Sunni-Shia violence erupted in the absence of any meaningfully politicized class cleavage, driving Sunni and Shia elites apart instead of together. Urban and communal the Iraqi civil war has certainly been, but it has lacked the class dimension necessary to cement collective action across Iraq's deeply fragmented elite strata. Since urban sectarian violence has signified Iraqi elites' factionalism, it cannot also solve it.

By focusing squarely on counterrevolutionary regimes that have confronted such dramatically different types of contentious politics, this book empirically encompasses the majority of postcolonial polities. But what of the cases where leftist revolution prevailed? Earlier chapters have already presented the argument that nationalist revolutionary movements tend to splinter after capturing power, ushering in a trajectory of fragmentation – as Burma and Indonesia began and would have continued to travel, I argue, had regional rebellions not so quickly emerged. Yet this contradicts the received wisdom that intense revolutionary struggles produce robust ruling parties, and hence durable authoritarian regimes. Does the continuing survival of authoritarian rule in post-revolutionary China, Cuba, North Korea, Vietnam, and Zimbabwe not indicate that cross-class revolution can be the midwife of lasting political stability as surely as counterrevolutionary elite collective action?

The "easy" response is that politics is rife with equifinality. Even if there is indeed a revolutionary route to authoritarian domination, this would not falsify my claim that counterrevolutions against endemic and unmanageable types of contentious class politics produce especially durable authoritarian Leviathans. Such an argument would strengthen my case for adopting a path-dependent approach to authoritarian durability, insofar as merely organizing politics through a powerful ruling party in the first place should exhibit inertial effects, whether or not that party is counterrevolutionary. Yet I prefer to propose a "hard" argument here instead. Although the revolutionary regimes mentioned earlier may appear to be as durable as counterrevolutionary regimes such as Malaysia and Singapore, and perhaps even more durable than such (now former) ruling regimes in South Africa and Taiwan, I would submit that these regimes' coalitional and institutional strength is overblown if not illusory. They are far more prone and vulnerable to internal fragmentation and factionalism than the domination cases discussed here.

To contrast the internal robustness of revolutionary vs. counterrevolutionary authoritarian regimes, it is essential again to distinguish a regime's *duration* from its *durability*. Following the conceptual work of Anna Grzymala-Busse, a regime's duration signifies its "temporal length," while its durability is best measured as "the vector of duration and stability." This suggests that "duration alone is not the best measure of regime durability, since it tells us little about the stability of the regime, or its ability to meet and overcome potential crises."[40] It is here where my concept of ordering power can shed light on revolutionary regimes as much as counterrevolutionary ones. Authoritarian regimes that order power have more weapons for pursuing political objectives, maintaining political stability, and surviving oppositional challenges than those that do not. Echoing Huntington's argument that polities lacking institutional capacity before confronting the disruptions of modernization are "presumptively unstable,"[41] I argue that regimes that do not routinely and consistently order power – extracting and organizing power resources from the societies they govern – are more likely both to suffer debilitating economic crises and to succumb to massive cross-class opposition than regimes that do. Even when post-revolutionary regimes *endure* for as long as counterrevolutionary regimes, we cannot simply assume that they are equally *durable* political arrangements.

[40] Grzymala-Busse (2008): 1.
[41] Huntington (1968): 398.

Mexico's long-ruling Institutional Revolutionary Party (PRI) regime illustrates these points nicely. Typically considered a highly durable post-revolutionary dictatorship, the PRI regime in fact enjoyed its greatest success at managing internal factionalism during its most *counter*revolutionary era of the late 1950s and 1960s, through the so-called Pact of 1958 – an elite pact that emerged, consistent with my stress on contentious politics, amid a massive strike wave "that, momentarily, reached the point of putting the political system in crisis,"[42] as Jose Luis Reyna has written. Tightened elite collective action provided the political foundation for coherent economic management, as "the powerful 1958–59 grassroots movement, far from provoking the macroeconomics of populism, only ushered in the most stable, rapid growth Mexico has ever seen."[43]

Yet after the labor threat passed and elite factionalism worsened, an era of squandering rather than ordering power began. The key mechanism was escalating competition for the presidency among political rivals backed by feuding factional business groups, or grupos. "After 1970, increasingly all-or-nothing 'struggle' among *grupos* tore the political system apart and repeatedly erupted in economic crises," Jonathan Schlefer summarizes. "As intra-elite power conflict turned all-or-nothing, *grupos* vied to buy support for their leader's presidential nomination via overspending, public bank lending, manipulation of the securities market, and other perilous gambles that erupted in economic crises."[44] Mexico thus suggests the propensity for post-revolutionary regimes to fragment from within, and to imperil their own survival by allowing the macroeconomy to be held hostage by factional rivals.

Yet if post-revolutionary regimes are more prone to internal fragmentation than their counterrevolutionary counterparts, why do so many of them exhibit such extraordinary endurance? Once again, it is critical to recognize how contentious politics drives political development – not only on the "front end" of dictatorships, but on the "back end." As I have argued throughout this book, cross-class democratic mobilization is the most powerful stimulant for authoritarian collapse, and the pivotal actors in such bouts of mobilization are communal elites: a polity's primary possessors of nationalist and religious credentials. Yet where a ruling party rises to power, not just through a leftist revolution, but through a *nationalist* revolution, nationalism can come to approximate a regime monopoly.[45] Without broadly recognized nationalist credentials upon which to base their protest movements, democratic oppositionists in cases such as China, Cuba, and Vietnam lack the symbolic power necessary to mobilize massive cross-class support for their high-risk activism. It is no coincidence, then, that every surviving post-communist authoritarian regime has its historical roots in a nationalist revolution – and that the only communist system to have collapsed despite having initially won power through a homegrown revolution, the Soviet Union,

---

[42] Cited in Schlefer (2008): 76.
[43] Ibid. 77.
[44] Ibid. 5–6.
[45] The following discussion draws on Slater (2009).

collapsed precisely through a monumental wave of nationalist mobilization.[46] In sum, the endurance of these post-revolutionary regimes is best explained by the failure of a symbolically powerful cross-class opposition to emerge, not by any lack of factional rivalries or institutional fragmentation within those regimes themselves.

The same might be said of the remaining authoritarian regimes in the world that are neither post-revolutionary nor counterrevolutionary in origin. In countries where decolonization occurred without any major upsurge in contentious mass politics – particularly in the long belt of Islamic monarchies running from Morocco in the west to Brunei in the east – to be a communal elite is typically to be a member of the authoritarian regime.[47] The weakness or absence of democratic movements in such cases is not so much a function of extraordinary regime cohesion, widespread popular support, oil-funded redistribution,[48] or a cultural commitment to authoritarian politics. It is simply that a past without viable popular movements has meant a present without viable political alternatives.

Leviathans without Authoritarianism

This book opened by invoking James Madison's timeless political dilemma: how might political institutions simultaneously enable a government to control society, while also obliging it to control itself? Unlike the failed and predatory states of the world that possess neither the virtue of capacity nor of accountability, the Southeast Asian cases considered here remain trapped on the horns of Madison's dilemma. In Malaysia and Singapore, citizens enjoy the collective fruits of development and stability, but not political liberty. These dominant Leviathans giveth, but also taketh away. By contrast, in the Philippines, Thailand, and now Indonesia, voters may freely express their opinions and choose their representatives, but weak states forestall the effective provision of widely desired public goods – such goods must be delivered, not just demanded. In short, nowhere in Southeast Asia can the general citizenry feel simultaneously confident that their

---

[46] Beissinger (2002).

[47] Owen (2004) underscores the authoritarian positioning of communal elites in Middle Eastern monarchies and republics alike. Republics such as Egypt, Iraq, Syria, and Algeria adopted "the Ottoman practice of bringing the religious establishment under state control by paying the *ulama* (the clergy) official salaries" (2004: 29), thereby bringing many pivotal religious elites into the regime's fold. In monarchical settings, Owen contrasts the survival of kings in Jordan and Morocco, who "managed the difficult transformation of putting [themselves] at the head of the local nationalist movement," with monarchs in Tunisia, Libya, Egypt, and Iraq, who "became so closely associated with the structures of colonialism that they did not outlast them" (2004: 16).

[48] For a provocative and broadly supportive argument that "[w]ealth generated through oil receipts is a catalyst for opposition to the state, rather than a tool to placate dissent" in Middle Eastern monarchies such as Saudi Arabia, due to the unequal and selective manner in which such resources are distributed, see Okrulik (1999: 297). To the extent that oil underpins authoritarianism in the Middle East, this may be due more to a regional propensity to invest resources in the state's coercive institutions than in public spending programs. As Bellin (2005: 31) argues, most regimes in the region "enjoy sufficient revenue to sustain exceedingly robust expenditure on their security apparatuses."

leaders have ample capacity to provide them with the fruits of good governance, and that they have ample opportunity to replace their leaders should they fail to do so.

Things did not have to turn out this way. By exploring the historical roots of both state power and authoritarian durability in Southeast Asia, this book has tried to demonstrate that the region's correlation between these two outcomes is fundamentally spurious.[49] Malaysia and Singapore do not have powerful states because they are authoritarian – they have both strong states *and* durable authoritarian regimes because they have consistently exhibited elite collective action, borne of particularly threatening and challenging types of contentious class politics that erupted after World War II. On the opposite side of the same coin, Thailand and the Philippines do not have weak states because they are democratic – they have both of these things because postwar contentious politics did not induce or inspire wide-ranging elite collective action. Since changing a regime does not require changing a state, the Thai and Philippine Leviathans were as debilitated under dictatorship as under democracy. By the same token, authoritarianism can be wiped away in Malaysia and Singapore without sacrificing the powerful administrative Leviathans that contemporary leaders have inherited.

What the citizens of Southeast Asia did not secure simultaneously, they may still secure sequentially. History provides numerous examples of authoritarian Leviathans becoming democratic, and of democracies undertaking state-building without becoming authoritarian in the process. The political histories detailed in this book have certainly been narratives of constraint. But by adopting a comparative analytic approach and by considering how things have gone differently elsewhere, scholars and citizens can turn the study of history into an avenue for better understanding the political constraints that bind them, and for more effectively pursuing the political changes that they desire.

---

[49] For a more normative extension of this analytical argument, see Slater (2008a).

Bibliography

Abinales, Patricio. 2000. *Making Mindanao: Cotabato and Davao in the Formation of the Philippine Nation-State*. Quezon City: Ateneo de Manila University Press.

Abinales, Patricio. 1997. "State Building, Communist Insurgency and Cacique Politics in the Philippines." In Paul B. Rich and Richard Stubbs, eds., *The Counter-Insurgent State: Guerrilla Warfare and State Building in the Twentieth Century*. New York: St. Martin's Press.

Abueva, Jose Veloso. 1979. "Ideology and Practice in the 'New Society.'" In David A. Rosenberg, ed., *Marcos and Martial Law in the Philippines*. Ithaca: Cornell University Press.

Alamgir, Jalal. 1997. "Against the Current: The Survival of Authoritarianism in Burma." *Pacific Affairs* 70:3 (Fall), pp. 333–350.

Alatas, Syed Farid. 1997. *Democracy and Authoritarianism in Malaysia and Indonesia: The Rise of the Post-Colonial State*. London: MacMillan.

Anderson, Benedict R. O'G. 1998. "Introduction." In Benedict R. O'G Anderson, ed., *The Spectre of Comparisons: Nationalism, Southeast Asia, and the World*. New York: Verso.

Anderson, Benedict R. O'G. 1998 [1988]. "Cacique Democracy in the Philippines." In Benedict R. O'G Anderson, ed., *The Spectre of Comparisons: Nationalism, Southeast Asia, and the World*. New York: Verso.

Anderson, Benedict R. O'G. 1996. "Elections and Participation in Three Southeast Asian Countries." In R.H. Taylor, ed., *The Politics of Elections in Southeast Asia*. New York: Woodrow Wilson Center.

Anderson, Benedict R. O'G. 1983. "Old State, New Society: Indonesia's New Order in Comparative Historical Perspective." *Journal of Asian Studies* 42:3 (May), pp. 477–496.

Anderson, Benedict R. O'G. 1978a. "Last Days of Indonesia's Suharto?" *Southeast Asia Chronicle* 63 (July–August), pp. 2–17.

Anderson, Benedict R. O'G. 1978b. "Studies of the Thai State: The State of Thai Studies." In Eliezer B. Ayal, ed., *The Study of Thailand: Analyses of Knowledge, Approaches, and Prospects in Anthropology, Art History, Economics, History, and Political Science*. Athens, OH: Ohio University Center for International Studies Southeast Asia Series No. 54.

Anderson, Benedict R. O'G. 1972. *Java in a Time of Revolution: Occupation and Resistance, 1944–1946*. Ithaca: Cornell University Press.

Anderson, Perry. 1979. *Lineages of the Absolutist State*. London: Verso.

Anek Laothamatas. 1996. "A Tale of Two Democracies: Conflicting Perceptions of Elections and Democracy in Thailand." In R.H. Taylor, ed., *The Politics of Elections in Southeast Asia.* New York: Woodrow Wilson Center.

Asher, Mukul G. 1994. "Issues in Forced Savings and National Economic Development: The Management of National Provident Fund Systems." In Al' Alim Ibrahim, ed., *Generating a National Savings Movement.* Kuala Lumpur: Institute for Strategic and International Studies.

Asher, Mukul G. 1989. "A Comparative Overview of ASEAN Fiscal Systems and Practices." In Mukul G. Asher, ed., *Fiscal Systems and Practices in ASEAN: Trends, Impact, and Evaluation.* Singapore: Institute of Southeast Asian Studies.

Asher, Mukul G. 1980. *Revenue Systems of ASEAN Countries.* Singapore: Singapore University Press.

Asher, Mukul G. and Agustin Kinantar, Jr. 1989. "Fiscal System and Practices in the Philippines." In Mukul G. Asher, ed., *Fiscal Systems and Practices in ASEAN: Trends, Impact, and Evaluation.* Singapore: Institute of Southeast Asian Studies.

Aspinall, Edward. 2005. *Opposing Suharto: Compromise, Resistance, and Regime Change in Indonesia.* Stanford: Stanford University Press.

Aspinall, Edward. 1996. "The Broadening Base of Political Opposition in Indonesia." In Garry Rodan, ed., *Political Oppositions in Industrializing Asia.* New York: Routledge.

Badgley, John. 1974. "Burmese Communist Schisms." In John Wilson Lewis, ed., *Peasant Rebellion and Communist Revolution in Asia.* Stanford: Stanford University Press.

Barnett, Michael N. 1992. *Confronting the Costs of War: Military Power, State, and Society in Egypt and Israel.* Princeton: Princeton University Press.

Barraclough, Simon. 1985. "The Dynamics of Coercion in the Malaysian Political Process." *Modern Asian Studies* 19:4 (October), pp. 797–822.

Barry, Coeli. 2006. "The Limits of Conservative Church Reformism in the Democratic Philippines." In Tun-jen Cheng and Deborah A. Brown, eds., *Religious Organizations and Democratization: Case Studies from Contemporary Asia.* Armonk, NY: M.E. Sharpe.

Barzel, Yoram. 2001. *A Theory of the State: Economic Rights, Legal Rights, and the Scope of the State.* New York: Cambridge University Press.

Bates, Robert H., Avner Greif, Margaret Levi, Juan-Laurent Rosenthal, and Barry R. Weingast. 1998. *Analytic Narratives.* Princeton: Princeton University Press.

Bates, Robert H. and Da-Hsiang Donald Lien. 1985. "A Note on Taxation, Development, and Representative Government." *Politics & Society* 14:1, pp. 53–70.

Beissinger, Mark R. 2002. *Nationalist Mobilization and the Collapse of the Soviet State.* New York: Cambridge University Press.

Bellin, Eva. 2005. "Coercive Institutions and Coercive Leaders." In Marsha Pripstein Posusney and Michele Penner Angrist, eds., *Authoritarianism in the Middle East: Regimes and Resistance.* Boulder: Lynne Rienner.

Bellin, Eva. 2002. *Stalled Democracy: Capital, Labor, and the Paradox of State-Sponsored Development.* Ithaca: Cornell University Press.

Bellin, Eva. 2000. "Contingent Democrats: Industrialists, Labor, and Democratization in Late-Developing Countries." *World Politics* 52 (January), pp. 175–205.

Bellows, Thomas J. 1970. *The People's Action Party of Singapore: Emergence of a Dominant Party System.* New Haven: Yale University Southeast Asia Studies, Monograph No. 14.

Benda, Harry. 1962. "The Structure of Southeast Asian History: Some Preliminary Observations." *Journal of Southeast Asian History* 3:1, pp. 106–138.

Bendix, Reinhard. 1964. *Nation-Building and Citizenship: Studies of our Changing Social Order.* New York: John Wiley & Sons.

Bermeo, Nancy. 2003. *Ordinary People in Extraordinary Times: The Citizenry and the Breakdown of Democracy*. Princeton: Princeton University Press.

Bermeo, Nancy. 1997. "Myths of Moderation: Confrontation and Conflict During Democratic Transitions. *Comparative Politics* 29:3 (April), pp. 305–22.

Boileau, Julian M. 1983. *Golkar: Functional Group Politics in Indonesia*. Jakarta: Center for Strategic and International Studies.

Boix, Carles. 2003. *Democracy and Redistribution*. New York: Cambridge University Press.

Booth, Anne. 1997. "The State and the Economy in Indonesia in the Nineteenth and Twentieth Centuries." In John Harriss, Janet Hunter, and Colin M. Lewis, eds., *The New Institutional Economics and Third World Development*. New York: Routledge.

Boudreau, Vincent G. 2004. *Resisting Dictatorship: Repression and Protest in Southeast Asia*. New York: Cambridge University Press.

Boudreau, Vincent G. 2002. "State Building and Repression in Authoritarian Onset." *Southeast Asian Studies* 39:4 (March), pp. 537–557.

Boudreau, Vincent. 1999. "Diffusing Democracy? People Power in Indonesia and the Philippines." *Bulletin of Concerned Asian Scholars* 31:4 (October–December), pp. 3–18.

Bresnan, John. 1993. *Managing Indonesia: The Modern Political Economy*. New York: Columbia University Press.

Brown, David. 1993. "The Search for Elite Cohesion." *Contemporary Southeast Asia* 15:1 (June), pp. 111–130.

Brownlee, Jason. 2007. *Authoritarianism in an Age of Democratization*. New York: Cambridge University Press.

Bueno de Mesquita, Bruce et al. 2003. *The Logic of Political Survival*. Cambridge: MIT Press.

Bunce, Valerie. 2003. "Rethinking Recent Democratization: Lessons from the Post-Communist Experience." *World Politics* 55 (January), pp. 167–192.

Bush, Robin. 2009. *Nahdlatul Ulama and the Struggle for Power in Indonesia*. Singapore: ISEAS.

Callahan, Mary P. 2004. *Making Enemies: War and State Building in Burma*. Ithaca: Cornell University Press.

Capoccia, Giovanni and R. Daniel Kelemen. 2007. "The Study of Critical Junctures: Theory, Narrative, and Counterfactuals in Historical Institutionalism." *World Politics* 59:3 (April), pp. 341–369.

Carr, Raymond. 1981. *Spain: Dictatorship to Democracy*. London: Allen and Unwin.

Case, William. 2006. "Manipulative Skills: How Do Rulers Control the Electoral Arena?" In Andreas Schedler, ed., *Electoral Authoritarianism: The Dynamics of Unfree Competition*. Boulder: Lynne Rienner.

Case, William. 2002. *Politics in Southeast Asia: Democracy or Less*. London: Curzon.

Case, William. 2001. "Malaysia's Resilient Pseudodemocracy." *Journal of Democracy* 12:1 (January), pp. 43–57.

Case, William. 1996. "UMNO Paramountcy: A Report on Single-Party Dominance in Malaysia." *Party Politics* 2:1, pp. 115–127.

Centeno, Miguel Angel. 2002. *Blood and Debt: War and the Nation-State in Latin America*. University Park: Pennsylvania State University Press.

Centeno, Miguel Angel. 1997. "Blood and Debt: War and Taxation in Nineteenth-Century Latin America." *American Journal of Sociology* 102:6 (May), pp. 1565–1605.

Chai-Anan Samudavanija. 1971. "The Politics and Administration of the Thai Budgetary Process." Ph.D. Dissertation, Department of Political Science, University of Wisconsin-Madison.

Chan Heng Chee. 1976. *The Dynamics of One Party Dominance: The PAP at the Grass-Roots.* Singapore: Singapore University Press.

Chandra Muzaffar. 1979. *Protector? An Analysis of the Concept and Practice in Leader-Led Relationships Within Malay Society.* Penang: ALIRAN.

Chaudhry, Kiren Aziz. 1997. *The Price of Wealth: Economies and Institutions in the Middle East.* Ithaca: Cornell University Press.

Cheah Boon Kheng. 1983. *Red Star Over Malaya: Resistance and Social Conflict During and After the Japanese Occupation of Malaya, 1941–1946.* Singapore: Singapore University Press.

Cheetham, Russell J. and Edward K. Hawkins. 1976. *The Philippines: Priorities and Prospects for Development.* Washington: The World Bank.

Cheng, Tun-jen and Deborah A. Brown, eds. 2006. "Introduction: The Roles of Religious Organizations in Asian Democratization." In Tun-jen Cheng and Deborah A. Brown, eds., *Religious Organizations and Democratization: Case Studies from Contemporary Asia.* Armonk, NY: M.E. Sharpe.

Chirot, Daniel. 1994. *Modern Tyrants: The Power and Prevalence of Evil in Our Age.* Princeton: Princeton University Press.

Chua Beng Huat. 1995. *Communitarian Ideology and Democracy in Singapore.* New York: Routledge.

Collier, Ruth Berins. 1999. *Paths Toward Democracy: The Working Class and Elites in Western Europe and South America.* New York: Cambridge University Press.

Collier, Ruth Berins and David Collier. 1991. *Shaping the Political Arena: Critical Junctures, the Labor Movement, and Regime Dynamics in Latin America.* Princeton: Princeton University Press.

Crone, Donald K. 1988. "State, Social Elites, and Government Capacity in Southeast Asia." *World Politics* 40:2 (January), pp. 252–268.

Crouch, Harold. 2001. "The Perils of Prediction: Understanding the Indonesian Transition, 1998–99." In Abdul Rahman Embong, ed., *Southeast Asian Middle Classes: Prospects for Social Change and Democratization.* Bangi: Universiti Kebangsaan Malaysia.

Crouch, Harold. 1996. *Government and Society in Malaysia.* Ithaca: Cornell University Press.

Crouch, Harold. 1978. *The Army and Politics in Indonesia.* Ithaca: Cornell University Press.

Dacy, Douglas C. 1986. *Foreign Aid, War, and Economic Development: South Vietnam, 1955–1975.* New York: Cambridge University Press.

Dancz, Virginia H. 1987. *Women and Party Politics in Peninsular Malaysia.* Singapore: Oxford University Press.

Darden, Keith. 2008. "The Integrity of Corrupt States: Graft as an Informal State Institution." *Politics & Society* 36:1 (March), pp. 35–60.

Darling, Frank C. 1971. "Political Parties in Thailand." *Pacific Affairs* 44:4 (Summer), pp. 228–241.

Doner, Richard F. 2009. *The Politics of Uneven Development: Thailand in Comparative Perspective.* New York: Cambridge University Press.

Doner, Richard F., Bryan K. Ritchie, and Dan Slater. 2005. "Systemic Vulnerability and the Origins of Developmental States: Northeast and Southeast Asia in Comparative Perspective." *International Organization* 59 (Spring), pp. 327–361.

Doronilla, Amando. 1992. *The State, Economic Transformation, and Political Change in the Philippines, 1946–1972.* Singapore: Oxford University Press.

Downing, Brian M. 1992. *The Military Revolution and Political Change: Origins of Democracy and Autocracy in Early Modern Europe.* Princeton: Princeton University Press.

Duncanson, Dennis. 1968. *Government and Revolution in Vietnam*. New York: Oxford University Press.

Edwards, C.T. 1970. *Public Finances in Malaya and Singapore*. Canberra: Australian National University Press.

Elster, Jon. 1989. *The Cement of Society: A Study of Social Order*. New York: Cambridge University Press.

Emmerson, Donald K. 1978. "The Bureaucracy in Political Context: Weakness in Strength." In Karl Jackson and Lucian Pye, eds., *Political Power and Communications in Indonesia*. Berkeley: University of California Press.

Ertman, Thomas. 1997. *Birth of the Leviathan: Building States and Regimes in Medieval and Early Modern Europe*. Cambridge: Cambridge University Press.

Etzioni, Amitai. 1961. *A Comparative Analysis of Complex Organizations: On Power, Involvement, and Their Correlates*. New York: Free Press of Glencoe.

Evans, Peter B. 1995. *Embedded Autonomy: States and Industrial Transformation*. Princeton: Princeton University Press.

Evrigenis, Ioannis. 2008. *Fear of Enemies and Collective Action*. New York: Cambridge University Press.

Faruqi, Shad Saleem. 1995. "Principles and Methods for Enforcing Accountability in the Malaysian Public Sector." In Patrick Pillai, Azreen Pharmy, Karen Neoh, and Kim Thiruchelvam, eds., *Managing Trust: Transparency, Accountability & Ethics in Malaysia*. Kuala Lumpur: ISIS/Goethe Institute.

Fawcus, Peter. 2000. *Botswana: The Road to Independence*. Gaborone: Pula Press.

Feith, Herbert and Daniel S. Lev. 1963. "The End of the Indonesian Rebellion." *Pacific Affairs* 36:1 (Spring), pp. 32–46.

Franco, Jennifer Conroy. 2000. *Campaigning for Democracy: Grassroots Citizenship Movements, Less-Than-Democratic Elections, and Regime Transition in the Philippines*. Quezon City: Institute for Popular Democracy.

Friedland, Roger. 2001. "Religious Nationalism and the Problem of Collective Representation." *Annual Review of Sociology* 27, pp. 125–153.

Funston, John. 1980. *Malay Politics in Malaysia: A Study of UMNO and PAS*. Kuala Lumpur: Heinemann.

Furnival, J.S. 1944. *Colonial Policy and Practice: A Comparative Study of Burma and Netherlands India*. New York: New York University Press.

Gallo, Carmenza. 1991. *Taxes and State Power: Political Instability in Bolivia, 1900–1950*. Philadelphia: Temple University Press.

Gamba, Charles. 1962. *The Origins of Trade Unionism in Malaya: A Study in Colonial Labor Unrest*. Singapore: Eastern Universities Press.

Gandhi, Jennifer and Adam Przeworski. 2007. "Authoritarian Institutions and the Survival of Autocrats." *Comparative Political Studies* 40:11 (November), pp. 1279–1301.

Gasiorowski, Mark. 1995. "Economic Crisis and Political Regime Change: An Event History Analysis." *American Political Science Review* 89 (December), pp. 882–897.

Geddes, Barbara. 1999. "What Do We Know About Democratization After Twenty Years?" *Annual Review of Political Science* 2, pp. 115–144.

Geddes, Barbara. 1990. "How the Cases You Choose Affect the Answers You Get: Selection Bias in Comparative Politics." *Political Analysis* 2, pp. 131–150.

George, Alexander L. and Timothy J. McKeown. 1985. "Case Studies and Theories of Organizational Decision Making." In Robert F. Coulam and Richard A. Smith, eds., *Advances in Information Processing in Organizations, Vol. 2, Research on Public Organizations*. Greenwich, CT: JAI Press.

George, Cherian. 2000. *Singapore, the Air-Conditioned Nation: Essays on the Politics of Comfort and Control, 1990–2000*. Singapore: Landmark Books.

Gerring, John, Philip Bond, William T. Barndt, and Carola Moreno. 2005. "Democracy and Economic Growth: A Historical Perspective." *World Politics* 57:3 (April), pp. 323–364.

Gerth, H.H. and C. Wright Mills. 1946. *From Max Weber: Essays in Sociology*. New York: Oxford University Press.

Girling, John. 1996. *Interpreting Development: Capitalism, Democracy, and the Middle Class in Thailand*. Ithaca: Cornell University Southeast Asia Program No. 21.

Goh Cheng Teik. 1971. *The May Thirteenth Incident and Democracy in Malaysia*. Singapore: Oxford University Press.

Gomez, Edmund Terence. 1999. "Tracing the Ethnic Divide: Race, Rights, and Redistribution in Malaysia." In Edmund Terence Gomez, Joanna Pfaff-Czarnecka, Darini Rajasingham-Senanyake, and Ashis Nandy, eds., *Ethnic Futures: The State and Identity Politics in Asia*. New Delhi: Sage.

Gongora, Thierry. 1997. "War Making and State Power in the Contemporary Middle East." *International Journal of Middle East Studies* 29, pp. 323–340.

Goodfellow, Rob. 1995. *Api Dalam Sekam: The New Order and the Ideology of Anti-Communism*. Clayton, Australia: Monash University Center for Southeast Asian Studies Working Paper #95.

Goodman, Allan E. 1973. *Politics in War: The Bases of Political Community in South Vietnam*. Cambridge: Harvard University Press.

Goodwin, Jeff. 2001. *No Other Way Out: States and Revolutionary Movements, 1945–1991*. New York: Cambridge University Press.

Gorski, Philip S. 2003. *The Disciplinary Revolution: Calvinism and the Rise of the State in Early Modern Europe*. Chicago: University of Chicago Press.

Gould, Roger V. 1995. *Insurgent Identities: Class, Community, and Protest in Paris from 1848 to the Commune*. Chicago: University of Chicago Press.

Greene, Kenneth F. 2007. *Why Dominant Parties Lose: Mexico's Democratization in Comparative Perspective*. New York: Cambridge University Press.

Grzymala-Busse, Anna. 2008. "Time Will Tell? Temporality, Causation, and Institutional Change." Unpublished Manuscript, University of Michigan.

Guevarra, Ruben. 1989. *The Story Behind the Plaza Miranda Bombing*. Quezon City: Katotohanan at Katarungan Foundation.

Hack, Karl. 1999. "The Malayan Emergency: The Role of Special Branch and Intelligence." Working Paper, Institute for Southeast Asian Studies, Singapore.

Haggard, Stephan and Robert Kaufman. 1995. *The Political Economy of Democratic Transitions*. Princeton: Princeton University Press.

Hamayotsu, Kikue. 2002. "Islam and Nation Building in Southeast Asia: Malaysia and Indonesia in Comparative Perspective." *Pacific Affairs* 75:3 (Fall), pp. 353–375.

Hamilton-Hart, Natasha. 2002. *Asian States, Asian Bankers: Central Banking in Southeast Asia*. Ithaca: Cornell University Press.

Hechter, Michael and William Brustein. 1980. "Regional Modes of Production and Patterns of State Formation in Western Europe." *American Journal of Sociology* 85:5, pp. 1061–1094.

Hedman, Eva-Lotta E. 2001. "Contesting State and Civil Society: Southeast Asian Trajectories." *Modern Asian Studies* 35:4, pp. 921–951.

Hefner, Robert W. 2000. *Civil Islam: Muslims and Democratization in Indonesia*. Princeton: Princeton University Press.

Heng Pek Koon. 1988. *Chinese Politics in Malaysia: A History of the Malaysian Chinese Association*. Singapore: Oxford University Press.

Herbert, Clifford F. 1994. "Role of Government in Mobilizing National and Public Sector Savings." In Al' Alim Ibrahim, ed., *Generating a National Savings Movement*. Kuala Lumpur: Institute for Strategic and International Studies.

Herbst, Jeffrey. 2000. *States and Power in Africa: Comparative Lessons in Authority and Control*. Princeton: Princeton University Press.

Heryanto, Ariel. 2003. "Public Intellectuals, Media and Democratization: Cultural Politics of the Middle Classes in Indonesia." In Ariel Heryanto and Sumit K. Mandal, eds., *Challenging Authoritarianism in Southeast Asia: Comparing Indonesia and Malaysia*. New York: RoutledgeCurzon.

Heryanto, Ariel and Sumit K. Mandal. 2003. "Challenges to Authoritarianism in Indonesia and Malaysia." In Ariel Heryanto and Sumit K. Mandal, eds., *Challenging Authoritarianism in Southeast Asia: Comparing Indonesia and Malaysia*. New York: Routledge-Curzon.

Heussler, Robert. 1983. *Completing a Stewardship: The Malayan Civil Service, 1942–1957*. Westport, CT: Greenwood Press.

Hewison, Kevin. 1999. "Political Space in Southeast Asia: 'Asian-Style' and Other Democracies." *Democratization* 6, pp. 224–245.

Hobsbawm, Eric J. 1994. *The Age of Extremes: The Short Twentieth Century, 1914–1991*. London: Abacus.

Hobson, John M. 1997. *The Wealth of States: A Comparative Sociology of International Economic and Political Change*. New York: Cambridge University Press.

Honna, Jun. 2003. *Military Politics and Democratization in Indonesia*. New York: Routledge-Curzon.

Huntington, Samuel P. 1991. *The Third Wave: Democratization in the Late Twentieth Century*. Norman: University of Oklahoma Press.

Huntington, Samuel P. 1970. "Social and Institutional Dynamics of One-Party Systems." In Samuel P. Huntington and Clement H. Moore, eds., *Authoritarian Politics in Modern Society: The Dynamics of Established One-Party Systems*. New York: Basic Books.

Huntington, Samuel P. 1968. *Political Order in Changing Societies*. New Haven: Yale University Press.

Hutchcroft, Paul D. 2000. "Colonial Masters, National Politicos, and Provincial Lords: Central Authority and Local Autonomy in the American Philippines, 1900–1913." *Journal of Asian Studies* 59:2 (May), pp. 277–306.

Hutchcroft, Paul D. 1994. "Booty Capitalism: Business-Government Relations in the Philippines." In Andrew MacIntyre, ed., *Business and Government in Industrializing Asia*. Ithaca: Cornell University Press.

Hwang, In-Won. 2003. *Personalized Politics: The Malaysian State Under Mahathir*. Singapore: Institute for Southeast Asian Studies.

Ileto, Reynaldo C. 1979. *Pasyon and Revolution: Popular Movements in the Philippines, 1840–1910*. Honolulu: University of Hawaii Press.

Ishak bin Tadin. 1960. "Dato Onn and Malay Nationalism, 1946–1951." *Journal of Southeast Asian History* 1 (March), pp.56–88.

Jackson, Karl D. 1985. "Post-Colonial Rebellion and Counter-Insurgency in Southeast Asia." In Chandran Jeshurun, ed., *Governments and Rebellions in Southeast Asia*. Singapore: Institute of Southeast Asian Studies.

Jackson, Robert H. 1992. "Juridical Statehood in Sub-Saharan Africa." *Journal of International Affairs* 45:1 (Summer), pp. 1–16.

Jesudason, James V. 1996. "The Syncretic State and the Structuring of Oppositional Politics in Malaysia." In Garry Rodan, ed., *Political Oppositions in Industrializing Asia*. New York: Routledge.

Jesudason, James V. 1989. *Ethnicity and the Economy: The State, Chinese Business, and Multinationals in Malaysia*. Singapore: Oxford University Press.

Jomo K.S. 1990. *Growth and Structural Change in the Malaysian Economy*. New York: St. Martin's Press.

Jomo K.S. and Edmund Terence Gomez. 1999. *Malaysia's Political Economy: Politics, Patronage, and Profits*. New York: Cambridge University Press.

Jomo Kwame Sundaram. 1986. *A Question of Class: Capital, the State, and Uneven Development in Malaya*. New York: Oxford University Press.

Kahin, George McT. 1952. *Nationalism and Revolution in Indonesia*. Ithaca: Cornell University Press.

Karl, Terry Lynn. 1997. *The Paradox of Plenty: Oil Booms and Petro-States*. Berkeley: University of California Press.

Kasian Tejapira. 2001. *Commodifying Marxism: The Formation of Modern Thai Radical Culture, 1927–1958*. Kyoto: Center for Southeast Asian Studies, Kyoto University.

Kasipillai, Jeyapalan and Bala Shanmugam. 1996. *Malaysian Taxation: Administration, Investigation & Compliance*. Petaling Jaya, Malaysia: Pelanduk Publications.

Kasza, Gregory J. 1996. "War and Comparative Politics." *Comparative Politics* 29:1 (April), pp. 355–373.

Kasza, Gregory J. 1995. *The Conscription Society: Administered Mass Organizations*. New Haven: Yale University Press.

Kaufman, Robert R. 1986. "Liberalization and Democratization in South America: Perspectives from the 1970s." In Guillermo O'Donnell, Philippe C. Schmitter, and Laurence Whitehead, eds., *Transitions from Authoritarian Rule: Comparative Perspectives*. Baltimore: Johns Hopkins University Press.

Keay, John. 1997. *Empire's End: A History of the Far East from High Colonialism to Hong Kong*. New York: Scribner.

Kerkvliet, Benedict J. Tria. 2000. "Foreword: Political Ironies in the Philippines." In Jennifer Conroy Franco, *Campaigning for Democracy: Grassroots Citizenship Movements, Less-Than-Democratic Elections, and Regime Transition in the Philippines*. Quezon City: Institute for Popular Democracy.

Kerkvliet, Benedict J. Tria. 1998. "Land Regimes and State Strengths and Weaknesses in the Philippines and Vietnam." In Peter Dauvergne, ed., *Weak and Strong States in Asia-Pacific Societies*. Sydney: Allen and Unwin.

Kerkvliet, Benedict J. Tria. 1979. "Land Reform: Emancipation or Counterinsurgency?" In David A. Rosenberg, ed., *Marcos and Martial Law in the Philippines*. Ithaca: Cornell University Press.

Kerkvliet, Benedict J. Tria. 1977. *The Huk Rebellion: A Study of Peasant Revolt in the Philippines*. Berkeley: University of California Press.

Kessler, Clive S. 1980. "Malaysia: Islamic Revivalism and Political Disaffection in a Divided Society." *Southeast Asia Chronicle* 75 (October), pp. 3–11.

Khasnor Johan. 1984. *The Emergence of the Modern Malay Administrative Elite*. Singapore: Oxford University Press.

Khong, Cho-Oon. 1995. "Singapore: Political Legitimacy Through Managing Conformity." In Muthiah Alagappa, ed., *Political Legitimacy in Southeast Asia: The Quest for Moral Authority*. Stanford: Stanford University Press.

Khoo Boo Teik. 1997. "Democracy and Authoritarianism in Malaysia Since 1957: Class, Ethnicity and Changing Capitalism." In Anek Laothamatas, ed., *Democratization in Southeast and East Asia*. Singapore: Institute for Southeast Asian Studies.

Khoo Boo Teik. 1995. *Paradoxes of Mahathirism: An Intellectual Biography of Mahathir Mohamad*. New York: Oxford University Press.

Kingsbury, Damien. 2003. *Power Politics and the Indonesian Military*. New York: Routledge-Curzon.

Kohli, Atul. 2002. "State, Society, and Development." In Ira Katznelson and Helen Milner, eds., *Political Science: The State of the Discipline*. New York: Norton.

Kuhonta, Erik Martinez. 2003. "The Political Foundations of Equitable Development: State and Party Formation in Malaysia and Thailand." Ph.D. Dissertation, Department of Politics, Princeton University.

Kuhonta, Erik Martinez, Dan Slater, and Tuong Vu (eds.). 2008. *Southeast Asia in Political Science: Theory, Region, and Qualitative Analysis*. Stanford: Stanford University Press.

Kurzman, Charles. 2006. *Democracy Denied, 1905–1915: Intellectuals and the Fate of Democracy*. Cambridge: Harvard University Press.

Lacaba, Jose F. 2003 [1982]. *Days of Disquiet, Nights of Rage: The First Quarter Storm and Related Events*. Pasig City: Anvil Publishing.

Lachmann, Richard. 2000. *Capitalists in Spite of Themselves: Elite Conflict and Economic Transformations in Early Modern Europe*. New York: Oxford University Press.

Lande, Carl H. 1986. "The Political Crisis." In John Bresnan, ed., *Crisis in the Philippines: The Marcos Era and Beyond*. Princeton: Princeton University Press.

Lange, Matthew. 2009. *Lineages of Despotism and Development: British Colonialism and State Power*. Chicago: University of Chicago Press.

Lau, Albert. 2003. *A Moment of Anguish: Singapore in Malaysia and the Politics of Disengagement*. Singapore: Eastern Universities Press.

Lee, Stephen J. 1987. *European Dictatorships*. New York: Methuen.

Lee, Terence. 2009. "The Armed Forces and Transitions from Authoritarian Rule: Explaining the Role of the Military in 1986 Philippines and 1998 Indonesia." *Comparative Political Studies* 42:5 (May), pp. 640–669.

Leith, J. Clark. 2005. *Why Botswana Prospered*. Montreal: McGill-Queen's University Press.

Lem, Truong Hoang. 1971. "A Test of Survival: The Case of South Vietnam." Ph.D. Dissertation, Department of Political Science, University of Southern California.

Lev, Daniel S. 1966. *The Transition to Guided Democracy: Indonesian Politics, 1957–1959*. Ithaca: Cornell University Modern Indonesia Project.

Levi, Margaret. 2006. "Why We Need a New Theory of Government." *Perspectives on Politics* 4:1 (March), pp. 5–20.

Levi, Margaret. 1988. *Of Rule and Revenue*. Berkeley: University of California Press.

Levitsky, Steven and Lucan A. Way. Forthcoming. *Competitive Authoritarianism: International Linkage, Organizational Power, and the Fate of Hybrid Regimes*. New York: Cambridge University Press.

Levitsky, Steven and Lucan A. Way. 2002. "The Rise of Competitive Authoritarianism." *Journal of Democracy* 13:2 (April 2002), pp. 51–64.

Liddle, R. William. 1999. "Indonesia's Democratic Opening." *Government and Opposition* 34:1 (January), pp. 94–116.

Liddle, R. William. 1996. "A Useful Fiction: Democratic Legitimation in New Order Indonesia." In R.H. Taylor, ed., *The Politics of Elections in Southeast Asia*. New York: Woodrow Wilson Center.

Lieberman, Evan S. 2003. *Race and Regionalism in the Politics of Taxation in Brazil and South Africa*. New York: Cambridge University Press.

Lieberman, Evan S. 2001. "National Political Community and the Politics of Income Taxation in Brazil and South Africa in the Twentieth Century." *Politics & Society* 29:4 (December), pp. 515–555.

Lijphart, Arend. 1975. "The Comparable-Cases Strategy in Comparative Research." *Comparative Political Studies* 8:2 (July), pp. 158–177.

Lincoln, Yvonna S. and Egon G. Guba. 1985. *Naturalist Inquiry*. New York: Sage.

Lintner, Bertil. 1990. *The Rise and Fall of the Communist Party of Burma (CPB)*. Ithaca: Cornell University Southeast Asia Program.

Linz, Juan J. and Alfred Stepan. 1996. *Problems of Democratic Transition and Consolidation: Southern Europe, South America, and Post-Communist Europe*. Baltimore: Johns Hopkins University Press.

Lipset, Seymour Martin and Stein Rokkan. 1990 [1967]. "Cleavage Structures, Party Systems, and Voter Alignments." In Peter Mair (ed.), *The West European Party System*, Oxford: Oxford University Press.

Loh Kok Wah. 1982. "The Politics of Chinese Unity in Malaysia: Reform and Conflict in the Malaysian Chinese Association, 1971–73." Singapore: Institute for Southeast Asian Studies Occasional Paper No. 70.

Lopez-Alves, Fernando. 2000. *State Formation and Democracy in Latin America, 1810–1900*. Durham, NC: Duke University Press.

Loveman, Mara. 2005. "The Modern State and the Primitive Accumulation of Symbolic Power." *American Journal of Sociology* 110:6 (May), pp. 1651–1683.

Loveman, Mara. 1998. "High-Risk Collective Action: Defending Human Rights in Chile, Uruguay, and Argentina." *American Journal of Sociology* 104:2 (September), pp. 477–525.

Luebbert, Gregory M. 1991. *Liberalism, Fascism, or Social Democracy: Social Classes and the Political Origins of Regimes in Interwar Europe*. New York: Oxford University Press.

MacInytre, Andrew. 1990. *Business and Politics in Indonesia*. Sydney: Allen & Unwin.

Madrid, Raul. 2008. "The Rise of Ethnopopulism in Latin America." *World Politics* 60:3 (April), pp. 475–508.

Madrid, Robin. 1999. "Islamic Students in the Indonesian Student Movement, 1998–1999: Forces for Moderation. *Bulletin of Concerned Asian Scholars* 31:3 (July–September), pp. 17–32.

Mahoney, James. 2003a. "Knowledge Accumulation in Comparative Historical Analysis: The Case of Democracy and Authoritarianism." In James Mahoney and Dietrich Rueschemeyer, eds., *Comparative Historical Analysis in the Social Sciences*. New York: Cambridge University Press.

Mahoney, James. 2003b. "Strategies of Causal Assessment in Comparative Historical Analysis." In James Mahoney and Dietrich Rueschemeyer, eds., *Comparative Historical Analysis in the Social Sciences*. New York: Cambridge University Press.

Mahoney, James. 2001. *The Legacies of Liberalism: Path Dependence and Political Regimes in Central America*. Baltimore: Johns Hopkins University Press.

Mahoney, James and Dietrich Rueschemeyer, eds. 2003. *Comparative Historical Analysis in the Social Sciences*. New York: Cambridge University Press.

Mahoney, James and Kathleen Thelen (eds.). 2010. *Explaining Institutional Change: Ambiguity, Agency, and Power*. New York: Cambridge University Press.

Mann, Michael. 1988. *States, War and Capitalism: Studies in Political Sociology*. Cambridge: Basil Blackwell.

Marx, Anthony. 2003. *Faith in Nation: Exclusionary Origins of Nationalism*. New York: Oxford University Press.

Marx, Anthony. 1998. *Making Race and Nation: A Comparison of South Africa, the United States, and Brazil*. New York: Cambridge University Press.

Mas'oed, Mochtar. 1983. "The Indonesian Economy and Political Structure During the Early New Order, 1966–1971." Ph.D. Dissertation, Department of Political Science, The Ohio State University.

Maung Maung, U. 1990. *Burmese Nationalist Movements, 1940–1948*. Honolulu: University of Hawaii Press.

McAdam, Doug, Sidney Tarrow, and Charles Tilly. 1997. "Toward an Integrated Perspective on Social Movements and Revolution." In Mark Irving Lichbach and Alan S. Zuckerman (eds.), *Comparative Politics: Rationality, Culture, and Structure*. Cambridge: Cambridge University Press.

McCoy, Alfred W. 1999. *Closer Than Brothers: Manhood at the Philippine Military Academy*. New Haven: Yale University Press.

McCoy, Alfred W. 1993. "'An Anarchy of Families': The Historiography of State and Family in the Philippines. In Alfred W. McCoy, ed., *An Anarchy of Families: State and Family in the Philippines*. Madison: University of Wisconsin Center for Southeast Asian Studies.

McHale, Shawn Frederick. 2004. *Print and Power: Confucianism, Communism, and Buddhism in the Making of Modern Vietnam*. Honolulu: University of Hawaii Press.

McKeown, Timothy J. 1999. "Case Studies and the Statistical Worldview." *International Organization* 53:1 (Winter), pp. 161–190.

Mietzner, Marcus. 2009. *Military Politics, Islam, and the State in Indonesia*. Singapore: ISEAS.

Mietzner, Marcus. 1998. "Between Pesantren and Palace: Nahdlatul Ulama and Its Role in the Transition." In Geoff Forrester and R.J. May (eds.), *The Fall of Soeharto*. Bathurst, NSW: Crawford House.

Migdal, Joel. 1997. "Studying the State." In Mark Irving Lichbach and Alan S. Zuckerman (eds.), *Comparative Politics: Rationality, Culture, and Structure*. New York: Cambridge University Press.

Migdal, Joel. 1988. *Strong Societies and Weak States: State-Society Relations and State Capabilities in the Third World*. Princeton: Princeton University Press.

Mitchell, Timothy. 1991. "The Limits of the State: Beyond Statist Approaches and their Critics." *American Political Science Review* 85:1 (March), pp. 77–96.

Moore, Barrington. 1966. *Social Origins of Dictatorship and Democracy: Lord and Peasant in the Making of the Modern World*. Boston: Beacon.

Morell, David and Chai-anan Samudavanija. 1981. *Political Conflict in Thailand: Reform, Reaction, Revolution*. Cambridge, MA: Oelgeschlager, Gunn & Hain.

Morrison, Kevin. 2009. "Oil, Nontax Revenue, and the Redistributional Foundations of Regime Stability." *International Organization* 63 (Winter), pp. 107–138.

Mortimer, Rex. 1982. "Class, Social Cleavage and Indonesian Communism." In Benedict Anderson and Audrey Kahin, eds., *Interpreting Indonesian Politics: Thirteen Contributions to the Debate*. Ithaca: Cornell University Southeast Asia Program.

Mortimer, Rex. 1974. "Traditional Modes and Communist Movements: Change and Protest in Indonesia." In John Wilson Lewis, ed., *Peasant Rebellion and Communist Revolution in Asia*. Stanford: Stanford University Press.

Nair, Shanti. 1997. *Islam in Malaysia's Foreign Policy*. London: Routledge.

National Economic Development Authority. 1979. *Philippine Statistical Yearbook*. Manila: NEDA.

Noble, Lela Garner. 1986. "Politics in the Marcos Era." In John Bresnan, ed., *Crisis in the Philippines: The Marcos Era and Beyond*. Princeton: Princeton University Press.

North, Douglass C. 1990. *Institutions, Institutional Change, and Economic Performance*. New York: Cambridge University Press.

North, Douglass C., John Joseph Wallis, and Barry R. Weingast. 2009. *Violence and Social Orders: A Conceptual Framework for Interpreting Recorded Human History*. New York: Cambridge University Press.

North, Douglass C. and Barry R. Weingast. 1989. "Constitutions and Commitment: The Evolution of Institutions Governing Public Choice in Seventeenth-Century England." *Journal of Economic History* 69:4 (December), pp. 803–832.

Ockey, James. 2002. "Civil Society and Street Politics: Lessons from the 1950s." In Duncan McCargo, ed., *Reforming Thai Politics*. Copenhagen: Nordic Institute of Asian Studies.

O'Donnell, Guillermo A. 1973. *Modernization and Bureaucratic-Authoritarianism: Studies in South American Politics*. Berkeley: University of California Institute of International Studies.

O'Donnell, Guillermo and Philippe C. Schmitter. 1986. *Transitions from Authoritarian Rule: Tentative Conclusions about Uncertain Democracies*. Baltimore: Johns Hopkins University Press.

Okruhlik, Gwenn. 1999. "Rentier Wealth, Unruly Law, and the Rise of Opposition: The Political Economy of Oil States." *Comparative Politics* 31:3 (April), pp. 295–315.

Olson, Mancur. 1971. *The Logic of Collective Action: Public Goods and the Theory of Groups*. Cambridge: Harvard University Press.

Osborne, Milton. 1970. *Region of Revolt: Focus on Southeast Asia*. Sydney: Penguin.

Osborne, Milton. 1965. *Strategic Hamlets in South Viet-Nam: A Survey and a Comparison*. Ithaca: Cornell University Southeast Asia Program, Paper #55.

Othman, Norani. 2003. "Islamization and Democratization in Malaysia in Regional and Global Contexts." In Ariel Heryanto and Sumit K. Mandal, eds., *Challenging Authoritarianism in Southeast Asia: Comparing Indonesia and Malaysia*. New York: RoutledgeCurzon.

Owen, Roger. 2004. *State, Power and Politics in the Making of the Modern Middle East*. London: Routledge.

Padgett, John F. and Christopher K. Ansell. 1993. "Robust Action and the Rise of the Medici, 1400–1434." *American Journal of Sociology* 98:6 (May), pp. 1259–1319.

Park, Bae-Gyoon. 1998. "Where Do Tigers Sleep at Night? The State's Role in Housing Policy in South Korea and Singapore." *Economic Geography* 74:3 (July), pp. 272–288.

Pepinsky, Thomas B. 2008. "Capital Mobility and Coalitional Politics: Authoritarian Regimes and Economic Adjustment in Southeast Asia. *World Politics* 60:3 (April), pp. 438–474.

Pierson, Paul. 2004. *Politics in Time: History, Institutions, and Social Analysis*. Princeton: Princeton University Press.

Pinches, Michael. 1991. "The Working Class Experience of Shame, Inequality, and People Power in Tatalon, Manila." In Benedict J. Kerkvliet and Resil B. Mojares, eds., *From Marcos to Aquino: Local Perspectives on Political Transition in the Philippines*. Quezon City: Ateneo de Manila Press.

Polanyi, Karl. 2001 [1944]. *The Great Transformation: The Political and Economic Origins of Our Time*. Boston: Beacon.

Polletta, Francesca and James M. Jasper. 2001. "Collective Identity and Social Movements." *Annual Review of Sociology* 27, pp. 283–305.

Prudhisan Jumbala. 1992. *Nation-Building and Democratization in Thailand: A Political History*. Bangkok: Chulalongkorn University Social Research Institute.

Przeworski, Adam and Fernando Limongi. 1997. "Modernization: Theories and Facts." *World Politics* 49:2 (January), pp. 155–183.

Purcell, Victor. 1965. *The Chinese in Southeast Asia*. London: Oxford University Press.

Rabushka, Alvin. 1973. *Race and Politics in Urban Malaya*. Stanford: Hoover Institution Press.

Ramage, Douglas E. 1995. *Politics in Indonesia: Democracy, Islam and the Ideology of Tolerance*. New York: Routledge.

Reid, Anthony. 1988. *Southeast Asia in the Age of Commerce*. New Haven: Yale University Press.

Rich, Paul B. and Richard Stubbs, eds. 1997. *The Counter-Insurgent State: Guerrilla Warfare and State Building in the Twentieth Century*. New York: St. Martin's Press.

Riggs, Fred. 1966. *Thailand: The Modernization of a Bureaucratic Polity*. Honolulu: East-West Center Press.

Rivera, Temario. 2001. "The Middle Classes and Democratization in the Philippines: From the Asian Crisis to the Ouster of Estrada." In Abdul Rahman Embong, ed., *Southeast Asian Middle Classes: Prospects for Social Change and Democratization*. Bangi: Universiti Kebangsaan Malaysia.

Robison, Richard. 1986. *Indonesia: The Rise of Capital*. Sydney: Allen & Unwin.

Robison, Richard and Vedi R. Hadiz. 2004. *Reorganizing Power in Indonesia: The Politics of Oligarchy in an Age of Markets*. London: RoutledgeCurzon.

Rosenberg, David A. 1979. "Introduction: Creating a 'New Society.'" In David A. Rosenberg, ed., *Marcos and Martial Law in the Philippines*. Ithaca: Cornell University Press.

Ross, Michael L. 2001. "Does Oil Hinder Democracy?" *World Politics* 53 (April), pp. 325–361.

Rudner, Martin. 1994 [1975]. "Financial Policies in Post-War Malaya: The Fiscal and Monetary Measures of Liberation and Reconstruction." In Martin Rudner, ed., *Malaysian Development: A Retrospective*. Ottawa: Carleton University Press.

Rueschemeyer, Dietrich, Evelyne Huber Stephens, and John D. Stephens. 1992. *Capitalist Development and Democracy*. Chicago: University of Chicago Press.

Rustow, Dankwart. 1970. "Transitions to Democracy: Toward a Dynamic Model." *Comparative Politics* 2:2 (April), pp. 337–363.

Salehuddin Mohamed. 1994. "Promoting Savings and Social Security Needs: Expanding the Role of the EPF in a Rapidly Expanding Economic Environment." In Al' Alim Ibrahim, ed., *Generating a National Savings Movement*. Kuala Lumpur: Institute for Strategic and International Studies.

Sandbrook, Richard. 1972. "Patrons, Clients, and Factions: New Dimensions of Conflict Analysis in Africa." *Canadian Journal of Political Science* 5:1 (March), pp. 104–119.

Sandhu, Kernial Singh. 1973. "Introduction: Emergency Resettlement in Malaya." In Ray Nyce, *Chinese New Villages in Malaya: A Community Study*. Singapore: Malaysian Sociological Research Institute.

Schiller, Jim. 1996. *Developing Jepara: State and Society in New Order Indonesia*. Clayton: Monash Asia Institute.

Schlefer, Jonathan. 2008. *Palace Politics: How the Ruling Party Brought Crisis to Mexico*. Austin: University of Texas Press.

Schmitt, Carl. 1985 [1923]. *The Crisis of Parliamentary Democracy*. Cambridge: MIT Press.

Schumpeter, Joseph A. 1954 [1918]. "The Crisis of the Tax State." In *International Economic Papers* No. 4. New York: MacMillan

Schwarz, Adam. 1994. *A Nation in Waiting: Indonesia in the 1990s*. Boulder: Westview.

Scigliano, Robert G. 1960. "Political Parties in South Vietnam Under the Republic." *Pacific Affairs* 33:4 (December), pp. 327–346.

Scott, James C. 1998. *Seeing Like a State: How Certain Schemes to Improve the Human Condition Have Failed*. New Haven: Yale University Press.

Scott, James C. 1972. "Patron-Client Politics and Political Change in Southeast Asia." *American Political Science Review* 66:1 (March), pp. 91–113.

Shefter, Martin. 1994. *Political Parties and the State: The American Historical Experience.* Princeton: Princeton University Press.

Sidel, John T. 1999. *Capital, Coercion, and Crime: Bossism in the Philippines.* Stanford: Stanford University Press.

Sidel, John T. 1998. "Macet Total: Logics of Circulation and Accumulation in the Demise of Indonesia's New Order." *Indonesia* 66 (October), pp. 159–194.

Sidel, John T. 1996. "Siam and its Twin? Democratization and Bossism in Contemporary Thailand and the Philippines." *IDS Bulletin* 27:2, pp. 56–63.

Sidel, John T. 1995. "The Philippines: The Languages of Legitimation." In Muthiah Alagappa, ed., *Political Legitimacy in Southeast Asia: The Quest for Moral Authority.* Stanford: Stanford University Press.

Siegel, James T. 1998. "Early Thoughts on the Violence of May 13 and 14, 1998 in Jakarta." *Indonesia* 66 (October), pp. 75–108.

Silberman, Bernard S. 1993. *Cages of Reason: The Rise of the Rational State in France, Japan, the United States, and Great Britain.* Chicago: University of Chicago Press.

Sillery, Anthony. 1974. *Botswana: A Short Political History.* New York: Methuen.

Slater, Dan. 2010. "Altering Authoritarianism: Institutional Complexity and Autocratic Agency in Indonesia." In James Mahoney and Kathleen Thelen, eds., *Explaining Institutional Change: Ambiguity, Agency, and Power.* New York: Cambridge University Press.

Slater, Dan. 2009. "Revolutions, Crackdowns, and Quiescence: Communal Elites and Democratic Mobilization in Southeast Asia." *American Journal of Sociology* 115:1 (July), pp. 203–254.

Slater, Dan. 2008a. "Can Leviathan be Democratic? Competitive Elections, Robust Mass Politics, and State Infrastructural Power." *Studies in Comparative International Development* 43:3 (Fall/Winter), pp. 252–272.

Slater, Dan. 2008b. "Democracies and Dictatorships Do Not Float Freely: Structural Sources of Political Regimes in Southeast Asia." In Erik Martinez Kuhonta, Dan Slater, and Tuong Vu, eds., *Southeast Asia in Political Science: Theory, Region, and Qualitative Analysis.* Stanford: Stanford University Press.

Slater, Dan. 2005. "Ordering Power: Contentious Politics, State-Building, and Authoritarian Durability in Southeast Asia." Ph.D. Dissertation, Department of Political Science, Emory University.

Slater, Dan. 2004. "Democracy Takes a Thumping: Islamist and Democratic Opposition in Malaysia's Electoral Authoritarian Regime." *Kyoto Review of Southeast Asia* 5 (March).

Slater, Dan. 2003. "Iron Cage in an Iron Fist: Authoritarian Institutions and the Personalization of Power in Malaysia." *Comparative Politics* 36:1 (October), pp. 81–101.

Slater, Dan and Christopher Haid. 2008. "The Worst Kind of War: Regional Rebellions and Political Militarization in the Post-Colonial World." Paper presented at the annual meetings of the American Political Science Association, Boston (August).

Slater, Dan and Daniel Ziblatt. 2009. "Revitalizing the Controlled Comparison: Extreme Variation and External Validity in Qualitative Research." Paper presented at the annual meetings of the Social Science History Association (SSHA), Long Beach (November).

Slater, Dan and Erica Simmons. 2010. "Informative Regress: Critical Antecedents in Comparative Politics." *Comparative Political Studies* 43:9 (September).

Slater, Dan and Nicholas Smith. 2009. "The Power of Counterrevolution: Contentious Origins of Dominant Party Durability in Asia and Africa." Paper presented at the annual meetings of the American Sociological Association (ASA), San Francisco (August).

Smith, Benjamin. 2007. *Hard Times in the Lands of Plenty: Oil Politics in Iran and Indonesia.* Ithaca: Cornell University Press.

Smith, Benjamin. 2005. "Life of the Party: The Origins of Regime Breakdown and Persistence under Single-Party Rule." *World Politics* 57:3 (Spring), pp. 421–451.

Smith, Martin. 1991. *Burma: Insurgency and the Politics of Ethnicity.* London: Zed Books.

Smith, Simon C. 1995. *British Relations with the Malay Rulers from Decentralization to Malayan Independence, 1930–1957.* Kuala Lumpur: Oxford University Press.

Snidal, Duncan. 1985. "Coordination versus Prisoner's Dilemma: Implications for International Cooperation and Regimes," *American Political Science Review* 79:4, pp. 923–942.

Snider, Nancy L. 1968. "What Happened in Penang?" *Asian Survey* 8:12 (December), pp. 960–975.

Soh Eng Lim. 1960. "Tan Cheng Lock: His Leadership of the Malayan Chinese." *Journal of Southeast Asian History* 1 (March), pp. 29–55.

Soifer, Hillel. 2008. "State Infrastructural Power: Approaches to Conceptualization and Measurement." *Studies in Comparative International Development* 43:3 (Fall/Winter), pp. 231–251.

Somboon Suksamran. 1981. *Political Patronage and Control over the Sangha.* Singapore: Institute for Southeast Asian Studies.

Stene, Edwin O. and Odell Waldby. 1955. "Administration of Public Revenues." In Edwin O. Stene, ed., *Public Administration in the Philippines.* Manila: University of the Philippines Institute of Public Administration.

Stenner, Karen. 2005. *The Authoritarian Dynamic.* New York: Cambridge University Press.

Stenson, Michael. 1974. "The Ethnic and Urban Bases of Communist Revolt in Malaya." In John Wilson Lewis, ed., *Peasant Rebellion and Communist Revolution in Asia.* Stanford: Stanford University Press.

Stenson, Michael R. 1970. *Industrial Conflict in Malaya: Prelude to the Communist Revolt of 1948.* New York: Oxford University Press.

Stenson, Michael R. 1969. "Repression and Revolt: The Origins of the 1948 Communist Insurrection in Malaya and Singapore." Athens: Ohio University Papers in International Studies, Southeast Asia Series No. 10.

Stockwell, A.J. 1986. "Imperial Security and Moslem Militancy, With Special Reference to the Hertogh Riots in Singapore (December 1950)." *Journal of Southeast Asian Studies* 17:2 (September), pp. 322–335.

Stubbs, Richard. 1997. "The Malayan Emergency and the Development of the Malaysian State." In Paul B. Rich and Richard Stubbs, eds., *The Counter-Insurgent State: Guerrilla Warfare and State Building in the Twentieth Century.* New York: St. Martin's Press.

Stubbs, Richard. 1989. *Hearts and Minds in Guerrilla Warfare: The Malayan Emergency, 1948–1960.* Singapore: Oxford University Press.

Suchit Bunbongkarn. 1996. *State of the Nation: Thailand.* Singapore: Institute for Southeast Asian Studies.

Suryadinata, Leo. 1989. *Military Ascendancy and Political Culture: A Study of Indonesia's Golkar.* Athens: Ohio University Monographs in International Studies, Southeast Asia Series, No. 85.

Tanter, Richard. 1990. "Oil, IGGI, and US Hegemony: The Global Pre-conditions for Indonesian Rentier-Militarization." In Arief Budiman, ed., *State and Civil Society in Indonesia.* Clayton, Australia: Monash Asia Institute.

Tarling, Nicholas. 2001. *A Sudden Rampage: The Japanese Occupation of Southeast Asia, 1941–1945.* Singapore: Horizon.

Thachil, Tariq and Ronald Herring. 2009. "Poor Choices: De-Alignment, Development and Dalit/Adivasi Voting Patterns in Indian States." *Contemporary South Asia* 16:4 (December), pp. 441–464.

Thak Chaloemtiarana. 1979. *Thailand: The Politics of Despotic Paternalism*. Bangkok: Thammasat University.

Thelen, Kathleen. 1999. "Historical Institutionalism in Comparative Politics." *Annual Review of Political Science* 2, pp. 369–404.

Thies, Cameron G. 2004. "State Building, Interstate and Intrastate Rivalry: A Study of Post-Colonial Developing Country Extractive Efforts, 1975–2000." *International Studies Quarterly* 48 (March), pp. 53–72.

Thompson, Mark R. 2004. *Democratic Revolutions: Asia and Eastern Europe*. New York: Routledge.

Thompson, Mark R. 1995. *The Anti-Marcos Struggle: Personalistic Rule and Democratic Transition in the Philippines*. New Haven: Yale University Press.

Tilly, Charles. 2004. *Contention and Democracy in Europe, 1650–2000*. New York: Cambridge University Press.

Tilly, Charles. 1992. *Coercion, Capital, and European States AD 990–1992*. Cambridge: Blackwell.

Tilly, Charles. 1985. "War Making and State Making as Organized Crime." In Peter Evans, Dietrich Rueschemeyer, and Theda Skocpol, eds. *Bringing the State Back In*. New York: Cambridge University Press.

Tilly, Charles. 1975. "Reflections on the History of European State-Making." In Charles Tilly, ed., *The Formation of National States in Western Europe*. Princeton: Princeton University Press.

Tregonning, K.G. 1979. "Tan Cheng Lock: A Malayan Nationalist." *Journal of Southeast Asian Studies* 10:1 (March), pp. 25–76.

Tucker, Joshua. 2007. "Enough! Electoral Fraud, Collective Action Problems, and Post-Communist Colored Revolutions." *Perspectives on Politics* 5:3 (September), pp. 535–552.

United Nations. 1953. *United Nations Statistical Yearbook*. New York: United Nations.

Utrecht, Ernst. 1972. "The Indonesian Army as an Instrument of Repression." *Journal of Contemporary Asia* 2:1, pp. 56–67.

Vandewalle, Dirk. 1998. *Libya Since Independence: Oil and State-Building*. Ithaca: Cornell University Press.

Von Vorys, Karl. 1975. *Democracy without Consensus: Communalism and Political Stability in Malaysia*. Princeton: Princeton University Press.

Vu, Tuong. 2004. "Late Leviathans: State Formation and Postcolonial Transformation in Pacific Asia." Ph.D. Dissertation, Department of Political Science, University of California-Berkeley.

Wade, Geoff. 2007. "Suppression of the Left in Singapore, 1945–1963: Domestic and Regional Contexts in the Southeast Asian Cold War." Paper presented at the European Association of Southeast Asian Studies Conference, Naples (September).

Waldner, David. 2008. "Democracy and Dictatorship in the Post-Colonial World." Unpublished Manuscript, Department of Politics, University of Virginia.

Waldner, David. 2002. "From Intra-Type Variations to the Origins of Types: Recovering the Macro-Analytics of State Building." Paper presented at the conference on Asian Political Economy in an Era of Globalization, Dartmouth College (May).

Waldner, David. 1999. *State Building and Late Development*. Ithaca: Cornell University Press.

Wedeen, Lisa. 2008. *Peripheral Visions: Publics, Power, and Performance in Yemen*. Chicago: University of Chicago Press.

Wedeen, Lisa. 1999. *Ambiguities of Domination: Politics, Rhetoric, and Symbols in Contemporary Syria*. Chicago: University of Chicago Press.

Weiner, Myron. 1987. "Empirical Democratic Theory and the Transition from Authoritarianism to Democracy." *PS: Political Science & Politics* 20:4 (Autumn), pp. 861–866.

Weiss, Meredith L. 2006. *Protest and Possibilities: Civil Society and Coalitions for Political Change in Malaysia*. Stanford: Stanford University Press.

Western, Bruce. 1997. *Between Class and Market: Postwar Unionization in the Capitalist Democracies*. Princeton: Princeton University Press.

White, Nicholas J. 1996. *Business, Government, and the End of Empire: Malaya, 1942–1957*. New York: Oxford University Press.

Wilson, David A. 1962. *Politics in Thailand*. Ithaca: Cornell University Press.

Winters, Jeffrey A. 1996. *Power in Motion: Capital Mobility and the Indonesian State*. Ithaca: Cornell University Press.

Wood, Elisabeth Jean. 2000. *Forging Democracy from Below: Insurgent Transitions in South Africa and El Salvador*. New York: Cambridge University Press.

Woodside, Alexander. 1999. "Exalting the Latecomer State: Intellectuals and the State During the Chinese and Vietnamese Reforms." In Anita Chan, Benedict J. Tria Kerkvliet, and Jonathan Unger, eds., *Transforming Asian Socialism: China and Vietnam Compared*. Canberra: Allen & Unwin.

Wurfel, David. 1985. "Government Responses to Armed Communism and Secessionist Rebellion in the Philippines." In Chandran Jeshurun, ed., *Governments and Rebellions in Southeast Asia*. Singapore: Institute of Southeast Asian Studies.

Wurfel, David. 1977. "Martial Law in the Philippines: The Methods of Regime Survival." *Pacific Affairs* 50:1 (Spring), pp. 5–30.

Yashar, Deborah J. 2004. *Contesting Citizenship in Latin America: The Rise of Indigenous Movements and the Postliberal Challenge*. New York: Cambridge University Press.

Yashar, Deborah J. 1997. *Demanding Democracy: Reform and Reaction in Costa Rica and Guatemala, 1870s–1950s*. Stanford: Stanford University Press.

Youngblood, Robert L. 1990. *Marcos Against the Church: Economic Development and Political Repression in the Philippines*. Ithaca: Cornell University Press.

Yawnghwe, Chao-Tzang. 1995. "Burma: The Depoliticization of the Political." In Muthiah Alaggapa, ed., *Political Legitimacy in Southeast Asia: The Quest for Moral Authority*. Stanford: Stanford University Press.

Zakaria Haji Ahmad. 1977. "The Police and Political Development in Malaysia: Change, Continuity, and Institution-Building of a 'Coercive' Apparatus in a Developing, Ethnically Divided Society." Ph.D. Dissertation, Department of Political Science, Massachusetts Institute of Technology.

Zakaria Haji Ahmad. 1976. "Police Forces and Their Political Roles in Southeast Asia: A Preliminary Assessment and Overview." Unpublished Manuscript, National University of Malaysia.

Zee, Howell H. 1996. "Empirics of Crosscountry Tax Revenue Comparisons." *World Development* 24:10, pp. 1659–1671.

Index

Other Books in the Series *(continued from page iii)*

Michael Bratton and Nicolas van de Walle, *Democratic Experiments in Africa: Regime Transitions in Comparative Perspective*

Michael Bratton, Robert Mattes, and E. Gyimah-Boadi, *Public Opinion, Democracy, and Market Reform in Africa*

Valerie Bunce, *Leaving Socialism and Leaving the State: The End of Yugoslavia, the Soviet Union, and Czechoslovakia*

Daniele Caramani, *The Nationalization of Politics: The Formation of National Electorates and Party Systems in Europe*

John M. Carey, *Legislative Voting and Accountability*

Kanchan Chandra, *Why Ethnic Parties Succeed: Patronage and Ethnic Headcounts in India*

José Antonio Cheibub, *Presidentialism, Parliamentarism, and Democracy*

Ruth Berins Collier, *Paths toward Democracy: The Working Class and Elites in Western Europe and South America*

Christian Davenport, *State Repression and the Domestic Democratic Peace*

Donatella della Porta, *Social Movements, Political Violence, and the State*

Alberto Diaz-Cayeros, *Federalism, Fiscal Authority, and Centralization in Latin America*

Thad Dunning, *Crude Democracy: Natural Resource Wealth and Political Regimes*

Gerald Easter, *Reconstructing the State: Personal Networks and Elite Identity*

Margarita Estevez-Abe, *Welfare and Capitalism in Postwar Japan: Party, Bureaucracy, and Business*

M. Steven Fish, *Democracy Derailed in Russia: The Failure of Open Politics*

Robert F. Franzese, *Macroeconomic Policies of Developed Democracies*

Roberto Franzosi, *The Puzzle of Strikes: Class and State Strategies in Postwar Italy*

Timothy Frye, *Building States and Markets After Communism: The Perils of Polarized Democracy*

Geoffrey Garrett, *Partisan Politics in the Global Economy*

Scott Gehlbach, *Representation through Taxation: Revenue, Politics, and Development in Postcommunist States*

Miriam Golden, *Heroic Defeats: The Politics of Job Loss*

Jeff Goodwin, *No Other Way Out: States and Revolutionary Movements*

Merilee Serrill Grindle, *Changing the State*

Anna Grzymala-Busse, *Rebuilding Leviathan: Party Competition and State Exploitation in Post-Communist Democracies*

Anna Grzymala-Busse, *Redeeming the Communist Past: The Regeneration of Communist Parties in East Central Europe*

Frances Hagopian, *Traditional Politics and Regime Change in Brazil*

Henry E. Hale, *The Foundations of Ethnic Politics: Separatism of States and Nations in Eurasia and the World*

Mark Hallerberg, Rolf Ranier Strauch, and Jürgen von Hagen, *Fiscal Governance in Europe*

Stephen E. Hanson, *Post-Imperial Democracies: Ideology and Party Formation in Third Republic France, Weimar Germany, and Post-Soviet Russia*

Silja Häusermann, *The Politics of Welfare State Reform in Continental Europe: Modernization in Hard Times*